Openings

Also by Jeremy Hooker

from Shearsman Books
Upstate: A North American Journal

Poetry
Landscape of the Daylight Moon
Soliloquies of a Chalk Giant
Solent Shore
Englishman's Road
A View from the Source
Master of the Leaping Figures
Their Silence a Language (with Lee Grandjean)
Our Lady of Europe
Adamah
Arnolds Wood
The Cut of the Light: Poems 1965-2005

Prose
Welsh Journal

Criticism
Poetry of Place
The Presence of the Past: Essays on Modern British and American Poetry
Writers in a Landscape
Imagining Wales: A View of Modern Welsh Writing in English

As editor:
Frances Bellerby: Selected Stories
Alun Lewis: Selected Poems (with Gweno Lewis)
At Home on Earth: A New Selection of the Later Writings of Richard Jefferies
Alun Lewis: Inwards Where All the Battle Is: Writings from India
Mapping Golgotha: A Selection of Wilfred Owen's Letters and Poems.
Edward Thomas: The Ship of Swallows

Openings
A European Journal

Jeremy Hooker

Shearsman Books

First published in the United Kingdom in 2014 by
Shearsman Books
50 Westons Hill Drive
Emersons Green
BRISTOL
BS16 7DF

Shearsman Books Ltd Registered Office
30–31 St. James Place, Mangotsfield, Bristol BS16 9JB
(this address not for correspondence)

ISBN 978-1-84861-304-1

Translation copyright © Jeremy Hooker, 2014.

The right of Jeremy Hooker to be identified as the author
of this work has been asserted by him in accordance with the
Copyrights, Designs and Patents Act of 1988.
All rights reserved.

For Mieke

21 April 1983
After the Poetry Festival at Cambridge from Thursday evening until Monday night.

Mieke—how aware of each other we were at once, how easily and naturally we talked and touched. We stayed up alone together all night on Saturday, at Göran Printz-Påhlson's, talking and making love. I walked back across Cambridge to Glen Cavaliero's on a grey, wet morning, streets almost empty, birds singing loudly and sweetly in gardens. Went to bed at 8 and slept on and off until 1, waking to the strange sensation against my neck of the tiny silver dolphin on a chain which she had given me, and the questions often in my mind since then—Is it true? Is it possible? Can we be so suddenly in love?

From the first I met old friends and made new ones: Glen, Clive Wilmer, Göran & Ulla, John Matthias, Michael Longley, David & Judy Gascoyne, Chris Sykes & Patrick Sullivan from Lumb Bank. Christopher Middleton has a remarkable quality of stillness; he is self-disciplined, a man who watches, listens, remembers people. It was characteristic that he should give a speech of thanks to the organisers at the end, and do it beautifully.

On Sunday morning I went with John Matthias to see Doug Kinsey's sequence of monotypes, *After the Fall*, at Caius. These will surely be widely known in time. If not, they should be, their images are at once so expressive and made with such craft and compassion. I have never seen a sequence of modern figurative paintings that has moved or impressed me more.

Jean Earle read first at the Festival. I read with her, Michael Longley, and Nassos Vayenas, from Rethymnon in Crete. For me, Jean Earle's reading was the most moving and effective of all the readings I heard. Not the best performance or the most applauded—far from it, there were several kinds of very accomplished performances. Jean Earle was inside her poems and they were in her; she read them from the inside, and almost entirely from memory, communicating the integrity of each poem by giving herself to it and not manipulating the audience. Other readers, notably Franco Fortini & Yuna Moritz, gave, in different ways, the emotional movements of their poems. Yuna Moritz seemed to be acting *in* her poems, not acting them for us. A fine distinction but a real one. I'm not moved by the poet as actor vis a vis the audience, although every good reading is to some degree an enactment. I was moved too by Peter Levi reading his elegy for Anne Pennington; it was as if we were hearing him reading to her.

William Empson was so indistinct that only a phrase or sentence was clearly audible, but although he read badly, it was strangely affecting to hear him read the famous poems—especially "Slowly the poison the whole bloodstream fills"—largely because this was an historical moment, and we were hearing him perhaps for the last time.

A few words and the livingness of all that has happened since last Thursday is reduced to images and shadows. Here a gesture, there something someone said… But I know this isn't the truth, any more than these notebooks which are, in a sense, my life… Love alone is true, both the current in and between people that is the real life of any time, and the knowledge lovingly held. In setting something down I have felt the current slipping between my fingers. Love comes only with sharing, going out from oneself, receiving another in, responding to the world together.

A cold, tiredness, my old fatalistic streak—a few days pass and I'm given miserably to doubt. Mieke, your dolphin touches my skin but I can't know that you haven't already gone back entirely into your old life in your work and your own place. I scarcely dare hope that the need which I felt in you was like mine, and the capacity to give and to accept is always with you, as in the special intensity of that time. I dream of a nature like yours, and I've no reason to trust my dreams. Nor any reason to distrust you.

At Hayford, Pennington
The photo of my grandfather, Tom Hooker, as a boy (c. 1885) with his uncle, Mr Humby, leaning on a donkey, in a group of estate workers, sitting or standing, each holding the tool of his or her work, was taken at Warsash House. This house, their workplace, was knocked down years ago, but I remember its dovecote, which, as a small boy, I walked past on the way to Sunday School. The School was on the way to the shore, and, apart from the dovecote, I can only remember the coloured pencils we were given to draw with, and one in particular, a stubby mauve pencil, which always comes to mind when I hear the word *mauve*. I've always associated the photograph with a Warsash estate, largely because the hedge behind the group stirs some strong but obscure memory of such hedges associated with the gravelly soil of the area. But it was only yesterday that my parents placed it for me, and incidentally called up some memories of my own.

23 April
On not hearing the cuckoo, or only a doubtful, very faint distant echo at the bottom of Hazel Road, but finding violets, stitchwort & bluebells on the bank by Kings Huts.

On Wainsford Common. Forced a scratchy way through undergrowth and muddy clay to the river, Sway Tower upstream as grey as oaks & alders not yet in leaf. Birds singing, but no cuckoo.

Under trees by the river, its brown eddies, gravel shoals, banks of silt and quick clear pebbly runs, and walking back—rich warm orange of berberis in the garden and my father in his old hat & overcoat stooping to a task—I see and feel how happy my life has been, and is.

24 April
Early morning. Dad, in his dressing gown, his mass of white hair standing on end, has just brought the usual morning cup of tea. Through my window, looking out at Penn Cottage and Wheathill, I can see the space between them filled with fresh

green leaves of the Buckles' horse chestnut tree. The phrase in my mind just now was "a shower of all my days". Time to make peace with you, Dylan Thomas.

Mieke rang last night: "I am just as insecure as you". As long as we feel the same!

Later, when I went to see Séan Street, he talked about his visit to Max Gate and the party on the lawn celebrating the publication of Michael Millgate's biography. He went into the room where Thomas Hardy wrote *Jude*, which was also the room in which he died. Eating strawberries & cream and drinking white wine on the lawn, Séan imagined quizzical eyes looking down from the blank windows. Like me, though, he's impressed by Hardy's complete absence. He left only his writings to haunt us.

Coming here a few weeks ago I felt restless and strange. Thanks mainly to my parents, I have come to feel at home again. The area no longer feels strange as it did when we were visiting or thinking about it from Brynbeidog, but is now familiar again. Not exactly as before, of course—I could never again find that unselfconscious participation which must precede all thinking about place; but without an unseeing, taken-for-granted attitude, either. For now, a certain magic, a preternatural sharpness about the look and feel of things, may have gone; but it has gone with anguish, with the intensity of that frustrated longing to come back.

25 April

Yesterday morning I took the children to Victoria Country Park. The water was high when we arrived, grey blue under a grey sky, and rough, in a strong wind. Yachts cut through the water on their sides, fishing boats dipped and rose at the bows, white horses were driven across the surface, and a big tanker with a black hull rode at anchor out on the middle. A broken sky of blown cloud; blown smoke over Fawley. The tide ebbing formed a waterline of gleaming orange stones, shells, countless fragments of smooth glass, white blue green. The IOW ferry as it passed looked small on the broad channel and against the farther shore. After the children had swung on a rope and played on the shore Emily sat at the foot of the wall and wrote a poem:

> the shells that roll under the sea
> the wav's that roll and seif [swerve]
> in the sun.

Afterwards I drove back to Wales, in rain, but as I approached Plynlimmon the sky was clear on the other side of the mountains, and I came down to a mild dry evening.

29 April

Setting out to walk to work I saw the postman arriving but decided to wait in hope until the evening or late afternoon—the difficult hour. Words of a psalm on the slate side of a ledger tomb near Llanbadarn church porch:

SO TEACH US TO NUMBER OUR DAYS
THAT WE MAY APPLY OUR HEARTS TO WISDOM

Jackdaws nesting in gaps alongside the slate clockface on the tower. The daffodils are dead now among the tombs & mounds. In places the graves form a wild, buried garden of terraces and ridges. Under grass, nettles and brambles many stones—whole families of stones—stand up with a solemn and touching dignity. Herb Robert with scarlet leaves are out in the walls, and overhead on the path uphill hawthorn leaves, blackthorn blossom, and occasionally—the freshest, sappiest green of spring—horse chestnut leaves. Dandelions have risen fiercely everywhere. Violets like tiny faces meet the eye with their look.

1 May
At Blaen Cwrt with Gillian Clarke and Dave Thomas; sawing logs in light rain; sitting by a big fire that shot sparks up the chimney, smoke curling "like fern" on the walls, while rain beat loudly on the tin and perspex roof. Sodden fields around, hedges & hedgebanks, sheep, misty distances—these and the earth underfoot, the shaly rock, mossed wood greening my hands, and sawdust, make me feel again the very ground of Brynbeidog. Here's the horse chestnut tree which, on my first visit years ago, was full of little black cats with green eyes, in crooks between branches, looking down through leaves.

19 May
A cold, wet, intermittently stormy May. Election fever gripping the advertising agencies.

On Tuesday I went with Dave to Cardiff for R. S. Thomas' 70th birthday celebration at the Sherman Theatre in the evening. After a showing of John Ormond's moving film, R. S. read. Trousers at half-mast as usual, his books & sheets of poems in a gas mask bag. He was evidently in good spirits, and quite relaxed afterwards, though his hands shook at the beginning of his reading. I spoke to him briefly; he'd heard that I'd been living in Winchester, and when I told him I was back in Aberystwyth, he said: "the right place for you".

Not a good month for me here, whether the right place or not. Shut in. Now I wait in suspense to see whether M. will be able to come tomorrow, or whether her brother's serious illness will prevent her at the last moment. I have been lethargic, depressed; a week ago I was blaming the department, our isolation in box-like offices, but then realized it was my withdrawal from people, my failure to write. Nothing truer than that we receive but what we give.

20 May
When Roger Garfitt came with Nigel Wells to read last night, Nigel was standing in for Frances Horovitz. Frances is weak; it was thought that an operation would clear her cancer, but it didn't. The months ahead will be critical.

M. rang this morning. She was called to her brother's bedside yesterday; he is in a desperate condition and there was clearly no question of her being able to come.

It isn't true to say I'm not disappointed for myself; the prospect of our being together for the next few days has helped to carry me through recent weeks. But the fact of a probable death, the fact of her grief for a dearly loved brother: these are stunning and numbing. Twelve days ago on her birthday, she was so happy. I read in Marcus Aurelius before getting up that a healthy state of mind is to be ready for anything.

21 May

To Mieke: in her brother's illness

All day the stillness
of a storm that will not break.
After sudden violence
of downpour, thunderclap,
the same clouds
shutting out the hills,
the sea a grey flagstone
at the town's back door.

I tried to reach you.
The shadow of my hand
moved on the paper
heavily, marking
the space between us.
I sensed you far off,
in a deeper stillness,
beside the hospital bed.

If I were Dafydd
I would send my seagull
over the mountains,
across England and the North Sea.
Where you lie with eyes open
in the dark it would come to you,
bringing love and sleep.

25 May
Wednesday
To Cardiff airport before dark—a big moon in the clear sky, hills in red light—to meet M.

Thursday
Mid-morning: went with M. to meet the children off the train at Cardiff station. Lunch outside a pub on Caerphilly mountain. Visited the castle, where Joe & Emily climbed on the walls, and were thrilled by the leaning tower, the moat, and the vastness of the place. A row on Roath Park Lake.

Friday
Took Joe & Emily to Llangwyryfon in the afternoon, and they visited the school. All the children shy of one another. "A bit embarrassing" (Joe). Saw Mari and met Bill Tyler in the road, waiting for his children. Drove past Brynbeidog. Just a glimpse of the house through the sycamores; but I didn't linger, the new owner was pulling in at the gate, and I didn't want to go in. Back in Aberystwyth we played the slot machines at the King's Hall before having a splendid spaghetti supper which M. prepared.

Saturday
To Harlech in rain, along tortuous narrow roads. Visited the castle, where the children walked round the battlements. Then had a picnic among the dunes at Shell Island, and rolled tyres on the huge sandy beach. Gathered starfish & shells. A cold wind.

Sunday
To see Gill & Dave at Blaen Cwrt on another damp morning. Left at 12. Picnic lunch by Llangorse Lake. After two more stops, at a motorway café, & for a snack in Devizes, we reached Pennington and my parents' home at Hayford early evening. I left M. there and took the children back to Winchester, seeing Sue briefly, and making the round journey in little more than one and a half hours. Supper with Mum & Dad. To bed in separate rooms.

Monday
Up at 5.30. Crossing the Forest we saw a fox disappearing into roadside undergrowth, and young rabbits along the verge. Donkeys at Brockenhurst. Time of cow parsley, snowy hawthorn, white & pink horse chestnut candles. Waited with M. at Eastleigh airport until it was time for her to board the plane. The sad poetry of an almost deserted departure lounge, squared linoleum like a runway, with at first one other passenger—a middle aged man—pacing slowly up & down.

31 May
I won't write of M. We speak and write to each other. I never dreamt of such warmth and fullness, or of the seeing and understanding that *are* a person.

I'm so blind in some ways or so self-doubting that it takes M. and Gill to make me see how important I am to Joe & Emily, how much they love me, and I often feel that the children understand me better than I understand them or myself. It was wonderful being with them, all of us together.

4 June
To Margam with Peter Lord for the opening of the Sculpture Park. My invitation came from Lee, and I walked round the Park with him & Kate & their boys. A fascinating place: landscaped parkland and gardens with rhododendrons and azaleas below high rocky bluffs; ruins of the Cistercian abbey; the burnt-out shell of the mock-Jacobean great house; the fine 18th century orangery. As we climbed through oak & beech woods and through heather & bracken on the open hillside onto high bare moorland, the smoking steel works of Port Talbot came into view, with the channel and the English coast beyond, and Gower cliffs to the west. It rained as we walked on the top and the day was close. Glynne Williams was at the opening, and I saw *Shout* and his other works. Lee's *Head of Staz* also impressed me, as did a magnificent Frink head. But there was a lot that was only whimsical or a formal game, clichés of contemporary sculpture, which looked especially vacuous against the medieval ruins and the modern industrial forms.

Peter was in a negative mood all day, partly because of his extremely critical yet ambivalent attitude towards art in general and sculpture in particular at present, and his conviction that work in the Park should be a response to its environment and the culture of Wales—which little was. We came back through Newcastle Emlyn, stopping for a meal in a new bistro. He then vented his frustration by probing me—it was more nearly an attack—about my lack of involvement with a people, and what he sees as my passive acceptance of English cultural conditions that make poetry inaccessible except to a tiny minority. I was too tired by this time to do much more than tug at the knot in my mind.

10 June
Tired and depressed after a long night listening to the election results. In the end what had once seemed unbelievable was made to seem inevitable, partly as a result of the polls. It's been hard in recent weeks to believe how serious the issues are: thought in Britain that can't be turned into a slogan or a mindless catchword is allowed no public existence. I know the defeatism & demoralization widely apparent on the left, where there's more passion in the hatred for Mrs Thatcher than in defence of humane values. The Election was won and lost mainly because the real passion of conviction was *in* her, and in reaction against her, instead of in any vision of the society we want.

15 June
> We live in a world of unreality and dreams. To give up our imaginary position as the centre, to renounce it, not only intellectually but in the imaginative part of our soul, that means to awaken to what is real and eternal, to see the true light and hear the true silence… To empty ourselves of our false divinity, to deny ourselves, to give up being the centre of the world in imagination, to discern that all points in the world are equally centres and that the true centre is outside the world, this is to

consent to the rule of mechanical necessity in matter and of free choice at the centre of each soul. Such consent is love.
> Simone Weil, 'Forms of the Implicit Love of God'

19 June
Cuckoo, from high on the wooded slopes of Cwmrheidol. Buzzard over Devil's Bridge, smaller than a winged seed. I sat with Peter in hot sun on the bank behind his house.

Midsummer Day
Climbed Pendinas with Dave in the evening, sun occasionally visible as a red bar through grey cloud. *Hush* of sea on the beach, hoarse and sibilant; the grey town shadowy & mysterious. M. rang late: a breath of laughter & wine.

27 June
In Winchester, memories of family life springing up to torment me.

Dusty the dog chased swallows on the rugby field, the birds keeping low as if to encourage him, then swerving out of reach. The limes over the stream were light and cool. Warm glow of red brick. Echoing strokes of the Cathedral bell. Did I ever really live here?

Took Emily for a picnic lunch to Horsebridge Mill, where Mary Casey lived as a child. A coot & its chicks on the clear waters of the Test below the bridge. The river and all the grounds are private so we walked along the lane, under elderflowers & wild roses, and ate our sandwiches in a gateway. We picked plantain and played "soldiers" with them, moving slowly from bridge to bridge and through Houghton. Emily's company and her enjoyment greatly cheered me. It was a delight being with her. Even so, I couldn't help realizing that I've never seen a more exclusive place even in Hampshire. And this only a few miles from where my grandfather, "Pop" Mould, as a boy, scared rooks from the corn.

Back in Winchester I sat with Emily in the park watching cricket; as we did last summer, down the steps from Monks Road and over the iron bridge, yards from the family home. Now I saw the place Sue & I living in Wales had long dreamt of. Like last year, Joe & his friends were swimming and playing fully clothed in the river by the School of Art.

Did I expect to be as "free" as Sue says she is, and to grieve no longer? I must learn to watch these feelings pass. And to love the children less selfishly.

A love like M's that draws me out… I've so much to learn, so much to unlearn.

To Emily

> A year later I see
> the hare in front of us
> on the misty downland ride,

keeping the same distance;
the ladybirds you counted
on weeds beside the wheat.

We sat at last to sketch a tree
but secretly drew each other:
father and daughter.
I caught the exact angle
and shape of your sandal.

A year later I see—
as though this morning
we had gone out early
in the dust and the dew,
leaving the others asleep.

30 June
Poetry reading at Leamington. A good evening with Keith Turner and friends.

I took Mother to stay overnight with her sister, Midge, who talked family history and brought out photographs. Sarisbury Green Carnival 1914, Pop Mould with his wife and young family driving in a procession of traps & carts, several of which belonged to him. Granny Elkins. The Fulford family (Mother's aunt & uncle & their children) at Bishopstone, the downland ridge behind them. Mother as a young woman dandling a child—Midge's eldest daughter—in the water at Brownwich (*Brinidge*, as Mother always pronounced it).

The mystery of other people's lives; all the greater when they are ancestors, strange familiars. How hard it is to believe in personal death, though nothing is more evident. Figures of the long-dead, in the fullness of their lives. But what they "say" isn't simple, whatever it is. There's a depth here I can't fathom. They speak of life as well as death, and of the mystery of kinship.

Pop was highly sexed, a great lover of women. Learning this, I felt immediate sympathetic recognition! Without this we must all look like period-pieces to each other across the generations: which is a total denial of life, and another instance of the picturesque. We are the same flesh.

Midge was born between two boys: James Mould who lived for 10 months, and another—possibly Charles—who lived 2 weeks.

Such unlived lives are the most haunting, with an excruciating pathos, all the more for the name belonging to no consciousness, no conscious claimant. Mother was shaken by Midge's insistence that Pop hated and ill-treated her because she survived and these boys didn't. For Mother, he is her model of patience and kindness, gentleness and generosity; she finds it almost impossible to believe that he could have treated anyone else differently. For me, remembering his blue, watery eyes, his benevolent domed head, he is suddenly turbulent, alive. I think especially of my brother Tony, and this grandfather is suddenly more "ours", and we are more "his".

Seeing more of the life of others, I feel myself too less knowable, impossible to contain in an image, and with this feeling life moves and expands.

2 July
Brockenhurst station. 6.30 a.m. A grey morning, the platform deserted. The second hand travels round the illuminated face of the station clock, and the minute hand jerks forward with a tick as it passes the 12.

Later, on the boat train to Harwich, I get into conversation with the young American sitting opposite me. Steve Kraus, from Minnesota: a doctor of tropical medicine who has already worked in Thailand, Vietnam, Cambodia and other places in the Far East, and intends to devote the next 15 years of his life to working in the Third World. We talked on the train and most of the time on the crossing to the Hoek. He comes from a large Catholic family and was brought up on a farm, now over 1000 acres, but it started with a grant of 5 acres from Abraham Lincoln to his great grandfather. Steve talked about the shortness of memory in America, and of the bitter and divided feelings arising from the Vietnam War, which are being suppressed. He was a student in the sixties; now his younger brother is a National Guardsman, and Steve remembers when the National Guards actually shot students. His America is the country of small communities, farms, the Mississippi, vast tracts of wilderness, like that in which his father taught him as a boy to hunt and shoot. Reagan's America, the Moral Majority, the materialist dream and even the great cities, are all alien to him. So is the American solution of throwing technology at Third World problems; for him, the first need is to understand the people and their cultures (he was reading a book on Buddhism and had recently spent a fortnight in a Buddhist monastery in Thailand) while the doctor's task is to treat the whole person.

We were on deck when the coast of Holland came into sight—at first, the flare stacks, tanks & cranes of a giant refinery, completely still, with no sign of life. Steve likened it to a city after a nuclear war, but it was friendlier to my eye. He was going on to meet his Thai girlfriend in Copenhagen, and we parted with an exchange of addresses.

M. was waiting when I got through Customs and drove me back to Groningen: misty vistas of long straight motorways, a first impression of flat meadowland, cows and windmills, canals, new, brick houses with stepped gables, all neatly ordered.

8 July
80 KORREWEG
On the roof garden looking out over aerials, chimney pots, red roofs of Groningen, church spires, the great gothic spire of Martinikerk, the water tower, trees and tower blocks. It is hot, hazy, after two similar days which ended in storm: rain, lightning, crashing thunder, but no relief; afterwards a thicker, more steamy heat. How quickly the full days go, days & nights of love! How soon I forget the feel

of days alone; even now when I'm no longer alone, but the distance between us creates longing! But now that's only a thought. Here's fullness, everything given.

9 July
Woltersum. The broad, brown canal under a silver-blue sky. Great barges low in the water, heavily laden, flying the Dutch or German flag. We sit on the bank beside the path and people on the barges and motor boats wave to us. Flat fields seen through gaps between poplars stretch into the distance on the opposite bank. Like a gallery of Dutch landscape paintings, the gaps frame a far view of trees grouped round red-brick farmhouse and barn; light through the gaps lies on the water in an arc, like the strokes on a clockface. A solitary gull settles on the water. All around us, the long summer grasses.

On to Eemshaven, to a meal of fish & wine in a restaurant raised on stilts high above the shore. Silver-grey mud, silver-grey water, tide coming in and the German coast across the sea becoming a clearer, more definite blue. Salt in the air after warm inland smells of hay & manure. Later the sun sinks, a smoky red globe, on a landscape of vast fields, dykes, windmills. The windmills haunt the land—if very tired or even a little unbalanced mentally, it would be easy to see them as giants or a strange, disturbing kind of creature; they have such presence, their sails (usually three are visible) raised like arms or wings, their towers shaped like helmets or shells. A Ruysdael painting of a windmill by the shore hung in my bedroom when I was a boy; now the image deep in my mind comes to life again.

10 July
To Emmeloord in the Polder: a mere 30 years of history in the towns and villages and on the surface of the earth, in a landscape designed by an architect and a geometrician. M's mother gave me a beautiful blue tile, a plant for my parents, and her blessing: "All is good".

11 July
In this flat country where so much is earth, water and sky the stones left by the Ice Age and either gathered together into small groups or placed singly in a garden or by the roadside provide a counterforce: a sense of the primitive and the irregular to set against the predominantly manmade order. This is even truer of the cromlechs—*hunebed*—like those we saw on the way back from Emmen: long narrow constructions of great boulders with passages underneath. At first, on the flat sandy soil, they look "out of place", as the cromlechs in the Preseli mountains or in Wiltshire or Ireland do not. But here depth of time emerges slowly as an impression on the mind while in those other places it's the first thing you see.

24 July
In Cambridge, at Kim Landers'. M. is asleep on a mattress on the floor beside me. After our travels in the last fortnight, an opportunity to set down a few impressions.

In Amsterdam, faces in the Rijksmuseum, a gallery of faces: *The Nightwatch*, *The Jewish Bride*, Rembrandt's mother, portraits by Hals, Vermeer's still-life figures, and the original of Ruysdael's mill. Faces in the city streets; a sweating hot-faced American evangelist working himself up in front of a crowd outside the station. Dark interiors, sunlight in the streets, opaque canals; a beautiful city, with many young, ravaged faces.

In Zeeland, drinking wine by candlelight in a garden surrounded by cornfields, beyond them a dyke and the sea.

Slow journey from Sheerness to Victoria stopping at every station; midnight arrival, exhausted, at Brockenhurst.

A day in Dorset. Knowlton, the ruined medieval church inside a Bronze Age circle. Tower against circle, stone against earth, reddish brown sandstone and white flint against grass and surrounding corn; encircled stillness amidst the crosscurrents of the fields.
On Hambledon: making love in a grassy hollow surrounded by purple thistles, fields below golden yellow, white, all the many shades of green; patterns within patterns, smoke from the first stubble burning but an as yet almost untouched summer, with dynamic lines in fields of straw, and house-high piles of bales in other fields.

Joe's birthday: at the Beaulieu Motor Museum. A good time for us all, beginning with lunch at the pub on the waterfront at Eling. Norleywood after dark, moon two days from full between black pines, *churr* of a nightjar from the woods. A sudden upsurge of sadness—for time passing, for Joe so open-natured and vulnerable, for all the days & nights when I'm not with them.

Hurst: horned poppies against the castle walls, deadly nightshade growing from shingle, a pair of terns trying to distract us with their cries. White, elegant lighthouse, ugly grey castle. The cottages and former pub are up for sale; we share a fantasy of living there, for a year if no longer, and plan our Hurst "book". Blue sky, blue sea, Island & Needles chalk-blue.

29 July
At Moor Farm, Reepham with the Grandjeans. The sculptor's house. Here in particular I notice forms: the shipshape red roofs of house & barn, with tiles like waves; the field track sweeping down to the house in its hollow ; fields of pinnacled corn, fields of sugar beet; sculptures in the garden and in the barn studio. Everywhere the presence of things made or being made. And the weather is hot: blue sky and a few brushstrokes of white cloud. High summer: deep country.
Our last day & night together for a while. Waking in the night I felt I could see time passing. The garden & fields were an eerie grey with looming, darker

masses of trees and shrubs; high up, a waning moon. Images may be like pebbles collected from places visited—hard and definite in the mind as pebbles turned over in the pocket. We had come in from an evening with Dick & Afkham Davis, who had been very welcoming although also very tired; now in the early morning half-light I turned over a few images from the past month… I am in the garden, Guy is sitting naked at our lunch table on the grass, M. is lying closeby reading Robert Gittings' essay on Frances Bellerby, Kate is playing music indoors and Lee is working in his studio with an electric drill on a block of stone. Two of the four brown chickens are pecking under the apple tree, which is full of sparrows chirping loudly. Earlier, walking with M. up the lane from the village, I said that we are never slow enough to see much—in a hedge, for example, the eye darting from butterfly to grass to flower to shadows of nettles and fall of light, sees nothing clearly. We are too quick in the wrong way; all around us is slow or fast as we are not. Peculiar shapes, shadows of apple leaves, sway and quiver on the typescript pages she is reading; a jet rumbles high up; the hens are still picking under the other tree, but Guy has gone indoors without me noticing, and now with ducks quacking on the pond I become aware of the garden behind me. But I could never *catch* this last month, not a minute of it; only live and work *from* the life we share.

14 August
A day beginning with my parents driving me to Brockenhurst station at dawn, a hare & rabbits by the roadside, sky hard and clear as a polished precious stone, with the scratch of a vapour trail, the high-flying jet momentarily a burning star when the sun caught it, ghosts of mist hanging at head height over gorse, deer beside the railway line through the Forest—and coming to an end with a train speeding through darkness towards Groningen, as I talked and drank lager with a young Dutch couple, the girl a student of Dutch and English, the young man a biologist working to develop a potato resistant to the night frosts of early spring. And in the meantime towns and landscapes slowly falling away, and the North Sea, at first soft, greeny blue with patches of sandy light, then a dark slate blue, creased, wrinkled, and approaching the coast of Holland, through lanes of tankers at anchor, past the spidery form of an oil rig, divided by wavy lines of scum.

16 August
Another early morning train journey—Groningen—Hanover—Berlin—a reflection of the round red sun travelling beside us on the water of a dyke, but now, as I write, the sun is higher, white, we have already crossed the border into Germany, though the flat landscape here is much the same, hares & lapwings in green fields, herons flying over water, barges on canals, here and there a relic of the war.

17 August
A visitor to Berlin first sees space—the size and layout of the city, with wide, straight roads, blocks of buildings, parks. He next sees history—in memorials

and place names, and in the public consciousness of history—the consciousness which, for example, rebuilds the Reichstag in its original monumental and barbarous form, and puts on inside it an exhibition of German history, where all day Hitler shouts again on film, the masses assent passionately to total war, and images of the ruined city shadow its present remade form—as if the ghosts of bombed & burnt-out buildings existed inside the present buildings. And if he sees history at first in individual names and actions—Bismarck, Walther Rathenau, the conspirators of 17 July, Rosa Luxemburg & Karl Leibknecht, Van der Lubbe—he is then overwhelmed by the sense of history as a force shaping generations and moulding individual lives even in their most intimate parts and in their apparent freedom of will.

Coming from the Reichstag yesterday, I was overwhelmed by this sense. And today I saw the power of world history in the Wall, and against it, unbearably poignant, wreaths for those who have died trying to cross. Without warning, tears came to my eyes at the instant I saw them and knew what they were, in that place of massive, impersonal power. In this city I can only see how little of ours is truly our own... Here history is no longer a word or a subject or a romantic preoccupation with tradition and ancestry, but a living power more terrifying than the most savage ancient god.

18 August

On the S-Bahn to East Berlin. First a long wait on the border behind a party of French schoolchildren. Then a long, hot day of walking about the city, with cool intervals in restaurants, under trees, at the graves of Brecht & his wife (simple, plainly lettered stones, near to sepulchral "houses"—family tombs pockmarked by bullets—and Hegel's grave).

Far fewer cars (none of them expensive) and people than in West Berlin; far fewer shops; no advertisements; none of the glitter, noise & garishness of the streets where everything is for sale. But the East Berlin we saw wasn't "grey" either. Here, wherever possible, the monumental architecture of an imperial past has been preserved, converted to use by the new order, and exists alongside the new—most impressive, the television tower, its long sensitive needle on a bubble of stone & glass reaching far into the sky. We watched young soldiers changing guard, goose-stepping, outside the building where the eternal flame commemorating the war dead is kept burning; their faces trembled; they weren't deadpan like guardsmen in London. We visited Berlin Cathedral, which is being renovated, its sombre dome reflected in the tinted glass of a large new building opposite. We looked down from a gallery onto the floor littered with debris, and high up into the roof, over religious plaques and sculptures still keeping their bright paint on the scarred walls. It made a sinister impression in its heavy grey stone: brother to the Reichstag, a massive embodiment of late imperial pride masquerading as a church of Christ, in a style borrowed from another time.

Hot and tired, we dozed briefly on the edge of a park. I lay flat out on the grass, my brother Tony nodded off close by. Mieke noted the astonished and disapproving looks of the other people in the park, where everyone kept to the paths and no one stepped on the grass. Later we took the S-Bahn to Treptower Park and walked to the Russian War Memorial—a formidable landscaped work, awe-inspiring, and moving. The difference between this and the monumental museum pieces scattered all over the city is that this means what it is.

But what could we really know, beyond the seriousness of purpose in all we saw? Buildings, memorials, fountains, statues of workers, open spaces: a cultural façade, with little to indicate what life feels like for people on this side. No signs of the sickness everywhere evident in the West, where the sight of madness or confusion is common on the streets, and in many faces the naked desire to exploit or be exploited, to consume or be consumed, is frightening. But our impressions here were of a carefully arranged front, the life behind it unknowable on a brief visit.

Walking from the theatre along Unter den Linden at night we saw a large shapeless yellow moon over the city roofs. The moon was dusky red when we saw it again from the train window, behind the head and ritual gestures of a tall man with a Slavic, Dostoevskian face, and a crippled foot. He was returning from the East drunk on vodka bought from the international shop (drinkers regularly make the journey for this purpose) and he talked loudly at us, not aggressively, but from some strange and lonely foreign place. "Atlantis" and "Einstein", often repeated, were the only words I understood. He was probably convinced in his mind he was offering us a key to a mystery.

We none of us have our meaning alone: I realize this very strongly here, and see its truth in many more ways than I could now say. And here in the West the constant pressure is to act as if only the contrary were true, and meaning something we stole or bought from others, or found apart from them, in our selves & our appetites.

The last evening of our visit Tony took us to Teufelsberg and Teufelsee. We had eaten and drunk well but were sober though dozy & heavy with the dream-like after-effects.

First, a huge, man-made hill, grey & dusty under dry vegetation, a space-age American radar station on the top. Berlin lay below us in every direction as far as we could see, extending beyond dark pinewoods in the foreground, and visible mainly as tall blocks, factories and towers, including the rival television towers of East and West. Whether there are really wild boar in the pinewoods, as Tony claimed, I don't know, but the idea of their presence contributed to the atmosphere. This was the end of another hot day and the sky was smoky blue-grey & tarnished rose, with a light that brought out the darkness of the woods and the buildings. We were standing on the only hill in the city—created from the rubble of its ruins after the war and concealing unimaginable things under the surface, besides the burnt-out trams & lorries that a man who'd worked on its construction had told Tony were there.

It was darker when we went to Teufelsee, where a few people were swimming naked in the brown, unhealthy-looking water surrounded by trees—white heads apparently without bodies moving across the surface. The lake is said to be very deep, and dangerous, and it looked both. Here we unexpectedly met an acquaintance of Tony, a painter perhaps in his thirties, who is himself confused and who has taken a great interest in Julie, for "spiritual" reasons. Julie was with him beside the water when suddenly she cried out in childish excitement, and continued shrieking with delight as a tiny frog hopped across the ground and the young man gathered it in his hands and placed it in the water. There was a strangeness immediately visible in his eyes but we could tell nothing of his mental state or its causes except from what Tony said as we drove away: that he has an unnaturally intense relationship with his father, who was in the SS.

This detail in this setting again touched the nerve that we felt running through the city, a painful, exposed nerve that many Berliners feel but fewer see or want to see. It may be that being with Julie made us especially sensitive to this, because she's more disturbed than ever and there's always tension in being with her. On another memorable occasion we walked in hot sunshine round the lakes of a local park in Charlottenburg, and saw first the well-dressed old woman who walks up and down Sybelstrasse every day from early in the morning, and is said to be looking for her son killed in the war. Then we saw the boy who sits on a park bench turned away from other people and feeds sparrows which land on his body and eat from his hands, while Julie, in a bad mood, was muttering to herself as she fed the ducks or collected twigs and plants and any rubbish she could conceal from Tony. Here we found a badly injured hooded crow and M. carried it back, nursing it gently in her arms. Julie, now walking beside me and concerned for the crow, kept saying how moving she found it and asking me: "How could you put this into words, uncle?"

21 August
We left Berlin at midday in sweltering heat. Through East Germany to Marienborn, armed guards checking passports, stations empty except for guards and the dogs they use to sniff under the train in case anyone is concealed there; more armed guards in West Germany, in different coloured uniforms… The heat continued fatiguing, and towards evening, nearing the Dutch border, a terrific storm broke in front of the train—sudden blaze of purple zigzags against dark cloud—and we went into and through it, rain sluicing the windows and all around us heavy darkness. Hours later, when after several changes we arrived very tired at Groningen the streets were wet and the storm was rumbling and flashing outside the city.

28 August
Day after the annual Bommen Berend festival in Groningen. Leaving at 8.30 a.m. from the beautiful waterfront in the centre of the town I sailed with Hans & Agnes in a party of people aboard an Aak—one of the old flat-bottomed ships, rather like a barge with sails, formerly used for carrying grain, stones, turf, etc. on the inland

waterways. We went in a convoy of similar boats, which shut off their engines and broke into sail—beautiful brown, dark-red or mushroom-white canvas when well out of the town, and carried us far into Groningen province, from Hoge Der A & Reitdiep to Hunze. A cloudy day, the breeze cold enough to make us shiver through our thick jerseys, but absorbing, and enjoyable. The waterway broadened between stubble fields, herons rising from rushes at the edge, between fields of maize, and pasture, with here & there a church among trees on a low mound rising above the wide-spreading flat land. We waited for bridges to open for us, at a sluice (where a German boy managed to fall in, and came out dripping, with a shamefaced grin) and eventually reached Zoutkamp, where M. was waiting to drive us back.

29/30 August
Night on the boat from the Hoek. Starry sky, big half moon over the coast of Holland, lights of the shore & refinery stretching out into a long line as the coast recedes.
    Well, I knew how it would be: once with M. time would fly. This summer has been the happiest of my life.
    The light was autumn when I left. M. found the first acorn in its cup and gave it me. We will never leave each other.

Morning. On the train at Harwich, nearly an hour before departure. In spirit I'm still in the rooms on the Korreweg...
    Back to a month of work. The danger, more than ever, to wish time away.

§

[N]obody can really wish to be born and to die in any time but his own. One can wish for oneself nothing but a share in the real joys and real sufferings of one's time.
    Christa Wolf, *The Quest for Christa T*

16 September
Over lunch today my parents talked with me about the threat of nuclear war: their opposition to Cruise and the multiplication of weapons that can only destroy the world several *more* times over, of the construction of fall-out shelters for administrators with money saved from the closure of hospitals, of their feeling for those with young children who feel the threat and their powerlessness most acutely. Their forthrightness surprised me. I found myself opposing the sense of inevitability (with the consequent resignation and even acceptance) with more hope. What I didn't say, and have hardly admitted to myself, is that in some people the impetus of the machine breeds a perverse, orgiastic excitement that *wills* the end. The Bomb is not only an external threat; it has entered into us in ways that have hardly been recognised yet.

After lunch, with these things in mind, I went out into the Forest.

Holmsley: over rounded, gravel hills following a leached-white, stony path that became a pony track through heather & bracken, expecting at every careful step to disturb or tread on an adder. In the valley bottom, near the first trickle of Avon Water, I walked along the abandoned railway track (having looked covetously at the deserted level-crossing keeper's cottage) and crossed to the edge of an inclosure. Sweet chestnut, including a fallen tree with dead branches among branches thick with leaves & prickly-coated fruit, birch, beech, oak, alder where it was boggy, firs and colonies of orange toadstools. Saw a grey squirrel, a dark butterfly flying up fast and high, magpies, a rabbit among gorse bushes, and heard and saw a green woodpecker. Play of light & shadow, movement & stillness, among leaves and branches and ferns: the quick and elusive spirit which the solidity and darkness associated with woods belie. Out on the heath again. Dark blue cloud masses, blue sky, revelations of the sun. Now, as I climbed back to the car, coming over the brow of the hill, a sudden burst of sunlight at my back flooded past me, and, with it, a fine rain blown from the same quarter by a wind from the sea. Before me, towards Wilverley, a rainbow, one foot apparently on the heath, the other lightly touching a distant wood. Refreshed, I sat in the car and wrote a card to M.

At night, though, the restlessness came back, as it often does. This is no time for lovers to be living apart. Yet on the way back from Holmsley, listening to the news on the car radio, but relaxed, my mind moving again to local rhythms, I'd thrown off the prevailing sense of time: no longer stages of growth, a lifetime, generations, but every year a series of crises, a wasting of energy, in the shadow of a meaningless end. "Progress" a sensation of being hurtled along a highway marked no through road.

19 September
Dad, unable to see well enough, had to discontinue painting in the morning's bright light & shadows. The eye specialist at his last appointment told him outright that he will go completely blind. Impossible with him to know whether he is preparing himself inwardly or wishing the problem away.

Late afternoon. A walk at Yew Tree Bottom.
On the way back I sat under a solitary oak on the heath and looked out, under its heavy branches swaying in the wind, over gorse & bracken, down over the slopes of the heath concealing the abandoned railway track, to the woods of Avon Water valley and along the valley to Sway Tower rising from trees, against the line of the Island and the sky.

Driving past the tower the other day I told myself that sooner or later it will be demolished, and imagined watching its fall. In this way too people prepare themselves, or try to, whether consciously or not, for the most personal tragedies. I do; but it doesn't begin to be enough: not enough to see human lives one after another, growth and decay, "ages" being made and superseded, or in the individual life phase following phase. This is usually how things look and feel; I know the sadness in my bones. But in any order based on love nothing is lost or superseded, "all is safely gathered in".

Only any human work, lifework, can produce at best only a very partial image, or glimpse, of this; reason, perception, imagination, at their greatest stretch, can only ever realize a fraction of all that's involved in a moment's experience, in one life with all its relations in and with the world.

Walking along the abandoned railway track, light and wind in my face, ponies on the bank above me, I remembered Simone Weil's statement, that it's not my business to think about myself, but to think about God, and leave God to think about me. Love as detachment. I had in my mind, also, an image of the closest human unity: the original family at-oneness which was a cause of Frances Bellerby's intensity, and no doubt a source of the belief in unity in creation which she came to hold. Love as attachment. But in each case a passionate human struggle: the action of love.

21 September
Imagine: a small boy from a poor family sharing a bedroom with his wealthy cousin, a mine-owner's son, in the mine-owner's house. The safe is in the room, and as the boy lies awake in semi-darkness the man comes in, opens the safe and takes out a wad of banknotes to give to his son. But first he crosses the room and runs the notes down the boy's face.

This happened to my father, at Dudley. The rich man's name was Ben Ganner. The same who stabbed Dad's mother to the heart—imagine—by telling her that her husband, Tom Hooker, had borrowed £5 from him sometime before and hadn't repaid it yet. His mine eventually failed, and he ended broke.

Tom Hooker, Thomas Alfred, had his second name from the poet laureate, Alfred Lord Tennyson. He was completely intolerant of anything he didn't understand, which included all the arts, but very skilled and industrious in his own work—gardening—which is also, of course, an art; loyal to his origins—at every visit he would sign the register at Lyndhurst church where he'd sung in the choir as a boy—and loyal to his friends, men he'd worked with, gardeners on other estates. He was a snob too—imagine—contemptuous of uneducated Yorkshire people with their way of speaking, and with detailed, admiring knowledge of the gentry who owned local estates. I remember taking him (or perhaps he took me) to a county cricket match at Bournemouth: a small, old, white-haired man who made me anxious that he'd get himself run over by his method of stopping the bus by stepping in front of it. But he was more than able to look after himself. He loved his cricket and had been a good cricketer when young. He was always kind to me.

I saw recently a photograph of Dad's O'Brien grandmother, the Irishwoman, wife of James Wastie. She had six children. A tall woman, with a strong face. On the other side his grandfather was a Welshman. How else explain the curiously un-English physical distinction, and the musical and artistic gifts, which appeared as a passion in the boy whose own parents had no sympathy or understanding for them?

No one, I think, really understands such "influences". An aptitude, an inclination, a build, a face, *flowing in*, without immediate contact, in some cases across generations, from one person to another. Then in one generation a gift may be realized, or ruined, or completed, that began in another. But where does a gift begin? Where do *we* begin?

How poignant to think of one life "completing" another which was perhaps spoilt by being unable to achieve completion, because of personal weakness or adverse circumstances! How encouraging and companionable to know that one is carrying through and passing on a gift, any gift for living, whether artistic or not! It must be our physical separation, greatly compounded by the estranging and fragmenting bias of the modern world, that has weakened, in many to the point of non-existence, the actual sense, like hearing or touch, of our living by and in and through one another.

Yet the knowledge that a person is many might make him terrified at not being *one*. Loss of a sense of identity may occur for many reasons, but it shouldn't occur for this reason. For, surely, the more I open up, the more I know myself a channel, the more I know in myself the presence of my makers, the more fully and securely am I myself. And the more open to mystery, for only to the most literal-minded, to those fixed in a scientific theory of the influence of heredity on the individual, is there in this any disproof of the existence of soul. I learnt from David Jones not to oppose creation as process and creation as free act, God the maker and man the maker, the things of which we are made and the unique person. But I leant in my thought from the beginning—hence its frequent tangle—towards both/and, not either/or constructions.

28 September

A hot day, mist of autumn light. A buzzard in the ash tree near the churchyard wall flew away quite leisurely as I approached. Peacocks & red admirals on the buddleia. A handful of sweet blackberries after breakfast.

Posted the typescript of Frances Bellerby's *Selected Stories* to Alan Clodd. I sweated over the Introduction, having been unable to settle to it until last week when my excuses for delay ran out. Why is writing so hard to start? I'm weary of the struggle to be concise and concentrated in prose, though I'd find it even harder to be expansive now.

30 September

To Mynydd Bach with Susan Butler and Ian Walker on a windy day for them to take photographs for the forthcoming *Poets in a Landscape* anthology. On the slopes of Hafod Ithel, among the rocks of "Arthur's Seat", by a ruin beside Llyn Eiddwen. Memories but no sadness at the time, rather an enlargement of spirit such as I've always felt up there, free from the pettiness of Aberystwyth & the university. But the following day, alone with the weekend in front of me—grief. I saw Brynbeidog again, and the world of family life when the children were little, and grief and incomprehension came flooding to the surface. I understand how people who are, or feel themselves to be, completely alone, can turn their faces to the wall.

2 October
Sunday evening. Peter Lord was here a little while ago. While he was here Dave rang from Cardiff: Frances Horovitz died this morning.

3 October
A closed-in day, but late in the afternoon a blade of light at the horizon, between sea and sky.

> I run with the dolphin
> I run with the sea
> I have outrun darkness
> do not stop me now—
>   Frances Horovitz, 'Dream'

9 October
Afternoon walk on the beach at Tan-y-bwlch. Tide out. Ystwyth in brown spate, the sea inshore brown and foaming white. A litter of whiplash kelp hold-fasts on grey stones. Walking away from the groyne, War Memorial, castle ruins, St Michael's, and Old College appear behind—all grey, and in front a fine spray blows across the grey shore. Here and there a beautiful pebble. I found a red one, bloodstone veined with white; but its colours faded in my pocket and I threw it back into the sea.

21-23 October
Academi conference on modern Welsh literature at Gregynog. I drove Ned Thomas over on Friday afternoon, and back again on Sunday.

Hywel Teifi Edwards' memorable lecture was something of a performance, due to the man's powerful personality, and probably also because of the tradition of nonconformist preaching behind it. He showed, with brilliant and witty illustrations, how pious conventions, arising from deference to English opinion of Wales, from the time of the Blue Books until well into this century, rigidly controlled what Welsh writers could actually say. How, in fact, they *edited* their humanity, purveying stereotyped ideal images of figures such as the collier and the shepherd, and of Welsh women. This lecture was the strongest manifestation of the spirit dominating the conference, which I called anti-idealizing. Little talk of the praise tradition or of the Welsh writer's advantages, but much of their challenges and struggles, in a confident, self-critical spirit. Hywel lamented the lack of a Welsh Gerald Scarfe, seeing *My People* as necessary and refreshing, not to say realistic.

There were frosts on both nights. Once I heard an owl, and another time woke before light and going to the window saw the full moon burning in a clear sky over the woods and frosty fields.. Later I went out alone, when frost was melting and falling in drops from leaves at the top of a beech tree on which the sun was shining, over pines on the other side of the sunken lawn, while I stood at its foot in shadow looking at the unfrozen leaves. Frost furred the sundial, a gossamer like a miniature silk rope hanging slack and moist from the gnomon.

On Saturday afternoon, walking through the woods with Ned, we saw a pheasant among fallen leaves, head standing out but the brown body almost merging with the colour of the woodland floor. This was close to the spot where I once helped Bryan Johnson and his wife and two friends search for a ring. One of his friends—his agent, I think—had dropped it among the leaves. We didn't find it.

Ned lectured on Waldo Williams. A lot of our talk was about him: his reading of Jefferies & other English writers, the time he spent in Wiltshire, Waldo studying English at Aberystwyth, the influence on him of English & German romanticism, Celtic Twilight and the Tree or Fountain or Fire of the early Romantics. In Ned's view, the symbol of the fire with its many sparks is the most democratic version of the great source of energy. As in Waldo's case, surely there has to be an actual community to which the poet *belongs*—but to what degree? Is *in spirit* alone ever enough?—before he can make actual, in his work of remembrance and celebration, a brotherhood of living and dead. All the questions for and about a poet that really matter arise from the question of whom he belongs to—the people, the "matter", what he receives and how he gives it back, hands it on, and to whom.

28 October
Met Mieke at Cardiff airport at 9.30 pm, and having driven down mostly in the dark, drove back in the dark to Aberystwyth.

29 October
To Black Covert on a beautiful day, sunny & still, to see the river running with reflections of autumn leaves, a dipper in the water. Then to Strata Florida (Ystrad Fleur) where we found the abbey ruins closed but walked in the churchyard to see the yew under which Dafydd ap Gwilym is said to be buried. The heart of the ancient tree is hollowed out like a cave with a floor of dark mould & stones, but the grain of the living wood is like the currents of a powerful stream. As we stood under it in the stillness loud tapping noises sounded from its branches, and looking up we saw a nuthatch pecking at the wood, and could hear another higher up. We then saw that the great tree was alive with birds. Sunlight falling on marble and slate gravestones made them shine like mirrors. Afterwards we scrambled down to the Teifi where it runs under trees and between moss-covered rock.

30 October
To Bristol in rain and mist for Frances Horovitz's Benefit Reading at the Colston Hall, where we heard—among others—Ted Hughes, Seamus Heaney, Anne

Stevenson (who was excellent), Charles Tomlinson, P. J. Kavanagh, and Roger Garfitt reading Frances' poems.

Next morning, after staying the night with Val & George Thatcher at Marshfield, we drove first to Avebury and then to Liddington Hill. It was the first time I had climbed Liddington, and seen the stone with a plaque dedicated to Jefferies and Alfred Williams. First we passed a pill-box, then left the Ridgeway to walk to the earthworks where the stone is situated. Below us, the sweep of the hill Jefferies climbed from his home at Coate; and Swindon and the countryside disappearing into misty distance. The roar of traffic on the motorway was with us all the time. As we turned to walk down a broader cloud break let the sun through, and the day brightened and became warm.

3 November
Even after two days and in dirty light the colours of the leaves & bracken have deepened and become more vivid, and the birch leaves are delicate, tiny yellow flames. Today we drove to Kilpeck making a detour to Abbey Cwm Hir. Tender sandstone animals—rabbit, hare, ram's head—carved on the church; bondsmen and ploughmen under the dark red ploughland.

On the way back we visited the church at Credenhill. A plaque on the wall commemorates Thomas Traherne but the church has the air of a church that doesn't expect visitors. It is an unadorned *working* church. The doors were unlocked; we opened them, stepped inside and turned on the lights to see a plain, attractive interior, partially restored, Sunday school papers & hymn books but no cards or guide books, the big bible looking a little crumpled and lopsided on the lectern. I've driven past many times over the years, meaning to look in, as I've meant to climb Liddington, and never done either before.

Came back to give a reading to the Alun Lewis Society in the evening.

4 November
Friday already! On Mynydd Bach today, Llyn Eiddwen a still mirror of the pale grey sky. Sounds carried far. A shepherd whistling to his dogs near the cairn sounded like a bird—high and shrill, beginning of a curlew's call. Dogs barking could be heard miles away. We drove past Brynbeidog: mid-morning, the post van at the gate, house visible through the sycamores, Beidog running between garden edge and field, forming a pool under the waterfall… But the hedges around and up the lane have been sadly butchered, with more wire fences strung out along the bare banks. Sue recently dated the beginning of the end of our marriage to the savage ploughing of the field beside the Beidog, once Mr Morrice's field. Today, the derelict marshy fields on the other side were their usual rich autumn gold.

From Mynydd Bach we drove again to Ystrad Fleur: rust red bracken, dark brown to dark gold oak trees framed by the rounded doorway (which Dad sketched and painted on my parents' visit years ago); red and brown and gold against grey stone. Ancient grave slabs of Welsh princes & abbots lying worn almost featureless—except for a cross on a fragment of headstone—in the grass.

Withering herb Robert growing here and there in crevices in the ruins. At the yew again: no nuthatch today, but a robin perched on a red post-box as we drove away.

7 November
Today, Monday, the three of us were up by 5.45. Dave & I watched from the roof of the airport as M's plane taxied into position on the runway and took off, its red tail lights disappearing into a misty dawn sky. Then we drove back. I had classes in the afternoon, and now write this tired, the loneliness without her like a presence in the house.

15 November
There's a terrible, pathetic irony in the way in which we bring up our children, not just protecting them but showing them a world that welcomes them, a world that for all its avoidable dangers is magical, exciting, in which life is a great gift, while all the time we live in fear.

All the time we are telling the stories of welcome, stories whose rhythm belongs to times which, whatever *their* darkness, could assume the naturalness of growth, child to adult, generation to generation. Of course, it is unthinkable that when we have children it should be otherwise; but even as we delight in them we know ourselves no shelter, no protection, and that all the good we want for them, the good we try to prepare them to give and take, may in an instant be horribly blasted.

Writing this, I have an almost physical sense of Joe's sunnyness—of his joy and openness since he was a baby. These have opened me to the goodness in life, the love in people, opposed to the power & horror of the machinery poised to destroy us, and the mentality behind it, the arrogant stupefied blank denial. I know the delight in him, the capacity to carry through into adult life his gifts of friendship, understanding, love. But I glimpse this in almost all children—and see adults shut in, self-centred, defeated; as perhaps we have to be to live for long with the official adult madness. No, I can't accept that; only to live we have sometimes to forget it, as I can enjoy the walk uphill, greet the grey donkey in a field beside the path, watch an oak leaf spiral down in the stillness, read, plan the work I mean to do, think of time to come, and so forget my anger at the morning's news, or even thread the anger & fear among other threads, and when I come to write these words, find a kind of pleasure in setting them down as truthfully as I can.

Yesterday, at my window in college, I saw the sun go down—a red ball, not, as usual, into a band of blue-grey haze over the sea, but into the sea forming the horizon. And, as it "touched" the sea, the rim "touching" it became elongated, like a drop of molten metal forming a stem on the disc from which it flows; and it was then, for a while, like a red balloon, and for an instant the scene had the gaiety of a fairground! As the stem formed so the top of the disc was slightly flattened. The image I saw then, again for an instant, was of a red glazed pot spinning on a potter's wheel. Then the sun dropped below the horizon and I watched until it vanished. Walking downhill later, the sky over the sea and behind Pendinas was a huge explosion of bright, deep orange light and the ridge against it was black and sharp.

Every time I look at Llanbadarn churchyard it looks more to me like a place ripe for a Stanley Spencer resurrection! Strangely, thoughts of death arising there don't make me morbid or melancholy. There is, perhaps, a reassurance in the slate, in the sober, caring words, the shapely ledger tombs, as in the solidity of the great square tower, and the yew trees spilling berries on the flat slabs, feeding the mistle thrushes. A reassurance of time and process, of lifetimes in the centuries, all of this slowing the mind, giving it substance to rest on—a counter-force to seeing in and behind everything the terror of the last days or minutes, and even in the radiance of light itself the final flash.

20 November
Dad, on his 82nd birthday, remembered most vividly his eighth: in Derbyshire, huntsmen in red & black riding with hounds over the fields; the coachman's daughter & another child came to tea; beside his plate a present from his mother, his first paint box and brushes.

Sunday evening. Back at Llanbadarn after the long drive. I sometimes think that all my experience can be summed up by the one word, *returning*.

21 November
A brilliant, cold day. I lectured with some difficulty on David Jones in the morning, and spent most of the day in my room, feeling blocked up.

Some weekday hours in this cold autumn blaze, when there are few people about, the town seems less a town than a naked, elemental place: stone buildings & streets which the winds have abraded and the sea has washed. In Winchester I felt the past everywhere underfoot and all around me: a schoolbook English history but all jumbled up like the bones in the cathedral mortuary chests, with now and then a living moment almost as if seen in the very beam of its own light. In Aberystwyth, between Pendinas and Llanbadarn, the past is almost as densely and visibly compacted, yet I've never felt it here with anything like the same intensity.

Brynbeidog apart, there's nothing here that moves me as I'm frequently moved in the south of England, where it takes very little—a tree, a wall, a house, a stretch of road, a particular weather or light—for the past to surge up in me, not only the past, either, but that peculiar feeling which is one's life, *here, in these things*.

Another cold night, brilliant and bitter. I sit close to the wall radiator; when I listen, I become conscious of the noise of the fair in town. In the first months of this year, such a sound would have made the memory of family life flood through me; as merely to drive down any street would bring back the action of driving to or from Brynbeidog, and that whole world—the entire family life—would in an instant be there, and not there, gone, everything gone. Memory doesn't describe the sensation of loss, constantly experienced afresh after a fraction of a second of disbelief. Now, however, I have come to accept the fact of the children & Sue being in Winchester, and have come to see their own lives as I couldn't do while holding them here, frozen in an image in my mind. There's gain then, a chance of developing relationships with my children, of something like friendship perhaps with Sue. A chance to welcome as the winter begins, making of my remaining months here not the limbo it has often felt like recently.

23 November
Frost sparkling like mica on the tombstones. Smoke the colour of frosted grass hanging in the meadows.
"If only" are among the most dangerous words.

§

The self is no mystery, the mystery is
That there is something for us to stand on.

We want to be here.

The act of being, the act of being
More than oneself.
  George Oppen, 'World, World'

The isolated man is dead, his world around him exhausted.
  George Oppen, 'Of Being Numerous', 10

29 November
Another bad day: tired, tense, it was all I could do to get through a lecture yesterday, and I had to force myself to walk to college this morning.
 Unnatural life: seeing hardly anyone to talk to for days on end, when Dave is away, working at several things simultaneously—reading, reading, burying myself in notes, but no writing apart from journal and letters—and hurt and bitterness working up into the stale, tired mind while I grasp for life at my contact with M., but can't be with her now. So the self crushed small and airless struggles miserably.
 Life for me, as a man, without the woman, is a poor thing, a struggle to keep purpose, sometimes a desolation and even desperation. Yes, there are times when it seems that almost any woman who attracts me will do; that it's woman and not the person who is important. But this isn't true. It is M. and Sue who, in very different ways, occupy my feelings and thoughts, the one giving all and sustaining me, the other still connected with me in spite of our conscious separation. The words just aren't available for what really happens in a life! I can't say how the life current and the person are one—how we are both man or woman and ourselves. I understand

well that sex is a force that moves all life, and affects everything in the individual, not just the obvious "sexual" relations.

1 December
Better today. The way I've been thinking and writing recently—not letting go, not making anything—is deathly. Thanks mainly to Dave, I came out of it last night. Nervous this morning in town, I began to look about me, and by mid-morning the depression lifted, as the sky lifted, low sun flooding the hills with white light.

4 December
Sunday at Blaen Cwrt helping Dave plant rose bushes, two apple trees—a Blenheim & a James Grieve: inseparable for me from the poetry of my father's naming of things—and a rhododendron outside the gate. Sawed wood and stacked logs. Low white sun, mild blue sky; frost melting during the morning. A large flock of lapwings with some fieldfares & a few gulls foraged in the fields around. A treecreeper climbed the ash-tree, bird and bark almost the same colour. Occasionally a lapwing's eerie whistling cry. Mossed sycamore and chestnut: I love these and the mossy earth banks. It was good to dig the earth, crumble peat in my fingers, lift damp branches onto the sawing horse and put my body into the work.

The poets—David Jones, George Oppen, R. S. Thomas—have understood the crisis of language and form; each in his way fills "love" with love…
   How different from each other Oppen, Jones, and Thomas are! Yet they—and especially Oppen and Jones—have this in common: they know that the crisis of language and form is absolute, and each in his struggle revalues certain words, and creates a world with meaning. Most poets work with words whose loss of meaning they are unaware of. True poets *start* from the gap between "word" and "world", and could not avoid it even if they would.
   "Modern man in the death-grip of his false communities": here, as in many other instances, Ronald Gregor Smith, in *The Free Man*, shows how acute his understanding of the crisis is. He is no more academic than Buber or Bonhoeffer. Yet part of my trouble with him is this "man"—"modern man"—"Renaissance man"—which I don't find in the others, perhaps because when they use similar terms the abstraction is countered by the lived history with which they fill them.

Ezra Pound's *Gaudier-Brzeska*: the act of generosity that kindles life, by the man big enough not just to recognise genius in another but to love it.
   I have learnt more about sculpture from this memoir than from any other book. It is also a key to the modern movement in poetry.
   Pound no doubt sees the difference between his conception of a new Renaissance and Gaudier's conception of barbarism, but he does not bring it to a focus. There is terrible irony in the latter: the sculptor working to shape the *mass* of clay or stone, exalting energy and will; the man in the trenches seeing the war as "a great remedy", as if it were a sculptor working with the *masses* of humanity,

"numbers upon numbers of unimportant units". And, of course, he is destroyed with them.

The contempt of the modernist for the crowd evades the question Oppen, almost alone, has asked: the question of the reality of the artist's self, and therefore of his work, in relation to the people. I believe that the artist who sees himself as a form-maker surrounded by a largely formless humanity which may excite his contempt, and, perhaps, fear, simply hasn't gone deep enough in questioning himself and his art. He hasn't got to the roots of his own humanity: the foundations we share with others, which intimately affect the reality of the self and the work.

30 December
I came to Holland with the children on the night boat on the 27th, and today the sun is shining, as it did in England on Boxing Day. I've never known happiness like this before—except at all times with M. But now it's especially good, with our children getting on together so well. Often recently Carlyle's words of not belonging have been in my mind, which have become peculiarly my own: "the fearfulest enchantment… a world not your world". Now I remember other Christmases: the restless looking ahead, always wanting to be somewhere else, at some other time. Only with M., here, wherever we are, with our families, do I feel completely at home.

5 January 1984
Noon, the day before we leave. As usual, the time with M. has flown.
    Exactly a year ago today, I left Sue & the children in Winchester to return to Wales.
    This afternoon M. and I drove to Lauwersoog, by the North Sea. We walked on the dyke between meer and sea, the water grey, choppy in a cold wind, turbulent below sluices which stood above us against the sky, like a piece of futuristic architecture; a dangerous sea, darker grey shapes of sandbars and islands visible not far out. Nearby I saw my first windmill working, the great sails turning with the motion of a giant acrobat rolling over & over. Here also a stork's nest on a chimney.
    Flat fields rising to the line of the dyke, extending in every other direction as far as the eye could see, meadows, fields of heavy clay; long vistas of ditches, wind sharpening the water to a glinting edge, wild geese in the fields. Once we saw an exotic sight: a brown woolly llama and two ostriches instead of the usual sheep and hens and ducks in a farmyard. But to me the native scene was stranger. Farmhouses and barns with long sloping roofs, a group of buildings among trees, with a ditch like a moat; the vast level expanse of land stretching out around them, with a hint of wildness here & there, a memory of the sea in water and reeds; some red and yellow in foreground vegetation, against green and brown. All winter-dulled, heavy, sodden, but with a delicacy in grey sky, naked branches, feathery rushes, spire of a church at the horizon, and the helmet and sails of a windmill. And

approaching the sea the waterbirds—a world of birds—and rooks on the dyke, and large hawks hunting over marshy places.

11 February
Today I worked in college, typing the essay on George Oppen. A walk back in the evening, perfectly happy, the light lasting almost an hour longer than in midwinter, and the air more springlike.

Under all I feel in myself an acceptance: something I have *in* myself, *with* M., and *with* my children and parents and friends, something far more real and lasting than bitter words or the abandonment of a career or the prospect of financial insecurity.

The pity has welled up mightily at times, pity and self-pity. Yet I feel now an acceptance and grasp something that is more important than these feelings, and stronger than my own softness, something altogether closer to the bone. And it has to do with purpose, with living *on*, with not allowing the bitterness and hurt and anxiety to become my life; and it doesn't mean rejecting the past. It means too that I am letting myself *be* loved, with M., with Joe and Emily; admitting it, feeling it, and feeling life-giving springs rising in me. It's knowing how much I can lose that I don't need in order to *live*.

15 February
Set out to drive to Cardiff airport in the late afternoon, ridges sharp and all things intensely real in clear light, with a bright moon almost full over the mountains. Kite flying steadily over the road: a bird like the spirit of the hour. Ran into fog between Rhayadar and Builth and only came out of it, suddenly, with a quick spontaneous thought of Wordsworth on Snowdon, on the road climbing from Brecon into the Beacons. Looking back, the valley was full of fog, like smoke from a damp bonfire, but in front of me a star flashed greenly over a clear-cut, black ridge.

Fog became thicker and was more widespread as we drove back. I was stopped for exceeding the speed limit in Abergavenny but the policemen was courteous and sympathetic and I got off with a caution, driving on with a good feeling from the incident. And at last coming out of the fog on the road to Llangurig.

22 February
With M. to the Hywel Dda project at Whitland. Peter Lord and Glyn Rees met us on site and we looked at the fine pavements and walls in the rain. Peter's work is larger than I expected, and impressive. If nothing happens at this late date to prevent completion, this will be one of the notable things of Wales.

25 February
Breakfast in Winchester on Emily's ninth birthday. Afterwards M. and I drove via London to stay with Lee & family at Moor Farm in Reepham.

26 February
A morning walk with Lee & the boys near Blickling Hall. A view of the Hall from the front, the beautiful, arrogant dark red Jacobean brickwork deep-set between broad yew hedges. This, on the site of the house where it's said Ann Boleyn was born and spent her childhood.

In the evening Kate returned from a night supporting the women at Greenham Common. Apparently, every doctor in the country has received a letter from the government asking them to make provision for the possible event of a nuclear war—e.g. by stocking sufficient supplies of heroin tablets for families to use among themselves. How soon the unthinkable has come to be thought and talked about.

As I sit here in the kitchen at Moor Farm, writing or looking out at the pond or across the lawn where a moorhen is feeding, I can hardly believe that this is in the same world—a robin has just flown up into the bare, greenish branches of an apple tree—as that in which the threat exists. But I know it is.

All the time now a double vision: of the goodness of things, of the natural order and the things we share in love, and the omnipresence of an insane mind with power over us.

27 February
This morning Lee produced a copy of the book that shaped my imagination. *Britain's Story Told in Pictures* begins with a cave man chipping flint & a sabre-toothed tiger and ends with the Whitehall Cenotaph and a "modern" (c. 1914-18) British submarine. This must be an earlier edition of the one I had, in which I remember a Spitfire & searchlights. Mother bought me a copy from Woolworth in Fareham when I was about five, and though I haven't seen one for more than thirty years, the images have often come back to me. The pictures and their juxtapositions, together with an early visit to the museum Below Bar in Southampton, first excited my feeling for history.

29 February
Back from Cambridge, where we stayed overnight with Kim Landers and I gave a reading with Rodney Pybus at King's. A small audience consisting mainly of friends and acquaintances including Clive Wilmer, Heather Glen, and Göran and Ulla. Only one or two students.

How often is a woman walking with a child aware of what she represents? Not often, I suppose; immediate cares would usually make impossible the detachment necessary for awestruck self-seeing—that moment out of time which comes with dream-like super-clarity, when a person sees him or her self not as "I", but I-who-am-a-man or I-who-am-a-woman, involved in some activity which people have always been involved in. How much more awesome, though, when the activity not only represents continuity but is essential to the continuation of life. But of course, in the case of woman and child this is by no means all, and words of analysis are particularly clumsy. The image reaches beyond words; it is perhaps the strongest and deepest we can see: as I saw it this morning as we passed one then another woman holding a child by the hand and walking along the pavement. And I was made more than usually sensitive, I suppose, not only by seeing Joe and Emily, as I often do, but also by the intensity of Kate's feeling for her children, when she was at Greenham; and also because being with Lee always intensifies my grasp of images. A woman and child are a reality before they are an image; the image doesn't invent them, it points to something immeasurably deep and powerful. But to *shape* the image so as to invoke the reality: it would be worth the effort of a lifetime to achieve this once or twice.

9 March
Here are the daffodils M. bought on St David's Day, a generous armful. But they have begun to wither now.

Last night we stayed at a motel near the airport and this morning she returned to Amsterdam on the 7 o'clock flight. Yesterday we drove back from Scotland—from Dundee to Cardiff—mountains & fells still streaked with snow; here & there a view of beautiful country—on the border, in Cumbria, through the "riven sandstone" of the West Midlands, Malverns misty towards dusk—but, for the most part, a tense and weary dream of heavy lorries and motorways.

We drove up on Monday, and the next day, at St Andrews, I gave a talk and a reading, "poetry of place", to students and staff of the English Department. They entertained us well. No doubt it accorded with the propriety of the place that we were put up respectably in separate rooms at a guesthouse.

On Wednesday morning we drove to Dundee; which they'd disparaged at St Andrews, but I took to the town immediately, when we saw it rising on hills across the river, busy and workaday, with a raw industrial aspect and a certain grandeur. I gave a lecture on *In Parenthesis* to a small group in the morning. Lunch in the staff canteen overlooking the road bridge, and the railway bridge over the Tay: a dark blue-grey day, the railway bridge shadowed by pillars of the first, ill-fated bridge. We were staying with Peter and Claire Easingwood, who in the afternoon took us for a walk on a beach a few miles from their home at Tayport. A wide, blue-grey sea; windrows of open-mouthed, smooth white shells, a dead seal with ribs exposed; also a large, rusty bell buoy washed up, which we looked at blankly for a long time, until I suddenly saw what it was.

In the evening I read with a dreadful Canadian poet, an elderly man who's done a lot—apparently, indiscriminately—to publish younger poets. I felt sorry for him; which was needless, since he evidently had every confidence in himself, as well as an adoring wife. When audible, he was embarrassing, and bad. I'd rather have been elsewhere, but had to follow him…

Back in a day's drive to Cardiff, with many new impressions. But now again I see, more than anything else, the small plane taking off into a mild, early morning sky, the sun just risen. I drove back numb with tiredness, and have since spoken to M. on the phone—the distance again, after three weeks of constant companionship.

14 March
Celandines, dandelions and primroses in the churchyard.

A growing day, but shut in by cloud. Late afternoon, flat disc of the orange sun appearing through mist, a dull orange glow illuminating one corner of the sea, off Tan-y-bwlch beach, the rest hidden. I walked downhill tired, dispirited, and as I passed in front of the church and glanced up at the tower, saw a faint, mushroom-skull moon.

With tiredness sometimes comes a feeling of great weakness: Tennyson's infant crying in the night is literally true, not a poetic figure. Yet it also strikes me that at those moments I have a chance of understanding that doesn't come with security and well-being: a chance perhaps of grasping the fact of being alive, the wonder and enormity of that fact, and the demands, and possibilities. And my mind is so made that that always points back to poetry…

18 March
Thursday afternoon. In Cardiff, at the BBC for the launch of Dai Smith's *Wales! Wales?* and afterwards to a reception at Oriel for the launch of *Anglo-Welsh Poetry 1480-1980*. Talked with Emyr, Roland, John Ward, and Wynn Thomas. I'll miss this particular world when I leave Wales.

In Winchester on Friday. Yesterday I took the children to lunch at Hayford. Dad has sunk deeper into old age this winter. Now he was sitting close to the radiator, unable to work in the garden because of the cold. As we sat together talking I looked at his pictures on the walls and saw again the colours and forms, and how good they are—a depth of yellow in the sky of *The Road to Keyhaven*, and the pattern of the forms, the rich blue of an Avon scene, and other paintings which I've loved dearly for many years, especially the red houses by the pond at Pilley, and the waterfall on the Beidog, with a view of Mynydd Bach through trees. All are so familiar that I usually enjoy them without really seeing them, but on this occasion, aware perhaps that he could not see me well, I looked at them with wonder.

After lunch I took Mother and the children to the shingle-bank, along the road from Keyhaven. The tide was farther out than usual, the sea calm, the sun silvering a light mist. There were wild geese on the mud among gulls and waders.

This morning, to Farley Mount with Joe and Emily and their friend Gavin and the dog. The same softly clouded atmosphere, textures & shapes of the land visible only for fairly short distances. I wonder at this too: it is so beautiful, I can never find the words for it. And I wonder now that I was ever there… But it's no good tormenting myself—after the long drive back, the memories, the vast loneliness (as it seems to me) over and behind the mountains, and my narrow loneliness at Llanbadarn by myself, writing these notes, hearing an owl calling…

As I saw the beauty of the chalk, its skeletal whiteness, and the actual skeleton of some animal lying under yew trees at the roadside, so I felt the limitations of my love of the unpeopled land. There's a sense in which I do go deep in southern places, and in which feeling that goes into the ground, and comes to me from the ground, is the stuff of my imagination; but if I once settle for this alone, for being cut off from my society and isolated in an empty landscape, or a landscape whose presences are all past, then I deserve to be a small poet or to dry up entirely.

Owls who-whooing in trees somewhere beyond the orchard. The owls of Llanbadarn, M. called them and lay awake hearing them on the nights here.

21 March

Charles Tomlinson, in response to the copy of my essay on George Oppen which I sent him, has written to tell me that Oppen is suffering from a disease from which "his mental faculties have *totally* disintegrated—he cannot even sign his own name". He goes on to say: "Physical or mental suffering is one thing. The abolition of a mind is quite another. Mary says that he *seems* to be happy. A terrible word that 'seems'".

23 March

I was awake at cockcrow, and before, reading. The cocks answer each other from the orchard, and more distantly, across the farmland separating the village from the town. I love to be awake, hearing that raw yet comfortably haunting call, as the dark turns. This morning, through the window and the streetlights reflected in the glass, I could see a few dim stars in the dark blue sky; and later, with the dawn, opened my window wide for the birdsong to pour in.

It rained, and a strong, cold wind rose during the day. I stayed in my room in college, stale, and working in a desultory way, and later introduced the course and the place to a group of prospective students. Otherwise I've seen no one except Dave to talk to all day. He left for Blaen Cwrt this evening, and I got a take-away from the Indian restaurant. Spoke to Joe & Emily & Sue on the phone, to my parents, and several times to M., and to Hans & Agnes, who are celebrating my birthday in Groningen. So now the day which began so early comes towards its end, and the wind has dropped and it is still again. I have a glass of bourbon (Emily's gift) beside me, and look up at Lee's dramatic drawing for the Labourer sculpture over the fireplace; the heating has gone off and I'm beginning to feel cold: my forty-third year: I find it startling, even—absurdly—rather frightening, when I say it in my mind, perhaps because I don't feel it, and wonder where the time has gone.

11 April

Drove to Tackley in the afternoon to see Kim and Oli Taplin. Before supper Kim & I walked beside the reedy, dark-flowing Cherwell and over the fields. We talked long and late, and when I went to bed I read Kim's series of poems based on nuclear weapons sites in Britain. Their homely stone house set deep in the country seems in another world; but nowhere is, and in any case Upper Heyford isn't far away.

12 April
A glorious day in Oxford with Robert Wells, walking about the city under a blue sky in warm sunlight.

Walked in past the Castle mound & Castle, and the police station where Dad's uncle Ralph Wastie had been Chief Constable, and, years later, Dad's brother Roland was deputy Chief Constable. I had my own memories too, of staying with Tony when he lived in Clark's Row (long since pulled down) and fishing in the Thames, and meeting Tony's friends, who were mostly Communist Party members or Irish navvies. But it was another Oxford that I saw today: the historic, beautiful city.

Robert's small room in Corpus Christi looks out one way to the Cathedral, and, in the other, to a distant view of the Radcliff Camera. We walked to the house he was brought up in, on the corner of Logic Lane, and went in and up the stairs (the house is divided into student rooms now), where he knows every creak and door knob, as I know Hayford. From there, we walked in and out of colleges, down back streets and in gardens all day, talking and looking, and seeing so much that I can record only a little.

At University College, where we trespassed: "the dead Shelley & the living cell". A very dead Shelley in marble, and, as we looked at it, Robert remarked that this was the college in which Boyle had made his discovery. In the chapel, stained glass by a Dutch master, the figures magnificently substantial, solid, even stolid, an Eve who was all there, a muscular Adam, Jonah and a heaving, mountainous whale. In another chapel we saw window glass said to have been painted by Sir Joshua Reynolds, the figures delicate, graceful, even a little effete, eighteenth-century aristocrats in saints' robes.

On the walls of many buildings I was surprised to see beasts, and fantastic faces, which are clearly of the same school as the Kilpeck figures. Their leers & grimaces, mockery, agony, and tenderness, *on the outside* of buildings, comment on all that learning, with its pretensions and solemnity and worldly ambition, would shut out, as if the university city were one great cathedral and these its impish critics.

In the Ashmolean we saw the Alfred Jewel; and I noticed an ancient Greek torso of a boy, perfect in its lines as Joe.

Magnolia against old stone walls, long, waxy tongues against warm yellow limestone. Spires, towers, pinnacles, great trees (ilex, beech, acacia), and the little beasts & faces; cool rational buildings in the time of Wren or later, against or between medieval colleges or churches. Eyes down and eyes lifted, between the detail and all around us that we could not "take in".

In New College chapel, Epstein's *Lazarus*. The shrouded body, monumental as a standing stone, but with the head lying on the shoulders twisted, as if looking round and down, but with eyes closed, mouth in death closed grimly on pain—

this gives it a presence, a meaning, at once frightening, solemn, and sad, yet the whole is charged with an energy not yet released, but which at any moment will wake in this heavy sleeper, wake in slow power, or with a motion that could spin the great body like a top, bandages flying free like garlands on a maypole…

The only modern art that can have a proper place in the old churches, with medieval stonework & woodwork, or with paintings like the El Greco in New College chapel, is sculpture by the modern masters who learned from the primitives and from natural forms.

It was returning along Addison's Walk, and seeing deer in the large park belonging to Magdalen, like a lord's estate, that I raged against our class society, feeling its knots tighten in my mind. But when I thought of Raymond Williams' *Second Generation* it was of what Williams excludes, as he sees the city in terms of class privilege and lack of privilege, but leaves out the beauty; and leaves it out, perhaps, because the very words that describe it, words like "nobility", "grandeur", "grace", "awe-inspiring", belong to a world of values he rejects, and the history has compromised. How hard it is to tell the truth about England! Knowing how entangled my own feelings are, I distrust the clear-cut rejection, as I reject the acceptance at face value of "tradition", the complacent view of the privileged eye.

Jude seeing the city from a barn roof; Jude jostled on the pavements by ghosts; Jude working on the outsides of colleges, as we saw workmen doing, and as Tony worked. But if I was given a place there, I think I could love Oxford—but not the university town alone.

At St Peter's in the East (now a library), the church where Robert's parents were married. A patch of white violets—Jefferies' white violets—growing behind a crumbling tombstone, near the entrance to the crypt, where we descended briefly into the gloom. And in the garden at Corpus Christi gold & green moss growing on an ancient stone in the sun, and the young, bearded gardener telling us he had unearthed the stone, and the best things, like the moss, happened in spite of his work.

Robert is working on his translation of Theocritus. As we were talking in his room at teatime, a young man called in who has a lectureship in English for a year at Christ College. He is doing research on seventeenth-century poems and had recently been examining use of the oak tree—apparently very common—as symbol, image or subject in poetry of the period. We talked about scholarship, Robert claiming not to be a scholar, though he has a higher ideal of scholarship than almost anyone else I know, and is scrupulous and thorough. The young lecturer, who hopes to get a permanent university post next year, commented ironically on his "grasping for a foothold on the slippery rock face" from which I'm voluntarily descending.

In a glass case at the Bodleian: Traherne's handwriting, small but neat and clear, with a few stylistic alterations, in brown ink very slightly faded, in the manuscript of the *Centuries*.

Once, while we were standing near an old building, we looked up and saw a large hawk climbing, then circling and hovering over the city. At that moment the confusion of detail fell away and the place was simplified, restored to wholeness under the sky. In memory, I see the hawk catching a glint of gold from the sun, and the image brings to a focus the perfection of the day.

13 April
Another lovely day, with soft wavy lines & tendrils of cloud in blue sky. Hawthorn coming into leaf. On Pennington Common, nailed high up on pine trees in the copse: PRIVATE PROPERTY KEEP OUT. Like a blow in the face. I wrote some of my first poems there. We always understood the copse was private, but that didn't bother us much. Standing at the edge looking in this morning, I thought of the boys who had played there and who were killed in the wars, and wondered if the owners who put up such notices would keep out ghosts if they could.

17 April
From Gatwick, a stiff frost, the car windows iced over, to Heraklion. With M. and our children, driving past orange sellers beside the road to Rethymnon, scent of orange blossom from orchards, the fruit sweet and juicy. Flowers beside the sea: marigolds, mallow, yellow horned-poppies, sea holly, soft hare's tail grass, a field of scarlet poppies. Purple reefs of seaweed under the surface of the sea.

18 April
To Arkadi fortress monastery, which was blown up by a patriot in 1866, killing more than 800 Christian men, women and children and twice as many attacking Turks. Over limestone crags, hooded crows on the ascent, and oranges, lemons, tangerines, silver-leaved olives and white anemones. We glimpsed three large birds, which may have been eagles, circling a neighbouring crag. Inside crumbling walls of orange stone, a church prepared for Easter, with lilies. Outside, a woodpile of olive trunks & branches, and a pigsty. A mausoleum up a flight of steps, containing glass cases full of skulls.

In Rethymnon, swallows & martins tearing the air with their screams.

Good Friday
Thunder in the night and drenching rain most of the morning, the children painting Easter eggs. Later, with a head cold and badly hung over after a "Cretan evening" at the mountain village of Axos (the best of it the drive through vineyards & olives, and the drive back, with Joe, who had had red wine, maintaining that "me and Dad and the baby are the only sober ones"), I walked by the sea kicking over pebbles, cuttlefish bones, globs of tar, bamboo roots sodden with salt water and shaped grotesquely, like witchcraft images of the human form. Mountains behind me, and, on the coast, half-built hotels, like ruins; to the west the Venetian fort (at first glance, from a distance, like Calshot!). Sea bottle-glass green under a grey sky. The sun appearing made my eyes water.

At night, the purring of cicadas.

Easter Saturday
Cavernous waves breaking, rolling over, and with a dive or leap that looks Dionysian in its destructive ecstasy, plunging to a chaos of foam. Crested with foam the waves come in one behind another and the water heaving between them is veined and webbed with foam. Turning over they are smooth for an instant and full of sunlight & sand. Light rides on crest and underlip.

Midnight. The crowd waiting outside the packed cathedral grows until the square and streets around are filled. We listen to the service relayed by loudspeakers to us outside. Occasionally a loud banger goes off, making us jump. The procession emerges when the priest announces that Christ is risen, and candles are lit from group to group, hand to hand, and points of light move everywhere in the crowd and are carried carefully through the streets. Fireworks explode noisily and colourfully over our heads. Driving back, we see families and small groups of people carrying their candles from other churches—blobs of light moving along the roadside in the dark

Easter Monday
Over the mountains to Chora Sfakia in rain, descending by the deep Imbros ravine and on a narrow, twisting road with frightening drops and a view far out across the Libyan Sea. Down to the small harbour, blue & white fishing boats with yellow nets, the clear water dolphin-blue and green. White mountains rising steeply above.

Frangacastello. Another crumbling, orange ruin of cruel and savage memory, a fortress on the coastal plain, massive under its walls but the size of a toy under the mountains rising huge and cragged, white where the sun catches them, small, white-walled villages perched here & there.

24 April
What to say about Knossos? Tourists & old dust. Towering snowy clouds & blue sky. Apricots & sparrows, a dead, naked fledgling lying on the stone. A cool fountain playing far off, on a patch of artichokes.

From the hills above Heraklion we bumped down a twisting, steep, red dirt track to Fodele, a cool village by a shaded stream, among orange groves. Allegedly the birthplace of El Greco, whose long bronze head, pointed like an olive, I caressed. Blue beehives outside the village, the hillsides humming.

25 April
A walk with Emily along four or five miles of beach to Rethymnon. Sunny & warm. An old man in black crouched on the sand as if praying, cork floats of a fishing net a little way off shore in front of him.

26 April
To Khania with M. & Joe & Emily while Bethan & Elin went to Axos again. Harbour water the colour of a thundercloud. Violent downpour as we ate in a dimly lit taverna. Lightning in the east as we drove back.

27 April
Alone with Joe & Emily, I got the car stuck across two narrow roads in Rethymnon in the morning. Emily, very embarrassed, hid her head in the back. To my great relief, a smiling young Cretan got out of his van (I was blocking his way) and directed me while I backed out.

M. & I took the old road to Heraklion in the afternoon. At first towards snow covered Ida, smooth & pure, and almost filling the sky. Richly fertile valleys—but in one field a man was breaking the orange earth with a pick. We stopped to gather wild flowers. Blackbirds were singing and the silver-green of olives made the transition from the greens of grass and vines and trees to the limestone heights. A scary climb and then descent to Heraklion, with a burnt-out bus abandoned beside the road at the bottom of a steep incline.

In Heraklion we climbed to the grave of Nikos Kazantzakis on the top of the walls and placed the flowers among other bunches behind the big wooden cross. Clocks in the city below began striking six, a jet climbed over the island of Dia; blue sky, blue sea, sun over the mountains white in a mist of light. Loud traffic noises, dogs barking, someone hammering on tin, the town looking all higgledy-piggledy, as if built in any available space, anyhow: patterns of past and present which we sense but probably no one—not even Kazantzakis, in whose day it would have been more compact, simpler—could grasp. A goat and kids on the rampart below the memorial garden.

28 April
Every day of sun the poppies blaze more scarlet against the blue sea. After a clear, starlit night, fresh snow on the mountains in the west.

At Gortyn, St Titus' basilica, with sparrows, ikons, offerings; columns and sarcophagi; a headless female statue—all among gnarled olives, figs, cypresses, poppies, a lemon tree. Again, on a hot day, with children who want only to get to the beach, I fail to find the temple of Apollo, but exploring with Emily find instead the shade of a plane tree beside the stream, which is where Zeus is said to have "married" Europa.

At Phaistos, a friendly man at the gate asks Emily's name and tells us he has three daughters but no son. No son, he repeats, and asks us to come again when he isn't on duty and drink some wine with him.

More dust, pot holes, broken road surfaces, here & there boys playing football on the road, in Mires the road completely blocked by people on market day. Mules, goats, sheep; donkeys standing in the shade, donkeys ridden side-saddle by old women dressed in black, donkeys heavily laden. An old shepherd asleep on a bank, the sun shining on his bald, brown head, his sheep grazing around him.

In Spili, a Venetian fountain, water gushing from the mouths of dozens of lions.

Magnificent Kedros in cloud on the upper slopes on the way back

29 April
A drive with M. & Emily into the Amari Valley, at first in mist or cloud.

At Thronos, cocks crowing & a smell of pigs & sweet flowers. Between Thronos and Asomaton we found a small, whitewashed Byzantine church standing alone in the valley, reached by a stony track with an olive grove on one side and fields on the other, and guarded by a dog barking in an outbuilding & a tethered Billy goat, his rope just too short to let him reach us. Big, black & yellow bees hummed loudly, diving deep into the abundant yellow flowers of Jerusalem Sage. Mountains stood at a distance, with a high snow-covered peak to the south. This above all is Crete—the manmade, beautifully proportioned, shapely, on a human scale, honouring God or the gods, within a fertile circle, beyond it the great circle of mountains and sea, wild, savage, nonhuman.

All was light & warmth inside the church, under a dome of thrush-egg blue, shaped like the inside of an egg, with a bird's nest in one of the openings and blue sky showing through the others. There could be no lighter or airier or more beautiful picture of heaven. Below, to one side, was a case let into the floor and covered with semi-opaque, dusty glass through which we could just see, at the bottom, human bones, like a litter of sticks. The church stood within a semi-circle of cypresses. There was a sound of running water from the field's edge nearby.

Later we saw a hoopoe twice in the same place, on the road and in the eucalyptus trees beside Moni Asomaton, on the way to and from Amari.

At Amari, a priest passing in a car gave us a warm smile of greeting and children led us to the old belltower standing above the village. Emily and M. came down from the tower minutes before the bells rang the hour. If they'd still been there, they'd probably have been knocked off the platform!

30 April
Early morning. The sea very pale turquoise, gentle waves bringing in the light. A sea the colour of cloudy glass, making, when it tilts, a window through which stones & weed inshore can be seen.

Later, a walk with M. uphill to a village. Out of the sun's heat into the shade of olives—Herculean trees, gnarled, knuckled, as if bulging and twisting with muscular effort to achieve their enormous productivity; black nets lying at their feet or folded between their branches, waiting for the harvest, feed the gladiatorial fancy. One tree has a huge root system, like petrified lava.

We see white snails on sword-like artichoke leaves, stuck together in masses. One big green lizard disappears into a crevice in a rock wall. An old man walks beside a donkey laden with olive wood. Deep in an olive grove, down a path patterned with sunlight & shadow, a tiny church, with paintings of St George and the dragon inside. The grove is full of birds & flowers.

A village like many others: narrow, labyrinthine streets of whitewashed houses, old doors, people in groups, an old woman dressed in black, sitting alone and talking to herself. Lemon trees, apricots, figs ripening. Again, seeing men and women working, an old woman gathering herbs by the roadside, a man in his orchard, I realize that most words and thoughts are superfluous, unreal. In our society a vast amount of mental and emotional energy is spent on false relationships, between each other, with ourselves, with our work, if we have any, and in pursuit of false "needs". I know in my mind the cloud, the waste, the dreams that mean nothing but can consume a life.

At the centre of the village, near the war memorial, the lean, strong, stone-carved face of the *palikare* who ignited the powder magazine at Arkadi.

1 May
Back in Winchester on a sultry evening. A coppery sun over the downs, on the Cathedral and the Guildhall roof, the Alfred statue and the deep, shadowy green of St Catherine's Hill. Hawthorn flowering, leaves on trees that were bare a fortnight ago.

2 May
Dawn. Birds singing loudly, distant cuckoo a soft pulse in the chorus, instead of the donkey hee-hawing outside the apartment and the sound of the sea from beyond the field of scarlet poppies.

Winchester to Hayford, Hayford to Wales—through a thunderstorm in Herefordshire. Purple lilac in the small, stone-walled garden at Llanbadarn, purple tulips from the bulbs M. gave us, and behind the garden an orchard full of white & pink apple blossom. The beginning of fullness, at once delicate and rich. The owls of Llanbadarn calling at night.

5 May
During the past two days in college R. S. Thomas read his poems and gave a lecture on 'Ends and Means in Poetry' and I was able to talk to him after both occasions, finding him communicative and humorous. What's most apparent in his work now is his sense of an end: holocaust, end of the century and of the millennium, the end of his own life. This, of course, develops a strain evident in his work for some years, but the latest, unpublished poems are his most direct, explicit, and terrifying. Even if we don't destroy ourselves, he doubts the continuation of poetry as we know it into the next millennium, anticipating the complete extinction of "deciduous" language and the total triumph of science & its terminologies. At the same time, he acknowledges that new genius can never be foreseen. But what, he asks, will the love poet praise in woman, when to speak of her swan's neck would be meaningless? Her genetic potential? He finds very little in contemporary English poetry that isn't clumsy and ugly. We disagreed about the merits of a certain kind of "flatness", focusing on our different evaluations of William Carlos Williams; but I share most of the questions he raised—his way is to question,

not to answer—and was moved by his feeling for poetry, shown in the instances, and actual words, he constantly brought us back to—in Shakespeare, Milton, Yeats, Eliot, Stevens, Hughes, Larkin, Hill. And chastened to be reminded that the modern poet is usually content if he can achieve just one of the effects which the great poets of the past combined.

10-11 May
In Colchester, where I read with Rodney Pybus and Peter Scupham at St Mary's Arts Centre as part of the Essex Festival. Closeby, a magnificent brick water tower, "Jumbo", captured my affection.

I stayed with my old friend Herbie Butterfield, who was so kind to me when I first went to Aberystwyth and he was a colleague. He lives with his two younger daughters, a beautiful red Burmese cat, and Wally, a wildly affectionate mongrel dog. We stopped up late talking and drinking his home brew.

This morning, with his daughter Milly, he took me for a long drive round. First to the university at Wivenhoe Park, where the grey brick towers have the sinister aspect of skyscrapers in the relatively flat country. We then went to Dedham and crossed the Stour into Suffolk. A day of Constable clouds, massed and broken, cloud over cloud, white and grey in a blue sky. New leaves on the trees, cow parsley by the roadside, masses of red and white and pink blossom. After winter the sky on certain days in spring comes close in peculiar intimacy to the earth, when the cloud shapes are themselves like masses of blossom and correspond with the shape and colour of blossoming trees. The sky is then a roof of the human home. This is what Constable shows; his is a natural world (though a man-made landscape) but it encloses and even embraces the human, as do earlier Dutch and English landscape paintings, but Constable is at once the most natural and homely.

As we drove round we also passed police cars waiting for miners' pickets on the way to nearby ports.

12 May
Set out with Ned Thomas to lead a small party of Alun Lewis Society members on a literary outing to border country.

First stop Bredwardine, the Wye landscape exuding richness and white with apple & hawthorn blossom. A large cherry tree in flower beside the path to the church was particularly beautiful and a fine plane tree standing close to Kilvert's grave.

At Kilpeck the dry, pink earth was patterned with boot & shoe marks that must have been made weeks ago. A cuckoo was calling below. I delighted once more in the carved faces & figures, especially the animals—ram, hare, and dog—done with an equivalent sensitive knowledge to that with which the Stone Age hunter carved reindeer in reindeer bone. Here I read Gillian Clarke's poem, 'Sheela na Gig at Kilpeck', which I think she wrote after our visit with Sue, Dave & the children four or five years ago. I noticed how many of the new gravestones commemorate people who died young. The shiny black stone of a young man who died aged 16 in the early 1970s pulled me up short as I walked away from the church, mind full of aesthetic and historical images, in that dreamy state it's so easy to fall into in an old graveyard.

At Capel-y-ffin, the chapel, though whitewashed now, is exactly as Kilvert described it, "squatting like a stout grey owl among its seven great black yews". When inside, despite all the differences, I was surprised to find myself reminded of the Byzantine church standing alone in the Amari valley. Looking at the squat, rounded stone inscribed "Remember Charlie Stones, Carpenter" in Eric Gill script I thought of Roland Mathias' poem inspired by it. Others, like David Jones, owe much to the Black Mountains and to the Marches generally, but Roland is the modern poet who has entered most deeply into this country—as deeply, in his way, as Henry Vaughan.

Climbing to a steep edge, it was like looking down through water, blue green, with different depths of colour according to movements of light & shadow, into the far, white sky. The Usk in its turnings shone below. Hang-gliders in the blustery wind hung still, like pterodactyls waiting for prey above a cliff edge of the ancient world.

Our last place of pilgrimage was Henry Vaughan's grave at Llansantffraed. The red sun was low now, the purple mountains sharp against a cloudless sky. Gnats were out, and bit us while we were in the graveyard; birds around and in the river valley whistled and piped and cried, with those *keen* evening notes which correspond with the sharp yet mellow tones of light on a fine evening in May. We found the grave slab under a yew, the stone and much of its inscription obscured by black stains and thick white bird dung.

15 May

Lee, in a letter: "I always wonder whether or not there is achievement in what I do, for in my study of the past I place myself and see my crudity. Ah we live in crude times. So many more machines and so *much* less order—moral order, spirit order. More intricate knowledge of parts and less of any concept of whole. Which is no kind of wisdom at all."

My mind's corrupt with misuse. Depressed by another critical dismissal—for my "empty descriptive" poems—I taste the bitter juice and feel the knock of my heart and the iron rim of defeatism cutting into my head. This is what comes of standing still, and my friends the working artists—Lee & Peter—who delight, encourage and inspire me, shame me too.

17 May

A walk with Simon Millward in light rain at Cwmsymlog, in a landscape of long-abandoned, ruined mines. Here, the hills have been turned inside out, and their grey, stony entrails spilt in heaps form a wasted image of the green, bracken-patched uplands surrounding them. Grey sky, grey shaly track between grey spoilheaps, past a tall, solitary chimney of rough-hewn, grey stone. A place heavy with a sense of men gone into the ground, their strength spent in pitiless harsh labour. One vivid yellow gorse bush; a flowering cherry growing out of the side of a mineshaft from which the stink of a dead sheep caught us—tufts of wool on brambles growing on the side. A climb through conifers which had the feel of an ancient battleground—rubble of ruined buildings and trees fallen or snapped off, like iron stakes, in brown gloom, impenetrable darkness further in, and fine mist rising like smoke from the tree tops; but also with a stillness like a waterfall's when it falls so fast that it appears motionless. We emerged at Llyn Pendam, rain-patter forming tiny circles on dark grey water below the foot of a great wall.

18 May
A beautiful day for a drive to Pembrokeshire.

At Nevern, the church folded in green trees, loud cawing of rooks from gaunt firs above the crowded graveyard. Grave on grave, with bluebells, stitchwort, herb Robert among them, slant stones leaning close together calling to mind Kilvert's description of the tombstones at Bredwardine, like "a crowd of men"—and they are like men, not women!—on the morning of the Resurrection. Time Passeth Away Like a Shadow on the sundial.

Red campion & ramsons by the stream running brown and clear. I walked beside it under the churchyard wall—what *is* the secret? In such a place it must have seemed to others too, generation after generation, since long before the Celtic cross was carved or the ogham cut in stone, that at the next moment meaning would be revealed, and understanding flood their minds. And some found it, no doubt, in what was given, while others, like me, feel the place itself is like a flower about to open but don't see beyond the actual flowers, and the trees and graves.

Bees hummed round their nest in a crack in the stonework halfway up the church tower. Church and churchyard lay cupped in warmth, but in the yews' shadow it was almost cold.

From Whitesand round St David's Head, sun & wind in our faces. Below us, a wide expanse of greeny blue sea lapping on sand and round the morsels of ancient rock it has still to consume. A driven sea, silvered & white-crested, vanishing into mist beyond the islands. An almost continuous lowing from the foghorn at the South Bishop Light. Sea campion & thrift on the headland; stonechats on gorse. Iron Age fields. Stone raised laboriously on stone, or effortlessly heaped up or scattered by sea and weather and movements of the earth.

28 May
Bank holiday Monday. At Hayford, after a rainy weekend in Winchester. How rich the leaves on the lime trees are above the stream at the bottom of Monks Road, and the cow parsley and grass growing on the banks, and the white blossom on the trees under which I used to watch cricket in the park, and did again. Summer brings back darkness to places that were open to the winter light, but in May it is at first a rich pattern of shadow and light. And memory clings to the leaves.

Along Nuns Walk Emily & I saw moorhens on their nests on the water, tiny yellow and red beaks appearing under the big beaks and black wings. The massive chestnut was again covered with white candles and blown petals were scattered on the path or sailed slowly down the bourne.

I'm always dragging my feet and looking back, but time passes and changes me anyway. I saw not only the waste but the perversity—the pride—of my sense of failure. It's been riding my back again recently—"giant with a giant on his back"— my poems see the truth long before I do, and perhaps see truths I don't see. This would be reason enough to write if I had no other.

Afternoon. At Barton with Mother. Sand martins swarming between the beach and their holes in the sand cliffs. Sky clouded, sea calm and grey, two or three sails on the long dark grey line of the horizon. The Island at first present as a barely visible shape, a thicker mist in the mist, but appearing like a landfall as the mist thinned; Hengistbury Head a long low grey mound to the west. Sea calm but not still, a skin rippling and wrinkling; grey but not grey, numerous subtle tones between greyish blue and dark slate.

29 May
Back to Wales on a day of white blossom, white cloud, soft blue sky, and every line and shape of the countryside sharp and clear. At Gaufron a round hill shoulder azure with bluebells. Stopped for lunch beside the Wye near Ross, and stopped again in Eardisley, where the Norman font is the finest I've seen. I was immediately aware of it in the empty church, like a person who compels one's gaze. Norman, but of the Hereford school, showing Viking and Celtic influences. A world turning round the huge stone fruit: fighting men with spears in the plaitwork, a mild-faced lion with an enormous tail thrust between his legs and resting on his neck, Christ harrowing hell.

10 June
Another weekend alone, the last in this place. Climbed Pendinas on a warm afternoon, in a fresh breeze blowing off the sea. From the summit, a fine view almost all round. Seaward, a small corner of the town—castle ruins, war memorial, roofs of South Marine Terrace—and the two bays. Out at sea a small craft making headway against the swell looks as if the whole sea were resisting it. From here, the town looks almost lost in its setting, with the University above the National Library on Penglais, the tower of Llanbadarn church with the village clustered round it below, and beyond, the hills rising above Talybont. To the south the long ridge of Mynydd Bach appears at this distance to be at eye-level though from there Pendinas itself would be a small mound… How beautiful it is! Once or twice recently I've regretted leaving, and have imagined living with M. in the country here. I've been proud, sometimes, to work in the University of Wales, and again now I think of the opportunities. But no, my life here was effectively over at the time of going to Winchester and I've been a revenant in the last eighteen months. In leaving I may be able to bring together and appreciate fully all that I value in Wales.

Early July
On holiday at Mudeford. Gold leaf, fire flakes on greenish silver mud, a pool of ox-blood water in Christchurch Harbour. My father, barely able to see, peers at a boat in the foreground and after detecting "the darkest dark" looks for "the lightest light" in the composition. When we first arrived I was full of bitterness, and walked round the front with M. looking at the sea & the Island as if they were a thin painted paper I could rip to see the emptiness behind them. I'd no part in them, no work, no living.

I was at school near here. When in the sixth form I'd often take a friend on the pillion of my motorbike to walk on the beach below Hengistbury Head at lunchtime and eat our sandwiches. For years I stood waiting for the yellow trolley bus opposite the Druitt library in Christchurch. All this area was as much where I lived as Pennington. I'm a holidaymaker but the accent of the local people is the voice of home.

Low tide. The sand & shingle spit across the Run extends a weedy green length further out to sea and two fishermen in waders haul in their net from beside the Spit. They work hard pulling it in slowly and laboriously against the water and the weight of rope, and it comes in full of weed and apparently empty of fish until the very end, when two large salmon are seen thrashing, silver against green. One of the men picks up a stone from the shore, and holding each fish in turn through the net, smashes it several blows on the head.

The Priory weathervane is a salmon, and one of the fine misericords is the head and shoulders of a salmon powerfully carved in wood. Salmon netted in the Avon and in the harbour entrance supplied part of the living of the community here more than a thousand years ago, and have done ever since.

Here swans enjoy the salt water equally with gulls. Jim told me the unlikely story that the only people to eat swans now, on Christmas Day, are the Queen (whose prerogative it is) and Sam Woodford, who for weeks before Christmas feeds them by hand at Great Ballard lake in New Milton, then on Christmas Eve... Jim has it by hearsay that they taste very good, something like goose.

This morning I saw eight cormorants standing together looking half-asleep on a mudbank. Jim says that when the tide is going out the water off Avon Beach is fresh. I've swum there once this time, with Joe & Emily; but the beach is crowded, and the best swimming here is from the sandy beach at Mudeford spit. It's a special place, with its comfortable shanty town of beach huts, open sea to the Island on one side and broad harbour surrounded by the Head and the Christchurch to Mudeford shore on the other, smelling strongly of salt and seaweed and mud.

9 July
First spots of rain after many hot, dry days. Aluminium masts & wires of shrouded dinghies tinkle like agitated sheep bells. The sky too is shrouded heavily with cloud and the Island's hidden. Now the rain falls straight and hard, big silver drops smacking noisily on roofs and road. If only I could look at and listen to all around me with sympathetic curiosity! There's an imagism that presents the signs

of the external world, reticent of the self out of respect for the world. And there's an imagism that excludes the self because it wants to evade personal difficulties or conceal ugly feelings.

A brief heavy burst and the rain stops.

Sunlight struggles to break through. The tide is low but not out; boats in the harbour lean on their bottoms or keels but there's water in shallow pools around them. The image in the second sense serves the self's image-making, suggesting clarity and precise definition where the self is in fact befogged and amorphous, prey to destructive forces that have no outlet. Or could it be that presentation of a world of clear hard lines will enlighten and discipline the self that perceives them? Possibly; but it could also lead to a diminished humanity, and unconsciously justify a monstrous self-deception.

I have fully to admit the humiliation of rejection, not only the pain of love rejected but the ignominy of hurt pride. The pain of a broken marriage comes in part from the confusion of mixed feelings. I have meant kindness or have justified myself when my heart & mind are a snake pit or the cannibal underworld of a murky pond. Dreams have revealed my true inner state. Yet right at the beginning I was glad to be shaken in my complacency; but soon forgot how persistent and subtle in its changes complacency is. It can be equally present in studied objectivity or close self-analysis.

Afternoon. A walk along the beach to Friar's Cliff and a swim in the sea with Jim. Beach almost deserted; sky over Hengistbury Head threatening a storm from the west. So much that is *thought* has no substantial existence; there's a great deal to be said for thinking with things and for finding oneself in relationships; as the mind concentrated on the sea's movements and the body acting in relation to them knows how to value thoughts rising passively from bitterness and defeatism.

10 July
Walked all day in the Forest, from Bolderford Bridge via Rhinefield to the Knightwood Oak and back by Puttles Bridge and across the open heath, where ponies & foals were grazing and the distances of heath and sky felt vast after time among the trees. The arboretum with redwoods & wellingtonia & other exotics, and walks & informative notices, is interesting, but I've never liked it much, and like it less now that it's more like an open-air natural history museum, as the Forest increasingly is. But it's still possible to evade the pedagogic hand of the Forestry Commission, and even in places only yards from a gravel or tarmac road to feel the depth and age of the woods or heath.

I saw again how impossible it would be to convey a true impression of the ancient woods of oak & beech without showing that they are movements of light and shadow and air as much as countless tree shapes; or rather that the natural "pattern" continually changing around one comes from the interaction of forces and things which together make a world of the most delicate and subtle movements, and strong deep-rooted forms. And this is only to sketch the surface, without regard to the interdependence of growth and decay, or of the many forms of life each with its own world in the world that human senses perceive; as for example insects under a scale of bark, a grey squirrel leaping from tree to tree, a woodpecker crossing a glade.

Supper at Hayford. Once when Dad was a schoolboy 6 or 7 years old, walking two miles to and from school every day, older boys stole the lunch his mother had made for him. He bawled, and a little girl asked him why he was crying. He saw her with wonder through his tears—it was the first time he had ever really *seen* a girl, and she was beautiful, *beautiful*. Telling the story today, he obviously sees her as he did then. Her name was Lily Lander.

11 July

From Lymington to Yarmouth for a day on the Island, seeing from the ferry red roofs & walls of Lymington, masts along the river & the "masts" of Fawley oil refinery, Burrard memorial, Sway Tower, Hurst Castle, the white cliffs of Dorset. Among the crowds at Alum Bay, showing M. & Elin the coloured sands. Tea with the Gascoynes in their garden at Cowes. I was less comfortable in their company this time. Judy was warm and welcoming as always, but with David, who is much more of an invalid than when I last saw him, I didn't feel like a friend exchanging ideas and experiences, but like a favoured listener. Judy produced photograph albums, and the talk of both was full of famous names—which is natural in view of their experience, but this time seemed close to name-dropping. I surmised afterwards that David lives so much on the past because he is not fulfilling the purpose of every truly serious poet—which he is—to write from every stage of life, developing until death. But I thought this as a warning to myself, not as a criticism of him. He must have consumed so much of himself in the intensity of his poetry and the horror and misery of his breakdowns. He told me again the story of his meeting with Berdyaev only three days before Berdyaev's death, and his pleasure in seeing that Berdyaev had a large photograph of Chestov—friend and passionate intellectual opponent—on his desk.

Towards evening we walked on the almost deserted beach at Freshwater. Wings of cloud shadow brushing chalk stack & cliff face, leaving the chalk brighter, shining against the heaving, deep blue and green sea. The mate on the returning ferry was old Henry, who looked much as he did when I worked with him, 20 years ago, with the same fussy gestures. No doubt he still cycles to and from East Boldre and lives the life of an old bachelor. Coming and going across the water for a whole lifetime! I can think of much less interesting and rewarding occupations.

16 July

In Dorset, at Gold Hill, Shaftesbury: a notice at the top on a huge collecting box in the shape of a Hovis loaf informs us that the 700 year old hill has been much used in films & adverts, most famously in the Hovis bread ad, but says nothing else about its history. There are Thomas Hardy ales in the off licence and elsewhere a bus with the name Thomas Hardy printed on the back. At Cerne Abbas the giant stands out boldly, a cow grazing inside his club, fields of large-eared wheat ripening at the foot of the hill.

Weymouth is crowded and full of bright, coloured trash; there are big, dead jellyfish, some like cellophane bags full of water & shingle, along the tide line. Chalk George riding away, and white cliffs to the west—where, sick in mind, I once walked, and met Gerard & Mary Casey on White Nose. There's no health in my thought when I walk on the esplanade disliking people, without knowing one of them, and forget that we're all equally being manipulated by the system that respects us no more than it respects "our heritage". Even in writing these words I hesitate, dizzy as if I'd come to the edge of a sheer cliff. Who are "we"? Whose inheritors are we? What do we inherit?

Class divisions enter into everything in this country, and the land itself, which has never belonged to one people, is everywhere deeply fissured. Many things that are aesthetically beautiful make the heart lurch sickeningly, both because their harmony brings out the jaggedness and mess of our social strife, and because the beautiful thing itself is often product and sign of possession by a class.

17 July

A brown butterfly flutters out to sea and is lost to sight among shining ripples and wave crests. Walking on the beach, I note the colours. Sea a deepening and darkening blue and green and purple as clouds slowly pass and change shape. Shingle washed by the waves a vivid orange, sand and shingle on the dry beach only duller by contrast, but bright in the sun. Cliffs of Hengistbury Head banded with orange sand, yellow and grey and greenish sand, with red-brown ironstone "doggers" jutting out like stumps of teeth or worn steps, and low in the cliffs, the dark almost black Boscombe sands, frequently covered with a green and yellow patina, which is presumably a form of lichen. White feather, naked tree trunk, smooth or smashed ironstone boulders on the beach. Beyond the oranges and yellows and reds of the Head, the great chalk beak of West Wight, and between and around them, the eye refreshed by cool colours of chalk and flint plunges deep into burning blue…

This familiar place is exotic, a flaming appearance on the face of massive forms, and at eye level and underfoot there are millions of years—gravels of ancient rivers which long before human memory changed their course, fossil urchins rubbed smooth by the sea, artefacts of the reindeer hunters, their camp site fallen to mingle with the beach drift after the iron mining of the last century removed the headland's own defences. I once thought it permanent, fishing from the groyne, which I now know is the protection slowing down erosion, and I can see, in cliff falls and worn shore, the shifts and changes of a mere thirty years. Even the ironstone doggers, that look so integral, "sometimes contain flattened tree-trunks, and the teeth and vertebrae of sharks".

Long before the priory, whose tower across the harbour creates an extraordinary sense of order and repose, long before the harbour itself, and before Avon and

Stour formed a single channel, a river tumultuous with fallen and uprooted trees had its mouth here. Man when he steps on the beach meets his absence; every stone was before him here and the death-wind blows comfortably from ages before his birth. Nor is there death alone in the wind's touch; it brings memories also of his slow formation, and enables a feeling of kinship with simpler forms, and with the ground of life itself, which even gives to death—if only for as long as the touch lasts—something of the beauty of sea and stone.

Tweoxneam. Twineham, between the rivers. Between the rivers became Christ's Church, from the belief that the Master himself had taken a hand in building the priory. Among the relics cherished there during the Middle Ages were "pieces of wood believed to have come from the manger and cradle of Christ", and earth from Gethsemane. Drawn in recent days to the tower, I have tried to imagine the place without it, the harbour an unbroken circle, the gravel and sand heights of St Catherine's Hill and Hengistbury Head showing the ancient connection, and a gap much greater than its breach in geological times—not merely the absence of this priory, but of the history that placed it there, leaving a great hole between the hunters of the glacial age and the work of the modern profiteers, visible in the towering hotels of Bournemouth. Nothing to connect the local earth with Gethsemane, or Golgotha, or Eden; only a world in which the salmon dying under the fisherman's hands is only a fish, twenty pounds of bloody meat. Masts and cross beams only masts and cross beams. Nothing between our struggle with nature to survive and our use of each other for pleasure. No knowledge, perhaps—however faint, however abused—that we are members of one another. How would the sea have looked then, I wonder, or the crumbling headland with its ages of buried settlements and its exposed and exploited iron.

19 July

Morning: a swim in the sea off the beach at Double Dykes. Sand, shingle, seawater, sun. I swam with my head underwater, the seabed a vague blur, and swam leisurely, and floated; then dried myself by immersion in sunlight, and plunged in the sea again. All day I could recapture the movements of my body in the sea, and the sea's movements around me.

A night out in Southampton with John Wiseman & his partner Yvonne. John drove us first to the slipway under the new bridge over the Itchen (its long graceful curve above us) where the shore is littered with green, weed-covered stones and bricks, and the old floating bridge, on which as a boy I used to cross to and from school; repainted dark blue, it has been drawn up on the hard and converted into a restaurant and nightclub. Then on a beautiful, still evening, the waterway stretching out pale blue to the Fawley shore, we walked on the shingle at Woolston, and I picked up a worked flint which I think is a prehistoric hand-axe. We ended the evening with John's home brew. I never felt more relaxed or full of hope, but inevitably much of our talk dwelt on the extreme precariousness of the future and the shrunken, perilous world we and our children live in.

20 July
Séan Street recounted a sinister experience whose irony Hardy would surely have appreciated. On a visit to Dorchester library to interview the keeper of Hardy's manuscripts he was conducted to the quietest available place. The ride in the lift felt motionless so that he had no sense of going either up or down, but when they got out he realized that they had descended and were now under the ground. They then entered a secret chamber furnished with strange apparatus, and he learnt that they were in the bunker reserved for local officials in the event of nuclear war. There he interviewed the librarian about the library's collection of Hardy's books and manuscripts and was able to examine several items of great value. Coming out of the heavily sealed chamber, the librarian remarked to Séan, "you'll never be as safe again as you've just been"—which on reflection I find not the least sinister part of the whole bizarre affair.

23 July
Late at night. At Reepham. M. went to Cambridge this afternoon and will return to Holland tomorrow. I'm alone for the first time in a month, and lie in bed with rain pattering on the window and a storm looming a few miles off and getting nearer. We drove here from Christchurch yesterday, a long, exhausting journey. Today Peter Fuller, the art critic, and his girlfriend, came over. He seemed very self-involved, and we found little to say to each other; perhaps it would have been different if I'd been able to be bold and out-going, but I doubt it. Sarah, a young graduate from Wimbledon School of Art is here too, and has been working on a large piece of elm which arrived for her this morning. It's a delight to see her serious, enthusiastic concentration in her work, as it is to see Lee's too. Tonight, Kate, Lee and I sat talking in the firelight (it's cold here in the evenings) as lightning pulsed and flickered in the night sky visible through the windows on either side.

Dawn. Sparrows chirping in the eaves. Quarter of a waxing moon.

Kate pointed out to me graffiti scratched on the bricks of this house: names, initials and dates, the earliest from the beginning of the nineteenth century. Moor Farm is much older; there's even a rumour that Anne Boleyn was born here. For me, it has something of the feel of Totleigh Barton, although filled with the lives of Kate & Lee & their children. The land is like a great, still pool of time. Beyond Huntingdon we saw the huge hedgeless fields of East Anglia stretching for miles without a break. But here the land gives a sense of enclosure, of hollows where time has gathered in great depth, accumulating in the earth itself, which generations have laboured over season after season. The new wheat looks very ancient—as it does everywhere, but here, more almost than anywhere else, I feel the touch and shaping of many hands.

Perhaps that is why seeing a sculptor at work here is so profoundly satisfying, and why Lee's works in barn and garden feel completely at home. He too is working because he needs to, and although not always using local materials, he is working with nature and shaping new forms for its rhythms and for primary human truths. Thus his *Woman pointing* is a strong image of the threat hanging over us all—everywhere the morning sky of Hiroshima—and a form containing woman's enormously powerful meaning. And although he feels he has never belonged in any place, I feel that he is drawing something essential for the creation of such images from being here.

Later. All morning we worked in and around the barn studio, clearing out chippings, using the gantry to lift sculptures, and trussing them securely to the car roof rack for the journey to London for a summer exhibition.

Scallops of the gouge: a figure some two feet high carved from *lignum vitae*, black-green and harder than some stones, "almost flintlike". Still rough, scalloped where it will be polished, and only partially defined, but already having strong presence. *Pathos*: Lee cuts down to release the naked emotion in the human figure—anger, grief, pathos, etc.—but always in sculptural terms. He spoke about the widespread misunderstandings of "organic form" and we looked closely at a hogweed growing close to the barn.

"Structure in nature is very clear; sculpture should aspire to three dimensional clarity." There's nothing loose or vague in nature, but in every thing a structure of definite relationships between part and part. The ribbed column of the hogweed stem has the strength and structure necessary to bear the branches which in turn are constructed so as to bear the slender, rayed branches from which the umbels grow.

"Clarity"—his primary value—is evidently the result of a coherent and integrated structure. It follows that the artist will learn nothing of value by imitating nature's appearances, but can learn much by examining closely actual processes of growth and structures of natural forms; but again, not in order to copy them, but to understand the relevance of their principles to the terms of his own art.

The African master blocked out the original form, achieving its proportions and its dynamics, and the apprentice "finished" the work. The Western apprentice blocked out the form, and the master achieved its finish. Hence the value of expert representation in the latter tradition, and the value placed on the underlying principles of form in the other. Lee works from the core, having a sense of the whole and the relationship of part to part forming it which determines the surface.

After lunch I drove to Aylsham via Cawston and visited Cawston church. This I found a place of impressive fragments: hammerbeam roof, wooden angels with goose wings outstretched high up, the Speed the Plough carved inscription, a head of the Green Man. But barnlike, empty, so that the words standing out on the altar cloth—*All in Christ shall be made alive*—were little more than words. Once the church would have been intimate, communal, a house of pictures & images, and being there would have been to be part of a living body. Now, for the visitor anyway, it's a kind of museum; and a museum might be equally fit as a place for solitary prayer.

Stayed the night with Dick & Afkham Davis at Aylsham. Little Mariam bawled when she first saw me, a stranger with beard & glasses: "I don't like that man". But by the following morning she was easy and friendly with me. Dick and I went for a walk before supper, crossing and recrossing the Bure and leaning on bridges, the water below dark, fast flowing, and low. Once a kingfisher flew across the river and perched for several minutes on a branch closeby, looking at us through the leaves. We talked a lot about poetry of course, and found considerable differences. I shared my thought about David Gascoyne, and Dick remarked that many great poets in the past were content to have written their poetry during a fairly brief period of their lives. He writes not for the future, but the past; by which I think he means that he writes in the formal poetic tradition he most admires, and judges himself (and consents to be judged) accordingly. He's currently hard at work on the *Shah Nama* (The Book of Kings), but claims not to be a scholar. So does Robert, but as someone said to him, every true scholar claims that he isn't a scholar. Dick is generous in his enthusiasms. On this occasion he introduced me to the poetry of Michael Riviere and Edgar Bowers, both friends of his; but he's also warm in his appreciation of poets who write in styles very different from his own.

27 July

My father dreamt he was singing in public, as he delighted to do in his prime, and woke realizing that he's 83—amazed at the fact—and that all his singing is over.

My mother dreamt that she was running downhill to catch the train to school; the road and bank of flowers beside it had changed, but the same man came out from the station to see if she were coming, and if necessary to hold the train for her.

Listening to them recount their dreams, I remembered that in mine someone had found me a job as a schoolmaster in a Southampton comprehensive, and I was taking it up nervously.

2 August

An outing with Mother. At Minstead church, a small, light, red brick building, where there was a small silver plaque commemorating a young officer who was married in the church in October 1914, and killed in action 24 days later. Under a large oak tree, tiny acorns forming in knobbly cups among dark green leaves, the grave of Arthur Conan Doyle, "Steel True/Blade Straight".

In Southampton: conkers on the trees and gulls on the grass in Watts Park; a brown and a blue-grey pigeon perched together on Isaac Watts' marble wig. Stained, uncared for memorial to the Titanic's engineers, and paths all bright-dark after rain, reflecting the cloud and sunbursts of a stormy day. At Netley, wind was blowing a near gale off the water beside the Victoria Country Park and yachts at their moorings tossed wildly. Crossing the new bridge over the Itchen, Mother remarked that her father wouldn't recognise the place if he could return to it now.

From Southampton we drove to the far side of Fordingbridge to the small downland village of Martin. W. H. Hudson based much of *A Shepherd's Life* on this village. And Pop was born nearby, in the cottage whose thatch came down to the ground and adders climbed up it, so that all his life he was afraid of snakes. This was on the land of Allenford Toyd farm, where his father was a labourer (and *he* too could sing, and sang in pubs at Fareham where he later lived, and won medals for singing. His father's drinking made Pop a lifelong teetotaller.) We saw the name Allenford, and drove up on to Toyd Down, but although we didn't locate the farm itself, Mother felt strongly that she was on her father's ground. Somewhere in these fields the three-year-old boy turned over his foot on a furrow; the man could never stand firmly on a stony surface.

I think there must be something in the blood from ancestral experience. Long before I'd read a book, at the beginning of consciousness, and at various times later when I'd no ideas about the past and no knowledge of family history, I was drawn powerfully to downland, to villages like Martin, and to the earth and chalk hills of Wiltshire and Hampshire.

4 August
Small green apples lie scattered over the lawn. Dad is in his studio spoiling paintings (including one of my favourites, which he gave to me) in the belief that he's improving them. But it's more important that he should work, and get satisfaction from working. There are hints of yellow among the dark leaves, and heavy grey raincloud, thinning to watery blue at the edges, hangs over the houses and trees. I've recently sorted some letters—a great hoard—going back 25 years or more, and found among them photographs, and diaries from the fifties: love letters, letters from friends, and from lost friends and dead friends. I can't describe the conflicting emotions these surprise in me, and I don't trust myself to try. It may be better to leave each occasion in its own time, and not respond later to words not meant for now. But I haven't been wise.

5 August
At Horseshoe Bottom, thoughts walking and pausing.

There is a shaping principle evident everywhere in nature, in structure, form, growth, rhythm. Here, in fern, gorse, pine, white stones from earth's formation, slow-moving clouds. It shapes man from the womb, from the seed, and from the seed of his ancestors, and *his* making is its manifestation in human terms. In man alone in nature can nature become conscious of itself, and choose to be self-consistent, in harmony with universal rhythms, or to express division and disharmony. The berries I can see reddening on rowans, each yellowing bracken frond, show fruitfulness and death. Man the maker is equally involved in this dying, but his work containing knowledge of death can also issue in fruit.

In man the shaping principle is intelligent and spiritual, but gifts of mind work with bodily gifts—a single power consisting of several interdependent faculties.

But is the shaping principle in Nature Spirit? Creation: God?

No knowledge of oneness except in recognition, in *experience*, of personal brokenness and division. Is this why much writing on the unitive vision washes over me? Why Christianity draws me?

I find most people proclaiming wholeness intolerable. But I find most people *proclaiming* anything intolerable.

Hand & intelligence are not separable in the sculptor. In fact the whole body, his person, all his faculties work together in conceiving and shaping the work.

I don't begin to see nature until I am physically active. Walking, senses coming alive, my mind clears. I feel that knowing the name of every creature & thing I see is part of seeing it, though all my seeing is partial. But now, walking, I am in the world and part of it.

7 August
Winchester—Waterloo—Liverpool Street—Harwich—Hoek van Holland — Amersfoort—Groningen.

9 August
A walk with the children on a sunny morning through the park and beside the waters into the centre of town. Joe photographed the rainbows in the fountains. This is where I shall walk every day.

In the afternoon we drove a short way out of town to a place where a still, greeny brown river joins a large lake and people were rowing boats & canoes. Here we rowed between the narrow banks and on the wide water and among lily pads and in mangrove-like places. From the riverbank, a view over meadows, waterways, cows, in the far distance a white windmill.

If I am alert this will be the best time for imagination and intuition: in transition, when all is still strange to me, strange as reality always truly is, before habit dulls it.

§

Brahman: the "voice of the rhythm which has created the world".
    (Sri Aurobindo)
"Ever since the creation of the world his invisible nature, namely his eternal power and divinity has been clearly perceived in the things that are made." (*Romans* 1:20)

16 August
Giethorn: village on water; village in a dream. Trees, wooden bridges, a network of peat-brown canals (mirroring rowan berries, balsam, leafy branches and sky),

thatched, camel-backed houses, brightly coloured flowers in the gardens. A faint, hothouse pungency from the soil; passages from shadow and narrow waterway to an area of reeds and broad lakes.

The village arose some three hundred years ago (though doubtless there was a settlement here much earlier) on peat, in a place deeply and extensively trenched by peat-digging, and lived by reed-cutting too (as in part it still does) and farming. Subsidence is continuous, many walls have cracked brickwork, and the houses are said to need renewing about every eighty years. They are renewed in the traditional style, but although some of the inhabitants are living by the old occupations, tourism is the main source of income now, and since a film was made here in the fifties (M's father had a part in it), it has become an expensive, "desirable" place to live, with famous actors & the like buying houses in the old village. The result, to me, is at once beautiful, fascinating, and not quite real: a model, too-good-to-be-true village, which I can imagine a Gulliver bestriding, looking down on neat miniature houses which appear to him as the small thatched duck's houses look to us; yet at the same time it is shadowed by the primitive, recalling an old pattern won from the struggle with water and earth, with a hint of the life Brueghel saw in the old men wearing clogs, and in the less well preserved thatch & brickwork. And for me it brings to the surface of the mind an early dream of such a place, where there's nothing to do all day except explore the waters and fish.

Stillness—as if a conker might fall from its case, and, landing with a mighty thud, shake the place to its foundations, rending walls, fissuring the ground, making the reinforced embankments cave in.

Giethorn is unique, yet also a microcosm of inland Holland, this country which is a large broken mirror reflecting the sky, where everything drags downward to the water and the earth. The country people for centuries have looked out, watching for danger, and have looked down, working and waiting. The flatness too contributes greatly to the feeling that here the force of gravity is so strong that nothing can leave the earth. In the heavy features of many Dutch faces there's something that seems only partly formed, as if the original clay were still being moulded.

Of course, I don't equate heaviness and slowness with stupidity and unattractiveness—quite the contrary. I only sense that in the Dutch the northern peasantry, which at one time we all were, is closer to the surface, more visible in the flesh. Holland isn't a country where one can expect to see Renaissance features—the face of a Medici—or to find belief in angels or the spirit in any of its airier forms. But here I become increasingly aware of a poetry of the material, and also see, in some architecture and design, for example, a fineness, a delicacy, that runs counter to these generalisations.

Sitting in the sun by the lake at Giethorn, while Joe & Emily were jumping off a paddle boat into shallow water, M. and I talked about Dutch identity.

M. has no sense of belonging here, and says that few people have. Holland has absorbed much from other cultures, and the Dutch have been absorbed *into* other cultures, as one might expect of a great trading nation. There is a great painting, but only instances of great books instead of—as in England—a great literature, and there are few historical events that have stamped themselves on the national consciousness and thus helped to form it. Dutch artists & intellectuals tend to go abroad as soon as they can, and in recent times many of them—e.g. Van Gogh, Mondrian—have done their best work abroad. I asked whether Holland is an unloved country. M. found the question disturbing—as to me the possibility is very sad—but could only say that it is unpraised.

§

Poetry is the mother-tongue of the human race, as the garden is older than the field, painting than writing, song than declamation… The rest of our earliest forebears was a deeper sleep; and their movement was a tumultuous dance… Senses and passions speak and understand nothing but images. The whole treasure of human knowledge and happiness consists of nothing but images. The first outburst of creation, and the first impression of its historian, the first appearance and the first enjoyment of nature, are united in the words, Let there be light. Herewith begins the experience of the presence of things.

Community is the true principle of reason and language, through which our sense-experiences and conceptions are modified. This and that philosophy separate things which cannot at all be parted: things without relationships, relationships without things…
   J. G. Hamann, in Ronald Gregor Smith, *J. G. Hamann:*
   A Study in Christian Existence

23 August
Another very hot, sultry day. Near Bourtange, on either side of the German border, combines harvesting grain, tractors on the roads; on the Dutch side, machines scooping up potatoes, heaps of potatoes by the roadside, a smell of potato-dust on the air. Bourtange, the fortress-village, "restored in its old glory", offering "the sights of a village which was known as invincible in the past". A shady square, a wooden windmill, synagogue & church, inside embankments and moat, all set out like an elaborate geometrical figure; cannons on the grass, and from guardposts on the bank, a long view across the fields and farms into Germany. Like a toy, and so carefully arranged that I even wondered for a moment if the cabbages in the gardens were real!

   As M. said, when the Dutch restore a place they turn it into something "too clean, too neat, too proper to live in". We walked about with other tourists in the heat, taking photographs, tiny black storm-flies sticking itchily to our sweating skin.

   On the roads around here, in 1940, the Germans came through on bicycles, or walking, and the farmers working in their fields could only look at them.

The soldiers as they came were all singing in harmony (which was what deeply impressed M's old neighbour, who had witnessed it). We drove over the border, passing numerous roadside crucifixes, which the soldiers must also have passed; except for a pill-box beside a river, there was no sign of the years of occupation— nor is there much in the landscape and architecture hereabouts to show that a border has been crossed. Yet it soon becomes apparent that it has—in the language, but also in a feeling of difference which would be hard to justify but is strong: the beginnings of an *assertion* that even the crucifixes state.

§

By close-ups of the things around us, by focussing on hidden details of familiar objects, by exploring commonplace milieus under the ingenious guidance of the camera, the film, on the one hand, extends our comprehension of the necessities which rule our lives; on the other, it manages to assure us of an immense and unexpected field of action. Our taverns and our metropolitan streets, our offices and furnished rooms, our railroad stations and our factories appeared to have us locked up hopelessly. Then came the field and burst this prison-world asunder by the dynamite of the tenth of a second, so that now, in the midst of its far-flung ruins and debris, we calmly and adventurously go travelling.
    Walter Benjamin, 'The Work of Art in the Age of
          Mechanical Reproduction'

25/26 August
Joe met an old Dutch sea captain who said to him, "Give my love to England and the English people".

We went with M's brother, Johan, to Zuidlaren. There was a good breeze and we took a sailing boat out on the lake. It was exhilarating to cut through the water, and as we approached the reeds, turn suddenly; but in making our last turn before going back, in the flurry of movement, my elbow jerked into M's face and knocked her glasses into the water where they sank and were lost.

The next day, almost windless, we took the children and hired a motorboat. The odd thing about the lake, and others like it, is that it is both very large and shallow, so that even in the middle people swim—as we did—well within their depth, and there's the strange sight of bathers lazing and playing as if at the water's edge but with a sea of water on every side.

27 August
A walk beside the canal through town with Joe & Emily. Wheelhouses with perhaps a bicycle or a pot plant—perhaps a geranium—inside, and tarpaulins covering the holds. Ropes, wire ropes, coils of rope. Between barges and houseboats, the greenest water I've ever seen, and thick, like a skin, but when looked at closely, alive with lights and movements, reflecting the wavering image of a warehouse

with rows of windows, or a "splash" of colour, the washing hung on houseboat lines. Here all is at once domestic—cats & dogs on the boats, curtained windows, a cobweb in the angle of a door—and redolent of centuries of trade on the inland waterways of Europe, and the seas of the world. The warehouses & merchants' houses divided from the water by narrow streets compound this dual sense of intimacy, even enclosure, of a depth of provincial life, and of a smell of the trading seas. It isn't only historical either (though the past here has a strong gravitational pull, countering the bright "flat" colours—reds & blues—of the modern city) and we watched fascinated in front of a high grain store while grain was pouring down shoots from several storeys into big lorries. Here, too, sunflowers: the blaze of August consuming itself in their faces, looking out from houseboat gardens over the green and shadowy water, and at an enormous brick water tower which is one of the most beautiful buildings in the city.

28 August
Still hot, but the weather beginning to break, a cave-mouth of blue sky between haze and clouds. Windsurfers on the water, their sails when they suddenly collapse, falling like exhausted butterflies. Willowherb bearded with seed that will soon be borne on the air. A smell of autumn under trees beside the lake at Paterswolde.

Later I walked with M. through the crowded & festive streets of Groningen and we had a good meal in the ship that has been made into a restaurant. I don't know how to say it, but I know with her a deepening of experience that makes all my words seem airy abstractions, as if I could speak only from the habits of an old life that is no longer my life, our life.

1 September
Hayford. I draw the curtains on a beautiful morning light falling on the apple tree, apples on the grass, a rake leaning against the tree. After the long journey back I stayed at Winchester yesterday night. Strange to lie in bed in the morning and hear the children laughing and talking with Sue & Roger upstairs in "our" old bedroom! Yet the acceptance that comes with time and change is stranger, when I think of it. Sue evidently regards me as a friend. I'm not sorry that this is how the marriage ends.

The divorce papers arrived in my absence, and I duly signed them.

Now, lying here, thinking of the weeks of sun & water, I remember evenings at Borgercompagnie with Karel & Tjitske and all the children, and especially one, when Karel put logs on the fire after the barbecue and we sat round the blaze until midnight, while the stars became clear in the sky and we saw at least four satellites moving across. Joe then spent four days with Karel and his family, going out with him on his photographic assignments, enjoying himself and learning a lot. At the end of the holiday he said he wants to come and live with us in Holland, where he likes the people and the "difference". There's a good chance that he will join us, perhaps early next year. In the meantime I have somehow to make a liveable relationship with Elin. Our virtual non-communication has been the one shadow—at times dark for both of us—during this summer.

Later. Took Dad to Burton where he judged a horticultural show, and went on with Mother to Tuckton Bridge, where we took the ferry to Christchurch Quay and visited the Priory. White swans on black water. A notice chalked outside the Priory: Please do not throw confetti in churchyard. Inside, I was struck by the figures of Sir John Chydiock & his wife Lady Catherine. They have the faces of ancient, battered pugilists, as for generations people took scrapings from the alabaster which, mixed with pure water, was believed to be an infallible cure for eye-infections. The Shelley memorial is (as Jim originally said) almost a Pietà; in fact, I'd say it's a Pietà pure and simple. Seen together from the quay, Hengistbury Head and the Island correspond closely in line and shape, so that looking up quickly as we came off the ferry I mistook the Island for the Head. Wherever we go in the Forest (purple with flowering ling & heather now), and indeed in a much wider area extending into Sussex on one side and Dorset on the other, my father has stories of the people he has known there, some of whom are still living. His working life after the war was one of the most satisfying imaginable.

3 September

First autumn gale, after a long airless drought. By Anglesea Corner in Lymington in early evening dark, blasts of wind from the sea, through the space where Wellworthy factory used to stand. Later, with Jim by the sports ground, we saw leafy tree crowns turned almost inside out by the wind. My spirit rose and soared. Driving back, rain, mist, and a smudge of orange lights in the windscreen. Now I lie in bed and imagine that in the wind I can hear waves breaking on the shingle shore.

5 September

Glorious autumn light in Winchester, falling through the avenue of limes, on the Cathedral, the war memorial soldier, the white gravestones, and in the city streets. A light to wake joy in the living. Now, about to leave probably for a long time, if I could see southern places—Forest, coast, Island, villages, Lymington & the streets of Winchester & Southampton—more intensely than I've ever done before, I would do so; but in this light, which surprises like an awakening, I know other seasons, other days, when I've been woken to the feeling that I'm seeing things for the first time. And this should continue for a lifetime.

Later in the morning I drove back to Hayford and took Mother out to Martin again, where we visited the church, to Rockbourne, and Cranborne, where smoke from stubble-burning hung thick and acrid in the air, while in other fields the last bales were being gathered and the stubble shone gold. I took her to Knowlton, too, but she felt a chill there, "heard" screams, and sensed an atmosphere of blood. Early in the evening I drove to Christchurch and left my car to the man to whom

I've sold it, so that now, for the first time in many years, I'm without one. I felt an affection for this Peugeot, because it was a pleasure to drive, and because of the many journeys between Winchester and Wales.

7 September
Drove with my parents in the dark to catch the 6.20 train at Brockenhurst. Dawn: low mist at half-tree height in the Forest, denser on heathland, where the top of a pine floated detached. A slow train stopping at most stations. Lyndhurst Road. Totton: gulls dotted about on mud & water at low tide, post at an angle and ribs of the old wreck sticking up out of grey water, a pair of swans sailing grandly upchannel. Redbridge: orange streetlights still on, but sky lighter. Millbrook. Southampton: in the voice of the station announcer—very clear—a sense of the whole life of the area—Fareham, Portsmouth, Eastleigh, Winchester, Micheldever, Hook, Romsey... 6.45 by the Civic Centre clock. Water paler at Northam, reflecting small fishing boats & cargo boats. St Denys: a brown sign on darkened brickwork—WHITBREAD/SOUTH/WESTERN/ARMS—an age and a world in this as much as in the most conspicuous things. Swaythling: more people going to work boarding at each station; gesture of a young man drawing deeply on his cigarette before throwing it down and getting on. Southampton Airport. A free journey, since the ticket office wasn't open at Brockenhurst and there was no ticket collector on the train or at the airport station.

Small Heron airplane waiting vibrating for take off. Airborne over Eastleigh: red roofs, then patterns of ploughed fields, green fields, woodland, all slowly passing below as if we're hovering. In cloud, and suddenly above it, in blue sky, cloud a broad woolly floor just below. Now, ground visible through thin cloud, beautiful cloud-shaped columns of white smoke from chimneys among small round "pill-boxes", no bigger than button mushrooms, the oil tanks of a refinery beside the Thames estuary. Over cloud again: a light smoky vapour with broken cloud masses below, dark blue of the North Sea visible between and below them, now whited out by vapour surrounding us. (Fear of sudden death isn't always fear of nothingness; it may also be vertigo: the spirit torn from the body, cast out on a vast space where it staggers and reels, falling like Lucifer, without even the fledgling's instinct to bear it up in the new element.) In turbulence, bumping: an erratic rollercoaster. Amsterdam below; square flat fields in strips, houses, water. Banking, descending. Down.

Later
M. met me at the airport. It was raining in Holland, and we drove through a misty, dirty light and almost blinding spray when overtaking. To Otterlo for lunch, (the journey had been comparatively so quick that here and for a while afterwards I felt, so to speak, as if I still had one foot on the tarmac at Southampton Airport.) After lunch we went to the Kröller-Müller to see the Van Gogh exhibition.

This was so crowded that it was often difficult to see the paintings and impossible to take time and look closely.

No more than impressions then (my discomfort in a crowded gallery compounded by my unease at viewing a lifework in this way, as a consumer.)

The great understanding of labour—how it shapes the human being, the relationship between man and worked earth—of the early sombre-coloured paintings of peasants; an understanding which only Millet among painters equals (Millet's influence apparent, but in Van Gogh there's a darkness that expresses not only his subject but also the enclosed, restrictive and depressive north, the north of a deeply internalised Calvinism.) He paints the gravitational pull, the sheer downward force of labour, and the strong unrefined human clay; the sun where it appears in the early paintings is a mere ember. But there's humour in some of the portraits, and even caricature, and the humour recurs almost until the end (e.g. in the postman whose beard is like two inverted flaming cypresses.)

Then in the south everything caught fire.

Sunwheels, sunbursts, stars like crystals or exploding fireworks, flame trees, blue flakes of the fiery earth. He heard the voice out of the whirlwind, he *saw* it speak, and showed it speaking. All is at once on fire and caught up in a fierce wind, charged with the fury of the wind. Surely a reaction here from the clay and darkness of the north; if he hadn't seen the dark, and known it in himself, he wouldn't have seen the sun. Of course, the late paintings are the work of a very great painter, and their vision is *true* to the dynamic forces of nature, perhaps to the supernatural, every instant a burning bush. There is loss as well as gain, though.

Now man is lost, or part of the dynamic force, no longer one slowly shaped by great toil and hardship, who in turn shapes the earth. The abstraction of the early paintings singles out man, and woman, the labourer (even the clogs connecting them with the earth are like parts of their bodies; but they are opponents of nature, too, their humanity defined by struggle with nature.) the abstraction of the later paintings emphasises another part: the force that man in order to live and work must only glimpse, or apprehend in a structure of belief as belonging to the universal order; which cannot be *seen* by the sower, though the observer may see the sower as himself part of it.

The greatness of late Van Gogh arises from the alienated self, and in what I've seen of his work there's no middle term (except perhaps humour) between the formation of the peasant in the northern darkness, and the presence in the southern sun of a God who consumes man. Human life is difficult but possible in the early paintings; in the later paintings it is not possible, except perhaps in the consuming moment, in the blaze of ecstasy or terror that extinguishes it.

9 September
Groningen. Sunday in Noorderplantsoen.

In the wind the leaves on the trees shake down light and are increasingly broken loose, spinning or rocking or turning as they fall. Rain and wind animate the lakes, whose soiled green water looks curdled on still days. A flock of geese converge noisily on a small group of people standing by the water—a young couple, a man on his bicycle with a child on the rear seat, and me. The geese stretch out their necks like long sinuous prehensile arms, but they are demanding not hostile, except to each other. The girl (I think of Emily) clutches the belt of her father's raincoat tightly. He keeps the bike still with one foot on the ground and stands watching as the disappointed geese—we have nothing for them—stop pressing around us, and some male and female birds turn fiercely on each other. The sunflowers in houseboat gardens by the canal are beginning to die; the water tower on the opposite bank, though solid and substantial, looks a little like the turret of a fairytale castle in its pinnacles and long windows and overall grace.

10 September
Saw David Wilkinson, professor at the Anglistisch Instituut, in the morning and accepted his invitation to run a series of weekly seminars on contemporary British poetry—specifically, on historical lyrical sequences (including my own *Soliloquies*)—at least until Christmas, while the member of staff who devised and should have taken the course is on sick leave. It's a great coincidence that this particular seminar should exist here and that I should be invited to take it, and a greater opportunity than I could have dreamt of to make contact with staff & students, earn some money, and continue the teaching that has always meant most to me.

§

> Tching prayed on the mountain and
>   wrote MAKE IT NEW
> on his bath tub
>   Day by day make it new
> cut underbrush,
> pile the logs
> keep it growing
>   (*Canto* LIII)

16 September
To Vries on Sunday morning, to a *Romaanse* (Romanesque) kerk—a large, beautiful church made of old and newer bricks, the earliest part of which dates from 1075, where we listened to a *Barokensemble* playing Purcell and Handel and early Dutch music. Autumn light through small rounded windows high on whitewashed walls and through tall pointed windows, with green squares among the squares of transparent glass. Electric "candles" shining on spider-shaped brass candelabra; mellow light and shadow on brick-tiled floors.

No altar, no ornament, no plaques on the wall, only hymn boards, what looked like a child's painting of a biblical city and an icon of a saint or apostle, its striking red and yellow near the pulpit forming the only bright spot on the walls. A twelfth-century font left in front of the church, which would have been at home in any Norman church in England, looked more like an ice-age boulder—one of the *keien* arranged under lime trees outside—or part of the fossils and prehistoric exhibits under glass at the back.

17 September

First seminar in the morning, in a room in an attractive, rather ornate 19th century building (stained glass, coloured tiles, grand stairways with wrought-iron railings) somewhat resembling Old College at Aberystwyth. I learnt from a professor that my old friend Jim Nosworthy had taught here in 1939. Jim sometimes talked to me about his time in Holland which led to his capture and internment by the Germans during the war. Now, especially in this lovely autumn weather, when memory seems most to take a ghostly body from the atmosphere of misty light, it's poignant to think of him here, a young scholar in his first post, and also to remember him as I knew him in Wales, at a time when, through his friendship with me and Carol, he seemed to be reliving the romance & poetry of his own past.

In the late afternoon we drove to Beverwijk where Johan is in hospital. (I write this in his sixth floor flat looking out between other tower blocks over roofs of part of the town.) We left the fine weather behind in the north; it was already mistier on the Afsluitdijk, the great dyke separating IJsselmeer (formerly the Zuider Zee) from Waddenzee—grey, with gulls hanging on the sea wind over the fast road, and the water choppy alongside. Nearer Amsterdam the mist turned to rain and a filthy greenish yellow leaden fog.

This morning, which is fine here, we walked on the beach at Wijk aan Zee, where there are miles of flat sand below the dunes. The subtle blue-grey sea was almost as flat. Big gulls rocked on the waves or flew low over them. A late butterfly flew with singular deliberation out to sea, and we found an exhausted grasshopper among shells & crab carapaces in the sand. The buildings and machinery and smoke of the steelworks at Hoogovens rose behind the dunes to the south, making the small resort look strangely unreal. Farther south, shadowy tankers entering or leaving IJmuiden. Mother & small daughter playing together on the sand!

19 September

Bergen aan Zee: sand drifts against pavements, sand between bricks in the herringbone-pattern brick streets, sand-wraiths rising from the ground and stinging our eyes. North Sea tumbling and foaming, flint-grey and grey and white as gulls; a statuesque oil rig out at sea, two windsurfers riding the waves. A line of foam quivering in the wind, blown in pieces across the beach.

At Alkmaar the great church was closed. Who in God's name do they think these buildings belong to? I felt like kicking the walls. I suppose they have a legitimate fear of vandalism; but M. says the Dutch Reformed Church is possessive and exclusive. Opposite the church we found a very fine cheese shop, which was of course open: cheeses on the stairs, cheese almost as big as car wheels, piles of rounded cheeses, yellow cheeses & cheeses wrapped in red cellophane, whole cheeses & cheeses which the *kaasboer* had sliced with his big curved knife.

20 September
My first Dutch class in the evening, in the language laboratory at the basement of the Faculty of Letters. How different from the school at Llangwyryfon, with Mari & Peter! For me, though, episodes of the same blankness, the same anxiety in case I can't understand a question, let alone answer it!

22 September
At Beverwijk again, to see Johan. Storm over the North Sea last night, at sunset a perfectly clear, pale blue shell-like expanse of sky between darkness over the sea and darkness over the land. Briefly getting out of the car on the high dunes, spray stung and blinded us and we staggered in the strong cold wind. This morning, when Johan came out of hospital, a thunderstorm that would not break; as it was in Aberystwyth on the day last year when M. was with him in hospital and his life was in danger.

It is easy looking down from the window of the flat at the spaces between blocks of flats, where there are trees growing, cars parked, and a few people walking or cycling, to fantasize a total breakdown of social order, bodies & wrecked or burnt-out vehicles lying about on the ground, gangs roaming a wasted urban scene, here and there a terrified individual or family barricaded in one of the few remaining occupied rooms.

In 1961, E. H. Carr, in *What is History?* affirmed his belief in progress: a subtle and qualified affirmation which nevertheless depends upon a positive view of the future. But now (and in this country where the sickness and disintegration as well as the virtues of individualism are perhaps more developed than anywhere else in Europe) I take my dis-ease and clichéd images from the general air, and in a lazy, almost thoughtless moment project a common, vague but draining fear: the nightmare just under the surface of the orderly streets, in the well-stocked shops, in escapist programmes as much as the news or documentaries on TV, in nicely appointed homes, that the end of our world will be the revelation that it is totally meaningless.

28 September
Eemshaven: a walk on the dyke with M. on a mild autumn afternoon. Here the dyke can be seen running east and west for a long way, with sea in front of it, and a large area of reclaimed marshy land behind. The industrial part lies to the west beyond this, and was visible from where we stood only by a row of cranes & a big tanker which from the low level appeared to be wedged into the land. Curlews flying between marsh and sea occasionally called. A big hawk hunted over the marsh, and there were sheep on the dyke, their droppings mingling with shells on its sloping tarmac surface, and numerous ladybirds on the dyke's grassy ridge.

I'd been working on the 'Winchester Mosaic', getting tense and despondent; but as we left the house and drove out of Groningen, M. telling me about her morning's work with a disturbed teenager & his parents, the flat land was at its most beautiful—mild blue sky and light cloud, black and white cattle in fields, sails of a windmill turning, tractors ploughing heavy clay, herons flying over, and a mist that softened rather than obscured, more light than mist—and I came out of myself.

My official connection with University College of Wales, Aberystwyth was finally severed today.

7 October
I learnt of George Oppen's death in July from the issue of *P.N. Review* which carried my essay on him.

Sunday bike ride round the lake at Paterswolde. Fine autumn weather still, with a slight chill in the air. Sweet smell of tobacco from Niemeyer tobacco factory (one of the smells of this town). Sun shining on brown water heaving in a stiff breeze. Over marshy waste ground between the Hoornsediep and the first buildings of town a hawk trying to hover was repeatedly attacked by a common gull, diving and screaming. The hawk was driven off, but soon returned when the gull settled on a post in the canal. A patch of sunflowers beside masses of dark grey clay dredged out on the canal bank (about 100 bombs from the last war have recently been found embedded in the walls of the Lopendediep in the centre of town). A grey cat sat watching a man fishing. We set off at 8 and returned at 10.

I spent the rest of the day working on the Winchester sequence, which I've been able to move on in the past 10 days or so: some extractions from and reshapings of journal entries, some original creation. I enjoy the work, but it disturbs me too, both because of the subject and because I'm uneasy about *using* experience in this way. But what is there really except experience to use? It's living on the past that disturbs me—only in Wales when writing the Mynydd Bach poems did I have a sense of writing of the present I was living. But of course the shaping (which is also understanding) is itself a necessary part of the living.

Standing with M. by the meer at Paterswolde, the windmill to our left and the broad expanse of water in front of us, I experienced a sudden but not unusual start: *once* at Mynydd Bach, *now* here. Already I've been in Holland long enough to begin to lose a sense of its strangeness, to accept it as known habitat, but from time to time I feel the strangeness powerfully. As I feel the change and all it involves.

14 October
Wolddijk to Bedum on a pleasantly grey, mild morning. Smells of earth, cows, cabbages—"red" cabbages, in fact, purple/blue/grey, colour of the local clay when it is freshly turned, and gleams. Many herons in fields and by ditches: a bird which is well camouflaged against grass as well as when in mud or water—partly because

of its colour, and partly because it is so thin—and then the great wings open (how could it have concealed them until now?) and it flaps away slowly, with graceful awkwardness.

The Wolddijk runs through a farming area, nothing but fields on either side as far as the eye can see, which is far even on a grey day, with churches standing up at a distance: spires ("fog-transfixing", Coleridge called them), a Rhenish tower, an onion dome. But small, neat houses continue at intervals beside the road, and the farms have moats of black water around them, and the farm roofs—typical of Dutch farms & barns alike—resemble mounds or well-shaped barrows, their long tiled or thatched surfaces sloping almost to the ground. In one place we passed an overgrown cottage, with an overgrown bicycle leaning against a wall.

Of course, I idealize people, some I idolize; which is a sure way of not knowing them. There is then a great danger of reacting only to the image, or the broken image, and therefore of never seeing or knowing anything except the self-creation.

19 October

Alone for five days while M. & Elin are in Paris during half-term. A ride across town on Monday evening—vivid cold colour in sky & water—to have a meal with Alisdair MacKinnon; Dutch class on Tuesday and Thursday evenings, and a brief visit from Hans & Agnes—but otherwise I've seen no one except Pip, the cat, whose company is a mixed blessing when he comes awake on the bed and chases his tail in the middle of the night, or climbs all over me, as he is doing now, biting the end of the pen…

I've worked at the Winchester sequence, and in working, even among the "bones", the "dust" that clogs the heart, even though I fear that this may be the most "closed" poem I've ever written—and so the opposite of what I hoped for, and believe in (but a poem mustn't be forced to fit a belief)—and even if it's really a small poem, I feel more *definite* than I have for a long time.

21 October

An exhibition of Russian ikons in an antique shop beside the Reitdiep, across the water (here almost solid with barges, houseboats, tugs) from the high building of Albion Mill, where on workdays a man is usually to be seen standing at the open doorway on the highest floor, supervising the discharge of grain by chute to lorries below.

Ikons and autumn colours, brown, yellow, gold. Many were conventional and even crude, bringing to mind Kazantzakis' account of talking with monks who were turning them out mechanically; but a few stood out for the force of their images and the beauty of their design. Several featured the eye of Hell. In another baby Jesus was being held in a blanket as if he were about to be given the bumps.

30 October
A full and relaxed week with Jim, who travelled here after grape picking near Rheims.

Wednesday, a drive with M. into Germany, where we spent most of the time walking round Leer, an attractive small town beside the broad Eems river. Here we saw workmen renovating a red brick road, placing brick beside brick: an operation requiring much patience and care over the centuries. Thursday, a long and in the end exhausting cycle ride: on the Wolddijk to Winsum, and back via Bedum and Zuidwolde. This was at first a beautiful day, blue sky with quickly moving and changing clouds, cloud shadows, a strong warm breeze blowing at our backs. As we cycled easily along, our shadows glided beside us, head & shoulders above brown water in the ditch, moving along the opposite bank. We were able to look closely at the sluices and tunnels and embanked waterways forming the drainage system: detail of great Dutch engineering. In Winsum we looked at one of the two windmills, De Vriendschap, its reed thatched *kop* (head) and sails appearing to bear down on us powerfully, as clouds behind reeled across the sky. Quiet: streets deserted at midday, dry crinkled leaves blowing over road and pavements. We walked by the river looking across at brick houses and orange tiled roofs crowded together on the far bank; a friendly teenager, who might have been male or female, told us a little about the town. Cycling back afterwards, we had the wind behind us for a few kilometres, then, for the rest of the way, it was in our faces, a strong wind from the northwest with little to break its force.

On Friday we visited the Drenthe museum at Assen. A student had recommended me to come here, after we had discussed the "bog people" in Seamus Heaney's poems. Here were three "corpses"—two headless things hanging together, made of what looked like very old leather, and bits of bone, and a young girl lying under a blanket, her small brown toothy head poking out at one end, and her tiny brown stick feet at the other. There were also a dugout canoe, and chariot wheels, and a fine collection of stone artefacts.

On Saturday Jim and I shopped in the fish & vegetable market, where I got what we wanted in some Dutch and English, and a mixture of both, and he cooked an excellent meal in the evening.

Sunday, to Lauwersoog; reeds the piercing yellow and gold of the wild field near Brynbeidog, but here of course there are far more of them—a world of ditches and reeds and clay where a short while ago there was sea.

Grey-green water, grey sky, pale grey sandy soil full of sea shells, where moles have thrown it up. (And how do moles learn of new land? And from how far away have they come, under old dry earth into new dry earth?)

Grey dusk in north Holland: line of a dyke against the sky, or a church spire and a misty windmill seen far off across flat, hedgeless fields, here & there a long mound of beets awaiting transport to the sugar factory in Groningen, clots of earth stuck to naked vegetable flesh, and in one place, where farmers were burning the leavings of a crop of maize, a fire, vividly animating a corner of the day, vibrant leaping red tongues licking at the mass of misty grey air. The strangely expectant look of unpicked cabbages, or a tumbrel of cabbage heads. Potatoes left to rot where the ground is too waterlogged to lift them. Yellow leaves, red flames, but over all greyness, beautiful and foreboding, like silt misting a great expanse of still water.

8 November

Thin but steady leaf-fall under a blue sky. The ground under the trees is thick with leaves, and leaves lie on bonnets & roofs of cars left alongside the park, and float on the ponds. Horse-chestnuts burn a beautiful yellow, copper, brown and gold.

Walking out in the morning, taking a break from work on the Mosaic poems, I was thinking about seeing. Oddly, it's only recently that I've become fully aware of my obsession with it, and this morning I thought of the eye as a devouring creature, which constantly and secretly feeds on all it sees, or chooses to see. There's something monstrous about it, an exaggeration of the one faculty in people who are disconnected from each other and self-alienated, so that the poet is in danger of seeing like the pornographer.

Vision remains for me a primary value, and I thought vaguely of Ruskin, and of the scale between acute perception, which is both aesthetic and moral, and madness, when outraged nature rises up violently against life narrowed to the point of sight. And thinking of this, I climbed onto higher ground, into a clearing among trees which overlook the ponds on one side and the road and fountains on the other, and came upon a sculpture which I hadn't seen before. It had been carved from a block of white stone, which was smudged and scrawled all over by graffiti, and represented a figure suggesting both beast and man. The figure was seated at, or rather attached to a table, for table and figure were carved from the same block; but the table was like any administrator's, and the creature's shaggy paw-like hands and forearms rested on it, as he sat hunched, staring from empty eye-sockets scooped from a rounded, brutal head. This was not unlike the Cerne Abbas Giant's, and as I looked closely I saw that, like the Giant's, it had more pathos than brutality.

I was held less by the sculpture itself, than by the eye-sockets and lower face, for someone had marked these with a dark substance, which ran crookedly from the sockets and down the cheeks, as if, like Gloucester, the creature had been savagely blinded.

Night
M. is in hospital. She had a cycle accident at midday, and was operated on for bleeding in her right arm. I saw her in the afternoon with Elin before the operation, and again with Bethan & Elin not long after she had come round early this evening. She will be in hospital for at least a fortnight. I was desperately worried before and during the operation, because she had trouble with her blood clotting after another accident a few years ago, but seeing her and talking to a young doctor alleviated the anxiety somewhat. But she is badly shaken and in pain.

8-16 November
Bright days, but colder; a feeling of coming snow as I've cycled to and from the hospital. Small sycamore in the tiny front garden blowing yellow, copper, green. M. has often had great pain which she has borne bravely. On Wednesday Hans drove me to Schiphol, where we arrived early and had an hour watching planes landing and taking off in spectral light while waiting to meet the children off the plane from Southampton. On Thursday morning M. came home until the operation, probably on Monday, to close the wound in her arm. Yesterday I took Joe to Sint Maartenscollege, the school he'll be attending when he comes to live here, and left him there for the day, returning in the afternoon to talk with his teachers, whom I find likeable and sympathetic. This morning, Saturday, I walked with Emily in the park, snow on fallen leaves, snow falling thinly through the trees, enough snow on benches for her to make snowballs, and the water shining black in raw, grey light.

Afternoon. I stood with Emily in the cold, a light snow falling, in a crowd waiting for Sinterklaas to arrive at the Stadshuis in the centre of town. It was worth waiting for the colourful actors in the ceremony, who brought an exotic touch—Catholic and southern—to the bleakness of the day, and good to see and share the expectancy of the crowd, but the wait was long and cold. As we stood there, the electric lights put up in the form of candles suddenly came on overhead and across the square. I love the winter festivals, Christmas in particular, when light and colour and the rich fruit of the year shine warmly in the dark and the cold which they need to give them fullness of life.

21 November
Up at 5 on a dark, wet morning. Took the children by train to Amsterdam, through haunting effects of lights and headlights—red orange, white—reflected or seen through reflections in the glass, moving, changing patterns and the long, dark stretches of countryside, until grey dawn after 7.30. From Amsterdam by bus to Schiphol, where I left them with a stewardess who conducted them to the plane. Then I made the journey back, sun breaking through and shining on wet fields, the day alternately watery blue and overcast.

24 November
Saturday morning. By the meer at Paterswolde with M, her first outing since the accident. Strong wind, masses of driven cloud outlined against pale blue sky, the meer dark brown and turbulent, waves heaving up into peaks, exploding in spray or breaking full of leaves against the bank. Ground sodden, plastered with dead leaves, trees by the water bare. A flight of ducks went over high up, as if the wind were speeding them like arrows. A few tower blocks on the far side of the water, and the chimney of the sugar factory, smoke streaming out horizontally (coming back we could smell it even in the doorway, a faintly sweet sourness, like soiled linen in the wash, or the bottom of a drained canal). A dark-bright world of sky

& water, waves darkening to a brightness it was hard to look at, and a solitary windsurfer, small and slanting fast on the stormy surface.

26 November
In the morning M. went back into hospital to be ready for the second operation on Wednesday. Later, in the seminar, I discussed Jeffrey Wainwright's 'Thomas Muntzer' with the students, and afterwards thought of the days when Jeff & I were at Aberystwyth together. In the evening Sue rang to tell me that the first stage of the divorce was completed today.

Peter Ackroyd's *T. S. Eliot* is the work of a good biographer, who knows that biography is "a convenient fiction since no one can probe… those hidden perceptions or experiences which run alongside the observable life but may not necessarily touch it".

I started reading the book with certain assumptions, and it dissolved or modified them, leaving me with an enhanced respect and liking for Eliot, and several more or less tentative conclusions:

1. Nothing can be concluded about any life.
2. This self-conscious man, enigmatic and evasive in the eyes of many of his close contemporaries, had a directness and absoluteness in his "spiritual life", and therefore a different understanding of the "self" existing in their social world, which are rare only in modern times, and appear eccentric precisely because of the compartmentalization of the human being into "spiritual", "sensual", "secular", etc.
3. A scrupulous and searching biography, which gives a deep sense of an individual life, nevertheless contributes to a feeling of incompleteness and even unreality by abstracting the life from the history of its times. Thus Ackroyd contributes to Eliot's isolation by failing to show—as I suppose all biographers must—how inextricably his life was implicated in his times.
4. Eliot's "self-making" was an instance of a pervasive modern need, observable especially among writers who do not find in their origins and everyday life a tradition to feed their creativity and form their self-image and identity in the world. Eliot was not empty but he began as a writer with an overwhelming sense of emptiness, which he had to fill.
5. The great writer who inspires one or more generations to see will also blind them to all that he himself does not see.
6. Objections to Eliot have to be earned, as Oppen and Williams earned them, and *made in the form of alternative ways of seeing*.
7. Eliot's influence (through his publishing as well as his writing) was more mixed than I may have suggested. For example, he published Idris Davies as well as Thirties' poets whose socialism made them no

more in touch with the people than he was. And he published David Jones, whose work makes available English (and British) "matter" which transcends Eliotic limitations.

8. Whoever Eliot was, he was a brave and admirable man. It's greatly to Ackroyd's credit that the qualities emerge strongly in a portrait with distinctly unattractive traits, and that the man whom, it seems, hardly anyone felt they knew is a moving figure. I was particularly moved, in different ways, by Ackroyd's account of the two marriages.

9. Eliot's poetry is part of me. (Janet gave me the *Collected Poems* in 1959.) I've "taught" him for so long that I no longer realized this; and it is the *poetry* that becomes part of one, the illusion of personal intimacy which arises from the work of other writers doesn't occur in Eliot's case.

10. His poetry proves on our nerves and emotions why he couldn't play the part of poet, but took refuge in the kind of worldly role his family & ancestry had prepared him for. I don't want to romanticize his isolation; he suffered it, and knew it from early on as a sickness in the culture, and a condition which the poet could recover from only in a common order, with a common language. I don't think it a dead question, even now, why he chose to become "English", and reading this book has made me think again about the "self-making" of modern writers and its implications. Generally speaking, Eliot could never rest content with "self" and "world" in any of the ways in which these are ordinarily assumed. Other choices are possible than those which Eliot made; but the choices have to be made in a life—in a sense, they cost a life—not groundlessly assumed as a stance from which to berate Eliot for his "defeatism" or lack of "human" sympathies

Early December
M. is now in her fourth week of almost continual pain.

Early evening: illuminated decorations over the Ebbingestraat shine like spiderwebs beaded with dew. A bright half-moon with an edge like a sharpened axe blade. A foggy dawn, pavements furred with frost, brick streets slippery and all standing cars opaque, sealed in.

For me, this is a time of work. I think a lot about family & friends in England, but at present rarely miss England itself. This obviously has much to do with the fact that I'm happy here, and like Groningen, but it also has something to do with the understanding that there's no work for me in the south of England now.

From here I can see more of the English tragedy. But if I can only be a spectator I'd rather look on from here than with comfortable people in southern England who complacently and self-righteously watch the miners fighting with the police and with each other: men fighting for their communities, the once great machine of industrial society grinding to a halt, and no public thought given to how we can make a life for all the people, instead of once more letting economic forces dictate the shape of a society, in which some people use them for their material advantage and others are used—as if economics weren't man-made and there were no other constructive human possibilities.

But it isn't as a spectator that I know England to be a poisoned and poisonous little island, but in the venom of the class system, in the currents of bitterness, hatred, resentment and contempt between classes, and the confused crosscurrents affecting those whose class is ambiguous. The tragedy is the extreme difficulty of love: that great love of the islands and the people must in reality be either vague and idealized to the point of abstraction, or highly selective, focusing on a few people, a few places, or loyalty to a group or class interest.

What is "a pattern of timeless moments" to men and women whose lives are constant struggle at the workface, or to the unemployed, or to those on the other side of the machine, using it for their profit? What is it to those who look for a world of meaning in society for themselves and their children, for all people, and who cannot find meaning in a tradition that excludes almost everybody? Meaning can't be made in a vacuum, its terms have to be available in the society and in England today they are hard to come by—you may be unemployed, you may make money, but if you want to make a life with other people that means something you have to be an exclusive specialist—a monk, a community worker, a miner, or perhaps even an academic—and if you want to cross specialisms towards a larger human community, you will have acute language difficulties and probably be labelled a sentimentalist or a crank. Yes: the rhetoric of denunciation is easy; it's finding a living image of a pattern which unifies that's hard.

Have I given way to complacency in leaving England, in not trying hard enough to get a place there—for I could do something other than teach? Or in not struggling to get a central influence in my "specialism", which I could have used to get a better hearing for writers whose work matters—as the ambitious Eliot succeeded in doing, because no one else wanted it enough, according to Peter Ackroyd? Well, I'm not Eliot, nor an attendant prince—and I don't suppose that what I believe in could be established in the seats of my successful contemporaries in that world. I can do nothing now but continue with the work I can do, without caring less about England because my angle of vision has widened.

8 December
Slept well after a bad tempered day in which I made no progress on my Eliot essay, and couldn't expect to, but read, with mixed interest and irritation, some essays by Guy Davenport. Dreamt again that I was back at Brynbeidog, but somebody else was working in the caravan—I could see his back from where I sat by the bank. Sue had written a poem and was using it on a Christmas card. I saw three versions and was dissatisfied with it but she took no notice. Now I was complaining bitterly that Sue took everything from me, even poetry.

A self-pitying dream though I didn't wake with that feeling. The details clung lightly to my mind as I went for a ride, needing fresh air, and cycled to Zuidwolde and back. A damp, misty morning, beginning to clear as I left the town. But first Korrewegbrug was opening as I reached it, to let through a long, pale grey barge, *Trude* from Rotterdam. Then I rode across fields—sodden leaves & grass beside the path, the refreshing look of new, turned earth, a heron hunched in a ditch, gulls chasing crows—and through the new estates at Beijum. Still thinking occasionally of the dream, I admitted how much Sue had helped me to write, both with her interest and acute criticism, and the long, settled life she gave me. Coming back by a canal, I passed two mongrel dogs at the gate of a small, houseboat garden, and thought, returning their curious, benign stare—well, they won't spend today struggling to make anything; which was momentarily an oddly comforting thought, since I usually see myself in comparison with other people doing unquestionably useful things!

14 December
Disturbed sleep towards dawn: a dream of death as falling endlessly through complete darkness.

17 December
A little snow overnight. Posted my Eliot essay to *Agenda* in the morning and took M. to the clinic for physiotherapy. The bandages are off the arm now, showing the wide and deep incisions. With painful exercise, use of the hand is gradually increasing, but it will be some time before full use is restored.

21/22 December
Left Groningen by train in the evening. After an hour's wait at Amersfoort, I stood on the train to the Hook, and there wasn't much room to stand. Some of the passengers were young soldiers on leave from Germany, crop-headed, foul-mouthed, clannish working-class boys. The boat was crowded too, but I had a cabin and slept on and off during a smooth crossing. We human beings en masse, whether loud or shut in ourselves, are an ugly sight, yet perhaps any one looked at closely, and certainly people showing consideration for each other, are beautiful.

On the train at Harwich, just before it started, in a lull among the tired, desultory conversations, a voice was faintly audible singing 'Away in a Manger', whether on the radio or someone on the train or on the platform, I don't know, but Christmas began for me at that moment.

24 December
At Yew Tree Bottom with Mother on an afternoon of beautiful sunlight, Sway Tower among trees standing up grey against the dark grey outline of the Island, bracken on slopes and a few yellow blooms on gorse. The sun was flaring red towards setting as we came away. Now, constellations are bright in a clear night sky and frost is forming on grass. I expect there will be children tonight who, looking

at the sky, imagine they see—perhaps in a shooting star—the sledge drawn by reindeer shooting across, as I did at Warsash as a boy.

Christmas Day
Took my parents to 7 o'clock communion at St Mark's. Poor old Pibworth, the vicar, read the service in such an extraordinary way—too fast, too loud, across the rhythm and with dramatic emphasis in all the wrong places—that it was very difficult to follow. When he began, I was afraid that I'd have one of the helpless giggling fits which often made evensong with David Hayter an agony of embarrassment for me when I was a boy. As it was, I found the performance so distracting that it practically emptied the words of meaning. Of course, worship isn't an aesthetic experience, but I couldn't make any observance in the circumstances. I was therefore at once disappointed and uncomfortable: not wanting to be a mere spectator, and knowing that Mr Pibworth meant every word, while even if he'd been the perfect channel, not every word would have meant something to me.

Afterwards, before breakfast, I walked round the "Triangle"—smells of decaying oakleaves in thawing mud by Yondy Corner, and of a field of farmer Morgan's cabbages (later we had one of his turkeys for dinner); barn owl fluttering to rest in the copse on the Common, Island downs rising at the far end like a local hill.

Slowly, I'm beginning to realize what uncertainties and demands I submitted to in giving up my job in Wales, as well as the advantages I gained. I can't reasonably hope to be a prolific writer, and in my present circumstances I've less chance of making a living by this means than when I was in Winchester or Aberystwyth. Yet in spite of the extreme unlikelihood of my work having any widespread impact on "the literary life" of England as it is today, I do have, much of the time, a deep-rooted confidence. Less in what I've done, more in the going on doing.

§

> Reason creates out of her own truths an enchanted realm of lies. We are all living as though under a spell and we feel it; yet we fear the awakening more than anything in the world.... [B]linded... by the "truths" which our ancestor plucked from the forbidden tree, we look on our efforts to remain in this sleep as the natural activity of our souls.... [A man] lives for his fellow-dreamers, in the hope that the "common dream"... will help still more to strengthen his assurance of the reality of illusions. Consequently men hate Revelation above all things, for Revelation is awakening... Philosophy sees the supreme good in a sleep which nothing can trouble, that is, a sleep without dream-faces. That is why it is so careful to get rid of the incomprehensible, the enigmatic, and the mysterious; and avoids so anxiously those questions to which it has already made answer.
>
> Leo Shestov, 'Gethsemane Night', *In Job's Balances*

Boxing Day
Fetched the children from Winchester on a bright, frosty morning. After lunch we went with Mother to the shingle-spit. A spring tide filled the estuary and was halfway across Saltgrass Lane. Blue sky, cloud moving over from behind the Island, coming up like smoke pouring from a huge funnel—white, grey, purple-grey— and breaking into oddly shaped fragments, one like an iceberg over the Forest. The sky in the west was a gradually encroaching sheet of cloud.

27 December
At Brockenhurst with Emily. The river was running over its banks through the trees, a swirling, brown flood carrying foam & bubbles. Emily, standing on a wooden bridge, said it made her feel sick to look down. The water in places where sun caught it was molten white, and ferns in stripes of light were golden. We went on to Hatchet Pond, where an image of the young moon folded and unfolded, writhing like a water snake, with the gentle wave movements, and the pond was yellow, red, gold in the setting sun.

28 December
Train to Winchester. Frost on Forest lawns & heaths, ice on ponds. Ponies cropping grass at woodland edges. Low tide in the Test estuary, mud and channels dotted with gulls & waders and silvery in the sun, a bird on a spar of the wreck's black and broken ribcage. Notice on a factory or warehouse near the airport: SOUTHAMPTON—HOME OF THE TRANSIT. Later I went round Winchester bookshops, bought a sausage roll & sandwiches for lunch, and ate them sitting in The Close. Perhaps because it has been a full week, I began to feel tired and tense, and near to tears for no reason. Old man's beard on the railings at the park end of Monks Road; dark glowing red brick—but I don't feel now that I've much contact with the place.

31 December
Groningen. Quite heavy snow overnight and in the morning. Took Emily & Joe to the park where they played with a sledge. Gulls & moorhens stepping daintily on ice on ponds. Later, a sound of sleigh bells outside—women pushing trolleys loaded with shopping from the supermarket over the brick surface of Balistraat.

The snow turned to rain during the day, but it was fine at midnight, when we let off our fireworks on the pavement outside the house, as people all over the city were doing. For half an hour or so the sky was full of coloured stars and pungent smoke, and fireworks were whistling, squawking, whooshing, and banging on all sides.

5 January 1985
Sun rising orange on the snowfields of Holland, flaring or warped and buckled in the windows of Amsterdam, as I took Emily by train to the airport. On my return the sun was burning white, and the trees beside the line were very beautiful,

especially the birches, which were like delicate glass flowers. Back in Groningen, I picked my way cautiously on foot from the station to the Korreweg. Only roads and cycle paths are fairly clear of snow, which hangs in lumps on hedges & bushes, and rises like an extra white roof on cars & house tops. Now Emily is back in England, and I miss her, as Sue will be missing Joe, who is living here with us. I remember walking with him in falling snow up the lane past Pencwmbeidog and seeing a magpie fly over, exactly like a Brueghel image. And now we are here, among the snowfields of the north…

7 January
Coming out of the hospital early in the morning, after taking M. for her treatment and before driving Joe to school, I looked up the road and was startled to see an enormous full moon, faintly rose colour from the rising sun. Moon at the city edge, just clear of roofs, but restoring space to the mind intent on near things.

14 January
Walked with Joe through softly falling snow, over frozen ponds in the park, to his bus stop early in the morning. The big trees look enormous in the snow, and human figures move darkly, with the caution and balance of Brueghel's hunters.

23 January
Again, recently, I dreamt of Sue and Brynbeidog, her partner, Roger digging the garden in front of the caravan (but humus, the ground there was heavy clay—and a stream ran *across* the edge of the field: but it was essential Brynbeidog) and woke bitterly remorseful and sad. Daylight comes and dream atmosphere and waking feeling begin to fade. But images from some dreams remain vivid lifelong, and are as much part of our real world as the daily things we are made of. "All our young lives": not quite. I am more completely happy now than I have ever been.

Afternoon. The rain of recent days has melted much of the snow, leaving patches to slip on on pavements, and eroded, frozen drifts, like soiled, worn alabaster. But today the sun is shining. Now, though, as I sit in the living room, the day suddenly darkens, and looking up, I see snow falling: thick and slow between the walls of Balistraat, and quick and slanting in the more open space of the Korreweg. An old man wearing an overcoat and cap walks past, and the snow on his cap is like soft white feathers. I read a little of Guillaume IX, the first troubadour, in an American translation, and it seems horrible: All male aggression, arrogance and possessiveness, a rich brutal but clever barbarian talking of "cunt" & horses. Perhaps it's better in Old Provençal, in which it evidently has rhythm & rhyme, and may possibly have more reason. Only now, for me, the words are part of the sudden darkness, as if the naked power of that world had risen up and held a blade before the sun…

"I will make a *vers* of exactly nothing…"

§

Poetry always remembers that it was an oral art before it was a written art. It remembers that it was first song.

There are two lines which confirm this, One is in Homer—or the Greeks whom we call Homer—where he says, in the *Odyssey*, "The gods weave misfortunes for men, so that the generations to come will have something to sing about". The other, much later, is from Mallarmé, who repeats, less beautifully, what Homer said: "tout aboutit en un livre", everything ends up in a book. The Greeks speak of generations that will sing; Mallarmé speaks of an object, of a thing: the idea that we are made for art, we are made for memory, we are made for poetry, or perhaps we are made for oblivion. But something remains, and that something is history or poetry, which are not essentially different.

   Jorge Luis Borges, 'The Divine Comedy'

2 February
Last Saturday I was with Joe in the park taking photographs—snow-capped sculpted bison, arrow claw marks of waterbirds in snow lying over ice on ponds, the blind man-beast alone on his hill—and snow was falling on us wetly out of a grey sky. On Sunday we all went to Zuidlaren, and Joe & Elin jumped on ice which began to crack, but stretched white and grey to blue trees in far distance, with a few houseboats locked in on the vast expanse of frozen lake, under a blue sky. But yesterday, and again today, the soft wind felt like spring, and the month of snow is almost forgotten.

Joe was homesick early in the week, but recovered after talking about it. He and I are in some ways very much alike, but fortunately he is open, and can show his feelings. He's very anti English, and disturbs me at times by talking remarkably like Tony. This, together with a letter from Phil Pacey, has reinforced my sense of the division that the Thatcher government has greatly increased within the nation: not caused, but widened to the extent of being more than a civil war of feeling. But of course, terrible damage can be caused with little or no bloodshed, and it has been, and is being caused in England.

I too have been more restless since Christmas, with memories of England & Wales rising unsummoned, seemingly at random—bubbles on the stream of the mind.

§

Rely only on yourself. Dig more deeply with your drill without fear or favour, but inside yourself, inside yourself. If you do not find the people, the earth and the heaven there, then give up your search, for then there is nowhere else to search.

   Boris Pasternak, *Letters to Georgian Friends*

The creative man has no choice but to trust his inner command and place everything at stake in order to express what seems to him to be true. This inner command is absurd if it is not supported by a belief in an order of values that exists beyond the changeability of human affairs, that is by a metaphysical belief. Herein lies the tragedy of the twentieth century. Today, only those people can create who still have this faith.
     Czesław Miłosz, *The Captive Mind*

9 February
To Lauwersoog with Joe & Mieke for lunch on a bright, cold day, an east wind blowing grey sand from polders across the road. Smashed windscreens and diamonds of ice scattered on ice still strong enough to bear a man's weight at the water's edge. Vast flocks of geese & ducks on the water and in the fields, or against the sky, dark flights which make the heart restless for the north. My parents' 58th wedding anniversary today. I rang them in the evening. After a fine spell, the day brought them snow. It is snowing again in the south of Holland, too, but here there's only bitter wind and ironbound earth.

15 February
Sun shines through the window onto a vase of yellow tulips on a glass table. There's a little snow on pavements, but the day is warm and bright. After a bad working week last week I've worked steadily, and at times excitedly, since my class on Monday morning, and am relaxing now after typing out what I think is the final draft of 'The Headland'.

27 February
I've been ill with a stomach bug since shortly after writing the above, and in consequence have eaten little. Wretched days, when at worst my philosophy hasn't been worth a rag, with periods without feeling sick or tired and miserable when I've written letters, or, today, a review. The best thing has been the Elfstedentocht, which we watched on TV: skaters vigorously and gracefully skating on dark grey ice on canals & lakes, small lonely groups detached from the main body of competitors, far ahead in a wide flat misty grey-brown landscape; at last, four together, suddenly fighting furiously for the lead on the last stretch...

10 March
Sunday morning. M & I walked through town and into the country in lovely warm sunshine. Snowdrops in one garden, but otherwise no spring flowers yet, but catkins & silky buds on pussy willow, and a few fresh green leaves close to the ground. We walked to a broad canal and back beside it—distant bridges shining mistily—and eventually by oil tanks and through an industrial estate into streets behind the Korreweg.

    I needed to get out in sun & air after several weeks spent mainly indoors. Work went badly at the beginning of last week, but on Thursday I wrote four poems which I think will probably be the last of 'Winchester Mosaic'. I never learn: the day before I'd been utterly miserable, nothing I did came alive and I felt a complete failure. This state of mind had a strong contributory factor in Michael Schmidt's negative response to several ideas for critical books which I'd put to him, together with his less than enthusiastic response to the information that I've a new book of poems near completion, and my apprehension that he may, in fact, reject it. It suddenly seems that I may be faced by the "wilderness" again, thrown back into the situation I was in ten or fifteen years ago, of looking for a publisher.

Damn it! I think I deserve a publisher's encouragement for my poetry & criticism, instead of being grateful for tactful but uncertain support. But then suddenly, on Thursday, all my doubts and all inclination to whinge vanished in an upsurge of confidence and I felt, especially in the poem to John Keats, something new—a liberation of figurative language after the long winter of my distrust of it. Heartened by this sense of a new freedom, and of the possibility of a richer more vital and inventive poetry, my fears and resentments melted—as the last ice has melted now on ponds & canals—and at the same time I felt the bedrock of what really matters—to write as I must, regardless of whether I can publish what I write or not.

15 March
Flurries of driving snow. In the morning I rewrote 'Master of the Leaping Figures'. Afternoon, with M. in the hospital, for the third operation on her arm recently; twelve storeys above the city, looking out over cranes working on the hospital extension, tiny cars and red-tiled roofs, in the direction of Germany.

17 March
Still winter in the woods at Appelbergen, near Haren, on sandy soil at the edge of the *hondsrug* (dogback), where the glaciers came to a stop. Masses of dead leaves under stunted oaks, looking as though nothing living could ever come up through them; small tight buds on trees, and nothing out except a few leaves on a little honeysuckle. Thin ice, patterned like frost on a window, or snowflakes, on dark water in ditches full of fallen branches. A cold wind especially at woodedge, where it brought a good smell of muck off ploughed fields—hillier than anywhere else I've seen in the north of Holland; warmer in sandy hollows in the woods, where the form of the land is like low dunes.

It was good to get out again, though I'm feeling distinctly off colour with a return of the virus which, in fact, I've not thrown off for more than a day at a time during the past month.

19 March
Snow, a heavier fall, settling, needling my eyes as I cycled back from the university at mid-morning. The Decree Absolute came today, though made on the 8th. Worked on the Ystrad Fleur, yew tree poem in the afternoon.

Is this what people mean by "mid-life crisis": the *physical* feeling I get of mental and personal limitation, when my head feels full, and dull and heavy? Or is it just tiredness, or a form of the defeatism that has plagued me for as long as I can remember? At times I'm sunk in myself, a heavy clay, yet at the same time am not "myself", not a channel freely expressing my being, but stopped, stagnant and impure. Christ! it sounds like constipation; which, emotionally, it is.

23 March
A day of cloud without rain, but the dark grey was more like the colour of April showers than of winter, and there was a smell of growth coming from the earth. I got up feeling sick after a night when I'd slept badly, and had read for long periods. Llewelyn Powys again: *A Pagan's Pilgrimage*, which has interesting and attractive passages, mainly after his arrival in Palestine, but is disappointingly thin, with a pompous style; and *The Cradle of God*, which begins by burying the power of the Bible in Powys' verbiage.

Felt better after a short walk with Joe & M. round the lake in the Stadspark, where witch hazels are in leaf, and mole highways cross the ground. Several friends came in during the day, Hans & Agnes briefly in the afternoon, Ellie & her son Marc, Neel, Tjitske late in the evening, bringing me flowers for my birthday.

Perhaps our language is all we have to understand with, and in words we articulate what we can of our feelings and instincts—all the non-verbal intuitions and forms of communication that reach deeper than we can say. So, the more I can put into words, the greater my sense of failure, from the correspondingly greater awareness that it is impossible to capture even the life that we ourselves live, let alone the lives of others. I can imagine a revelation that would astonish us with a familiar, yet strange vision: our lives seen as they are, from every hidden motive and remotest influence to every minutest detail, correcting our mistaken notions and distorted perceptions, completing our partial awareness. For me, the poem that works is the poem that gains a little more of this vision.

26 March
Wrote my essay on Gillian Clarke's poetry yesterday, and, today, took my last seminar—of the present session, at least—at the Instituut. I've enjoyed teaching the Dutch students, and we've done good work together. Intellectually, and in dedication and motivation, they compare very favourably as a group with students at the same level in Wales. Some subjects have been difficult for them, e.g. the special "Englishness" of *Mercian Hymns*, and I felt the difference from Wales this morning, when we discussed *The Tribune's Visitation*, but without anything like the same engagement with the culture/fact of empire opposition; but their interest and willingness to talk about serious issues have made the seminar useful and enjoyable.

28 March
Confirmation of my visit to Israel, in the form of a cheque from John Levy to pay for the flight, came first thing this morning.

To Amsterdam with M. for the day. Trains crowded: on the "balkon", between Hildersum and Amsterdam, a young man reading the Penguin *Wuthering Heights*, with front cover missing.

We walked across the city, which in many parts is very beautiful, and rather like Groningen, only on a much larger scale. Clocktowers, narrow streets and broad, brown canals, bridges, elegant houses by canals, and flower stalls backing with greenhouses onto canals; sex shops, peep shows, diamond traders, everything for sale—all the glamour and wealth, cultural impoverishment and stunned or desperate faces of a great modern Western city; crumbling sculpted classical figures over gateways; new pipes, and old rusty gravel-encrusted pipes on the pavement—dug up by workmen on a day when much of the city seemed to be under excavation, with sand thrown up on pavements & streets, and power drills vibrating against traffic noise and clang of yellow trams, which drag themselves round corners like caterpillars, only much faster!

We came out of the station to the strains of a bagpiper playing. A saxophonist was playing in the caverns under the Rijksmuseum, where the road goes through, and the arched high-ceilinged space was filled with the mellow sound. On our way back, a clarinettist had taken over in the same place, softly, hauntingly.

After a bite to eat we went to an exhibition of modern art, *La Grande Parade*, at the Stedelijk museum, which has been immensely popular and was still too crowded for comfort or proper attention. So much to see! We came out with aching eyes, yet I had only a few impressions, and knew how much I'd missed. What really impressed me, in this fleeting visit, was a Rouault, *The Clown*, which fortunately we saw almost at the beginning; a modern work through & through, but as if the face had *emerged* from the ancient world, from the wall of a catacomb, with crumbling plaster partly forming it. There were some Chagalls nearby, for me, one of the main attractions of the exhibition, yet, seeing them against the Rouault, I was disappointed—not by their poetic qualities, Chagall's superb and deeply touching imagination, but by their flatness as paintings. It was as if the act of painting were secondary, whereas Rouault, in his struggle with the medium, created an impression of the face emerging from the art, being won in the struggle, while looking as if it had always existed.

It's a paradox of communication that there's no way in which an exhibition can avoid selling an artist's vision, or a visitor can avoid buying it—and there was much in the show that offered itself to be bought and sold, in rooms we hurried through. A major difference between good modern art and its worthless simulacrum is that in the former the struggle can be seen, while in the latter the artist has his eye on the public, and the market, from start to finish.

After this, I was drawn into the Jackson Pollocks and very impressed by them. The Picassos in this exhibition, by contrast, were mostly examples of Picasso painting Picassos—which can also happen to a great artist when, or at phases during which, he has won a struggle, and makes a style of his victory… At the end, we almost missed the rooms that gave us some of the greatest pleasure—a Rodin, its presence like a hand gripping and stilling the head spinning with impressions, reeling from distraction to distraction: *Le Bourgeois à la clé*, with the face & body of a Savonarola, or a fanatical torturer. Mondrian's *The Mill* near Van Gogh's painting of fields near Montmartre, whose windmills look like a loving reminiscence of home. Monet next to Cézanne's apples & bottles. The colours of de Kooning opened my eyes to the colours of the city as we walked back

30 March

> The art I have practiced since my childhood has taught me that man is capable of love and that love can save him. That, to me, is the true colour, the true substance of art.
> Marc Chagall (1887-1985)

1 April

Damp grey morning, trees winter-bare, water in furrows and on grass. Ghostly anonymous headlights approaching and withdrawing across fields as the road neared or drew away from the railway line. Change of trains at Utrecht. Crossing on the *Prinses Beatrix*, blowy on deck, with a bit of a swell. Whitecaps on an ebony and silver sea. A double rainbow, inner bow very bright, moved with us across Essex. Then the moon, between half and three quarters full, travelling fast in blue sky behind and in and out of flaking cloud.

2 April

Winchester. Yellow forsythia in the Arthurs' garden, next door to my former home in Monks Road; daisies, daffodils, celandines by the chalk stream and in Holy Trinity churchyard, where elder is in leaf. A brimstone in The Close; soft air. Had lunch with Emily at The Riverside after walking by the Weirs. Evening: with Joe to see Emily tap-dancing in a show at the John Stripe theatre.

3/4 April

Hazy sun on St Catherine's Hill and the downs, shining on the Itchen and on railway lines. Dave was at Hayford. It was very good to see my brother, and in the afternoon I drove him down to Hurst shingle-spit and we walked to Milford and back and had a good talk. This morning I got up early to see him off: big old overcoat over torn oilskins, on a small moped for a 4 or 5 hour journey. After he'd gone Dad flew into a rage that seemed really insane, as I remember him doing in similar circumstances more than 30 years ago, except that this time it was directed only at Mother. I took her out in the morning and again in the afternoon, and she talked as she isn't able to with anyone else. Later in the morning he calmed himself somewhat in talking with me.

A horrible day—except that when it began I felt like running away, but didn't, and stayed to be of use. I came to England realizing that I've begun to be selfish with M, living in my work and through her instead of making contacts and really sharing her life. This morning, seeing Dad in such a state, which was all the worse to me after the affection that Dave's good nature released, and the sheer relief of being with him, and feeling Mother's predicament—I can't say how I felt. Except that this is the mess of close family relationships, this is the other side of "love". And I was afraid.

How can a father be so hostile towards his son? Jealousy? Frustration of age and failing sight? Yet, for a moment, I was in my mind a boy again, hanging on to him as he tried to go for Dave in an uncontrolled rage, trying to comfort Mother. As Dad talked to me he became very sorry for himself, and cried. There was no reason in what he said against other people, but as he talked I began to be aware of other reasons, and finally he said, with the candour and realism that are such rare qualities when applied to the self, that his creative life came to an end when he was about 75. I saw an astonishing duality: the deep understanding, wisdom even, the generosity, and the blind unreasoning rage, the peevish nerve-sick egocentricity.

It's in recent years that people have begun to break out of the images I've imposed on them, and the reality is frightening, yet brings too a possibility of understanding that was never there before, and with it a disturbing but fresh and renewing air.

Good Friday

> And he cometh unto the disciples, and findeth them asleep, and saith unto Peter, What, could ye not watch with me one hour?

A walk in the morning on the edge of Beaulieu Heath. Distant whine of a model airplane—a black dot climbing and diving—over the abandoned wartime airfield. Beyond, like darker mist in grey sky, Island hills. Hawk Hill: pines, open spaces under oaks, a clear gravel stream, or "gutter", chaffinches active at the edge of woods and the machine-gun "hammering" of a woodpecker. Back on open heath, I heard a curlew, and a biplane drawing an advertisement behind it circled Forest and coast.

When Dad was travelling for John Peed's seed firm in Dorset in the late 20s and early 30s, one day he met the head gardener of the Digby family at Minterne, and the man told him about his wife's suicide on Christmas Day. She had three children and was expecting another. After getting everything ready for the family, she walked out in the snow. They were able to follow her footsteps to the edge of the lake on the estate at Cerne Abbas. Dad remembers that the man blamed the Cerne Giant—"that thing"—for affecting her mind.

§

> "I say what I can say
> with only the feeble song
> of man
> in response to nature."
>   Olivier Messiaen

Messiaen says, "birds are true musicians. In the beginning they listened, and heard the sound of raindrops and the noise of the wind, and that is how they learnt to sing." In *his* beginning he had an extraordinarily close relationship with his mother, who was a poet and had premonitions of the music he would one day write. No fear or suspicion of nature for him, but everywhere reflections of the divine energy. A man centred in nature and the invisible. "Christ was radiant at the moment of Transfiguration. Christ was radiant at the moment of Resurrection. And we too shall be radiant when we rise again."

6 April

Afternoon: a walk in the Forest with Jim & Nicky & her daughter Carmen, & a neighbour's son, a small fearless boy who swarmed up trees, and a dog that climbed with him when it could. On the abandoned railway track at Longslade Bottom, across the bog and into trees at Hinchelslea. A small pool in a hollow among trees, probably once a marl pit: black water mirroring sky, reflections of Scots pines like black clouds. There was a fresh breeze and sun in a wide blue sky, with cloud from the west and a scent of the sea on the open plain, and smells of leafmould & mosses under trees. Birds are singing louder every day now and crumbling soil is alive with movement.

    Sun sharp on holly leaves, shining silver. Older holly trees are sometimes completely hollow, like a tree in cross section or a reed that a boy has cut with a penknife and scraped out all the pith. Some older oaks are amazing: hugely vigorous, with giant tortuously twisted trunk & limbs, dead branches among living wood, and gnarled dinosaur scales of bark. They suggest at once great strength and endurance and a great capacity to bear pain and go on living while partly dying or dead. Ferns grow in their crooks and every time we pull off a piece of loose bark we disturb countless lives.

Easter Day

At Taddiford Gap, where all but two of the wartime "dragon's teeth" have been bulldozed over and the concrete base of a gun emplacement, with circular marks, remains. On the slippery cliff path to Becton Bunny. There, on the beach, Jim scattered the beads of an African necklace which he'd used as a rosary, over the place where he and Linda had buried their "marriage-stone". Or as near as he could discover—the cliffs in this area are continually falling and changing the beach's geography. Even as we stood there, sand was crumbling and running down, and we had walked as far as possible from the cliff edge which in places was supported on nothing and all along showed fresh falls. This is a remarkable area, with strange shapes and vivid colours—red ochre and bright rust-orange gravel at the top, yellow and white sand and sand the colour of verdigris, and slippery or hard blue lias, which is in fact dark blue or even grey-black. The cliff edge is jagged, like pieces of a large, ill-fitting jigsaw, and looks from below oddly like a pagoda.

From Becton we walked to Barton along the narrow strip of shingle where the high tide sent tongues of water almost to the foot of the cliffs. A big sky full of sheets of rain cloud sweeping across and broken cloud where the sun came and went filled the space between the Island and the Dorset coast, but the rain held off as we came back over the golf course with the wind in our faces. Fallen cliffs, breakwaters—rows of stout posts standing out above the sea—gravel and gorse on the very edge of the cliffs: these are things that move me strongly and, in part, obscurely. They belong to love and friendship. Being with Janet at Hordle all those years ago gave me the beginnings of a poetry that was really mine. Less personally, breakwaters stir deep primitive feelings. The posts are vaguely human in shape and they stand for a massive effort that is only temporarily effective and has to be renewed over and over again; they become part of the elements, and at the same time are completely nonhuman, insensate, and like a strange thing *emerging* from the sea. They belong and do not belong, they become part of the sea against which they are a defence, the waters they are meant to break. A sleeping painter and a sleeping sculptor come awake in my senses here. When I came back the smell of the sea was on my hands.

10/11 April
In London. First to a pleasant leafy avenue in Golders Green, where I visited John Levy and discussed my coming visit to Gezer. Then to Millbank and the Tate, where I met Pat Adams, the education officer, and had a long talk about poetry and painting in connection with a competition and anthology which the Tate is preparing. Afterwards I had time to see only a few things, beginning with a long look at Munch's *Sick Child*. A Spencer Resurrection—the dead emerging from lifted grave mounds like tortoise shells, or looking out from tombs like boats, with dazed or wondering expressions on their faces, like voyagers gazing at the marvels of a new world. Perhaps because of its subject, there is also something of the Victorian funerary imagination about the scene: morbid, statuesque, literal, without light or vital rhythm. Rothko's room of maroon and black canvases, with the stillness and muted coloured light of a chapel. I would have liked to stay there for a long time but it was late afternoon and the gallery was about to close. I met Lee and we looked at Picasso's *Weeping Woman*.

From the Tate we went first by the river for a drink in a pub at Cheyne Walk, near Carlyle Mansions. Coming out, we saw Concorde beginning to climb over the city, sun shining on fancy struts and icing sugar paintwork of the Albert Bridge, and drove through Chelsea to his mother's house in Fulham. After a meal with her, an evening of good talk and drinking in a pub crowded with young people near Parson's Green.

Next morning, in rain, Lee took me to see his first major one-man show at Blond Fine Art in Princes Street. Here, looking at the few large carvings, the smaller carvings and reliefs and paintings, I remembered words from the Apocrypha which he'd quoted to me in a recent letter (and which in some form was an impulse in 'Master of the Leaping Figures'): "To the universe belongs the dancer". Now there was time for me to look again and again at each work, to feel the presence of each, and to take in the presence of the "world" which all together made. He has done great work and has the capacity to become a major British sculptor.

In the large carvings, in much of the work, tensions: power/vulnerability, shelter/exposure, terror/ecstasy. In several the raised arm becomes the dark threatening cloud, expressing his constant awareness of holocaust, "the last blast of light". Yet his power comes in part from his combination of this awareness with dynamic natural rhythms, the "earth dance", or from tension between these primal emotions. Several reliefs (*Secret*, *Sky and Earth*, *Three blues*) suggested to me Stations of the Cross. I don't think this was intended, and wondered whether this and other suggestions and echoes were merely my irrelevant importations.

No: because art of this order has correspondences with all forms of life and extends the tradition of art which has such correspondences. *The Bow Flown Away with the Arrow*, a relief whose original impulse was our experience of the swifts on the bridge at Ovington, as it was of my poem too. He expresses the space between human being and bird, the impossibility of the two being joined, and sadness at this.

The exhibition is in its last week and so far nothing has been sold except a painting which his father-in-law has bought. Lee is worried about money, I think; he didn't dwell on it, but it's clearly a pressing practical issue for him, and a threat to his ability to go on working and living as he does. We were in the gallery a long time, during which one man came in who was evidently there mainly for the children's book illustrations hung on the wall in one room, and two women asking for directions to the shop selling school uniforms that used to be where the gallery now is. Finally, a man came in and arranged to display one of the large sculptures in his garden and two of the smaller carvings in his house at St John's Wood, for a kind of private exhibition. This may lead to a sale, and was, from that point of view, the only hopeful sign during the whole exhibition so far, though it has had several good notices and reviews.

12 April
Walked with Kim Taplin from Brockenhurst station to Boldre and back. Primrose in the shelter of a slanting tombstone in Brockenhurst churchyard. Through oakwoods to Royden, river high and brown after recent rain. Boldre church was open and we went in, admiring the simple and dignified language of Gilpin's memorial tablet and looking at the great bible and the *Hood* memorials. Outside, a wire shaking on the flagpole on the tower made a sound of a sailing ship at sea.

Lunch at the Fleur de lys, then to the Shallows where half a dozen youths were fishing from the bridge. Back to Boldre bridge, across the river and uphill to Sandy

Down. Heath stretching from Setley towards Sway Tower—Latchmoor, place of corpses—is still brown with winter. All the time we talked and talked. Kim remarked how lucky I am to have been brought up here—memory on memory rises on this ground—and said the same of my parents and my relationship with them, after we'd had tea at Hayford and they were, as always, kind and welcoming. She is right on both counts: I've known it since I could first think about such things, but have occasionally forgotten, or obscured the latter by overreacting to a bad day. Seeing though her eyes, I knew and felt the truth.

But no one is made for constant happiness—at night, the tooth which had troubled me when I walked with Robert Wells in the Forest, and had then got better until it began to ache slightly when I was in London, now became very painful and I lay for a long time miserably awake.

13/14 April
To Mappowder to see Gerard Casey & Lucy, the youngest Powys. Already there's more green beside the roads. Now the first wave is gathering.

A violent hail shower lashed the Forest heaths, and in Dorset too the wind was blowing strongly. It was like autumn outside as I sat with Gerard in his front room, hearing wind blasting the windows, and it was even wilder in the night. In the morning, as we sat at breakfast, broken light was blown though branches of apple trees outside the window and wind whistled and shook the house.

Gerard's eyesight is bad: he can read for only about 20 minutes at a time, perhaps four times in a day. But he is more at ease than when I last saw him. He says that after 5 years he has now begun to accept Mary's death. He rested on the couch as usual while we talked, a powerful man in worn clothes, wearing two warm shabby pullovers—it was quite cold in the house, which in its comforts is like a village interior of thirty or forty years ago, and reflects austere living. He has always treated me like an equal, but on this occasion the give and take was even easier than usual, and there was no sign of his tendency to sermonise.

Lucy greeted me warmly. She is 94 now, is completely dependent physically, and soon tires. "I'm afraid it can't be hurried," she said gently to Gerard recently. He is very close to her. When he first met her, not long after her husband's death, she looked ravaged, like her sister Katie Powys. Now she is serene and becomes more serene with every year. She is attentive and kind, but there's steel in her, he says. As I was leaving, she took my hand again and asked me "to keep an eye on Gerard later".

We talked about Van Gogh. I told him my idea about Van Gogh being consumed by what he saw, and he said that Mary with her intensity could not have gone on living longer. In the morning he told me that when she died he turned not to the Bible but to the Greek Anthology (the 2nd volume of the Loeb classics which John Cowper Powys had given to Mary) and singled out three sentences: "I remembered how often we had walked down the sun." "He (or she) has gone into the divine sea."

"Beyond death I see the light of Olympus." We talked about nature, and paganism, and Llewelyn Powys, for whom he has no intellectual respect. He has no time for neo-paganism; "we can't go back". I brought up Charles Lock's words, which have impressed me, about Christianity's necessary apology to paganism, and Gerard remarked that the early Church was reacting against the gross sensuality of the Roman world, and we worship a nature we have spiritualised, which has a terrible side that we rarely see now. He has an acute sense of the pathos of existence, but believes that something beyond redeems it. Greek philosophy could not answer the questions Greek tragedy raised; only the New Testament could. He is less interested in Powys writings now; all three brothers seem to him eccentric, and he is increasingly only interested in the concentric, in what human beings have in common. He recalled Katie taking him to see old farmer Cobb of East Chaldon, who was also a Methodist lay preacher and knew Theodore, Llewelyn and John Cowper well and the old man saying: "They call themselves pagan, but I think they're three fine Christian gentlemen'".

In the evening I shared in the ritual when Gerard played Lucy a record before she went to sleep. On this occasion, Mozart, but my toothache had come on again acutely and I was almost unable to bear the pain. It kept me awake at night too, but at last I slept, and today it has been much better.

Saturday morning. Back to Winchester to pick up Emily and bring her with me to Hayford. I went through Shaftesbury and Salisbury. There are moments when I see things, as I did some trees & a church tower at Shaftesbury, as if within an older rhythm or way of life, as a person approaching on foot, belonging to the local world before any of our modern forms of transport was invented. Imagination, I suppose, yet the look of things speaks of another time.

15 April
In the lychgate of a church on or near the Halifax estate near Doncaster there was a skull in a glass case with the words "Me now, Thee tomorrow" written on it. Once, when Dad was passing through the gate with another young man, his companion took out a revolver—his father's, from the war—and shot the skull to pieces, and then fired at crows over the church.

16 April
In a cabin on the *St Nicholas*. Earlier: standing room in the guard's van to Waterloo, with others standing or sitting on the floor or on their cases, reading or writing or talking in small groups. How men together will often bring out the worst in each other, sneering, boasting, talking dirt, small minded & animal under their city suits, and apparently very pleased with themselves—but it is all apparent, what they really are remains hidden. I notice too how the "punters" with well-bred voices take every opportunity to talk down to working men when there's a malfunction in the system that carries their daily existence—say, a train being 15 minutes late—and how the same people talk scornfully of the unemployed. I've always

resisted believing in types, but a very short time in commuter England proves me over-delicate in this. This is a country where to think and to be thoughtful of others are increasingly rare.

The countryside is much greener than when we came, horse-chestnut trees, elders, brambles, hawthorn, all in leaf, and white anemones—windflowers—in woodland beside the track. A lovely spring day: blue sky & light cloud, warm, hazy sunshine, a sea breeze out at sea and countless eyes of light winking on the water. "A nice tone to leave England on."

Evening. At the Hoek, smell of the salt, sun-warmed sea. After the industrial waterfront, the same green in hawthorn hedges, but also, flatness and architecture apart, the difference from England. Canals, shadowy bridges, naked round walls of a sailless, converted windmill… but more than a physical difference: a language, a history, a culture, a people. And we are on the Nord-West Express, destinations Copenhagen and Warsaw. This is Holland, and it is also continental Europe: new distances in time & space, once the North Sea is crossed, and new crosscurrents, with England on the other side.

20 April
The unfolding horse-chestnut leaves are like wings of fledgling birds, with the same helpless look. In the barber's: an old woman next to me, having her hair rolled up in curlers, had the face of a Frans Hals portrait: white, with a large nose in a cluster of wrinkles & lines of good humour. Yet if we see reflections of the great realists' art in faces around us, that's because they first taught themselves to see and to reproduce the life around them.

Finished my essay on Roland Mathias today; in part, reparation for my early, inadequate piece. Long delayed, but worth the effort.

21 April
Evening. White sun in a cloudless sky, slanting on low lands. To Delfzijl with M. Blue-grey sand & shallow blue-grey sea, roughened by a stiff fresh breeze. Thumbprint wave marks on sand. Light of Emden, in Germany, across the water, and farther out, north and west, lights of the island of Borkum just visible on the horizon. Sunset purple as blackberry juice, then flaring to crimson. We had a meal at the Eems Hotel looking down on shore and water. I had sole with mussels in a sauce that was far too rich for me, and spent much of the night awake feeling sick.

23 April
Gezer, Israel
It is early evening, but quickly getting dark. Outside, a new moon and the smell of earth, voices of children playing. I am in my room at Kibbutz Gezer, a small room with two single beds, a wardrobe & a table made of a concrete paving slab resting on two breeze blocks, on which my Brazilian roommate, Edmondo, has stood his rucksack, and a carpetless, tiled floor. I'm drinking vodka from the top of a plastic

soap dish, furtively, because I don't know whether alcohol is frowned on here, but in any case it's the only thing resembling a cup I have.

First impressions: informal, young, apparently haphazard but probably pretty well organized, not a place for formal introductions. Lots of young bearded Americans; men, women, and children rather like 70s "drop-outs" to look at. But there's ceremony here. Tonight a flame was burning outside the dining room and a man & woman were singing and playing the flute…

As I wrote that, a siren went off loudly—but no one seems to be alarmed. Tomorrow is the commemoration of all who have died in the wars since 1948.

This morning Margo, a big girl who speaks English with an American accent, picked me up at Ben Gurion airport. I was surprised when she told me she is Dutch, from Arnhem. She brought me in a taxi to the kibbutz. I had got up at 5. Dawn in Groningen: familiar streets & signposts on a blue background: Winsum, Bedum, Hoogezand; the attractive blue & yellow trains at the station. Across Holland: a rowing boat drawn up on a canal bank, stern in the water; a barge waiting against a bank, seen across a field. Poplars. Willows. Thought on an early morning train: much of our life is sleep.

At the airport: police and armed security guards. All passengers for the El Al plane were searched and the men frisked. I talked in the departure lounge to a young Dutchman who was going bird watching at Eilat, apparently a marvellous place for migrants. In the plane I had a window seat close to the wing. Cloud: a smooth snowfield, a snowfield with blue clefts, little tufts or parachutes of cloud, but cloud below us all the way, land—snow-topped Alps, a serpentine road—and sea visible only occasionally.

Now, in this room, it is dead silent. But standing in the doorway I can hear night noises—insects, a cat crossing the grass, someone walking on a path, distant voices. The stars are bright in the sky and I can smell a eucalyptus tree and earth. It's hard for me to realize where I am. Four and a half hours in the air to travel a distance which could take pilgrims in the Middle Ages up to six months.

24 April

Memorial Day. I have come from early spring to midsummer: poppies, thistles, mallow, convolvulus, many red, orange and purple flowers and flowering shrubs whose names I don't know, and many beautiful birds which are strange to me. In the morning I collected my working clothes and then went for a walk by myself round part of the kibbutz, getting a view of surrounding hills, including Tel Gezer, the biblical site rising close to the kibbutz. One large field has a crop of young sunflowers, which they grow commercially.

At dinner Jan, a young Norwegian who was brought up in England, remarked that he didn't like sitting under the pictures of military scenes decorating bunting hanging from the ceiling. The man sitting next to him said that if it wasn't for them—meaning the military victories—we wouldn't be here.

Meal outdoors in the evening, in the cool of a hot day but with a pleasant breeze. Then folk dancing, which the women in particular threw themselves into with joy and great vigour, and the little children danced with them, or in circles by themselves. I have talked with a few people today and two or three have gone out of their way to greet me, but at present I feel at the edge of things—inevitably: people here are very distinctive in their belonging, and I always begin shyly anyway. But it has been a beginning, and I feel that I shall enjoy my stay here. The siren sounded again this evening: it commemorates the dead in war, and when it sounds everyone stops what he or she is doing and stands in silence for a minute or two.

25 April
Independence Day. Jan tells me that when Rabbi Meir Kahane, a right-wing extremist, came to speak at Ramla, a group of 20 to 30 people from the kibbutz attended the meeting and disrupted it. Afterwards a group of Arab women got in touch with them, and now periodically visit the kibbutz, so that contact continues.

Afternoon. Walked by myself to Tel Gezer, once an important fortress town close to a major crossroads: between Egypt and Syria on the coastal plain, and between Jaffa and Jerusalem and Amman. In the fields, brown, cracked soil, like old varnished canvas or parchment, with whitish streaks between rows of sunflowers where water has recently run. I climbed to some pine trees growing on the hillside, large slabs of limestone lying under them. Then, under a cloudy sky, in a strong cool breeze, I came upon bigger blocks of limestone heaped up formidably in long wild oats and wild barley and flowers. The path became dry, white, pitted with holes surrounded by a little fresh soil, where red ants swarmed in and out; in one place a beautiful piece of white mosaic sprinkled with dust. Water pipes alongside the path. Next, vines growing on upper slopes below the summit. Cactuses overlooked the sweep of an enclosed valley which was blue from flowers among grass, and alongside it another vineyard, which does not belong to the kibbutz, where I glimpsed Arab workers in long white headdresses tending the plants.

Tel Gezer: a place of ancient and modern fortifications. Concrete floors partly hidden in grass, a tangle of rusted barbed wire, a lead cartridge case among stones. A honeycomb of ancient stone & mud walls dug into the hill, or rising in ruins—walls made of great blocks of dressed stone, perhaps belonging to Solomon's time; also a line of standing stones. There were caves in the limestone too, some of which had been recently fortified. Corn marigolds everywhere, a stony dusty white soil at their roots and under grass. A pair of beautiful large birds with bright greeny blue wings flew from a mud wall that was like the face of a quarry. Then a hawk flew up out of a deep cleft in the ground, from out of sight, as I stood at the edge peering down, and shortly afterwards another hawk followed, each bird flying towards me but sheering off, and circling for as long as I stayed near.

From the summit I looked over at hills of Judea, and down on the Valley of Aijalon, of which it's said that whoever captures it will take Jerusalem. Descending, butterflies fluttered round me, a warm, slightly sweet smell rose from vegetation, and I could hear birds singing, crickets, and, very faint, Israeli popular music from a transistor radio far below. A hawk, wind-ruffled, hung over the Tel, hung, then lowered itself slowly to the height of grass tops, dropped, climbed again—preying as, no doubt, hawks have preyed here from long before the Assyrians, or before Solomon, or the row of standing stones.

> And this is the reason of the levy which King Solomon raised; for to build the house of the Lord, and his own house, and Millo, and the wall of Jerusalem, and Hazor, and Megiddo, and Gezer.
> For Pharaoh king of Egypt had gone up, and taken Gezer, and burnt it with fire, and slain the Canaanites that dwelt in the city, and given it for a present unto his daughter, Solomon's wife.
> And Solomon built Gezer...
> *1 Kings 9, 15-17*

26 April
Up at 6 to work. *Noi*: landscaping. I worked with Ricardo, a young Brazilian who is studying agronomy and has spent the last year or so seeing the world. We loosened the roots of a tree and removed some young palm trees that were growing too close together. And most of the time we talked: England, Israel, Brazil, unemployment, the destruction of the natural world, the possibility of nuclear war. He's perhaps half my age, and he's more pessimistic. He believes mankind always learns too late; which is hard to disagree with. Later, under the direction of Nancy, an American girl, we cleared branches from trees round the new swimming pool, which several people were enjoying themselves cleaning and generally preparing for use. Towards noon, I began to feel tired; mercifully a cool breeze sprang up then. Half an hour for lunch, after which I helped Shula gather some children's beds and chairs and other odds and ends into her store, bumping along on the trailer as she drove the tractor from place to place on the kibbutz. Finished work at 2.30.

27 April
Shaul is a New Zealander, perhaps about my age—difficult to tell—lean, athletic body, lean face, black beard, full lips, loud laugh like my brother David's, when he opens his mouth wide and shows his teeth. My first view, or, rather, hearing of him, occurred in the recreation room, each of us on opposite sides of a magazine rack, partly hidden from each other, when he was reading a newspaper, exclaiming to himself and from time to time letting out a roar of laughter. I thought to avoid him then, but we met this evening—he has the neighbouring apartment—and talked for a long time. He's very intelligent, ironical, often abrasive in manner, and I think something of an outsider here, but with a good deal of sensitive awareness of the other, I would say, a delicacy and tact with regard to things that really matter, and perhaps a tendency to play a somewhat brash, yet solitary part, without illusions. Self-contained, but also lonely, perhaps; as so many human beings are.

For even in a community like this, or perhaps especially in such communities, people have images which partly reveal but also partly hide their real personalities.

Shaul began defensively in describing himself as a New Zealander, and at the same time a little aggressively, anticipating a stereotyped English response, and, not getting it, quickly adapted himself to my level of thinking and response, but without denying his independence. He has very strong opinions of other people, likes & dislikes. Last night he said that one history has burnt out another in this country, and claims that the past is therefore destroyed here, or too fragmentary to be interesting; whereas the stratification, or jumble or chaos, or whatever it is, is one of the things that I find most interesting.

But a mere academic interest would be burned up here by the first molten drop of reality.

I slept badly again last night, and lying half awake between shallow dreams had disturbing thoughts of the first kibbutz—this is the third—here. It was overrun by Jordanians in 1948 and its members killed—I shall go to look for their graves this morning. They were, I think, eastern European Jews, and in my half sleep they became identified with survivors of the Holocaust, which some of them may well have been, and the idea of them fighting and dying here, where all is now apparently so safe and domestic—fighting to the death with the determination that perhaps only those who have once been dispossessed, who have had nothing, can know—became a little confused with Pharaoh burning Gezer and slaying the Canaanites.

In 1948 there was a border settlement; the Tel was, I believe, actually on the border. Immediately after the declaration of Independence the Jordanians attacked. Now, there's an armed guard who keeps watch at night—for thieves attracted by the unfenced kibbutz and the supplies that are fairly easy to get at. But of course, in this country no settlement can be taken for granted. The domesticity a little oppresses me here—couples, families, small children everywhere, the possessive care of the couples, but extended to a general intimate care of all the children. I sometimes feel there's something a bit cloying about this. Perhaps mine is the male's jealous reaction to the female's preoccupation with something other than him!—a setting aside of his *seriousness* as not worth regarding in comparison with the child's importance. D. H. Lawrence had this essentially childish masculinity to a high degree. But if I have it too, I'm more than reconciled to the maternalism (of father & mother alike, but almost as strong in the modern, liberated Jewish mother as it is traditionally in *their* mothers & grandmothers) by realising the history and the continuing, constant threat affecting their hope for their children, and specifically for the children of this land. This love has an edge of fierce protectiveness, which is both awe-inspiring and poignant. The more so when present in people who are not fanatics, but liberals, concerned with the rights of those who would destroy them.

A lazy Sabbath. Walking about in hot sun, reading, writing. Read my poems to a small group in the synagogue in the evening, and afterwards had a beer with Shaul.

28 April
Working in the dining hall. Just off the first shift: dish washing from 6.15—11. No time to stop to make notes, even if I'd wanted to.

Washed up and cleaned in the kindergarten after lunch. Then read, slept, read.

29 April
Early morning, rising sun a white globe over rocky hills, then a fiery halo as it rises higher and the eye can still bear to look.

Worked from 6 driving a tractor for Mark, the pest control specialist, while he sprayed a mosquito breeding area near the cesspool and then weeds round the cowsheds, using paraquat (extensively used in Vietnam). A hot, still day with an oppressive grey dusty atmosphere. Rested for an hour in the morning and was flat out for a couple of hours after cleaning up in the kindergarten after lunch.

Now (Tuesday morning), it's a week since I arrived here; the feeling that I don't fit in comes and goes, depending on human contact or its prolonged absence, among people who seem to know each other well and are generally much more extrovert. It feels as though I've been here longer than I have, yet still don't really know where I am. Coming here straight from the airport, talking all the way, remaining in the kibbutz and working here since, I've little sense of the country, apart from what the walk to the Tel revealed, but at the same time, through talking to people and through reading, Europe has become for me a much smaller, less politically significant part of the world, and from this distance and in this new perspective Mrs Thatcher & her government—representatives of England to the world—look even more unpleasantly absurd than they do in England.

30 April
Another hot day under a cement-grey sky. Working in the chicken house with Danny, who comes from New Jersey. I thought his face was familiar. Then it came to me: Elijah, in the great initial by the Master of the Leaping Figures in The Winchester Bible! The same build, the same features, the same curly black hair & black beard; only wanting in fierceness—hooked finger, lean body electric with spiritual power, blackness of hair crackling with life. Yet the similarities were remarkable. Nine hundred years ago, in Winchester, or in his travels in Europe, the artist probably saw a man, a Jew, who might have been the twin of the man I worked with today.

May Day
The Khamsin (desert wind) lifted during the night and today was cool. A holiday in honour of Labour Day, but first a little communal weeding in the morning. After lunch I went with Peter to look at his sculptures—figures cut out of sheet metal—and spent much of the day with him. An American, probably in his early forties, Peter is very critical of the kibbutz and especially of his fellow Americans. According to him, they're mostly interested only in baseball and leading regular

lives, and pay lip service to the principles of the kibbutz movement. He says there's considerable tension between them and the Brazilians. He himself is ambivalent towards both the kibbutz and Israel, *and* America, seeing advantages and disadvantages in them, but finding more meaning here. He claims to be clear about his ambivalence.

In the afternoon he took me on my first outing—through Ramla to kibbutz Netzer Sereni, where his girlfriend's parents live. This is a much larger kibbutz than Gezer, though Peter tells me that it too has big economic & social problems, the latter mainly between the generation of founders, who are loath to relinquish control, and the younger generation. A group from Buchenwald was among the original members of the kibbutz and a number of them are still here. He pointed out two of them to me and we looked at a sculpture commemorating victims of the Holocaust. Thinking of these people living their lives there, several of them daily re-enacting rituals belonging to their camp experience, I felt an unutterable misery—there's no word for it—mixed with the earth and air in that place.

The kibbutz itself is attractive, and interesting, with the pleasant, colonial architecture of a former German Templer settlement occupying part of the site, and orange-red soil bearing many trees—carob, fig, eucalyptus, oranges, mangos, avocados, loquat. As we walked round, the moon's frail skull gradually brightened in blue sky between large islands of cloud. To add to the atmosphere of romantic decay a pair of green parrots flew in and out of tall trees in the old garden which the Templers had once laid down.

Hardly anything or anyone escaped Peter's criticism. His father was a professor of educational psychology, and his lack of respect for all systems and theories seems to derive from his father's worship of academic authority, even though last year's truth is this year's discredited idea. Peter's questioning makes life uncomfortable, and is, I feel, motivated by concern for the truth—or conviction that the truth is unknowable, and refusal to accept pretenders to the truth. Intellectual life in Israel has a similar acutely critical and self-critical spirit; at least, thought on the left has, as I find in the writings of Amos Oz. There's probably more agonized talk here than anywhere else in the world. Perhaps this has something to do with the fact that in Israel, since very early times, silence—the silence of the absolute—has been felt and tested more intensely than anywhere else.

2 May

Early start in the Dining Hall. Work over by 2. A lovely day, warm with a fresh breeze. Swallows high up in blue sky, small as bees. In the evening, walked in view of Tel Gezer—like Hambledon, it draws me; though unwritten, Hambledon too no doubt had an equally dramatic history—at least, to those who experienced it. Past graves of defenders of the kibbutz: a small walled garden, one wall composed of their stones inscribed in Hebrew, side by side, a line of cypresses rising above. Moon indistinct, a partly blown dandelion clock, and an airliner turning over rocky hills, which reminded me of the mountains of North Wales seen from Mynydd Bach in a certain light. And perhaps because I was tired, and lonely too,

I felt heartsick for Brynbeidog seven or eight years ago, when the children were little, and when my life was much more real than it seemed at this moment. Came back to the apartment and had a long talk with Eddie, mainly about Brazil, before going over to supper. As always, friendly human contact pulls me out of myself as nothing else can.

3 May
This morning in the Dining Hall I made pancakes, and enjoyed doing it well, making them quickly & efficiently, not keeping people waiting, and was delighted by compliments. As, in a way, I enjoy cleaning too: having a job and doing it systematically. Table by table: first take off everything that's on it, then brush the surface, then wash it down, and afterwards dry it, next the chairs... Methodical, repetitive, a simple art; and a necessary job, *my* job. Good to finish again in the early afternoon. Read, sleep, read, shower.

Robert Alter says of Charles Reznikoff that his "sense of exclusion from the continuity of Jewish history" wasn't absolute, since "if you can talk about being in exile with such feeling, that may mean that at least some small part of you belongs, after all, to a realm of rootedness against which the condition of exile is defined". Yes: but tell that to the Jews in Babylon. Also, it fails to take account of the feeling of being at home in Brooklyn that many of Reznikoff's poems give. Unless we are to understand that the exile is the person most at home in the city streets; which may have been true of Reznikoff in New York.

4 May
Ofra, Peter's girlfriend, lent me 'Gezer Diary' from the archives, typescript accounts by participants and eyewitnesses of events leading up to the battle for Gezer on 10 June 1948, the battle itself and the aftermath for survivors in captivity. One witness records the blowing up of houses & wells and killing of Arabs in neighbouring villages, which were subsequently abandoned, as acts of reprisal for the killing of a member of the kibbutz and for harassment.

Late afternoon/early evening. A walk with Shaul to the Tel. Another lovely day, the light much clearer than when I was there before. As we climbed, Ramla, its ugly tower blocks transformed by distance, came into view on the coastal plain, and beyond, mistily, the buildings of Tel Aviv and a long shining blade, the Mediterranean.

Shaul pointed out a rusted tank track near the prickly pear cactus, and nearby we saw several hummingbird hawk moths sipping at flowers. He pointed out the monastery of Latrun in the Aijalon valley, (the name, from the original Crusader foundation, which is a ruin nearby, came from *Domus Bene Latronus*, the House of the Good Thief). On a hill far on the other side of Latrun he showed me what he believes is an outer suburb of Jerusalem. Before reaching the summit we had passed the site of an Arab village abandoned in 1948, with little but a heap of potsherds to show where it had been.

From the top of the Tel we saw five storks standing on the ridge not far from us—at first glance they looked to me like heads of fawns emerging from the grass—and though they flew off at our approach, at first laboriously, slowly flapping their great black and brown wings, we saw them again—but now there were six—on the other side of the hill as we returned along the path. Shaul told me that they migrate from East Africa, along the Syrian-African rift (on which Jerusalem stands), to the area of the Elbe. As we descended the sun went down red-gold over the Mediterranean and at the top of the hill, turning, we saw the yellow full moon rising over the Judean Hills, in the direction of Jerusalem. Earlier, he had quoted Joshua: "Sun, stand thou still upon Gibeon; and thou, Moon, in the valley of Ajalon".

Now, at 10.30, there's a total eclipse of the moon, part of which is still dimly visible, like a bloodspot under skin.

5 May
A day's journey in the truck with Richard, who comes from California. Set out on the sandy coastal plain, with orange groves beside the road, and a lot of traffic. Here, and on all the busy roads, there were many soldiers, men & women, hitching lifts. Netanya: yachts on the sea; a lorry in front of us almost bursting with grapefruit. Caesarea: an electricity generating station near the town, pylons & cables across a wilderness of dunes, fish ponds, and the ruin of a Roman aqueduct. Mount Carmel (the vineyards of God), where Elijah hid in a cave from Ahab. We crossed the mountain, which is well wooded with cypresses & pines, every tree having been planted by hand on bare rock. A new Arab village on the mountainside prompted Richard to talk about improvements in standard of living, education, medical care, and so on, which many Arabs living in the State of Israel enjoy. He acknowledged exceptions and problems, but was attempting to balance the account biased in the other direction, which he claims liberal Jerusalem newspapers give.

On the other side of Carmel we drove down the Jezreel valley, a broad, fertile valley, with fruit trees and fields planted with cotton and wheat, and made our first business stop at a kibbutz. Now, lower Galilee was in front of us. Our next stop was at kibbutz Messilot near Bet-Shean, where we picked up 75 young olive trees from a large nursery (which also supplies, in an openly secret way, Jordan and Syria). To reach here we passed Mount Tabor—a hill shaped like a cone—on our left, tower blocks of new Nazareth appearing on the summit of a neighbouring mountain. On our right Mount Gilboa rose above twisted remnants of the old Haifa-Damascus railway line and date palms were growing round fish ponds in the valley.

From here we could see the hills of Samaria and the West bank, and the cloudy outline of Mount Gilead ahead. Afula Elite: a city of tower blocks perched on a mountainside, characteristic of the coming together in Israel of ultra modern settlement with primeval rock. Returning along the same road I noticed hay baled in the shape of wheels in fields below the mountain that hid Nazareth from us.

Lunch at an Arab café at the base of Mount Carmel. Afterwards a short drive to the industrial area near Haifa, where we called at a foundry—a yard full of bits of rusted metal and dust, where a man wearing goggles, a blue boilersuit and an Arab headdress was working with a welding torch. Ahead of us, a faint outline of the hills of Lebanon. Then through Haifa, the ancient and modern town built on the side of Mount Carmel and beside the sea, a waterfront of cranes & containers opening on blue and glittering water. Back along the coast road, passing ruins of a large castle overgrown with cacti, the sandy waste near Caesarea again, and a space round a golf course where villas of the well-to-do have been built on one side and shabby blocks of flats stand on the other. Approaching the outskirts of Tel Aviv we passed a memorial on the spot of the bus massacre, and bypassing the city, came back onto the old road to Jerusalem which passes Gezer.

I come back with my mind full of pitted, grey-white limestone mountains under the sun, mountains that are not big even compared to the Snowdon range, and seem hardly bigger than the Black Mountains, but are charged with a human history, and a more than human history, which would make one rock too much for the mind to grasp. Name after name, like a sound of approaching thunder, a threat of earthquake, and still the mountains with new cities & villages clinging to them stand in the sun. But what they are is precisely what the mind can't grasp, can't fit in an image or a name, and master. Nowhere on earth is there a poetry of place equal to this; but it is more than poetry—the condition all true poetry aspires to but can only point toward.

Another image imprinted on my mind: two young soldiers, a man and a woman, crossing a side road by the busy highway near Tel Aviv. They are walking hand in hand, and this together with the laughter in their faces, a delighted unselfconscious intimacy, surprises me as they catch my eye, which is beginning to glaze with heat off the road and the long journey.

6 May
An overcast day, cool at first. Worked with Shimshon and three other volunteers, hoeing between young olive trees, breaking stony soil and hacking at tough-rooted fennel, releasing its pungent smell, thistles & other weeds. We hoed for two hours before breakfast and continued weeding afterwards. After lunch, Diana & I worked with Shimshon planting the olives which I'd helped collect yesterday. This was hard, hot work, and we went on until it was finished, making a long, exhausting day. But satisfying too, especially when we could see the results of our work and think that the olives will probably grow there for many years to come.

Shimshon is an interesting man. His name is adopted (it is the Hebrew for Samson), and he is a black American from New York, and a Jew, and now an Israeli. He's one of the few people here to have a strong feeling for the land & the trees, and he's also knowledgeable about the politics of the Middle East and clear and articulate about his political opinions, which don't exactly fit any of the main categories—but then the complexity of the situation is bound to evoke a complex response in the sensitive and intelligent participant.

Shimshon pointed out to me where the 1948 border ran, on the far side of the field of sunflowers next to the field we were working in. He set the battle of Gezer as an episode in the larger conflict: the fight between peasants for the land, the war between rival national armies. There were three Arab villages here in 1948: Abu-Shusha, on the Tel, El Kubab & El-Biryeh. The sites of the latter two are now occupied by moshaves and Abu-Shusha has gone leaving little trace. Reading the early pages of 'Gezer Diary' again, I realize that before the battle kibbutz Gezer was an isolated Jewish settlement surrounded by Arabs, and that retaliatory action led to the abandonment of the three Arab villages, again before the battle. Briefly, all four settlements here were destroyed in June 1948, and the Arabs left their places for good.

§

> The landscape of Samaria—the stony ridges and the fertile vales, the terraces, the vineyard with its watchman's hut, the Arab stone-built villages growing on the slopes, the flocks of sheep at the foot of Mount Baal-Hatzor, the desert breath from the rift to the east of the mountain plateau—all these weave a Biblical charm draped in stillness, as though in these places everything has already been said, once and for all, and not a word can be added; one can only join the silence of these olive trees and the stones.
> ...
> And then I study the elusive cunning of the Biblical charm of this landscape: and isn't all of this charm Arab, through and through?
> Amos Oz, *In the Land of Israel*

7 May
Sorted washed clothes. A pleasant job to begin with, but after eight hours in a hot room, working repetitively and feeling the effects of yesterday, I was near to dropping.

Slept on & off for a couple of hours afterwards, then finished reading *Judaism Despite Christianity*, the correspondence between Eugen Rosenstock-Huessy and Franz Rosenzweig, in 1916, when they were both soldiers in the German army, Rosenstock at the Western Front, and Rosenzweig in Macedonia. The letters are remarkable, not least because they scarcely mention the war. It is present, nevertheless, as the disintegration of the secular world, which each man takes for granted, as he attempts, with absolute seriousness and total concentration of purpose, to define his religious belief against the other's, but on the maximum common ground possible. There's much in the correspondence that I can understand only dimly, if at all, and I was irritated as well as bewildered by the writers' frequent use of Latin & Greek and the obscurity, to me, of many of their allusions. But where I occasionally sense the desire of two very clever men to impress each other, there is, in reality, a life of the mind that speaks poignantly of their vanished world. For both were Jews, and though Rosenstock was a Christian, and his friend had to *recover* his Judaism, they belonged to a European cultural tradition which their people has assimilated and contributed to, and this was, above all, German. Indeed, Rosenzweig at one point expresses his great gratitude to German culture. The retrospection of a later reader touches the letters with the most bitter and tragic irony. But this in no way diminishes the integrity of each man's answer to his existential challenge, and the concentration of mind and spirit shows up, by contrast, all that is essentially meaningless in man's exercise of his powers of evil and destruction.

> "…as a Christian one has to learn from someone else, whoever he may be, to call God 'our Father'. To the Jew that God is our Father is the first and most self-evident fact—and what need is there for a third person between me and my Father in Heaven? This is no discovery of modern apologetics but the simplest Jewish instinct…"
> Franz Rosenzweig

> "Christianity redeems the individual from family and people through the new unity of sinners, all who are weary and heavy laden. That is Christianity, and its bond is equal need."
> Eugen Rosenstock

8 May
Worked with Mark again in the morning, spraying pesticide on pupa & eggs of flies in the compacted dung of the cowsheds, as he turned it over with a hoe. Mark, from New York, is a deliberate, steady man. He is Peter's antithesis, in his measured, rather pedantic speech, and even in the neat cut of his moustache & beard. He takes a great interest in his work and, grateful for my interest and companionship, explains in detail what we are doing, the pesticide, alternative methods, and other related matters. He has been a member of the kibbutz for 11 years, having joined just after it started.

I asked him about socialism in the kibbutz. He described the society as egalitarian: a difficult equality has been achieved between men and women, and his group, the original members, decided to maintain material parity among themselves, so that while some came from wealthy families and some did not, all were more or less equal in material terms here. Exceptions were made—for musicians with their musical instruments, for example, but not in the case of private record players. This seems to be about the situation now, too. The system is democratic: there's a committee for every function, and those who find this burdensome, but participate, nevertheless, as Mark does, prefer to get on with their own special work without interference, as much as possible.

Naturally, likes and dislikes exist here just as they do in the outside world, but the kibbutznik has to work with his fellows, irrespective of whether he likes them or not. Those who aren't suited to the life eventually leave, and Mark claims that some people stay longer than they should, and it becomes evident to others that they will leave before they realise it themselves. In his view, the main problems facing the kibbutz are that it doesn't have enough permanent members—and at present the large number of children to be looked after makes the problem more acute.

Finishing an interesting 4 hour stint with Mark, in the heat of a Khamsin, before 11, I felt glad that I'm working here, hard though it sometimes is. *Now* is the time for me to be doing this—earlier I could have done it but lacked initiative/opportunity; later I would have become too soft. Especially working on the land, I think of Dad and Grandad—again & again when treading down earth round the young trees I saw them doing the same.

Eddie says we work too hard here: on a bigger, more prosperous kibbutz there would be more time to read and think. No doubt he is right. But for me personally the demands are beneficial, though I've been either bored or close to exhaustion at times, and they aren't what I expected as a kind of "poet in residence"!

After working with Mark I went back to the clothes department and worked with several Brazilians. They are lively and noisy, a complete contrast to most of the Americans, and the time passed much more quickly today, as I gave Claudio some help with his English. It was a relief to have a good day. Two or three times in the last two days I've felt that I might not be able to go on. I was anxious and lonely at night—driven too far into myself by tiredness to be able to make contact—and I've had bad dreams almost every night so far.

Evening: Lag Ba'Omer. A bonfire, sparks flying into the dark. We stood round it eating marshmallows and drinking wine or lemonade. Later I rang M. on her birthday; she'll join me for a holiday on the 17th.

9 May
Unusual work here starting at an odd hour, in Berel's studio, helping him to print a lithograph. We started at 4 a.m. to avoid the heat, but in fact the day didn't turn out to be hot. Tedious work but providing a good chance to talk.

In the evening I held a poetry discussion at Peter's house, where we got together a roomful of people most of whom hadn't done anything like this for years, or perhaps ever before. I did a lot of the talking and, not surprisingly, discussion was halting at first, but several people joined in more & more as the evening went on, and at the end we agreed to meet again next week.

10/11 May
Another early start with Berel. Positively a mind-numbing task, and if it hadn't been for breakfast and occasional cups of black coffee I might have gone to sleep on my feet.

In the late afternoon, after a rest, I went up to Jerusalem with Shaul. Rusted wrecks from the 1948 war at the roadside; natural terraces, hard hills, a deserted Arab village clinging like a swallow's nest to cliffs outside the city.

Through the Jaffa Gate into narrow, covered streets & bazaars: to me, a strange new world of sights and smells, and a world more humanly various than any I've ever entered before. We took bed spaces in a hostel on the Via Dolorosa, on the roof, looking out on the gilded Dome of the Rock, the Mount of Olives, a dense cluster of cone-shaped, stone roofs, most with tall TV aerials, and with goats on the flat roof of a house below.

Via Dolorosa: a first impression of raindrops & dust under low stone ceilings. We walked to the Damascus Gate—bunches of bananas, like coils of yellow snakes, on steps—and into the modern city. Outside Herod's Gate a wedding party went past in a convoy of cars & taxis horns hooting and blasting. At the Western Wall at evening, hundreds of Jews praying, Jews striding together down the middle of the road, regardless of everything & everyone round them, in possession here, in their city. But I noticed that the Arabs are equally at home, but in another way, impossible to define; less conspicuously, more "naturally", merging with stone passages as Jews dressed in black, and especially Hasidic Jews with their eighteenth-century dress, show no wish to do—everything about them signals their apartness, only here it's their being apart that brushes other people into the shadows.

After dark we walked again into the modern city, to Meah Sh'earim, where the ultra-orthodox live. There were barriers across the roads (drivers have been stoned for driving through on the Sabbath) and few people outdoors, but singing & chanting burst from lighted synagogues throughout the district. I felt like a trespasser—I was also very tired—and was glad to get back to the hostel and go to bed.

Then, at about 4 in the morning, a Muezzin! The singing came from a minaret close by and answering echoes could be heard from other minarets in the city. There's nothing I've ever heard before with which I can compare this—rising and falling, hypnotic, melancholy, lyrical, beautiful: song of a world that's utterly different from all I know.

Tea in an Arab café in the morning. Then a walk to the Lion Gate (or Dung Gate), where Shaul pointed me in the direction of Gethsemane before leaving me to walk alone for a few hours while he went to visit friends. First I went to the tomb known as Absolom's, where I was alone except for an Arab boy; and while we stood there not understanding each other very well an old Arab leading a donkey laden with packets of toilet rolls came down the dusty track. Dust, grey dust, the Kidron

Valley full of graves, and dust, above us the Gate of Mercy in the great walls of the old city.

Across the road at the Basilica of the Agony of Jesus Christ I went into the church, stepping into purple darkness caused by dark stained glass windows—"an art lover's woe"/religious kitsch—and as I was about to look at a rock set in the wall a priest turned me back, as Mass was about to start.

The garden of Gethsemane was pretty with tastefully tended roses & olives, and quiet except for parties of tourists clustered round their guides and thronging the paths. Across the road, through a locked iron gate, in a garden with high walls crowned with broken glass, I saw a sign announcing the spot of the betrayal nailed to a tree.

Up the steep hill in the sun, to the Mount of Olives Hotel, and an Arab selling camel rides to tourists, outside the Chapel of the Ascension. Turning, I looked over a patch of waste ground where a carrion crow was pecking among bottles, tins & cartons, and down across the valley, over the walls of the old city, and up the valley to blocks of the new city rising on the hillside. Mount of Olives: olives and cypresses, rusted iron and rusted oil drums, carrion crows… nothing unexpected in the trade on temple and church, in the cynicism and dirt, and all the time I was thinking that this was where the eternal entered time, and seeing both the great beauty of the city and something of the depth of time, stone heaped on stone, dust on dust, composing it.

Later, waiting for Shaul at the Damascus Gate, watching the people. Arab women in beautiful coloured dresses, stepping gracefully poised with bundles on their heads through the crowd, or squatting with baskets of vegetables in the gateway; Hasidic Jews; Arabs in European clothes, some with Arab headdresses; tourists; soldiers; Arab boys on donkeys; a wild-looking American in a red shirt, holding a black case with "Elijah" written on one side, and "Try Jesus By Faith" on the other. I walked with Shaul and his friends to the Church of the Holy Sepulchre, and went in. There I stood for a while watching a Greek Orthodox service, but I'd seen too much and couldn't take in any more.

Back to Gezer, walking up from the road and breathing in the smell of earth and cornfields with relief.

12 May
5 a.m. In the truck to the local co-operative—much arguing and pushing—to fetch vegetables for the week.

7.45 a.m.—noon. Working with Shimshon, painting pipes at the irrigation plant by the road, and learning more about the history of Gezer from early times, and about politics and peoples in the Middle East. Apparently, a German was the first European to own the land at Gezer; which he bought to effect an idealistic plan of farming and settlement, sometime about the middle of the last century—and was killed by Arabs. Later, there was a (more effective) English presence here.

Prominent among settlers in 1948 were communist Jews from European resistance movements. Close to where we were working and talking, two belated storks were going over stubble, meditatively.

13 May
Gathering stones. Spreading fertiliser by hand. Weeding. The sunflowers turned to the sun look as though they are turned to each other, a silent conversation of golden faces.

14 May
Worked with Shimshon weeding rows of olives, pruning the young trees. Learnt today about the histadrut (he had been up late listening to the election results) and talked a little about England's social problems, and about trees. The second cool day in succession, overcast, with a little unseasonable light rain. A moment of conscious happiness: walking slowly with Shimshon across the kibbutz to fetch fertiliser, talking, feeling the earth underfoot, and seeing the fields running down towards the road, and the Judean Hills misty in the distance. I touch something in the communal life here that I've been looking for all my life.

Walked at dusk over the fields with Shaul, to find a tree where an eagle lives, which Shimshon had told us about. And there it was, the tree, a buckthorn standing alone at the edge of a field of maize on the northern slope of the kibbutz, with the great mound of the Tel rising into the sky above; and as we approached, what might have been a branch shaped like a large bird, moved and spread its wings and glided quite leisurely into a grove of olive trees further down the valley. The lights of Tel Aviv were sparkling below us far to the south as we walked back, and a few scattered lights like watch fires were burning in the mass of hills north and west. Again, I thought of Welsh hill country; there's the same hardness here, a hardness in the land itself which, together with the political situation, has helped to make a hard people. Integrity and determination are hard, so are obstinacy and cruelty; all are to be found here.

§

"Nothing unreal is allowed to survive."
(Virgil, in Hermann Broch's *The Death of Virgil*)

15 May
In the factory, washing out used glue containers, putting tops on plastic bottles; outside with Henning, dismantling old machinery, cutting through iron with a power-driven saw. Henning is Danish; a lean, even gaunt man, with a drooping blond moustache. He's a Christian fundamentalist, and a reader of Revelation. Once, at breakfast, he told us matter-of-factly that the world will end in a nuclear war soon. He lives near Jerusalem for this reason. His beliefs are completely out

of place on the kibbutz (he's no socialist either, and worked on May Day because he doesn't recognise it), but he fits in well. He likes to argue, but is a most good-natured and considerate person. He's one of the people that I've come to feel very much at home with, and shall miss when I leave.

Had a beer with Brian in the evening and talked with him about his poems which he'd given me to read. Brian is from Montreal; he's a close friend of Peter, but although he shares much of his friend's criticism of Gezer, he defends the leaders' conservatism. In his view, their caution is a response to the precariousness of the foundation—it could all still fall apart, as the second kibbutz did—and he believes that things will change when security is established. We sat in his apartment, between a larger than life-size portrait of Bogart on one wall and a portrait of Gandhi on another, and had a long talk about the poems and the kibbutz.

Work & companionship: Gezer has entered into me more deeply than I would have thought possible at the beginning, or on days when I felt like running away. Will the intense concentration of my time in this place give it the quality of a dream when I am outside it?

16 May

Another morning spent washing up—better forgotten. My last full working day.

A self-appointed spokesman for the commune movement in Britain arrived on the kibbutz to lead a discussion. A tall man looking somewhat like Lytton Strachey, with a high domed forehead and long hair, carrying a handbag and a woman's green hat, he came attended by two women—amanuensis and bodyguard, according to Shaul—and claimed to have "one of the best brains on the planet". He believes that all but the intelligent should be discouraged from breeding. I avoided him.

17 May

Light work today, washing up & cleaning in the children's room. Met M. at the airport at 5. After a party at Brian's house, we held another poetry discussion, which was lively and went on until after 11.

18 May

Set out to climb the Tel with M. in the morning. As we were standing by the war graves in the cemetery, a pine marten—I think it was a pine marten: a long, brown and white mottled animal with a small alert triangular head—made its way sinuously across the grass close behind us and passed fearlessly into undergrowth. Bird tracks in dust on the path and sunflowers shimmering in the hot sun: a sun dance, flowers pulsating and even appearing, at a distance, to be jumping up and down. Full-faced sunflowers or sunflowers with dried heads hanging, heavy with seed, bees yellow with pollen climbing up out of them.

Passion flowers, white with fine, purple antennae, were out among the rocks. Lizards too, lying flat on warm surfaces or looking out dragon-headed over the rock's edge. Yellow butterflies, yellow flowers and grasses; a dove purring in a pine tree. A new Arab village, some houses still being built, stands on a hillside facing the Tel and the site of Abu-Shusha and looks down on the Aijalon Valley and the coastal plain. A hoopoe was standing on the highest mound of the Tel, and beyond a stork was descending like a hang-glider, and high above the stork an eagle was circling. Big green grasshoppers bent the grasses, which, in the heat, were *alive*— with insects, birds, reptiles.

Rounding a bluff we found ourselves close to four storks, which rose with a flap of their wings and floated round the Tel, over the rocky valley. Swallowtails were flying all about us, and M. found numerous herbs—sage, fennel, oregano, camomile, thyme, blue pimpernel—most of which we could smell before we saw them. Then, a rustling among dead thistles, we looked down cautiously, expecting to see a snake, and there was a tortoise! A wild, green shellback, which kept its head extended and seemed to be looking at us steadily with its black eye.

19 May
To Jerusalem, where we took a room in a shabby hotel near the Jaffa Gate. (This turned out to have been a bad mistake at night, when we were well bitten by mosquitoes.) Walked in the old city. On Temple Mount, stone surprisingly cool under our bare feet, as we entered the Dome of the Rock. Inside, in rich half-darkness from beautiful stained glass windows, the gilded, intricately patterned dome contrasted strangely with the great slab of rock which it rises over and covers.

I found the Aqsa Mosque more moving—light and spacious, with Arabs sitting reading, or praying or even asleep, against the base of great marble columns or against the walls, and swallows weaving in and out of columns under the roof. In the Islamic Museum I noticed the calligraphy, in many sizes, each a work of art, in copies of the *Qu-ran* made of gazelle skin; and the cloak of a warrior riddled ("ridden" the label below said) with bullet holes; and armour and a helmet on which Persian poems were inscribed.

It was hot, and in the afternoon we slept and half-slept, vaguely aware of the commotion and music outside occasioned by Jerusalem Day, and the voice of "Elijah" exhorting us to love our enemies. When we eventually looked out and saw a procession it was a funeral: a Christian funeral, crosses draped with flowers & leaves, and wreaths carried at the front, and an open coffin which men bore on their shoulders in the middle of the procession, so that we looked down on the face of the corpse: an olive-complexioned man, his body covered by flowers.

At 5 we made the short walk to the Yemin Moshe district, near the windmill, a pleasant area of quiet, leafy terraced streets, where we called on Yehuda Amichai. He greeted us kindly and we sat and drank wine with him for an hour or so, talking mainly about Gezer and Jerusalem, and a little about poetry. Raucous music was coming up from the valley between Yemin Moshe and the old city—"the valley of hell", in English, he said; and of Jerusalem, affectionately, "a big bad poem". What he loves about the city is its life; it isn't a museum, but a place where people live, and lack of respect for the holy places reflects this.

I asked him about the attitude of academics here to his work. He is taught in the university, and theses are written on his work, but he couldn't teach there himself, because he hasn't the academic qualifications. Poetry sells very well in Israel, and he could just about live by his writing, he said, but in fact he supplements his income by visits abroad, especially to America. At sixty he has a new family—two small children—as he told us with a rueful twinkle, half hiding and half showing his delight and pride. Leaving him, we climbed on up the steps feeling light with wine and his gentle welcome.

20 May
After breakfast of coffee & cheese pastry in a café we moved into a small Armenian hotel, also near the Jaffa Gate. We then walked in the new city and took a bus to Mount Scopus. After a rather aimless walk round the university campus we walked along the road to the Mount of Olives, passing through a lot of Arab schoolchildren, who took a friendly interest in us. The same Arab friendliness was evident later, when we walked to the fruit market at Bethlehem, and were the only non-Arabs there. We'd intended to go to Bethlehem anyway, later, by bus, but at the foot of the Mount of Olives we met a very persuasive Arab taxi driver, and went with him as driver and guide there and back.

Hard, white hills, bone-dry, Herodian dominating the country on our left. At Rachel's Tomb, women weeping against the cloth draped over it; soldiers at the gate, and a guard at a rooftop post across the road. A poster: "King David's Cinema, Now Showing *Jesus*". Other signs which seemed too good to be true, like The Good Shepherd Stores. Our guide showed us a factory where olive wood figures of camels and donkeys and holy figures are made. In Bethlehem he handed us over to another guide for the purpose of seeing the Church of the Nativity.

Once again I had a sense of taking in only a little. Or, rather, only a few things came alive for me. The rocky fields where David was a shepherd. Stooping under an ancient doorway, low to keep animals out, on entering the church. Pillars stained brown like old canvases, with paintings on them, including a magnificent tall lean Elijah with a beard to his navel. Brown and old-gold icons, a brass hanging lamp with a Tsar's crown—his gift to the church—at the top. Fragments of the mosaic floor of Helena, Constantine's mother, well below the level of the present floor. A black Madonna, over stone steps which we descended into the manger, a place like a cave, where we each lit a candle. Crusaders' presence in stonework & symbols, and different architectural styles of Armenians, Greek Orthodox, Catholic. All in all, a house of many ages and several different styles, containing many symbols, but with an overall coherence and simplicity, and, like the Dome of the Rock, built to protect something of primal simplicity.

From there we were taken to the Shepherds' Field, a small, insignificant-looking piece of ground in rocky hills—which made me realize I've always imagined the scene as taking place in *English* hill country—and, beside it, some olive trunks which our guide said were 2,000 yeas old. With their tense, densely concentrated swirling lifelines, they looked it. Earlier, on the Mount of Olives, we'd paid 200 shekels each to visit the Chapel of the Ascension, which contains a squared off area of rock that is supposed to bear the imprint of Christ's foot, and has a tub of grey sand full of candle stubs beside it, but overhead, in the beautiful, austere shell of the domed roof, a sparrow had built a nest and was chirruping.

Driving through Jerusalem, our guide pointed out the no-man's-land, in the Valley of Hinnom, in the battles between Jordanians and Jews—yesterday, in Yemin Moshe, we'd seen gun emplacements, which are kept as memorials by the Jews, as so much in this city is—and he pointed out reminders of the British presence too. He moved constantly back and forth between events of his own youth and manhood and things of thousands of years past.

> And not forgetting:
> the cockerel on an old bed
> standing in an orchard,
> the donkey lying
> in a pool of dust,
> not bothering
> to look up at us,
> on the Mount of Olives.

21 May

Started the day feeling pleased with ourselves, having bought a necklace of amber beads at a considerable reduction in the old city. Then it dawned on us: they were plastic! Another very persistent young Arab offered M. a necklace for nothing, if he could see it against her skin. We got to the Damascus Gate without further mishap, and caught an Arab bus to Jericho.

Encampments of open-sided tents, with sheep & goats as well as people inside, on the mountain. Dusty limestone, pale yellow sand or mudstone mountains, with patches of pink, orange, red. Landscape that is essence of dryness. Then the plain was below us—oases, above all the oasis of Jericho, with beautiful red acacias sheltering buildings, and hibiscus & bougainvillea among date palms, and a distant view of the Dead Sea.

Old Jericho, mounds & hollows above the green oasis of the new city, beside box-like mud and straw houses of a refugee camp, many empty, their former inhabitants having gone to Jordan. Above, the Mountain of Temptation, its great, rugged sides banded with reddish-brown rock, and with caves like dark eyeholes.

Looking at the refugee camp, wretched though it is, it isn't difficult to understand how city after city of mud and straw walls could fall on the same site, sifting down through time. At Shalom Al Israel, the mosaic of a synagogue 1400 years old, with an Aramaic inscription which says, in part: "He who knows their names and those of their children and of their families may He inscribe them in the book of Life". At Hisham's Palace nearby, another mosaic, which looks as though it might have been completed last week, though the Palace was built in the 8th century: the Tree of Life, full leaved and bearing apples, between two gazelles and a lion leaping on a gazelle. This palace, with ornamental pool, Dancing Room, Guest Room, Mosque, Hot Room, was evidently the work and possession of a Caliph who felt no call to renounce the world.

Waiting for a bus on a desert road outside Jericho, I glanced at a soldier in battle dress getting out of a lorry with his rifle over one shoulder and what I thought was his helmet under his other arm. As he came towards us I saw that it was a huge watermelon.

The bus came at last and took us along the shore of the Dead Sea, under the cliffs and caves at Qumran of the Scrolls—a turquoise sea, the hazy Mountains of Moab a mirage on the farther shore. And when we got in the water, at Ein Gedi, we found it oily, smelling vaguely of suntan lotion, at first burning in every scratch & gnat bite, but warm, and relaxing to float in.

22 May

Early morning dip in the Dead Sea. Water ruffled, unlike the mirror-stillness yesterday, and the jagged cliffs above—edge of the Wilderness of Judea—stood out more clearly, humped, camel-coloured cliffs, evidence of terrible rending. As we ate breakfast, violent sonic booms shook the restaurant, as they had the church of the Nativity at Bethlehem.

Bus to the Jericho/Jerusalem junction, with the same driver as yesterday, on his return journey from Eilat, but this time involved in what sounded like a violent political argument with a man and a woman seated in the front, voice raised and hand gesturing in the air as we sped downhill and swung round bends. At the junction, we got on a crowded bus to Tiberius, which followed the road between the mountains of Samaria and the Jordan Valley.

Sea of Galilee, salt smell of a dark blue-grey, living sea on a day of desert cloud. Boats, fish rising, swallows hawking close to the surface, boys diving in, and, as we watched, a girl caught a fish on a hand line from the seawall. Later, we had an excellent fish meal in a restaurant near an old mosque, and in the noise of videos from surrounding restaurants and shops. Night, on the roof of the hotel, a new moon over the western hills and lights twinkling on the far side of the sea.

23 May

By bus to near Tabgha, traditionally the site of the miracle of loaves & fishes. A walk between tomato fields and orchards, but tourists in buses had preceded us to the first sanctuary, where Mass was in progress, so we didn't see the mosaic, because I was too impatient to wait. On to the next sanctuary close by, a new, small chapel on the shore. Once round the buses and past men selling "religious" gifts at the gate, it was quite peaceful, but my bad blood flowed thicker when we came on a dreadful poem, in English, fixed on a ruin inside the gate, and its sculptural equivalent by the water. But there was a black lizard standing up with one foot and one leg on the edge of a black basalt stone, returning our look. And a white crane, with long wispy hairs at the back of its neck, fishing in shallows near the chapel, and a brilliant blue kingfisher in tropical vegetation nearby. Here I dipped my face in the water, and we looked inside the chapel, at bright new stained glass and a great rock—traditionally the spot where Jesus appointed St Peter head of the Church.

The walk to Capernaum was even hotter. There we saw excavations, columns & broken columns, pine needles lying on the basalt remains of St Peter's house. But the heat was too much, and the other tourists, the hymn singing & recitations of Germans & Americans at the other sanctuary, the bad art which with its sentimentality creates a sick feeling of unreality, but above all the heat. So we got on the boat waiting to return to Tiberius—which we shared with a party of French tourists, and the boat stopped on the water for a reading of the Gospel passage of the stilling of the storm, but mercifully there was a breeze, and the water was no longer the dull silvery blue which it had been when seen from the shore, but olive green. Now, as I write in our hotel room, the Khamsin has thickened and dust has reddened the heavy grey sky, but it is evening at last.

Later. As we sat at a seafront café table eating our meal, under a sky that had become an even heavier yellow reddish grey, and watching tiny fish swarming blackly round pieces of bread thrown on the water, suddenly the wind got up. Trees overhead swayed and opened, lights went out, waiters jumped to catch glasses & bottles blown off tables, napkins soared into the air. A cloud of sand & dust swirled downhill through an opening in the wall covering our plates & glasses with sand grains. The sea had instantly risen in high waves, and in the uneasy calm that followed we could see a black line of wind approaching across the water. Thunder & lightning far off, the song of a muezzin from a distant part of the town, a few drops of rain.

No one could understand it; such conditions were unknown at this time of year. A waiter remarked that it might be due to Libya's explosion of a nuclear device in the Sahara. Meanwhile a warm breeze continued to blow, and as we walked back we could see the moon, misshapen and partly obscured by sand in the atmosphere.

24 May
For me, the strange violence of the evening broke the day's oppression, and in retrospect I felt the reality of the walk to Capernaum in the heat, the black basalt, the ruins among shady trees by the water. Somehow, the eerie natural violence made the miraculous history more real. I could see Christ and the disciples out on the water in a sudden storm.

From Tiberius by bus, a steep climb to a high land of yellow cornfields and variously cultivated valleys, evidently worked since early times. From Kafr Kana (Cana of

Galilee), a small hillside town, to Nazareth. Limestone hills, a much softer, more fertile country than the hills of Jerusalem, with figs & olives growing on orange and rust-red soil and in the town, where there were also many cypresses among houses and around churches on the ridge, and jacaranda trees—still beautiful, though their blue flowers are much thinner on the branches than at Gezer a few weeks ago. Nazareth was crowded and full of traffic, so that we passed through on the bus at less than walking pace.

At old Acre, we found the sea breaking on rocks, and the window of warm dusty air of recent days was suddenly flung open, letting in a deep cool freshness. We walked slowly round the old city, up and down narrow alleys, beside seawalls of honeycombed stone, looking through gaps at the sea breaking over ruins of older walls. The town of alleys, mosques, and minarets is oriental, but, near the walls, it constantly reminded me of the English south coast too. This was due mainly to massive stonework, usually Crusader at base though often Turkish, and to many deserted, half ruined cavernous buildings with vaulted ceilings, like the medieval cellars in Southampton, and sudden openings on sea and coast, on an oil refinery and the towering buildings of Haifa on the slopes of Carmel in the distance. Close to the fishing harbour we came on the torn and rusted iron ribcage of a large ship half sunk in sand, just off shore, near a broken-down iron pier. Farther out, a ruined tower on an island—Tower of the Flies—might have been part of the medieval defences in the Solent.

As we looked into crypts and walked under or on the walls, passing through iron-plated, nail-studded gateways and in and out of alleys, in the relative quiet of the eve of a holy day, I felt Acre to be a haunted place. But what we actually found haunting our room in the Youth Hostel, a former villa with marble pillars and floors and stairways looking out over the sea, was scores of mosquitoes, which kept us miserably awake.

25 May
Today we discovered the city under the city, St. Jean d'Acre of the Hospitallers under the city of Arabs and Turks and Ahmed el-Jazzar. At first, I felt I was going into a place like the crypt of Winchester Cathedral, but then found the underground buildings were like a great labyrinthine castle combined with a great cathedral, and because they were underground, silent, almost bare, and in half light or darkness, they were literally like nothing on earth, yet kept a space for the past. The muteness of the great stones is a kind of eloquence, but with so much that has been made, that is, in fact, a human world, I find myself hungry for some sign or word of explanation, something in which the makers speak. And at last we came on a broken marble dedication, in Latin, which in English reads:

> In The Year 1242 After The Incarnation Of Our Lord, The XV KLS Of October, Past Away Brother Peter De Villebrede, Eighth Grand Master Of The Hospitallers After The Recapture Of The Holy Land (*Sancte Terre*). Let His Soul Remain In Peace, Amen. In His Time, The Duc

Of Montfort And Other French Barons, Were Released From Egyptian (*Babilonie*) Captivity, And Richard Duc Of Cornouailes Reerected The Fortress Of Ascalon.

In His Time: which has somehow been preserved by the Turks who filled in the buildings with dirt and rubble and used part of them as a sewer, and by the excavators who have partly opened them again.

Later, we had another experience that played disconcertingly, but humorously, with time. Passing the Khan-el-Umdan after dark, we glanced into the courtyard and saw that a play was being performed. Pausing, we heard that it was in English, and I realised it was *Measure for Measure*, with Angelo, the only character I could see, (Isabella was hidden by a column) dressed in Victorian black frockcoat & trousers. Judging by the little we saw and heard the performance was no match for the imposing setting.

26 May
From Akko to Haifa, where we got lost walking purposelessly in the city, and from there by sherut to Tel Aviv, and eventually to Gezer. Again a feeling of homecoming as we turned up the road between golden wheatfields and fields of cotton and sunflowers, in the quiet, with the Tel rising above, and the mountains of Judea softened by distance. An American stopped his car to ask the way to the Tel, and I found myself explaining how to get there, how hot the walk would be, and a little about the place with the confidence of someone who has long lived here. But these days away have broken the spell of special intimacy that working on the kibbutz created, and I'll be able to leave now without regret.

27 May
Packed. Very hot, even at 6 in the evening, when we took a last walk round the kibbutz. Past the cemetery, where lizards, seeing us, scuttled up the trunks of pine trees. Across the fields to the eagle tree, but the bird wasn't there. Later, a party at Peter and Ofra's, to which Shaul and, later, Jan and Shimshon also came. Drank a lot of vodka.

28 May
Shaul was up early to say goodbye and Peter came with us to the airport. In much less time than it takes me to get by train and boat from Holland to England we were at Amsterdam.

Back to early summer, young fern, leaves, grass, fields of buttercups, all the lovely cool refreshing shades of green, and leaving behind the dusty fields white to harvest. Returning, I'm struck more than ever by what a small, relatively safe, green corner Western Europe is. Not that anywhere in the world is safe, but here, in contrast to the Middle East, is a neat, comfortably ordered existence, and, for the most part, a temperate politics without passion or imagination.

4 June

Back a week, I've had, for the time being, to put the experience of the past five weeks to the back of my mind, and concentrate on critical work—the struggle to enter with more awareness into George Oppen's 'Of Being Numerous', and the intellectual effort to grasp Jacques Maritain's philosophy of poetic knowledge. I come back willingly to this work, and to work on three lectures for the autumn. And hope that the experience of Israel will settle deeper in my mind. Already, though, I feel the old imbalance—worked mind, under-worked body.

But I have walked and cycled and swum, enjoying the beauty of Groningen and surrounding country at this time of year. Days of hot sun, but the vegetation is a moist, fresh green. Copper beech by yellow leaves, orange shutters and red brick, blue road signs, white or pink horse-chestnut "candles". The leaves are most alive now, moist, gleaming, delicate. I waited at a bridge over a canal for a German barge to pass, a large barge so laden that water half covered her name. Then cycled on a narrow path between thick creamy hawthorn and cow parsley, breathing in their warm pleasant faintly acrid smell. On Sunday I went out with M. in the car so that she could drive for the first time since the accident; which she did safely, but painfully. The doctors now think she will only partially recover the use of her hand.

What I said about the comfortably ordered existence in Europe was shown to be as silly as it is by the violence at the Brussels football stadium last week, which we together with millions of other people saw on TV as it was happening. It was frightening; and it's frightening that Thatcher and others who immediately expressed shock and outrage and called for punitive measures are completely incapable of seeing any connection between the violence and the emptiness and despair that their social and economic policies exacerbate.

15 June

We visited M's friends at Ezinge on a day more like autumn than summer, with a high wind pouring through the grass, blowing grey cloud about the sky, and shivering light on leaves in the trees. Yolande and Wilfred live in an old, red brick house surrounded by trees, but open to the fields around. The thirteenth-century, brick church and church tower, separated from each other to symbolise the body and head of John the Baptist, stand at a short distance, on the terp rising abruptly from the fields, like a large island. The fields stretch far round in every direction, but are broken up, there, into small plots, some with black and white cows in long grass, some with windrows of hay, like coarse yellow hair.

It feels like an ancient pattern, and is, though four hundred years ago Ezinge was at the edge of the sea. The terp has been built up over the centuries—five layers have been excavated, and the archaeologists in their enthusiasm, cutting down through the hill beside the church, strained and cracked the church walls. Human settlement has been traced back seven centuries before Christ.

Much of this, and more, we learnt from Mr Bosma who showed us around the church and tower. A frail old man—he is only 68 but he is dying of cancer—he stood in the church with the large key in his hands, his body wasted under his neat suit and raincoat, his face crazed with red veins, but clear and well defined. He showed us the tiny window at knee height, where lepers used to come to kneel at the wall outside to receive communion. He showed us the pulpit and family pew, of fine eighteenth-century woodwork. (I noticed the sensuous female forms of the angels carved between rails surrounding the pulpit, below the strong masculine figures of the evangelists carved on the pulpit itself. They were all there was of woman in that austere interior, where, according to Mr Bosma, the entrances had at one time segregated men and women, on the grounds that Eve had seduced Adam.)

He showed us the tomb of a young Groningen advocate, set in the church floor and finely lettered in stone script, like sloping handwriting, and a picture of the young man. A conventional portrait, but with enough self-consciousness in the face to give me a flicker of awareness that I was standing over his bones. He had managed to arrange for himself to be buried there four years after a decree had gone out from The Hague to prevent burials inside churches, on account of the fact that news travelled slowly in those parts. His wife who lived into her eighties had to be buried outside.

As Mr Bosma talked, and M. at intervals translated for me, I tried to conjure up the past. But the rows of chairs in the body of the church remained stubbornly empty, and everything stayed irreducibly as at that moment it was. Standing by the lepers' window, looking at our guide and listening to but not understanding him, I had a strong sense that we really are earth, and return to earth. At the same time I knew the utter distinctness of each face that has gone—the fact of distinctness, for of course I saw nothing but light through the windows, grass outside, and we three in the church.

This is the incredible thing I break my thought on—Gone, the living moment that was, lives shaped through years that were theirs. I don't mean the hourglass and skull carved on the pulpit. That's a story told to frighten children, like a scarecrow put up to scare the birds. A true story, but with a truth that freezes us, that may kill the freedom to live, as knowledge of personal death should not.

I only half know what I mean. The truth of the old language touches me, yet in churches of that kind, in a bare Protestantism, I'm not deeply moved—for me there's nothing between the skull and the wintry light. Earth is real, the generations that are earth, and the handiwork of wood and stone, the names and messages on the stones, but where I want to meet others in belief, there's nothing.

Tired at last, Mr Bosma rested against a table and told M. about his cancer. He's living on "borrowed" time, since he'd been given until January to live. He lives in faith, without fear, and this church is everything to him, and showing it to interested visitors is his greatest pleasure. According to Yolande, he has a dominant wife, and is only too glad to be in the church for that reason too.

16 June

According to George Steiner, Heidegger's apprehension in *Being and Time* shared common ground with Nazism. For example, "Heidegger's rhetoric of 'at-homeness', of the organic continuum which knits the living to the ancestral dead buried close by, fits effortlessly into the Nazi cult of 'blood and soil'".

Steiner quotes Heidegger, in 1933, on the "hard clarity" with which the philosophers, reunited to the *Volk* through the National Socialist Revolution, will return to the question of the meaning of human existence. And he comments, "Heideggerian 'resolution' has more than a hint of the mystique of commitment, of self-sacrificial and self-projective élan preached by the Führer and his 'hard clear' acolytes".

"To produce poetry that is hard and clear" (Ezra Pound) was the main aim of Poundian Imagism and Vorticism, which was influenced decisively by T. E. Hulme and Gaudier-Brzeska. In Pound, Hulme and Gaudier the strong masculine will is evident, the artist's desire to master his materials and express his emotion in terms of formal arrangement. Gaudier's perception of mass in sculpture seems to blend with his idea of human masses in the war, which he sees as "remedy", the instrument of a necessary reduction: "It takes away from the Masses numbers upon numbers of unimportant units". Pound, remembering him in 1934, wrote, in cold anger: "What we call social necessity is nothing but the temporary inconvenience caused by the heaped up imbecilities of other men, by the habits of a dull and lazy agglomerate of our fellows, which sodden mass it is up to the artist to alter, to carve into a fitting shape, as he hacks off unwanted corners of marble".

The aim of these notes is not to judge the men, but to question the leaning of Imagism and Objectivism, a leaning that may exercise some unconscious internal control even when the writer's political and social commitments are directed the other way.

Pound wanted poetry to use the language of common speech. In fact, though, he follows Hulme in demanding an exactness which is not common, but expresses the artist's different seeing, "the exact curve of the thing". Clearly, this differs from what a democratic poet's aim might be. The "I" of the Imagist is always his own; the eye that sees and the "voice" are his. Hence Oppen's means to sincerity, which is close to authenticity in Heidegger's sense. His poetic, embodying his morality, commits him to exactness that selects, and excludes: he cannot give over his poetry to other "voices"; he cannot be "inclusive", as Olson and Williams are. But Oppen's mind is not directed by masculine will; it is open to the feminine, and receptive to wonder, to letting "this in which" appear. At the same time, he is concerned to expose the hidden "sources" of capitalist power. He is a love poet, and he was a communist. But

> "Whether, as the intensity of seeing increases,
>   one's distance
> from them, the people, does not also increase"
> I know, of course, I know, I can enter no other place

Isn't such "distance" inevitable in the "seeing" of Objectivism, with its roots in the aesthetics of Hulme and Pound, but not necessarily in all "seeing"? Oppen's poetry has a spiritual intensity reminiscent of Simone Weil, and Kierkegaard's "Single One". How therefore could his speech voice humanity's being? Isn't it *bound* to distinguish him from "the people". In spite of his politics, in spite of his heart even, isn't he bound to see the people as "they", *das Man*?

Heidegger, too, is shot through with paradox, especially in the masculine/feminine oppositions which he seems to hold without resolving in his thought, oppositions between creative violence and wise passivity. But his milieu and origins were radically different from Oppen's. And Oppen seems to accept the city as his natural habitat. Or does he? Isn't he, rather, a "nature" poet living in and writing from the city, but constantly adverting to earth under pavements, and sea under pier, the original wilderness?

"The language of poetry naturally falls in with the language of power." Thus Hazlitt, writing in cold anger in response to the repressive politics of 1817. Of course, he was talking about a different poetry, Shakespeare's, with roots in the hierarchical world order of church and kingship. And Hazlitt at that time wasn't pausing to think about the poet of unaccommodated man. But the question is relevant to the poetry of this century too. Was there something inherent in Pound's poetic method that led him to admire Mussolini? Was that method really akin to the hard clarity of Heidegger's Nazi-inspired philosopher? These were men who wanted to give form to the chaos of their times, Oppen, as a communist, wanted to change society. Was there, then, a contradiction between this and his and Mary's stated aim of entangling themselves in the roots of their time, among the people? He was not, like Pound, a patrician, or a conscious elitist, but perhaps, as he sought authenticity, he had to disentangle himself from the "public".

I suspect that the answer to the question about distance from the people was implicit from the beginning in the kind of poetry he wrote. Or, to put it another way, that personal authenticity and social alienation are inseparable in that way of seeing.

Modernism: the separated vision. 'A Language of New York' brings this home to me as surely as *The Waste Land*. Oppen's language is idiolect, not dialect, and, like Heidegger, he puts tremendous pressure on certain "small" words, driving the reader down to the roots. And what are absent from 'A Language of New York', and the language of 'Of Being Numerous', are "common" voices. There, in the subways, is *talk*, rootless speech. It seems the poet cannot be with others in speech, though he can name them; and his voice alone sounds in the poem, determining what can be said. Oppen sees the problem; but to what extent does his seeing cause it?

Early July

I spent the whole of June working on my essay on 'Of Being Numerous', which I finished a few days before we left for England on 2 July. Again, I lived in the work, becoming shut in and nervous, almost deaf and blind to the world around me.

How shall one know a generation, a new generation?
Not by the dew on them! Where the earth is most torn
And the wounds untended and the voices confused,
There is the head of the moving column.

Who if they cannot find
Their generation
Wither in the infirmaries

And the supply depots, supplying
Irrelevant objects.
    —George Oppen

In East Anglia. Mountainous, green hedgerows—the best year of the wild rose I can remember. After the flat land the English countryside, with dead elms in the hedgerows, is immediately irregular and various, a place of corners, hills & hollows, mysterious, with dynamic broken rhythms. It was on the narrow road just out of Norwich that the uncut roadsides looked like green mountains, on the road where I thought of Michael Munday, my friend and colleague who died young, coming home to his city.

At Corpusty, an abandoned church on a hilltop. Belfry boarded up, windows closed with sheets of corrugated iron, pantiles slipping and a mouldering stone porch. Tombstones sunk to their heads and shoulders in nettles, grass & fern. Near the gate, where the grass is not so thick: *In Sweet Memory of Dawn Beloved Daughter Aged 8 months.* There were red flowers and dried grasses by her stone. She would have been twenty-one this year.

In Lee's studio. Paintings and sculptures of faces looking up fearfully, fingers pointing. Room in shadow, but here and there a brilliant spot of light on the floor, from gaps in the barn roof. Halves of a swallow's empty egg under the nest high on the wall, above the paintings. A set of elmwood heads and one in walnut wood, all staring up. A painted relief cut in an old gate, Christ suggested by a Velázquez *Flagellation*. Figures painted on the bottom of what was once a solicitor's desk. The large sculptures from the show were there, too: all a family of images, a growing body of work—which Lee was pleased that I said; he's more strained than I've seen him, and has only recently won relief from financial difficulties. He's also having to promote his work as much as he can, to "hustle", as he says.

    He's asking how to express things through figures, but beyond appearances and naturalism. The body is a medium for expressing emotion, felt physically. He wants to hang onto the subject while transforming it into another reality. I saw the influence of Picasso in the staring faces—Lee said that he was always "hitting up" against Picasso in what he was attempting to do. He admires Picasso very much; he is the modern artist who has opened up the way.

Hot days. Digging, sweating, weeding an overgrown strawberry bed near the sculpture of the fox & goose. Looking up, eyes cleansed by sweat, I saw the trees and woods as a depth of blue shadow—July in this, beyond the delicacy of midsummer, as when I helped Dafydd bring in the hay—and the sharp angles of red-tiled house & barn. Malevich, the white cat (Lee professes shame at the name; the other, grey, cat is called Gris) lay near in the shade of raspberries. White cat, pink nose, pink ears showing through fur, eyes like translucent pebbles. She caught a vole and brought it to show me.

Chickens, ducks & ducklings. Moorhens & baby rabbits on the lawn. Partridges & lapwings with their chicks in the fields. A hare like a small deer.

Sweet Dawn. The word "ancient": light shining on dust and spider webs in window panes, a thick hawthorn hedge outside, and a glimpse of a wheatfield and woodland beyond. Gold dust motes. Red and blue lupins, moorhens in the grass. Saxthorpe, Edgefield, Corpusty, Baconsthorpe, Little London. Church towers, all with an air of abandonment, standing apart, the few unbroken strands lying slack on the surrounding landscape. Yet I would re-enter the pattern, come back to wood and earth and stone. But even if I could it would be no good breathing a finished air. What Oppen says about one's generation is true, that we know it by its confusion and wounds, and if we don't find it, we're lost, abandoned to irrelevance.

Lee and a few friends are my generation, a few friends and more unknown friends. It's difficult, but I find no contradiction between this and a refusal to abandon the past. Only we have to understand what is "past", and always to distinguish nostalgia or a longing for the dark from the life in the things. There's a great difference between England and America in this; perhaps it's easier for an English poet to "go" American, but to me that's merely another form of irrelevance. It's hard to understand—we enter a church and trace the meanings in inscriptions and stained glass, a worm-eaten Flanders cross, feel something of the world stretched on the cross that this house is, and outside a jet fighter from a USAF base blasts across the sky, over wheatfields where poppies growing together look like bloody wounds.

Remember Eternity in gold letters over the church clock at Reepham.

5 July

A walk to Holkham beach with M. & Elin, Lee & the boys. When we got there, down a long track between fields, through a pinewood, passing close to the Queen's lodge, it began to rain and to thunder and lightning. Lee at once directed us to make a shelter of driftwood planks, fish boxes, a plastic sheet, etc. in the dunes, and arranged and built most of it himself. This kept the rain off us and we huddled together in high good spirits under the roof while the storm came close and then moved away. Then, in a fresher air, we played rounders on the sand, and the sea, which I've rarely seen on this coast, began to come in.

Evening, the distant sea where the sun caught it flickered like flames. Then mist, sun a red-gold ball over the sea, glimpsed between pines, and as we walked back, past musty elderflowers, hay, and cow pasture, smelling strongly after the rain, Cuckoo! Cuckoo! So I wasn't to miss it this year after all.

On the way back we stopped for a drink at an old pub (Lord Nelson) at Burnham Thorpe, and sat outside with our drinks at he edge of the playing field, looking across at the church where Nelson's father had been vicar. It was a haunted place beside a small stream in misty evening light, with swallows skimming over the green. As Lee told the children the stories—telescope to blind eye, and so on—I could feel something of the sea's pull for the boy, as if it were actually plucking at the still earth around us.

6 July

A long, unpleasant drive from Reepham to Hampshire, breaking down with a snapped off exhaust pipe a few miles from Ely, and with the engine cutting out whenever we stopped at a crossing or traffic lights. At Hayford I found my parents noticeably older. Dad sees very little now, and Mother was dizzy yesterday morning, and looks thinner than when I last saw her. They welcomed us with strawberries out of the garden, which Dad says is more beautiful than ever this year. It is still beautifully kept, though Mother says he can no longer see to weed. Afterwards, very tired, we came on to Christchurch, where we have a flat near the Quay and Priory for a fortnight. Riverside looks out to the river & boats over a putting green, which our landlady owns.

Early to mid July

We have all been a bit strained in this house. There have been good days, all together, with Emily & with Jim or John & Yvonne, but I've too often been touchy, anxious and withdrawn. M., Elin, and Emily have also been adversely affected in different ways. There have been tangible reasons—more problems with the car, growing up, my usual sense of estrangement in such circumstances, concern about my parents, the difficulty of finding things to do that interest everyone. Perhaps it's mere superstition that makes M. and me sense another reason in the house itself, in the unhappiness that must have been experienced in these rooms.

Early on, at a casual meeting, our landlady told me that her husband had committed suicide. He drowned himself in the river by the Quay about two years ago. She spoke of him without apparent sympathy, even with a suggestion of contempt, as a man who had been afraid of everything and everyone, of young vandals, for example. She accosts them boldly, and works hard at running her business by herself. She is Russian, a woman whose age is very hard to tell—she makes up, wears flowery clothes and has a grey, clipped poodle called Sasha, but there are marks of age on her skin. Her husband had "slight problems", she told me in her quaint English; and she told M. she's been married three times, and each husband left her money. She believes the neighbours spy on her through binoculars. Whenever we meet her she is on the wing, always busy, with no time *now* to stop and talk—but with time enough to leave us with some intriguing, discomforting fragment.

Fear. One morning I was alone at Mudeford. Tense and anxious, I walked to the water, neither in myself nor in the world, but in the grey region in-between, not thinking or seeing, nerves strung taut, mind turning repetitively on the anxieties of my tense body. How much of life I've wasted in that region!

The day was clouded, mild, silvery blue. And as I saw it, so I was able to relax. A little, low cumulus smoked over the Island, east of West Wight, where Tennyson's Memorial was visible as a dot. From the sandspit to Avon Beach, in slack water beside the Run, perhaps a hundred swans were feeding, dipping long hooked necks into the sea. A fish smell and piles of black lobster pots on the quay. Again, I saw men hauling in a net, pulling steadily against its weight in the water, and finally beaching a salmon.

On other days we've been swimming off the sandspit, or I've gone crabbing with Emily. One day we caught one of the usual green shore crabs, but with all four legs missing on one side. It brought back the cruelty that sickened me, when men and boys fishing would dash crabs against stones or seawall or tread on them.

The first day Jim was here, when we went swimming at Mudeford, he told me that he's rereading Tennyson, especially 'Maud', and finding there many things that he feels, and are important to him, things that perhaps Tennyson alone among poets expressed. I share his admiration. Love of Tennyson has been with me early and late. We agreed that he wasn't a father figure we needed to "kill", as Yeats and Eliot and all who felt oppressed by Victorianism had to. Indeed, if we need to "kill" anyone it might be Yeats and Eliot, though the word's far too strong for the critical, sometimes exasperated, love I feel for them. But Victorianism hasn't been a problem for us, and we can even regard it as a kind of picture, with the fascination of a world both near in time and spiritually very distant.

Another day, walking back from Mudeford, I sat down on Hengistbury Head to read a Jefferies' essay, 'Walks in the Wheatfields', and was surprised to be reminded of his hatred of the church, "these repellent structures" which have no use in the world. It's a late essay, full of pain: the form in which I think he was making his most original poetry. That feeling, too, like Tennyson, was at once near and far. Near in his anguish, his loneliness, in the intensity of his questioning; far in that his anger against the church, like Hardy's, and his belief in the disproof of science were as Victorian as the tension in Tennyson between the experience of disintegration, the darkened mind, and the need for a positive vision. As we have lost—indeed, never had—both the faith in science and the need to maintain an order crazed with contradictions, so our questions are very different. Yet there's something in Victorian seriousness, and in the felt and acknowledged confusions and sense of loss in men like Tennyson and Jefferies and Hardy, that I feel closer to than I feel to Yeats' occultism or Eliot's irony.

Alone at Mudeford on a morning of sun, shadow, wind, and sudden waves of blinding light. Wind offshore drove the glitter, millions of dancing points of light, towards the Island, which rose up dark and distinct. Light danced where wind blew on the sea, over the smooth, slow-moving waters of the Run at high tide. Masts & wires jingled, and all was fresh and beautifully clear.

In the afternoon we walked in the Forest near Burley, through pinewoods where multitudes of red ants were crossing the paths and had built large anthills, some taller than Emily, of fallen pine needles. In one place a small carrying party was dragging off a lobworm's mutilated corpse. Butterflies & small moths fluttered along the paths, where bells were falling from foxgloves. Only an occasional bird broke the midsummer quiet.

It was at Solent Mead two or three days ago, on our walk back from the Head, that Emily and I found a St Peter's school tie—my old school tie!—fastened to a fence post. I wondered whether someone at the end of his schooldays, light-headed with joy and relief at the thought of never having to wear it again, had taken it off and hung it there.

I've recently had the idea of a fictional character—but applicable in a way to myself—who desires *to turn his life into a stone*. On one hand, the possibilities of the obvious irony, that his finish will indeed be a stone. On the other, the need to explore the desire to find or make images in the daily flux, to crystallize life's movements in words that are clear and hard and shining.

19 July
Salmon weathervane against sky and cloud, over pinnacles shaped like the "swords" of swordfish. Walked with Emily across Solent Meads and the Head to Mudeford in a strong, warm wind blowing cloud about the sky. A world of glorious colour. Teazles, spines tipped with purple, washed, whitish purple blackberry flowers, purple thistles, coarse yellow ragwort, white convolvulus, pink mallow. From the Head we saw whitecaps out at sea, white foam on the beach, sea breaking white over the groyne, and purple shadows spreading and changing shape on the broad, blue and greeny blue waters between Wight and the dark blue Purbeck hills.

How many shades of purple and blue! And no word for harebells or heather. One white sail in the middle of the bay echoed the white lighthouse at Hurst. Light, colour, wind; and the sheer physical being, the material substance of forms. West Wight & the Needles: the great mound of blue-white rock humped up out of the sea; earth in its utter nakedness, which is earth and more than earth…

Appearances slip from me, I exult in it all, and in the irreducible being of bedrock things.

What it is to be alive on an earth one loves. And never to be able to say it, never come close; even the brightest, most substantial word is a mere husk of time and place, an impression, a glimpse of the surface, never a word from the inside, where the foot meets the ground, where the mind lives in the world, not separated in a thought or image locked in the skull, but living as a native element…

Yet, though I'd set out knowing how I poison myself, as we came down from the Head I found myself walking almost blind, composing a mental reply to a petty review of my book of essays. But that doesn't matter. What matters is being alive in the world. And the day, and our stay here, ended with an enjoyable supper with my parents, who were lively and loving and in good spirits.

20 July
I was awake in the middle of the night finding it difficult to breathe and thinking I might die. Another night, between sleep and waking, my mind was congested by thoughts I could hardly control. M. also had bad nights in the house, which we were glad to leave. Then, as if we hadn't had enough bother with the car, I managed to hit the gatepost at Hayford and buckle the side when we called in on the way to Winchester.

24/25 July
Kerarno, Brittany
Hot, almost continuous sunshine after recent clouded days. Days of swimming in the sea and lying on beaches.

At Locmariaquer, *le grand menhir brisé*, ("largest artificially shaped stone in Europe"). The great stone broken into five pieces and shaped like a giant phallus looks as though it has fallen from the sky. It has enormous presence in its fallen state and must have had an extraordinary effect when standing, when it could have been seen from far off across the Morbihan Gulf and on the Quiberon peninsula and from beyond the Carnac alignments. I don't think we can come nearer to the recoverable truth of these things than Joe did, when he said that the people who raised the megaliths must have really believed in their religion.

The town cemetery is just behind the menhir and the two large tumuli close-by. We entered one of these, the *Table des Marchands*, finding for ourselves the mysterious signs carved on granite in the passage, including a fine axe which also looks curiously like a plough furrowing the underside of the capstone. Swallows circling overhead in grey light seemed to prefer this spot to any other around.

26 July
Today we visited the alignments and walked part of the way along them: stones which in places look like the heads of ancient tombs in a long-abandoned, overgrown graveyard. They appear above gorse & fern, and stand elsewhere high above ground, with, here and there, a tourist posing himself or his children for a photograph on top of one, or a stonechat flitting from stone to stone. The vastness and mysterious pattern of the construction are astonishing, even in its present fragmentary form. It easily swallowed us all, whether on foot or horseback between the stones or in cars on the road alongside; as their combination of utter silence and absolute, unknown purpose swallows our speculations.

27 July
At *Les Pierres Plates* looking across slate-grey water to a dark island. With the small light of a torch we glimpsed more carvings in the tunnel, which otherwise

was pitch-black, and from the little I could see they looked like abstractions of the human form. Enough to bring me back into daylight with an enhanced sense of pattern in the world outside, in the wave-shaped curves of the beach, and the echoing curves of windrows of dark brown wrack. Greeny blue sloes bound with travellers' joy grow round the tomb, and sea spurge, sea holly, and yellow horned poppy on the beach in front, and in the water swaying rafts of bladder-wrack.

Seeing nodules of red and white quartz in the granite menhir standing at the entrance to the tomb, I wondered whether the great stone constructions, which in their bare or lichen-encrusted surfaces seem designed to lift up the nature of stone, were originally *painted*. If this were the case, presumably some method for detecting the fact would have been discovered by now; but supposing it has not, and the alignments originally alternated red and blue, or some other arrangement of symbolic colours (rather as medieval churches were internally quite different from what we see), how different they would have been from our usual conception of them. In which case, again as with naked, imageless, bare stone church interiors, it would be we, with our romantic sense of the picturesque, who would be worshippers of stone, not the people who *used* stone for some purpose beyond our ability to imagine.

Afternoon: a boat trip to Locmariaquer among the islands of the Morbihan Gulf. A passing view of Gavrinis, whose tumulus our guide described as "tombe d'un grand personage", which sounds so much *grander* than any English equivalent! Most of the islands are apparently associated with modern grand personages—generals, marquises, and the like. On one small island of megaliths some stones were standing in the water, with gulls & cormorants perched on them.

28 July

It rained and wind blew strongly most of the night, and we got wetter and wetter in our leaking tent. Rain continuing in the morning decided us to leave early for home; in fact, before breakfast, which we had at a café beside a river at Auray. Then a long drive across Brittany and Normandy, the extent and depth and *solidity* of the northern countryside revealing itself to us; a solidity of earth and the stone farmhouses together, though there are also many decaying mud-walled outbuildings & dwellings, of the type which was fairly common in the New Forest when I was a boy. These called to mind Jericho, too, and the countless dissolutions of the human fabric forming the ground of any long-settled place.

At night we stayed at a hotel at Les Andelys, a small, old city by the Seine, under a steep chalk bluff crowned by a ruined castle, built by Richard the Lionheart. Beechwoods, downs, wheatfields surround the town, and the approach from Evreux, after a landscape of wide, flat fields, is rather like the upper Itchen valley. This is beautiful, fertile chalk country—all the stranger for its familiarity, a shared, conflicting, different history joining and separating the broken geology of France and England, and on both, like cloud shadows continually passing, and like entrenched field patterns, the Norman presence.

29 July
Les Andelys—Amiens—Arras: Picardy, land of the Somme. I felt how Edward Thomas would have loved to see the ripening orange-red rowan berries, and the summer sky of towering clouds which turned to a lowering dark blue roof of storm cloud as we neared Arras, and broke in downpour smoking across the fields, and almost blinded us as it pelted down on the road. There are small memorials here and there, but the large cemeteries are set back from the road, and the mounds & ditches in the fields might be prehistoric in origin, so that it is the names above all that call back the War, with a deceptive, grim poetry—true only for those who were there, who may "tiptoe" when they name the place. For us, if not exactly tourists to the devastated areas, which are no longer devastated, it is in fact the first savage wound in the substance of our spirit

After Arras, we stopped again at Ghent, where some kind of festival was in progress. In a square of medieval and Renaissance buildings a Peruvian group was singing and playing—drums, flute, an instrument like a mandolin—to an appreciative crowd, in which a few men, women and children, who may have been Peruvian, were dancing happily. A sound between a shout and a sob in the voice of the principal singer brought a foreign, passionate lyricism to echo among the well-proportioned, ornate, dignified bourgeois surroundings. They were small men dressed in their national costume filling the square with their music. A large stone statue of a man, rising high over the crowd, had one hand raised as if he too had joined in the dance.

Back to Groningen after dark.

5 August
At Hayford, with my parents. A clear, starlit night, moon in yellow haze, after days of rain. It was wet with a strong wind blowing when we came over three days ago. Next day, when I came here from Winchester, the sun shone intermittently while wind blew clouds about the sky. At Milford with Mother, sea a greeny blue race of white horses driving towards the shore, the chalk face of West Wight & the Needles like frozen foam. Yesterday it rained all day and strong wind blew down conkers, leaves & branches, as if it were autumn. I got wet twice walking to the village and back, and had a drink with Jim in The Sportsman in the evening.

Today, Mother's 79th birthday, I drove her & Dad to Bransgore for lunch at The Three Tuns. Dad could see almost nothing and had to be guided everywhere.

8 August
Early morning, looking out of my bedroom window over the gardens of Hayford, Penn Cottage and Wheathill: green gardens, a few prematurely fallen apples and white clover on the lawn, round the wooden seat, and against the wall of Dad's studio. Later, I saw his recent paintings through the window—in fact, earlier paintings which he's spoiling while he thinks he's improving them—and walked round the garden, which has a wilder richness of grass & flowers this year. Roses,

pansies, a lovely purple clematis on the garage wall, all the many colourful flowers whose names Mother always tells me and which I always forget.

9 August
Left Winchester with Joe on the crowded 7.20 for Waterloo. "No More Hiroshimas" chalked across a human silhouette on a wall.

Leaving London from Liverpool Street: grey sky of smoke & low cloud, but little evidence of industrial energy, rather an atmosphere of lassitude, even dereliction; office blocks with lights glimmering, crowded carparks, few people visible. Arriving at Waterloo the other evening my first strong impression was of the number of drunks on the station and the general air of shabbiness, despondency, and quiet, reckless despair. Rain-streaked windows, a wet countryside beyond the city, bedraggled cornfields. I write this on the *St Nicholas* at 2 pm., still at Harwich two and a half hours after the scheduled time of departure, where the boat is stalled with mechanical failure.

10 August
Back at Groningen after a journey of 28 hours. It was dark when the boat came in—we'd seen the sky darken, an orange streak to the west, and even on the North Sea in view of the coastal lights there was a feeling of vastness in the expanse of water, a scattering of white and green lights of shipping, within distinct lines of far horizons. The boat's movement was majestic, accentuated by a few accompanying gulls hanging on the wind.

More chaos at the Hook, where our crowd off the boat ran into the crowd waiting to board. I got to a telephone and rang M. No answer: she'd already left for the station to meet us, and Elin, as I learnt later, was out. Eventually Joe and I lay down on the floor under the stairs in the station, and after an hour or so, much to Joe's annoyance, for he had gone to sleep on the cold floor, and in any case was greatly enjoying the misadventure, a porter came to tell us we could sleep on the train on which we'd leave, for Amersfoort in the morning. So we stretched out in a carriage, and slept on and off until 6.30. Four and a half hours later we arrived at Groningen. Joe had helped to turn what would otherwise have been very tedious and irritating into good fun, and was good company during the whole journey, which he hoped would be prolonged by another failure or mistake, like our getting on the wrong train at Amersfoort. Happily, he was disappointed.

Back from rain to more rain, and in the evening a heavy thunderstorm.

14 August
Midsummer haze: a body for the light. Morning train to Rotterdam with Joe & Mieke to see her publisher, Willem Donker. It was hot in the train, hotter in the crowded plastic tents of the *Fenomena* exhibition, in the gardens below the Euromast, where I went with Joe. Then, out of a clear sky, thunderclouds gathered behind the mast. But the storm didn't break until we were on the waterfront at Willemsplein, waiting for M. & Willem. Then a great dark cloud sailed rapidly

up the waterway, covering the farther shore in darkness and swallowing up the barges, which bored through with lights burning. Even under the trees' dense foliage, where we pressed ourselves against the glass wall of a narrow bus shelter, torrential rain swept down, exploding in large silver cones on the brick pavement and quickly forming pools. At the same time lightning flashed over the city and thunder crashed, briefly drowning the noise of the downpour. It was like a ghostly premature nightfall, with house lights, car headlights and lights on the water glimmering in violent, rent darkness.

Afterwards, sky grey but no longer dark, a light rain falling, Willem took us to see Zadkine's great sculpture, *De Verwoeste Stad*, which has been moved from its former site and is at present in a temporary resting place. Before seeing it I had asked Willem whether it commemorates the rebuilding of the city after the war, and he replied, no, it commemorates "the heart burnt out of man".

Standing by it, I saw what he meant: a bronze Atlas, mortally wounded, its heart ripped out, but with cylindrical thighs expressive of great power, giant body contorted and hands raised to heaven, a figure that is not defeated though it reels in agony.

Willem is proud of his city, which has been rebuilt, partly in terms of a futuristic architecture, mainly in the last 5 years or so. It was his grandfather's city and his father's, who established the publishing business. He remembers seeing it lying flat in 1945 (as I saw the centre of Southampton). Later, he saw the Zadkine sculpture in pieces, waiting to be put together and raised up. Sometimes he leaves his office during the day and walks on the waterfront watching the ships; then he thinks of his grandfather and father, of the river that will go on when he's dead, and he feels glad to be "a minor part, but a part of it".

§

If we study Japanese art, we see a man who is undoubtedly wise, philosophic and intelligent, who spends his time how? In studying the distance between the earth and the moon? No. In studying the policy of Bismarck? No. He studies a single blade of grass.

But this blade of grass leads him to draw every plant and then the seasons, the wide aspects of the countryside, then animals, then the human figure. So he passes his life, and life is too short to do the whole.
Vincent Van Gogh

Late August
I've been a fool, letting myself feel depressed and defeated by the fortunes of my "name". As if "Jeremy Hooker" were a balloon floating about in the world, batted about among strangers, and blown up or deflated, or pricked or ignored, while I merely suffer what happens to it, as though it were my life out there...

To Van Gogh the word "artist" meant: "I am seeking, I am striving, I am in it with all my heart".

28 August
Bommen Berend Dag. Berend was the Bishop of Munster whose siege of the town in 1672, when he bombarded Groningen with canons, was relieved by the citizens under the command of a Swiss captain. It's *always* fine on this day. And it was today, when I walked into town with M.

Flags flying on the Martinikerk and A-kerk and on other churches and many buildings, crowds of people in holiday mood and summer clothes out on the streets. We walked back through the park, where there are weeping beeches by the water—tall, round-shouldered trees with leafy branches hanging down like long, dark green hair—and fed bread to a pair of muscovies, which caught it like dogs, the male wagging his tail. A pair of black swans, guarding two fluffy, grey cygnets, dipped their long red beaks and necks in the water. A middle-aged man lying flat out asleep on a bench, with a sherry bottle standing on the ground beside him, his head pillowed on one arm, which stuck out stiff and straight as a salute; his trousers, slightly drawn up, exposed brown shoes and socks that expressed absolute abandonment.

In the evening we went up on the roof to see the fireworks let off on the other side of town, behind and to the side of the soft, ruddy light illuminating the Martini Tower and under a hazy full moon. In the windless night we could hear the crackling of roman candles as well as bangs, and one kind of high-climbing rocket exploded in a large circle of bright green stars, which, as it turned white and faded, looked like an enormous dandelion clock.

6 September
In the evening we attended a poetry workshop at Ruinen, in a large, converted farmhouse belonging to a doctor who has a strong interest in metaphysics. It was in Dutch, of course, but my contributions in English were welcome, and with M's help I was able to follow what was going on. About twenty people were present, men and women of different ages, and we sat round a long wooden table in a comfortable room which had been artistically redesigned, with a small pool set in the stone floor and a modern sculpture on a pedestal, where formerly cattle had been kept, adjacent to the farmer's living quarters.

The workshop was conducted by Simon Vinkenoog, a Dutch poet who first came to prominence in the 1950s. He spoke to me of his friendships with Christopher Logue and Allen Ginsberg and of entertaining many writers, including David Gascoyne, at his home in Amsterdam. Evidently for him, as for me, for a while, the fifties was a time of revelation—he mentioned Mailer's 'The White Negro' with awe, as well as Ginsberg.

Simon insisted on the necessity of internationalism; but to my mind this is a common weakness of modern Dutch poetry, and while I don't forget that I've only sampled English translations in anthologies, a depressing amount of what I have read has relied heavily on American models, and exists in a kind of psychic no place, with the result that, in striving for subjectivity and novelty, it all sounds much the same. Of course, the same is true of a lot of English poetry written since the fifties, only in Holland during the same period there has not been—as far as I know—any equivalent to the "grounding" of poets like Bunting, Hill, and David Jones, or, for that matter, of the Americans, and notably William Carlos Williams, whose techniques Dutch poets have imitated.

I'm not dead to what I might learn from the spirit of Dutch internationalism, which has long-established qualities of outward-looking and tolerance. It's the internationalism that loses the anyone anywhere—the genuinely common—in the no one nowhere that I oppose, not the internationalism that seeks to know and understand others. I've also to remember that writing here responds to a different history, and a geographical situation that has made the Dutch far more outward-looking than the insular English.

14 September
Jim arrived for a visit yesterday and today we went for a cycle ride round Paterswoldemeer.

Jim later remarked that the south of England I want to go back to doesn't exist, and never did. I don't think I ever idealized the south or my "belonging" there anyway, and I understand well what Jim means when he says he can breathe here, as he can't in Lymington, where "class" makes the very air suffocating, because I feel the same. I don't think I have any illusions about England. But still the fact remains that I'm drawn back, not in grief and almost in panic as I was sometimes in Wales, but in the certainty that my place is there. The need to be there is part of me.

23 September
On Friday, to clear our heads after drinking too much the night before, we cycled out of town along the Starkenborghkanaal, stopping to watch oil barges passing, and the level of a lock being lowered, with a strong rush of water into the brown canal, to let a small cargo boat through. The narrow cycle path on the west bank runs for a long way through a tunnel of green trees—still green, though leaves have been falling thinly for some weeks—and we cycled pleasantly there in a kind of dream. Next morning we walked across town and spent several hours at the museum. After looking with particular interest at a photographic record of excavations at Ezinge, and especially at the 8th century ritual burial of two horses & a dog—the arrangement of bones set in clay looking like a large, strangely beautiful insignia—it was a shock on going upstairs to look at the paintings to walk into an exhibition of Arnulf Rainer's *Hiroshima*. Outside, beds of salvia burned bright red against dark green horse-chestnuts touched with bronze.

Late September
Morning. As I open the front door the sun blinds me, shining through a spiderweb slung across an angle of the entrance. Stepping back I see the web, with strands that, seen at a certain angle, are prisms. Across the blue sky, a single curving vapour

trail. We walked in the park, where the reflections of house fronts and cars were so bright and sharp that for an instant the mirrored images looked real.

In Wales I became intensely conscious of light. Here, I've become more conscious of the human clay. Clay gone back into the earth, clay of the generations, clay from which we can shape ourselves. Shaping/making/exploring; but suppose the truth was revealed once in time, as Christians believe, and exists eternally, wouldn't this direction lead away from it—for it is only necessary to "be still and know"? Or does the way in Keats' vale of Soul-making lead back to the original image, which is God's within us, though we obscure and deform it?

7 October
Cheltenham. Lunchtime reading with David Eggleton, "the mad Kiwi ranter", at the Axion Centre. David, from Auckland, is part Polynesian, a slender dark young man. He was diffident and nervous in conversation, but recited his long wordy fast moving satirical poems from memory, standing confidently in front of our small audience.

At 4, I gave my lecture on Hardy & J. C. Powys to a packed Town Hall. Shortly before—fool—I glanced at Martin Booth's malicious comments on my poetry in his critical book, but was able to suppress my feelings, together with the usual nerves, as I stood on the platform.

8 October
Alone in the Town Hall canteen in the afternoon, I got into conversation with a big, black-bearded, long-haired, rather shambling man. He asked me, very politely, about my interest in place and what relation it bore to my academic experience, and listened attentively to my answer. Then I asked him about himself. Initially, his account was deeply impressive and, even when I found it hard to follow, he gave it reasonably and calmly: he was a representative of both "Her Majesty the Queen" and Mr Cyrus Vance and was working for them under cover as an inspector in Cheltenham; he was "behind" the Festival, and he was a don and a priest, though not in Holy Orders, but a "go-between" (I think he meant with God) like the Archbishop of Canterbury; he was re-organising world education, and he assured me that what I had told him about the relation of my academic work to "place" would be taken into account. His role grew in importance and complexity as he talked, unfolding it between us with effortless seriousness and candour, and looking me steadily in the eyes. Eventually Alan Hancox appeared and found a pretext for detaching me from my companion. Shortly afterwards I gave my lecture on Jefferies, again to a full house.

After the lecture I drove Kim back to her home at Tackley, and shared a meal which Oli had prepared, enjoying it with the whole family.

9 October
Lay in bed hearing, at intervals, trains approaching and rushing past. Slept at last, but shallowly, because still mentally active after my lecturing and talking.

Got up and drew the curtains when I heard the household stirring, and looked out on rain soaked furrowed arable stretching away from the wall, autumnal rook caws, late gnats dancing over brown earth; from the other window, pollard willows lining a ditch through the hummocked green field, once the site of a medieval village. Then I remembered how, in the dark, we had driven through Bladon, past a sign to the Hanboroughs and past Wastie's garage, which was once my Wastie grandmother's country.

10 October
Winchester. Elizabeth Bewick was very encouraging about the 'Mosaic' poems. This was heartening after Robert Wells' initial cool response, but it may be that Elizabeth's involvement in the subject, together with her feeling for me, affects her judgement. I find it difficult to see the poems clearly.

Took Emily out for a meal in the evening, but when we came in we couldn't get on together. I had stupidly asked her whether she missed me, and she clammed up. It's worse than ridiculous for an adult to take an emotional tone with a child. I'm afraid the truth is that I'm rather jealous, because at present Roger has inevitably taken my place with her

§

> Some astronomers suggest that the universe started as an extremely thin gas, gradually contracted under the force of gravitation to a superdense mass, and then exploded. In other words, it began an eternity ago in the form of almost complete emptiness, went through a contracting stage to the "cosmic egg", exploded, and is going through an expanding stage back to an eternity of almost complete emptiness. We just happen to be living during the very temporary period (an instant in eternity) of the fullness of the universe.
> *Asimov's Guide to Science*

Dad, at eighteen, was a torchbearer at the burial of Lady Halifax. He carried a torch of flaming tar as she was borne to the vault. Afterwards pails of beer were brought for the bearers; it was so thick that a stick would stand up in it. This was at Hickleton near Doncaster.

There was also a boy called Piggy working on the estate. He was a great poacher, and he got the sack after Lord Halifax had walked into one of his snares and was tripped up. Lord Halifax owned Hickleton colliery. One night, during the First World War, striking miners got into the glasshouse on the estate and stripped it of grapes, cutting the vines.

13 October
From Horseshoe Bottom, smelling of pony droppings, fungi and pine needles in the morning, to the littered, dirt-stained pavements of Golders Green in the cold, bright flares of sunset.

Later, on a starlit night, I walked out to a quiet, clean, prosperous area, along Finchley Road and up Hoop Lane, past the Crematorium, which I first thought was a palace or at least a mansion, to the Meadway. There Carol Rumens and I were guests of honour at a party given by the Friends of Israel Educational Trust. As I arrived at the house, Kate & Lee, to my surprise and delight, drove up. I had invited them, but hadn't expected they would be able to come. Pat Adams from the Tate also came at my invitation. I enjoyed the party, and had a warm response to the brief account of my stay at Gezer, which John Levy unexpectedly asked me to give.

14 October

A beautiful autumn morning driving and walking with Lee. Along the Embankment, the river in Monet light, a faint, misty blue. New gold leaf shining on the face of a scaffolded Big Ben. Statues: Cromwell, Churchill's turned back, Epstein's Smuts, a dark, striding figure, with a gull perched on his head. Through the East End. Whitechapel. A new mosque, sweat shops. Jack the Ripper's hunting ground at Spitalfields (Brick Lane, Fournier Street). The Blind Beggar & the Krays' territory. Along the Mile End Road, past Queen Mary College, where Mother accompanied me when, years ago, I went for an interview. (I wonder how different things would have been if my A level results had been good enough for me to take up the conditional place I'd been offered. My friends who studied in London became Londoners.) To Bow, where we called at a wax factory to get some wax for Lee to use in his modelling.

Back via Waterloo to Winchester. Sunset filling downland fields with light, becoming concentrated in a red globe, disappearing and leaving a flaming afterglow and a sense of cold light dying on a vast sea, as I drove back.

15 October

To Lepe with Mother & Dad for lunch. High tide just on the turn. Sea and sky a soft blue-grey, the Island a darker blue outline, wooded and undulating. Dark-orange, wet shingle, pale grey shingle & sand, with hopping flies; a windrow of black-green wrack and a coarse red weed like mopheads. A clouded, muffled day, waves breaking gently with a rhythmical splash and shingly backwash, ships crossing silently at the entrance to Southampton Water or moving through the channel with a distant throb. To Dad who had painted here, "no colour today". "The sky touching the earth".

A drink with Jim at Lymington Community Centre in the evening. He is making us some beautiful goblets, fired red, from Barton blue "slipper".

§

Man stares at what the explosion of the atom bomb could bring with it. He does not see that the atom bomb and its explosion are the mere final emission of what has long since taken place, has already happened....

What is this helpless anxiety still waiting for, if the terrible has already happened?

The terrifying is unsettling; it places everything outside its own nature. What is it that unsettles and thus terrifies? It shows itself and hides itself in the *way* in which everything presences, namely, in the fact that despite all conquest of distances the nearness of things remains absent.

Martin Heidegger, 'The Thing'

18 October
Drove to Aberystwyth for the Academi conference. Arriving at Llanbadarn before Dave had come home from work, I walked in the churchyard. A still day, a little smoke oozing from chimneys into a smoke-grey sky, low over Pendinas. Yew berries on grave slabs. A jackdaw on the weathercock. So Teach Us To Number Our Days.

When Dave came back I had a cup of tea with him, then went to the buffet at Staff House, where I met Roland and Ned and Raymond Garlick and other old friends and acquaintances.

19 October
Slept in my old room, hearing a distant cock crowing in the early morning. It's strange that, after only a moment of strangeness, nothing is strange—as if I'd never been away, or as if my life in the place had been waiting for me to resume it.

Two good lectures in the morning, in Old College, where all the lectures were held, with the sea outside the window. Wynn Thomas on R. S. Thomas: the most penetrating analysis of R. S. I've heard or read. No doubt partly on account of the emphasis of my talk on "poetry of nearness", I was particularly struck by Wynn's observation that there's *no distance* in Wales, so that all Wales is exposed as a border country. Raymond Stephens then spoke on R. S. Thomas and Patrick Kavanagh, bringing out the attractive qualities of Kavanagh and his poetry.

Having arrived late at the forum in the afternoon I wished I hadn't gone at all, since it went boringly over ground that's familiar to me. Given the strength of the literature, it's a great pity that the need to analyse or agonize over the "Anglo-Welsh situation" should often overwhelm and even bury the literature.

20 October
Goats in the walled orchard at the back of Dave's garden, two white goats & one brown one, cropping the grass, reaching up to chew leaves on the apple trees. If nothing is strange, this is largely because so much is the same: the curtains, cracks in the plaster on the wall... And perhaps the odd thing is, I have retained the happiness, and even the misery seems to have become part of it.

Following my lecture, which was well received, and the final discussion I had lunch with Raymond & Beryl Stephens, sunlight falling bright and warm on their hillside garden. It was very good to see them again; they are among my kindest and best friends.

I spent the evening with Dave and we stayed up late. He is working hard, on Blaen Cwrt as well as in his practice as an architect. It was a good evening, reminding me of our best times together, and of his great charity and understanding, which always make me ashamed of anything small and mean in my mind.

21 October
Left Aberystwyth under a cloud-veil, the Rheidol valley filled with light. Fog on Plynlimmon, fog lightening or thickening during most of the journey, dense on the climb to Birdlip, then a sudden break into sunlight and falling leaves. Afterwards the fog came down again, shrouding Liddington, but in Winchester the sun was shining and the atmosphere mellow. Took Emily for supper at the Recreation Centre and played cricket with her in the park, sun setting red behind a thin film of bonfire smoke from a garden in Hyde. Then she went to club with her friends, and I felt good that she is really living there. All the difficulty over her in my mind dissolved and blew away, and I felt happy for her, as I was with her. Now I saw her, a child deep in her daily life, anxious to be with her friends and popular with them, and was content.

22/23 October
After a night of little sleep we got up in the dark and Tony drove me to Brockenhurst station. We sat in the waiting room by the fire and talked—but it isn't talk alone that brings people together; almost all that matters most in human relationships is indescribable. I couldn't say what I saw in my brother's face, the look as we sat there, and later as I saw him standing on the platform as my train drew out. It isn't possible to describe what is between people, in the "place" where we are at home with each other, where differences of opinion and even quarrels are reduced to nothing. It is seeing the other person, not self-love, because a face kindly reflects our own. But we see them *in* the relationship—that is the "place" in which we both are, looking at each other. The place a look can bring us back to, from confusion and misunderstanding, reminding us that we are only truly ourselves when we are there. It can't be described, not even the way a particular look can travel with us. The moments that reveal what we live by can't be described.

Later, in the train: blue, ghostly dawn; a tall, thin, dark, bespectacled young man going up to the city, standing in the carriage aisle clutching a copy of the *Financial Times*, veins standing out on his hands like branches of a tree, while I listened to an amiable elderly engineer telling me about his work and travels in the Far East and his houses and what they cost.

Much later, after getting a breath of air in a fresh breeze on deck, and watching Harwich and the gulls wheeling and diving in our wake drop away, and after sleeping in my cabin, towards the end of the long day, I was reading (in Maurice Nicoll's *Living Time*) about shadows of images in Plato's Cave, as the Nord-West express rolled smoothly through the night in Holland, and looking in the window through reflections of my face and of my companion in the carriage, a friendly middle-aged lady who was going to spend a holiday with her sister in Amersfoort, and at lights moving out of shape in the countryside under a clear, dark sky with a gibbous moon.

§

Think that you are not yet begotten, think that you are in the womb, that you are young, that you are old, that you are dead, that you are in the world beyond the grave, grasp all that in your thought at once, all lives and places.
Hermetica

§

The modern man (in so far as he is truly modern) is a radical individualist, who will not admit that he is not—as far as knowing truth is concerned—self-sufficient. Self-sufficiency is the core of modernism. The entire development of the modern mind is like the story of Robinson Crusoe; it is an attempt on the part of the single man to live his own independent life, to find truth by himself.
Emil Brunner, *The Word and the World*

If my experience has taught me one thing, over and over again, it is the complete insufficiency of the self.

3 November
So far I've barely glimpsed the surface of this city: reflections on canal water.
Last Sunday M. & I walked in the Sterrebos (Star Wood), a small park that was formerly part of the wood to the south of Groningen. Tall oaks, probably between 100 and 200 years old, and large beeches round a pond, a few families out for a walk in the sunlight. At the edge, facing the road, the big sculpture commemorating the Jews of Groningen killed during the Second World War. This consists of six bronze hands, twisted, tortured, open or partly clenched, all reaching skyward, standing in a row on concrete pedestals inside an open shelter made of concrete blocks, which contributes to the sombre, poignant effect. It is a powerful work, though unfinished. A seventh pedestal stands empty; the sculptor, Waskowsky, drank himself to death before he had made the seventh hand. He was about my age, and, according to M. who knew him and liked him, a quarrelsome, violently emotional man who got into a dispute with the civic authorities over the cost of the monument, which hastened his end.

On Friday morning I was the "subject" of Rudy's English class, reading them a few of my poems and stimulating them to ask questions. Several of the women were painters, and an older man, in his sixties, had in recent years—he was a retired carpenter—begun to write poems, mainly in the local dialect, Gronings, but also in standard Dutch, and a few—touchingly illiterate—in English.

When Rudy came in this morning to give me my Dutch lesson he told me that the man had been a soldier in the colonial war in Indonesia, When he returned to Groningen he was so upset by the killing he had done and seen that for a year and a half he walked in tears about the city. Starting to write restored his emotional balance. This, together with the classes, keeps his mind alive, and prevents him, in terms of a hard Dutch expression, merely taking up someone else's place.

In the Vismarkt this morning, a material world to look at, handle, and savour—as the market holders cut slices of cheese for buyers to taste and we finger vegetables and fruit. Brick pavements greasy with rain and fallen leaves round the stalls, the gilded spire of the A-kirk shining in sunlight above the dignified façade of the Korenbeurs—survivors of an older Groningen, the old city still in place among post-war concrete and glass. Among all the fishes with sightless eyes, eels in yellow plastic crates, still just alive, slowly moving their bodies against each other, coiling and uncoiling. I imagine a terrible gasping, and cannot bear it, thinking of a barely conscious, dull-flickering dream of the sea.

7 November

A morning walk in woods near Onnen, on the *Hondsrug*. Here the uneven ground of small sandy hills looks much wilder and higher and more dramatic than it really is, against the general flatness. But the oak & birch look ill-nourished, starvelings that have sprung up too close together, tall and thin but without bulk. They swayed gracefully in the strong wind, leaves like moths or sudden flocks of birds flying round us. We walked to a café at Appelbergen, with a small menagerie of goats and geese and other animals outside, and cats lying comfortably on the bar & tables inside, and a big shaggy dog that barked at us but soon made friends.

I have been reading Tom Nairn's *The Break up of Britain*, with its incisive diagnosis of the effects on native nationalisms—Welsh, Scottish, English—of the rise and fall of Empire and its contribution to the making of the British State. In the main, I accept his diagnosis, but in places it makes me obscurely uneasy. At the same time I've been immersed in post-war "historical" poems—Geoffrey Hill's sequences, *Briggflatts*, *City*, *Remains of Elmet*, and poems by David Jones and Tony Harrison—and thinking about the crisis of English national identity, in the light of these poems and of Nairn's book and Seamus Heaney's perception that contemporary English poets are "afflicted with a sense of history".

For all the differences between the poets, one thing they share is their difference from the historian. In certain respects, Nairn sees England clearly, and being an outside observer, as well as historian and political theorist, helps. He sees the confusions of English nationalism, and the sense of direction that "history from below"—the presence of the people in English history—could contribute. But the poets write, in different ways, from *feeling*, which, irrespective of whether they are mainly conservative or mainly socialist in outlook, roots them in the English experience. None of their Englands is as clear-cut as Nairn's, none (unless it is Harrison's) would reject so much, sloughing off "backward" traditions, cutting a new, "progressive" shape from the old, inert and encumbered material. They give "speaking pictures": the particular, not the general "truth of things", as Philip Sidney, confident in the universal, saw the difference between poetry and history. They give images of their troubled love.

Reading Nairn I find myself, again, defending mystery and a certain "darkness", and seeing the difference (which helped to disillusion me with the academic world) between the critical intellect and the poetic imagination as the difference between the observer who assumes that he is standing in the light, and the person who knows that he has to feel a way in the dark—more, that he is part of that dark. Yet I want to defend mystery without indulging a vague romanticism... Poets owe a great deal to historians and, in England since the war, the work of historians has been more important than all but the best poetry—thinking of E. P. Thompson's "epic", *The Making of the English Working Class*, I'm tempted to say more *poetic*...

9 November

To Nijmegen with M. on a bright, windy day, a whirlwind of plane leaves flying up from the pavement, and leaves in drifts against trees and fences in the city. We spent the day with Rachel Blau DuPlessis, her husband Bob, who is an economic historian, and their little daughter Kore. Small, dark-haired Kore is the centre of the household and there was gentle, touching comedy in the way that Rachel & Bob jumped to humour her every whim, and talked to her—as intellectuals, and especially intellectual Americans tend to talk to their children—with a mixture of adult reason and exaggerated, coaxing deference. We ate lunch with them and talked in their flat and while we walked in woods outside the town not far from the Rhine in the afternoon.

Rachel & I had got in touch as a result of our mutual interest in George Oppen, of whom she was a close friend in his later years. She told me that after he had returned from Mexico and was writing again, he deliberately sought out a number of young poets as his "audience", in order to test his poems against their responses and to enter into dialogue with them. Their words, as well as Mary Oppen's, are in his poetry. She told me a little about his final illness, too, which filled him with violent anger—an effect of the disease—but didn't result in physical violence, as it often does. Both she & Bob testified, as much in their tone as in what they said, to his great personal and moral presence and to their feeling for him. Rachel is a feminist and highly intellectual and both she & Bob are left-wing, possibly Marxist, and certainly owing a lot to Marxism. She is also, as poet, critic & teacher, passionately involved with poetry, and I found it very refreshing to talk with them about poetry & history, sharing enthusiasms and indignations, and giving and receiving recommendations. This is what I miss in being outside the academic world, though, much of the time, I missed it inside as well.

Just before we set out to drive back a fine double rainbow appeared against an inky sky on the other side of the city, bows drawn tenuously across tumultuous cloud at the apex, but bright against darkness, and with one foot on the red-tiled roof of a noble building. On the way back we crossed the great bridge over the river at Arnhem.

18 November

I am walking with Jim in a Dutch landscape, by a dyke & a waterway through flat fields. It is misty, and suddenly a tower appears through the mist in front of us. We walk up to it and examine it closely. The stone it is made of is white as bone, and has been cut in long slender strips, set upright in the ground and interlaced, forming a tall, rather narrow structure, which is hollow inside. The stone has been carved all over its surface, and the carvings are in the form of heads. Formally the effect is of a number of uprights or interlaced totem poles, but the overwhelming impression both of the carvings & the hollow tower as a whole is medieval. Shortly afterwards we are in a pub, where we are evidently visitors among a crowd of locals. The tower is the subject of conversation. The locals say that it is in the way and should be knocked down. We say that it's beautiful and argue that it should be left alone.

The scene stands out clearly from a longer dream which dissolved when I woke. Now, writing it down, associated images float into my mind: Sway Tower, Winchester, an ugly conversation between two workmen which Jim & I overheard years ago in a pub at Minstead… But if these were formative, it was the absolute reality of landscape, tower and argument that existed for me at the time.

20 November

My father's 84th birthday. A cold day. I wrote letters, worked on my lecture, went for a short cycle ride. Ice & leaves on ponds, a glitter of bright but cold sunlight. At night, the first snow in the north of the country. This morning it had turned to rain, leaving thin white veins in the brick streets & a scattered white on the garden, like spilt salt.

26 November

Stars scintillating in the cold last night as I walked with M. to the Anglistish Instituut, where I gave a lecture—'The Presence of the Past'—and a poetry reading to a fair-sized audience. I shall be glad to relax for a while now, before revising my talk as an essay.

Letter from Emily in the morning, with a lovely poem about a rabbit sitting on a hill in the dark, "the small body fading away in the black. I saw it running away from me. The ears alive and listening for a rustle, I saw it disappearing into the darkness."

"I saw the rabbit on the hill top. It wasn't a Dream, oh! no, not this time. It was a wonderful sight on the hill that night in the dark."

2 December

In the market: the pleasure of skill. A girl chats to a customer while her fingers expertly fill and tie a bag. A man slices a fish without pausing in his talk. Scales confirm measurements made more or less accurately by hand & eye. All the time, skilful movements accompany every conversation. These skills that are an integral part of things may be little noticed, but without them everything would be different, our common world without ease and pleasure, chaotic.

I think the contemporary English experience is more extreme than most poets realise. But this is only revealed, in poetry, by poets who write from a deep level of the self: not the everyday taken-for-granted ego, but the self seeking its ground in primary relationships.

When human communication continues only on the surface, and the need for a deep common purpose is frustrated, the mind becomes a cave haunted by shadows.

There's a great difference between poetry in which the self is concentrated in the writing, in the work's integrity (in George Oppen's Objectivism, in Mary Casey's poetry as prayer, in David Jones' "very things") and poetry that the poet uses to conceal or evade a groundless self. Geoffrey Hill may sometimes be ambivalent in this respect. His extraordinary sense of literary traditions and their evasive, idealising tendencies, and of the ambivalence of all language, makes it difficult to know where he stands, and what he stands by. Yet I feel that Hill, in his very elusiveness and difficulty, is more fully present, and present at a deeper level in his poetry than the many who say "I" easily or without much effort in their poems.

10 December

Headlines: the Reagan Administration uses Britain's agreement to participate in star wars research to demand more spending on it from Congress. Reduction in the higher education budget threatens to cut 18,000 student places in polytechnics & colleges in Britain. Obituary of Robert Graves, with Philip Larkin and Geoffrey Grigson, the third famous English poet to die within a week.

By train to Leeuwarden on a damp, grey day, water standing in fields, earth thrown up from freshly dug ditches. Farms surrounded by trees, islanded in broad green country intersected by dykes. The train stopped at small places like Grijpskerk in the middle of fields.

The work that has made it is evident in the land—there could be no landscape more human—yet, in general, perhaps because of the overall regularity of features, the past is not easily conjured from it, or doesn't start up, as it does in olive grove or vineyard or English hedgerow. In the farm buildings, though, it is present more than in the land.

Cees van de Meulen met me at the station at Leeuwarden and we walked to the school he teaches at, Rijksscholengemeenschap, which is where M. went to school for a year: a large, old building in the middle of town, but apparently not large enough—several classrooms are square wooden buildings in the form of houseboats floating in a row on the canal beside the school, which is soon to be moved to a new site. Cees, a cheerful, kindly red-faced man in late middle age, is married to a Scotswoman, who is Joe's maths teacher. He speaks fluent English with a strong Scots accent; in fact, when he first visited me to invite me to the school I thought he was a Scot.

When we got to the school almost the first thing I did, after being greeted civilly by the headmaster, was to get shut in the toilet! The outer door had a loose handle, and having closed it behind me I couldn't open it again. Fortunately, after a short time, Cees came and let me out. I then went into the canteen, where the chairs & tables had been arranged for my talk with about 80 pupils. Cees & other English teachers had been discussing some of my poems with them, and I found them quick to ask intelligent questions, and responsive and attentive. He walked back to the station with me afterwards, and we talked over a coffee, mainly about his holiday home at Oban. And he gave me a copy of his only published poem, a translation into Dutch of Belloc's 'Matilda'. All in all, it was a very enjoyable visit: touching in the warmth & courtesy I received, and encouraging in that I felt I really had communicated with the pupils & teachers. Of course, they had been well prepared. All the same, it was evidently a successful visit for them too.

Returning, the late afternoon sky was a washed, mild blue with flights of duck against it, and jet fighters. Looking out on fields & water, with the planes going over and my experience at the school fresh in my mind, I was struck by the absurd monstrous wickedness of the system pretending to defend them, the children, all of us—the system pretending it is devising ever more secure defences for the people, while in fact securing the continuation & growth of the military-industrial machine.

Perhaps there has never been shelter for man: the medieval powers built only in stone, wood and metal, the physical reach of their arm was limited, but for the least noticed peasant or the cunningest outlaw, there was no hiding place from the wrath of God. One main difference is that the god we have made seeks no one's soul, but threatens every being & every object with the same indifferent destruction..

18 December
At Hayford.

Grey, leafless woods in Wainsford valley. Grey, almost white, skeletal mare's-tails, like steeples broken in half, hanging down. Red hawthorn berries by black sloe, a wren chirring in brambly underwood. Whine of a motor-driven saw in the woods towards Efford.

The pool under and by the bridge has filled in, but below the bridge, under the great horse-chestnut tree, where it used to be shallow, the river is excavating a new pool. Gnat dance and water flow: life naked, visible in process and energy.

Crossing St Mark's churchyard the first gravestone I came on was that of Moses and Elizabeth Pressey. I remember the old man working at Turvilles' Nursery, or cycling back & forth, with a slow dragging sideways movement due to his bad foot, crippled when a load of coal fell on it. And the little old woman who long survived him, living in their cottage facing the Common, which I passed shortly afterwards.

Light yellow in late afternoon, half moon growing sharper, sky a clearer blue.

20 December

A walk from Hordle cliffs to Milford on the beach and back along the road.

Strong wind. Light rain-mist & spray, no visibility beyond Barton, the Island now veiled, now more distinct, then vanishing behind me. Sea grey, greeny grey off the Island, with a dark green buoy leaning against wind and waves. White waves beginning far out, intervals of grey water, waves diving on waves, breaking on the breakwaters' black wooden fences. Gulls, rooks and jackdaws held themselves precariously on the updraught at the cliff-edge, hovered, let themselves sail rapidly up, or dived with effort, wings stiffly held in. A rook trying to land was momentarily a tangle of wings and legs, like a glove being pulled inside out.

23 December

To Hurst Castle and back along the shingle-spit with Jim.

Bright light, a strong wind off the sea.

Hurst deserted except for two fishermen, probably father and son, who had put up a small tent in the shelter of the castle walls. Close to the entrance of the old part—Henry VIII's fort—a huge rusty cannon has been hauled out and stands pointing towards Keyhaven. On this side, landward, thin grass over a long-disused railway line—the short track to carry provisions & armaments from pier to fort—a pile of railway sleepers by the seawall, the lighthouse gleaming white alongside concrete shells of Second World War bunkers.

Seaward, fleshy sea-beet clinging to shingle, the Race surging where the shore ends, and redbrick Fort Albert facing on the Island across the water. High walls made of blocks of Cornish granite, with gunports bricked up between sheets of rusted iron, and barbed wire to deter climbers on the more accessible places: the brutal harmless face of an obsolete technology, Victorian, but holding Tudor memories, and memories of imprisoned king and priest. A massive weight bearing down on shingle, but holding firm only yards from the sea's edge, where black stumps of old defences are gradually disappearing under the new breakwaters.

Everything except the granite corrodes and wears away. The place is sterile, ugly, brutal, yet here the words name an austere elemental beauty.

It was dusk and quickly becoming dark when we turned back, the Needles' light glowing red like a cigar, the lights of Yarmouth clustered behind us and the lights of Bournemouth shining beyond the dim outline of Hengistbury Head.

My great-grandfather, James Wastie, of Church Hanborough, owned a huge pig which, when he was old and ill, became a great trial to his daughters who had both to look after him and feed it. The doctor had forbidden him to drink beer, which he was very partial to, and only when they bribed him with a glass of beer did he agree to sell the pig. When he was near the end, Dad's Aunt Kit asked him if he wanted to die. "Nobody do, do they."

Peter Levi tells me that Kit Wastie is still a living legend in Stonesfield, where she kept the school for many years.

A few stories—all that remains—little enough to know those lives & that world, yet I too came by that way, partly through them.

§

We are like the chrysalis asleep, and dreaming of its wings.
Samuel Palmer

Christmas Day
Drove my parents to Communion at St Mark's on a dark, wet morning, but did not attend myself. Later, as it got lighter, I went for a walk before breakfast, a southerly wind making clearings in rain-cloud. At Yondy Corner, calves standing forlorn at a gate, eyeing me curiously, brown curls matted on bony foreheads, hair plastered down on wet hides. A few gorse flowers—tiny yellow mouths—out on the waterlogged Common. A robin & one or two thrushes singing.

After breakfast we opened presents, and Dad & I drank brandy; he wept copiously at the tape of my Hardy/Powys lecture, which was the only tape we had to try out the radio-cum-tape recorder I'd bought them. David rang, and I spoke on the phone to Joe & Emily in Winchester.

Drove out alone through Burley to Vinney Ridge after lunch, and walked through young conifers into the great, ancient woods of birch, oak & beech, with a scattering of holly & a few yews. Sun through branches on the slope, marking also the chalk rim of the gravels, and the sea. Red-brown bracken & fallen leaves, vivid green star clusters of moss. None of the greater, and few of the lesser trees are without a maim, many of them more fearful than diseased or ivy-strangled limbs. A great oak stripped of bark, another split in two, resting forked branches on the ground, like a figure bowing. A recumbent, carved beech torso, as if the tree were giant effigy and bier. An enormous rotten beech stump, streaked black and green, fungoid, the touchwood interior riddled with beetle and crumbly as cheese, apparently long-dead, but with a living branch.

Boxing Day
From Puttles Bridge by Oberwater with Jim. River in flood, a turbulent current, brown as strong tea, and water making islands of trees.

Talked with him about being "at the edge" & the "thinness" of my experience, especially compared with some people of an older generation, and with my father above all; groundlessness, belonging & not belonging. He helped me to get things in perspective.

From the river we drove to Boldre church, which was locked. Walked round the church in the dusk, one flowering tree—a Japanese cherry—glimmering whitely among graves.

28 December
Much colder, the sky cloudless. Heavy frost on the open Forest. Driving into Southampton with Emily, approaching the traffic lights at the end of Tebourba Way, we saw what looked like silvery puffs of smoke in the sky. I took the first for an explosion, but, when it was repeated, saw it was a flock of doves wheeling, catching the light.

In Watts Park the statue of Isaac Watts looks newly whitewashed. From there we worked our way Below Bar, through crowds brought out by the sales, visited stores, and had lunch at George's.

In Holyrood, the shell of the bombed church which is a church of memorials, a tablet marking "the valuable and heroic service" of the Merchant Navy in the war over the Falkland Islands—which of course isn't called a war—has been placed on the wall opposite to the fountain commemorating the crew of the *Titanic*. For the first time I noticed the Charles Dibden memorial, weathered on the outer wall.

Driving out of town, a glimpse of the sun going down startled us—a red ball, sinking beyond the bows of a giant oil tanker and behind Solent Flour Mills.

Waking up cold in the night:
   Is poetry possible without a "people"?
   Clearly, most poetry now is written without one.
   What does that tell us about poetry and poets?
   Where do we go from here?

30 December/New Year's Eve
Dawn at Hayford: red sky & cockcrow. A hard frost, the garden pond frozen solid. Gull shrilling on a neighbouring chimneypot, the robin that gives Mother joy coming to the windowsill. Thistledown caught in apple tree twigs.

In the evening Joe & I met Jim in London and returned with him on the night-boat to Holland.

Snow on the ground at the Hoek, deep in the south but only a light dusting as we travelled north. Dawn purple and rose madder on snowfields.

At midnight we saw the New Year in with a party & fireworks.

6 January 1986
Snow has fallen, sometimes heavily, since the beginning of the year and children are out in the park sliding down man-made hills on sledges or being drawn by their parents, with the shopping, along pavements.

Jim left on Saturday, but we had several good walks in & round town and visited the Scheepvaartmuseum. This brings vividly to mind the days when the province was an important part of a great seagoing nation, exploring, trading, colonising, from the time of the Friesian fleet through the Hanseatic period to that of the East & West Indian Companies. It is full of old, handled things redolent of practical skills: not only models and parts of cogs and tjalks and schooners, but also pottery, coffers, compasses, turfs and other materials and instruments.

Some of these things still have echoes on canals among barges & houseboats in the city, but the immeasurably larger world they were part of is far from us, though it was *the* world until fairly recently. One painting shows a Dutch & an English man-of-war firing at each other broadside on, with men on their decks discharging their rifles against each other. It looks quaint, a piece of picturesque or fancy-dress history, though to those involved nothing could have been more serious.

Before Jim left, we went for a walk with Joe, who brought his camera. The sun was shining on the snow, which squeaked and creaked under our feet like a rope being strained taut, as Joe said. We walked by the canal, where some boats had small Christmas trees tied to their masts; in one place, free of ice, an Indonesian man was standing on the bank fishing in black water. Back through the Indonesian neighbourhood behind the Korreweg, at first by blocks of flats next to the canal which have symbolic figures—earth, sea, the town, etc—sculpted on their walls.

Twice we went to drink leffe, a delicious, dark brown Belgian beer from the barrel, in an old pub by the Korenbeurs. Here, an old pub is known as a "brown" pub, which couldn't be more appropriate in this case: a large sombre homely room, walls painted dark green and brown, with a painting depicting old ships with dark red canvas sails in a haven, a ceiling the colour of nicotine, billiard tables at one end, and a spacious arrangement of chairs & large & small tables, with carpets on them. All looked smoke-stained, but also as though the smoke were time, which has burned there slowly for centuries. It was here that Jim mentioned the "wildness" of God—like a child, like a tiger—which made me think of Blake, but for some reason he didn't elaborate and we talked about something else, leaving the idea to echo in my mind. He also said that the devil is a moralist, which I think I understand.

13 January

> What is the price of Experience? Do men buy it for a song?
> Or wisdom for a dance in the street? No, it is bought with the price
> Of all that a man hath, his house, his wife, his children.

> Wisdom is sold in the desolate market where none come to buy,
> And in the wither'd field, where the farmer plows for bread in vain.
> William Blake

I need this, as I need to break the despairing picture which I made for M. the other evening: the thinness of experience I have to draw on, the baselessness under me, the intellectual isolation, the feeling that, because of my strong attachment to my parents, I've somehow failed to live my own life, the critical intelligence, developed at the expense of my poetry, which shows me what I "represent"—life without substance, because not rooted in anything greater than the self, a mind given to books & nature, but not belonging to any living community or movement, always at the edge.

Even as I made the picture I knew that it wasn't the whole truth—so my despair wasn't complete; there was, as usual, some indulgence. Yet I had to make it stark and clear.

Reading Blake again quickens and strengthens me, as it always has: his fear & trembling, his "Annihilate the Selfhood in me: be thou all my life!", the imaginative boldness, the wisdom and excitement of *The Marriage of Heaven and Hell*, the mind ranging the height and depth and breadth of Albion in *Jerusalem*, and grounding the vision in actual English places and contemporary conditions—as I itch to open myself in Thatcher's Britain, instead of letting myself be driven to the edge. And perhaps what I see negatively is my spectre: a creation of the critical mind from all the fears and anxieties, defeatism and self-pity, self-imposed limits, the emotional prison that is the obverse of loyalty & love. And perhaps if I could see myself in Blake's terms I could cease to feel myself trapped in an individual predicament, whose very specialness makes it hopeless, as though I alone were condemned to a unique fate.

> All things acted on Earth are seen in the bright Sculptures of
> Los' Halls, & every Age renews its powers from these Works
> With every pathetic story possible to happen from Hate or
> Wayward Love; & every sorrow & distress is carved here,
> Every Affinity of Parents, Marriages & Friendships are here
> In all their various combinations wrought with wondrous Art,
> All that can happen to Man in his pilgrimage of seventy years.

For, surely, it is only the Selfhood that can feel, in its blindness & pride, that things can happen to it that do not happen to Man; indeed, that it is not an *actor*, but an originator, unique in a way that no one is. I think I must have blindly nurtured some such image of myself, which is the sculpture or petrifaction blocking me. Thus I recount my experiences, as son or former husband or once unhappy lover, as anxious father, as emotionally divided academic or ex-academic, as isolated writer, or as "exile", etc, as if they weren't "stories", sculptures of Los' Halls, but utterly peculiar to me, private possessions, and therefore inhuman.

One thing I have understood from my very spectre and must not lose sight of is that for us loss of contact with each other, through *suppression* of the social sense, takes the place of suppression of liberty in Blake's time. The difference from his time is that we live at a later stage of the same historical process he knew then.

Mid-January
Attended a two day conference celebrating the centenary of English Studies at Groningen, which was well attended by lecturers from all the English departments in the Netherlands, together with a few from outside. Here I met Richard Hoggart and sat at table with him and his wife during the special dinner. This was the more interesting in that he was among the handful of working-class academics whose work in the fifties had a strong influence on the attitudes of my generation in universities, and while I am thinking mainly of *The Uses of Literacy*, his book on Auden (which he proudly told me was the *first* book on Auden) also had, for me, a special significance. Now, he has recently retired as Principal of Goldsmith's College, a job which he took up after a period as Assistant General Secretary at UNESCO in Paris, and he and his wife have a comfortable house at Farnham, where he entertains what is evidently a large circle of family and friends.

What mainly struck me about Richard Hoggart was his warmth and friendliness. He is probably more used to talking than to listening, and he told many good stories arising from his experience as an academic, at UNESCO, and as a defendant at the *Lady Chatterley* trial. As he talked, he frequently touched the person he was talking to, and sitting between me and Angie Fry, he would often take the arm of the one he was addressing.

I felt that I was with a confident, successful, friendly man, one who knew how to get what he wanted from other people, and how to avoid being manipulated. I was also struck by his amiable egotism: all the famous people he has known, what they said to him, what he said to them, all the stories he told which reflected his own qualities, or reflected badly on those who had opposed him and, in his early days, tried to exclude a talented young working-class academic from the corridors of power.

The voice, a little like my father's, was that of an educated north countryman who has spent a lot of time in southern England. But he is much more sophisticated and more worldly than my father, as was shown by his account of his chairmanship of a committee examining pornographic video films. In speaking of this, though, he protested his "innocence", even his original ignorance, since he had to ask someone else what homosexuals actually "do" to each other! The exclamation mark was his, but I felt he was telling the truth.

31 January
Two images from recent days: There is a cut near here, between a high brick wall and a laboratory in which men & women in white coats can be seen sitting or standing between shelves covered with glass bottles and other chemical apparatus

and pouring some liquid into similar vessels. Among the graffiti staring at them from the wall one stands out, written boldly in chalk:

> THIS TOWN IS
> NO FUN
> AND NEITHER ARE YOU

A short distance from here along the Korreweg one of the uncurtained windows shows at night an old lady sitting in the middle of a room neatly arranged in typical Dutch fashion, with old, mellow-polished furniture. On the wall beside her hangs a reproduction of Vermeer's painting of a woman—a maid—pouring milk from a jug.

4 February
More snow on Sunday. As we drove to Emmen in the afternoon, the snow was like flour scattered on fields & evergreens. The pavements are *spiegelglad*—mirror-slippery. Going out late this afternoon after a day's writing—I began work on the book of essays yesterday—the bright cloudless sky took me by surprise. It was made higher, vaster and clearer by several jets drawing their white comet-tails high up across it, like a few tiny silver fish alone in a big lake of clear, blue water.

14 February
With M. by car to Den Haag. First, we went to the museum to see the School of Barbizon exhibition.

I was attracted by paintings by Corot and Daubigny, and by a painting of trees by Theodore Rousseau, but was held by Millet, especially by his painting of a mother feeding her child. In a way, this repelled me—the big child with knees exposed on the mother's lap, red-faced like the mother, and with open mouth, the mother holding a spoonful of pap in front of her face and blowing on it. It was ugly, the mouth of the feeding child, stickily open, the coarse clothes and plain features; yet not ugly. The ugliness was in the eye of the beholder, looking for idealised expressions, perhaps expecting them all the more because this is a kind of Madonna and Child, not a parody, but realistic, a painting of poverty, hardship, coarseness, and care. I remembered Van Gogh's ambition to paint people with the equivalent of a halo, but Millet was more down to earth, with a harder truthfulness, perhaps without the idea of "peasant" that Van Gogh brought to *his* realism.

Among the sepia photographs of Barbizon and the painters was a full-length portrait of Millet, a heavily built man with a big beard and a big belly: the farmer's son who painted the people he came from. There were also photographs, one above the other, of Millet's and Van Gogh's *The Diggers*, Millet's people having their feet firmly on the ground, Van Gogh's being figures of firestorm and whirlwind, the earth swirling around them.

After grey skies and the dark greens of rock colours it was a shock & a delight to stand in front of Van Gogh's *Garden at Arles*. Then we looked at the Mondrians, especially some lovely landscapes, a "windmill" (he saw the extraordinary life of those being-things) and trees (the subliminal crown of thorns).

Later we walked by the North Sea, sun going down round and red and the wind bitterly cold.

Stayed the night in Den Haag with M's friends Valentine & Hans, who have a new baby and two small boys. Seeing the children & the children's things brought back the time when my children were little, and I felt wretched and remorseful.

Before Valentine & Hans rented the house, a mother separated from her husband had lived there with *her* two small children. Then, one day when the children were out with the husband, she hanged herself in the room we were sitting in. But here were no "bad" feelings, for Hans & Valentine—the place was completely filled with their family life.

The next morning Valentine showed us round the city centre. Bright day, with a bitterly cold, Russian wind. We walked up and down the Lange Voorhout, past embassies & palaces, then through the parliament courtyard, past the iced-over moat, with coots diving in one corner where the ice had been broken. All the buildings dignified, prosperous, historical, the town quiet, a place of government, diplomacy, administration, without the commercial thrust and untidy vitality of Rotterdam or Amsterdam. Several greened, bronze equestrian statues—at least two of Willem 1—and something of the feeling of London's more decorous and well-to-do squares; the same spaciousness, the same light.

To Amsterdam in the afternoon, where we met Johan and went with him to the cinema to see *Chorus Line*, afterwards walking through the busy, brightly lit streets, under coloured advertisements (and an electrically illuminated cross, high up over the rooftops, tilted on its side in the dark), past a small open-air skating rink where a few people were skating.

Next morning, after spending the night at Beverwijk, we visited the Turkish market and sat out of the cold at a café table, eating delicious shoarma and shish kebab and enjoying the oriental atmosphere created in the huge market hall, in what is otherwise a functional commercial area outside a dull north European town. Then we drove back via the Afsluitdijk, seeing groups of skaters on almost every canal or lake, and on the edge of the IJsselmeer, too. It was a little like glimpsing Averkamps: it isn't possible to escape from paintings in this country, even supposing one wants to. What I'm much less sure of is what lies under the surface: what the deep places of the Netherlands are—though of course they too are no doubt revealed by the great painters. I feel that the "poetry" which discloses spirit is visual in this country, whereas we learn most about the English through careful attention to their words.

15 February
I read in *The Guardian* today that John Tripp died on Sunday. He was a difficult, necessary man. Once or twice he gave me support when I badly needed it. He

could be very funny—when I last saw him, at Aberystwyth in October, his reading made me cry with laughter. For all his anger & bitterness, I knew he wasn't hard; indeed, I found him soft, sentimental, warm, with a not very convincing cynical exterior. The true man is in the poem about David Jones which he dedicated to me, and in other poems about those he admired: soldiers of goodness and truth.

2 March
At last, a warmer day, bright and still. Dogs and geese and people on ice in the park, and one heron standing up among other waterbirds clustered round a man throwing them bread. It looked too stiff and slow to get any food and may have been starving. Sticky buds on chestnuts, aconite leaves above ground, blue tits active in the trees.

3 March
Dawn start for England. Half moon in clear sky and a thrush singing from somewhere on the other side of the Korreweg. Red-tinged ice with gulls on it. As the train left Groningen the sun rose, at first appearing slightly flattened and elongated, like a red Chinese lantern. I write this on the *Beatrix*, by a window of the observation lounge, the sea calm and sun shining through light mist. It is late afternoon and we are an hour or two from Harwich. On deck the breeze is refreshing and not cold. Inside, the boat is a small, shabby microcosm of the larger society, with regular announcements of the films showing at the cinema, bars, a casino, a duty-free shop, and generally half-hearted attempts to entertain the people and take our money. Almost nothing except money-making devices to represent either England or the Netherlands, and therefore little sense of crossing between two countries. The choice is between guilders and pounds sterling: that's all. I'm tired, bored and crabby, but have been content to read or look out at the frozen countryside or sea all day.

5 March
To Hayford after a wet day in Winchester with Emily, shopping for her birthday present and going to the cinema in the evening. On Winchester station, a few people standing or sitting apart or walking up and down, not talking: all of us *strangers* to each other. Are any other people on earth such strangers?

6 March
A long talk in the car and a short walk on Milford beach with Mother on a fine, fresh day. She tells me that Dad is very difficult now and she sometimes wonders whether her strength will hold out. She tells me, then laughs acceptingly. There's nothing to be done except listen and talk and take her out when I can: he's completely dependent on her and now, as always, the slightest criticism of him would be turned into a greater burden for her. In some ways he is so wise, yet in this, the most important thing of all, selfishness prevents him from understanding anything.

7 March
I'm at Waterwynch House Hotel near Tenby, waiting for Anne Stevenson and our "students" to arrive for a creative writing weekend. Outside my window, waves are breaking gently on a small stony private beach and I can see, through a gap between low cliffs, a dim outline of the Gower coast in evening light, across Carmarthen Bay. When I set out to drive here this morning the top of Salisbury Cathedral spire was hidden in mist. Later, a dark-bright day, clefts of snow on the Black Mountains, with great clouds rearing up behind them, as I used to see cloud rising on Mynydd Bach and rolling inland along the ridge in broken masses, opening the day with downpours of light, then closing it up in a cave of shadow. The trees are still leafless, of course, and the country spacious between their bare branches, but somehow they're no longer winter-stark. Life is springing in them though it is invisible yet.

12 March
The days have been so full since the weekend at Tenby that it already seems a long time ago, but it was a successful and most enjoyable weekend. Anne was fighting off the onset of 'flu but still took her part fully, and the "students" were a pleasure to be with.

I had little chance to get out except for an early morning walk on the beach and a walk through the woods, where the first daffodils were out, and onto the cliff edge, where I watched fulmars planeing up and down over the sea. And the only chance I had of speaking to Anne alone was at the very last, when we walked on the beach and I asked for her support in the event of my finding myself without a publisher for 'Master of the Leaping Figures'. She kindly agreed to help.

On Sunday afternoon I drove to Aberystwyth where I stayed with Ned, who is now living at Llandre. We had long talks on Sunday night and again on Monday, and on Monday morning I saw several former colleagues in the English department.

Parking outside my old room opposite the pier: the great grey face of the United Theological College—there were times when, walking from "Strathmore", ascending the prom to this building left me breathless with panic—a yellow notice in an upper window: The Wages/of sin is/DEATH/but the gift/of God is/ETERNAL LIFE. Sea leaping in spray against the seawalls, a distant cry of gulls. Outside Old College the two familiar statues, both black with green streaks: Thomas Charles Edwards, holding an open book in his right hand and holding his left arm extended with finger pointing down—the very image of the pedagogue as preacher; the old Prince of Wales, arms folded high across his chest, with a self-conscious smile on his slightly turned face—indeed, his head sits a little awkwardly on his neck, as it well might, since it has been removed by dissidents but found again and restored on more than one occasion.

Tuesday: to Swansea, where I gave a seminar on David Jones for Wynn Thomas in the afternoon. Afterwards he drove me round the city, up the steep streets, including Cwmdonkin Drive and we had a drink and a snack together before my reading in the evening. Back with Wynn to his home near Gorseinon. He is an exceptionally kind, intelligent and sensitive man. I thought so when we first met in Swansea in 1974, but this was the first occasion when we have had time for long talks. In the morning before setting out early for Lampeter I met his attractive wife, Karen, and their little daughter, Elin.

14 March
Left Lampeter yesterday morning, rooks cawing in their nests in trees beside the Canterbury building. A warm, growing day with mist-veiled sunlight that darkened, cleared. Driving down narrow lanes, through Nebo, with sheep in fields behind bare hedges and the ridge of Mynydd Bach to the right, my heart ached. The moment of intense feeling, of love or loss, the moments in which we are most conscious of people and places; the moments we most want to hold, but can't, when we feel what it is not to be able to live for ever, or keep for ever those we love: then we can only be thankful, the only response is gratitude. There is nothing that will keep the time, and trying to hold it will sour and distort it, will press us in *our* feelings of regret, *our* pain, instead of letting the time be and the others exist with us in it. But the time is somehow "kept" in the only way possible—its unique being is allowed to be—if let go with an open heart, in gratitude. I think I can understand in these terms what Gerard meant by saying that he could see Mary only in God.

Buzzards & crows circling the valley & rocky mountainsides by Cadair Idris. Sun shining on the mountains of slates at Blaenau Ffestiniog and at Bettws y Coed, where I stopped for lunch, and walked in warm sunlight and a fresh breeze. Then on to the North Wales coast, and down from the mountains to the world of caravans & arcades & pleasure palaces on the coast between Rhyl and Prestatyn, but also with thoughts of Emyr Humphreys' great novel, *Outside the House of Baal*.

Here, in Prestatyn, I'm staying with John Davies & Marilyn & their small daughter Ceri. I will always think of John as my "first" student, because he was indeed one of the first, and the one I knew best then, when we discussed our poems together & in a small group, sometimes including Jim Nosworthy & Jeff Wainwright, in a back bar of the Cambrian Hotel, and a little later when he was working on Alun Lewis. He has published several books of poems since those days, and while he once wrote essays for me, I shall shortly be writing an essay on younger Anglo-Welsh poets, which will be partly about him. John has also been twice in America—last night he talked enthusiastically about Richard Hugo's poems—and he has learnt to make wood carvings, mostly of birds, which are very fine. He is still one of the funniest & most perceptive storytellers I've ever met.

My route through the country in these past days has been like passing from link to link of a chain of friendships, and even the friends I haven't met, or those who are dead, have been links in the chain, either because I've remembered them, or because someone else has spoken of them. And now I recall feeling that Wales—

Mynydd Bach and the physical landforms—was completely other, and that, in contrast to the south of England, it shut me out by being everything that I'm not. It didn't shut me out from an easy identification, which I never wanted, but in the sense that it made me define my difference. And of course I defined that largely by my being from the south of England. Yet the truth is that in Wales I found my spiritual home as a poet as I have found it nowhere else.

But I mustn't cultivate a "timeless" image of Wales. As both John & Ned have said, things have been very different here since the Devolution debacle of 1979. It seems that there are several poets who have, since then, lost all sense of direction and are unable to write in the altered circumstances. At the same time, there are other, mostly younger poets, those who are more *socially* than culturally conscious, like John himself, who are able to respond to the terrible deprivation of their people, to the wasting of Thatcherism and failing industry, to that nakedness under the acid rain that Gwyn Alf Williams speaks about movingly at the end of his history of Wales. And I feel close to even the rawest of these, but nothing but contempt for the "ludic" boys & girls who are currently fashionable in England. Interestingly, John feels strongly the need to write poems that his mother and his neighbours would understand—rather as Wilfred Owen didn't want to write anything to which his men would say "non compris"—although he well understands the difficulties and the limitations of this.

Evening John drove me to Buckley where I gave a talk on some contemporary British poets (Larkin, Bunting, Hill) at the library. We arrived to find three or four people in a large room with chairs arranged neatly in rows. One of these was the mayor, a pleasant, dapper, dark-haired young man with a distinctive Merseyside accent; he was wearing his glittering chains of office and had been invited to introduce me. In the event, though I was made welcome, there wasn't much introduction, because the intense, anxious young lady representing the library introduced the mayor, and the mayor introduced us to Buckley! By this time more people had arrived, including my former student, Glenda Beagan, who brought me one of her new poems, and I was relieved for the organisers' sakes—especially for the nervous young lady—that there was a fair-sized audience and the talk was a success. Afterwards a mother and her teenage daughter came up to me—the daughter who is studying Larkin at school had persuaded her mother to come—and told me with unaffected enthusiasm how much they had enjoyed the talk. This is the kind of thing that makes it really worthwhile to put in the effort.

15 March
The end of my week in Wales and the long drive back: Prestatyn, Llangollen by the Horseshoe Pass, Shrewsbury, and back on the familiar road through Hereford and the Cotswolds and Wiltshire. Stopped for lunch in a pub in Dymock. Two countrymen who had worked together on the same farm 40 years ago and had only met again recently were reminiscing, warmly naming people & places and sharing what they knew of the people's histories. One knew the girl serving at

the bar as the daughter of an old neighbour and they both turned to her with enthusiastic questions.

After lunch I stepped into the sandstone church—Anglo-Saxon & Norman but much restored—beside the pub. Utter silence. An item of the Table of Benediction to the Poor of the Parish caught my eye: "Thomas Murrel gave for ever to ten Poor Widows of this Parish of Sober Conversation the Interest of ten pounds". I wonder precisely when the time began that well-to-do people could assume that what they gave was "for ever", and when it ended.

Information about "the Dymock poets" was available in the church. They too seemed to belong to a far-off world although the fields outside would be much the same as when they walked there, with the same red earth on their boots. The fact that I'm at present rereading Edward Thomas' pre-war prose, in which he affects an unreal timelessness, no doubt helped to produce this impression. There were snowdrops under trees in the graveyard and beside the wall, near an oak planted by children of the parish to commemorate the Coronation of George VI.

It was a grey day during much of the journey, but as I entered the Forest at Bramshaw the sun broke out and shone against a bank of dark blue cloud. Blue sky over the coast, Sway Tower & the Island downs standing out as I came over the ridge at Marlpit Oak and saw what I instinctively think of as "my patch".

16 March
A walk in the morning with Jim from Saltgrass Lane along the shingle bank to the White House and the Marine Café at Milford. Mist concealed the Island and the Needles' foghorn sounded repeatedly. (I could hear it distantly from inside the house before setting out.) Sun gleam on the stream flowing from Sturt Pond at low tide and on the breaking waves. Orange wave marks on shingle. Jim talked about Rose Windows, which he uses as a kind of mandala, and about the symbolism of the rosary he has made. He has recently had news of his son Christopher who is at Arnewood School; he has heard that he plays the violin well and sculpts with enthusiasm.

It was a lovely morning, fresh and warm and salt. Turning out of Fullerton Road after I'd left him, I suddenly felt, my God, how real everything is! It was the sense I had in Wales, which suddenly gathered to a head and broke into consciousness: at once a sense of people and of the substance of our world, of things and the ground under our feet. And at that moment I passed the cemetery: which made no difference although by then I was making distinctions, thinking that not *all* things are equally real. It's the things between us, the world known in love & friendship, in which we know our lives and gather up the self in the substance of the world.

I took the feeling with me to Winchester in the afternoon, when I walked with Emily (who skated on her rollerboots) by the clear, grey bourne to Abbots Barton and went to see her swim at the Recreation Centre in the evening.

17 March
Morning in the Winchester bookshops, where I got a copy of *Dawn in Britain*. Celandines under low hollies in St Bartholomew's churchyard, a dandelion at the base of the wall of the King Alfred, crocuses on the banks of the bourne and by walls remaining from the monastery. Lunch with Elizabeth. A brimstone & a pair of tortoiseshells in her garden. After lunch she drove me—dangerously—to Stockbridge Down where we walked in warm sunshine under tall, slow moving, white and grey, chalkland clouds in blue sky. A sound of distant gunfire from Salisbury Plain. Tractors harrowing finely-turned fields. No blackthorn flowers, but the stones of last year's sloes, which the birds have eaten, hanging like white buds on the branches.

18 March
On the *St Nicholas* just out of Harwich, with a tiny sun gleaming on grey water and glittering on low waves through fog. It was misty when I set out early this morning—by taxi to the station, with a bag heavy with books—and on the chalk ploughland with beech trees and brown fields turning finely green, on all the rich land north of Winchester, and in London and the east.

I feel we *know* people in what we share with them, and neither as isolated selves or as selves with which we identify. Perhaps at the greatest depth we know them *in* God. Or as Martin Buber says, what we know is *between* us. Thus, trying to disclose one's inmost self by talking about it, or to understand another by listening to his or her self-analysis, produces far less real knowledge than if one meets on a ground in which both are passionately involved, or goes for a walk and shares the place and the day.

23 March
My 45th birthday. Read I. B. Singer's *The Penitent*: a strong, clear book, but over simple in the author's relation to his character's moral bullying and evasions. Tony rang in the morning and Emily in the afternoon. Cycled to the station with Joe for the Sunday papers and a cup of coffee and had a short walk in the park with M. A windy day, with masses of high white cloud driven across blue sky. Yellow aconites out in the park, and crocuses and snowdrops, later than in Britain. Friends came in in the afternoon and we stayed up late drinking and talking; my most enjoyable birthday for years.

After my reading in Aberystwyth Laurel Brake said that my talk about "reality" had disturbed her, because, in contrast to modern ideas about the way in which our minds construct "reality", I seemed to be invoking belief in authority. At the time, I denied that this had anything to do with authoritarian politics, and said that I was aware of the modern ideas, and sceptical of them. Ned then drew me out on the religious implications, with which I think he sympathises. I might also have said that I couldn't live with the belief that we—mankind—construct all meaning, and therefore without awe at a power and an order greater than ourselves. I've always *felt* reality to be other than a human construct, though I've come in recent years to be aware of history and society as enormously important shaping forces.

While away, I saw this too: that while I don't think I've made poetry my religion—unless as an idol representing my purpose in life—I *have* replaced religious observance with poetic observance. One of my tasks now is to think out the relations—legitimate and illegitimate—between poetry and religion.

I well understand the desire of Singer's hero to return to the tradition of his parents and grandparents. Only in my case it would be hard to say exactly what the tradition was, and harder to locate its continuation into the present. The connection with the land has gone irrevocably. The connection with the church was more tenuous, and despite my emotional attachment to the Church of England, I don't feel at home there. There have been few occasions when I've felt of any large group: *these* are my people. If I were either Welsh or Jewish, as I felt in Wales and at Gezer, it would be different. But not, I think, so different that I would become a fundamentalist who identifies corruption with the world outside my group, as Singer's Joseph Shapiro effectively does, in spite of his recognition that evil exists in his sect too. Ultimately, he can't draw me to an equivalent penitence, strongly as I feel the need of it. It is rather the real Jew, Charles Reznikoff, with his feeling of exile yet also with a tender regard for the people & things of the streets in which he finds himself, who moves me to recognise my needs. It is he, and it is my Welsh friends too.

Easter
It is easy to see the limitations of others' ways of thinking and seeing; far harder to see one's own. Thus, in seeing Edward Thomas, in *In Pursuit of Spring*, cycling through the south country recording natural observations and impressions, in 1913, picking up practically no sign of the forces in his world that would soon violently and horrifically transform it, so that anyone looking back now sees the massive iron structures of imperial powers about to collide, sees them shadowing the green roads and villages he cycles through; in seeing this, I saw also the history—the idea of history—which bounds my vision of place and wondered what it excludes, what I am blind to.

Perhaps it is the violence and horror, which Thomas couldn't see then, that, for some of us, makes the words of Christ live, as for many they did not, during that long and seemingly endless peace before August 1914.

Waking up this morning, I realised that mine is a poetry of broken connections: that I have written so far in the gap between my ancestors' and parents' attachment to the land, which defined their sense of belonging in terms of place and temporal continuity, and the life without this attachment, but with feelings shaped by it. At least, some of my poetry has been about this, either directly or indirectly, and sometimes unconsciously. Or, to put it another way, the broken connections have determined my choice of ground.

Easter Sunday
M. a lot better after flu. Drove her to the dyke near Eemshaven—a tanker & cranes standing in apparent isolation at the edge of land. Warm sun, cold wind, cloud shadows racing us on the roads, and racing darkly on pale, brown-grey mud, on water and rows of posts exposed at low tide. We walked by the water crunching shells underfoot, disturbing a flock of hundreds of oystercatchers, their white parts bright as white ships far out on the sea near Borkum. Only a few people out on the dyke; a solitary motorcyclist scrambling on a rough track between tyres on the landward side.

From Eemshaven we drove behind the dyke on narrow roads, sometimes hardly wider than the car, between a canal and a ditch with vast flat ploughed fields running away far inland, with a windmill or a spire on the horizon, and a few farm houses & barns shaped like small, man-made hills islanded on the land. A "Saxon" country, as the place names and churches show, and somehow, by association, the small red brick and red tiled villages have a Saxon look. Certainly the settlements were originally Saxon.

Eventually we came to Noordpolderzijl: a sluice, a handful of red brick houses including an inn on the landward side of the dyke, surrounded by a great flat sea of sodden ploughland intersected by canals and ditches. On the other side of the dyke a long narrow harbour has been cut into mudland. Here a dozen fishing boats—some of them old, wooden boats—were moored in olive green water to the seawall. Cold and refreshed, we sat in the inn crowded with cheerful families & couples and drank beerenburg before driving back through the Saxon villages and landscape to Groningen.

2 April
Today in the Rijksmuseum, Amsterdam, looking first at 15th & 16th century paintings:

> The intense concentration on event in the Christian story, in canvases peopled with medieval figures; but never merely costume-drama: *this* truth—on *Calvarieberg* or in the stable—is the truth of all time, not an historical subject. "We" now are there.
>
> The nakedness of the Christ-child; his ugliness, like a little pig or a miniature adult. They did not see babies or children.
>
> Portraits: faces possessing a world, rings on fingers, hands resting on skulls—death and judgement circumscribe their world—these are not the burgher faces of Rembrandt and his contemporaries.
>
> Geertgen tot Sint Jans (1460/65—1490/95), his *boom van Jesse*: tree springing from Jesse's richly cloaked loins, above him, all in the richest, most beautiful medieval clothes, David with harp, exotic figures among

the leaves, Mary & Jesus at the top, an angel on either side. There is a peacock, and—most noticeable—several of the young men wear bright-coloured, striped stockings. It was all a vivid, intricately patterned design, an extraordinary work of medieval abstraction—yet in my (admittedly limited) art books there's no mention of it, and no reproduction in the museum.

In these rooms I frequently found myself smiling and even laughing with delight at masterwork, and also, sometimes, laughing with amusement at gaudy medieval *kitsch*.

The material vision is never *only* material. Surely there is more of the Netherlands in these rooms than there is of any other country in its national gallery.

Stupid to leave no time for Rembrandt! But already we had looked at too much. It would be worth a visit to the Rijksmuseum just to look at the hands of Rembrandt's mother in his painting of her.

Afterwards M. & I walked back to the centre—crossing canals smelling faintly of the sea—where we met Elin & her friend Linda by the war memorial. Rush hour; a trumpeter playing across the street, his music sounding over the noise of traffic; grey-blue pigeons almost the same colour as the *kejen* (paving stone mosaics) they were picking over. The girls hadn't been waiting long, but had already been offered heroin & cocaine. (Almost the first thing we saw on leaving the station was two guards persuading a young man not to lie down on a tram line.) Then we visited the great store, *De Bijenkorf*, and walked footsore about its apartments.

Evening on the train: cloud shadows & shadows of bare trees sharp in water beside the track, beams from the sun's gold disk flying across puddles and ponds, canals and ditches. I realised that in moments of such clarity we may have the illusion of seeing things as they really are, but the clear-cut image or luminous detail is not true to the thing itself. For life both fills the thing from within and connects it to the world surrounding it. The moment of perfect clarity may symbolise a spiritual state or a state of mind, but as a perception of the world it is a strictly limited visual impression born of a particular way of seeing in a particular quality of light. Therefore (I now realise) the "pure" or clear-cut visual image reveals the seer and the relation he desires to have with the world, but does not necessarily reveal anything of significance about the world.

23 April

Remember the days of old, consider the years of many generations;
ask thy father and he will shew thee; thy elders, and they will tell thee.

I find these words, in which the past speaks to me, strangely comforting; at the same time I don't know how those who lived in the continuity of generations can help us now. People in the past have known great terrors; but was there ever an equivalent feeling of being exposed *at the edge of time*? We look back at those who believed the world would end, and to us they seem deep in time, folded in what we call the Middle Ages. Perhaps we will be looked at in a similar way, by people to whom "modern" means a past age, as "modernist" to describe the arts already does. Yet it is impossible to see from here how people will get back into the stream of the generations and lose the taste of the separated self, and the sense of oneness with others only in the common terror suspended over all.

I have been thinking along the line of Heidegger's idea of the abolition of nearness: if man once put God to death then the worst has happened. And it seems a thought I've no right to, because made only of words. It is not a conviction demanding all I have, but a refuge from present fear: the worst *has* already happened, it is not still to come. Yet surely the thought also implies that we re-enact the killing with every denial of God.

It is scepticism, not faith, that draws me to Christianity: scepticism of every other belief and idea, but especially of modern faiths or philosophical systems claiming to be the Truth. That, and the recognition that all I value has an obscured Christian source.

24 April
Cycled to Haren to give several readings at Sint-Maartenscollege.
After I'd read a few poems and talked about my sense of the past and the historical awareness which is common in modern British poetry, one student, a young man with black hair and a knack of asking attacking or difficult questions, asked me: "Don't the British believe in the future?"

In a letter from Wynn, the quotation from Emily Dickinson which I often half-remember:

> "Nature is a haunted house, but Art a house that tries to be haunted."
> (Letter to T. W. Higginson in 1876)

And another, which Wynn quoted to me outside the pub in Swansea:

> "I hope that you have power, and as much of peace as in our deep existence may be possible.
>   To multiply the harbors does not reduce the sea."
> (Letter to Perez Cowan in 1873)

27 April

Sunday. Celandines out all over the park, daffodils & windflowers in places.

Blackbirds singing in trees and on housetops.

Pellets of blossom on blackthorn. Horse-chestnut leaves—green fledglings opening their wings. On other trees green buds spike the branches—soon they will form a green mist to the eye, now they are like beaks of young birds.

Chairs & tables under coloured umbrellas outside cafes on the Grote Markt.

Warm tarry smells from black decks of barges.

High, grey-white cloud mountains dissolving in a flux of covering grey.

A shower darkened the Ebbingestraat as we walked back, raising a cold, faintly acrid smell of wet dust.

Spring in the west brings a new lightness to things—for a time the world belongs to the birds and leaves and flowers, and the heart is borne up with them, a new spirit wakes in the body. I know from other years that this is a time when depression can poison the system and rest heavily on the mind, perhaps because growth sets off the severed lifeless limb, and lightness in things makes the self know the weight of its burden.

This year I have felt little of this, but noticed and thought more of the presence everywhere of mad power—posters in the streets advertising the war games of mindless men, men with greased, muscular bodies playing with deadly machines, the English countryside shadowed by bombers, occupied by bases over which we have no control, the technical sophistication that can reduce millions of people to targets on a screen, and will do nothing for populations starving in the world's desert places.

Spring comes to the west—every clod of earth is a world of abundant flowering life—and the peoples are a flight-path of warplanes that could destroy them without warning. Where is mind in this? That is a question to madden and blind with impotent rage. Where is mind in the way Reagan says the word "America" and Thatcher says we will not "cower" or "cringe"? Where is mind in the decision to *bomb* a problem whose roots are deep in complex unjust political situations and which can never be eradicated by violence? What the bombs kill are people, children & women as well as soldiers. And the political situation which produces terrorism hardens and extends its root-system. Where is mind in the slogans and insults we may die for? In a world in which "sophisticated" describes weapons and intelligence can say what it likes, but is always on the outside of the barbed-wire enclosures and ministerial offices, with no check on the controls.

Spring in the west: our lives out of our hands—all power behind the walls and barbed wire we can only claw at, where mind doesn't penetrate. Always now the double vision, infinitely more complicated and bewildering than one thing superimposed upon another, yet with a brutal simplicity: the one unique person, place or thing/strategic number, blip on a screen, or expendable blank space.

§

> The first *cywyddwyr* sang so that others could sing after them. Like the architects of the great medieval cathedrals, these carpenters of song initiated great designs that would never be completed in their lifetime.
> Emyr Humphreys, *The Taliesin Tradition*

2 May
Radioactive dust from the nuclear power station near Kiev is falling out over Europe, drifting in the air over us, as, in two or three days, people have put off their winter clothes and dressed lightly, emerging in festive brightness to cycle along the Korreweg or sit in party mood outside cafes. Reassurances that there is no danger to health also fall from the air—and no one knows if they can be trusted, or what may be seeding in the bones—as, suddenly, the small square of public grass across the road, Bernoulleplein, is bright green in morning sunlight, and, on the far side, trees, unseen until now, are green and ochre leafy domes. Yellow forsythia, white cherry blossom, creamy magnolia, pink flowering shrubs make gardens along the road bright and sweet. One garden is wild with dandelions, which also grow between stones beside the pavement and seem to be shooting up at the edge of sight. Today I saw the first wasp. At dusk a high, clear sky with a few bright stars, reflections of a row of white street lamps mooning in black water.

4 May
Afternoon. Red sycamore leaves unfolding, like tropical insects, on our small tree in front of the house.

A walk with M. in woodland near Glimmen on a pale bluewhite day with a cool breeze:

powdery grey sand underfoot
delicate sprays of beech leaves, each leaf with tiny silky hairs at the edge
all the trees in leaf: alder, sycamore, hawthorn, elder, cherry, rowan; only oaks leafless, or with shreds of dead, brown leaves hanging down; rooks cawing, small birds chirping or singing—chaffinch, great tit, long-tailed tit, warblers perhaps; white wood sorrel, scrolled, green lily leaves essence of freshness in beech leaves, their effect, as M. saw it, looking up through branches, *pointillist*; solitary horses whinnying to each other from fields on either side of a long drive between beech trees, the smooth, grey trunks inscribed with initials & lovers' declarations

From Glimmen we drove slowly, on a pot-holed track, to Zuidlarenmeer, where we had beer and a *broodje paling* on a café terrace beside the lake. Kingcups on the damp banks of drainage ditches. Skylarks rising singing, curlews circling and calling, over marshy fields.

6 May
Finished the essay on young Anglo-Welsh poets. Fell into a black mood after another letter from Michael Schmidt which suggests the probability of Carcanet

turning down my book of poems if I submit it, and began to consider asking to be released from my contract—which I feel he would welcome.

7 May
In Drenthe: green fields, black earth.

On nature reserve heathland near Beilen, I walked towards what I thought was the noise of rooks in the distance, but eventually came on water surrounded by tufts of dead, white moor grass and found the noise was a large number of seagulls loudly clamouring.

Once, through wind sighing in the firs, I *almost* imagined I could hear a cuckoo very far away, but it was only somewhere deep in my mind.

We drove through Zevenhuizen on the way back. M's father hid in the woods there and worked with the Resistance during the war. He was born of Friesian parents living in Germany and was conscripted into the German army. But he deserted when fighting in Russia, stole some horses and began the journey back, travelling at night, and living off the horses as they died one by one of exhaustion. The journey took him at least nine months, but he made it without being caught and lived in hiding, striking at collaborators and the occupying force, during the rest of the war. He would never talk about his return from Russia, but M's mother said that when he got back he had holes in his legs through to the bone.

12 May
M's fortieth birthday on the 8th. We celebrated with friends and a good party.

Jude & Peggy James arrived with their two young grandsons on the same day for a short holiday.

They were interested in everything. Jude in particular has the same gift of infectious interest as Jim.

We made several excursions. North to Appingedam, where kitchens of houses overhang the canal, and where, on a fine day, people were hanging bedding out of windows to air. To Delfzijl: the fish in the sea aquarium looking more melancholy than any creatures I've ever seen. At Noordpolderzijl we noticed the plaque commemorating the sluicekeepers since the beginning of the 19th century. One family supplied the keeper for three generations, from the 1890s until 1975.

To Drenthe on a windy, damp day, magnolia petals lying like shells on pavements, a chiffchaff singing in woods. We followed the Hondsrug route, looking at hunebedden: at Annen, Eext (a dark-gleaming shellback), Drouwen, Borger. Then to Orvelte, a village closed to traffic, and frozen in time (or several times), a museum of old shops, farms, barns, agricultural practices. We visited a granary, and saw cheese being made in another building. Housemartins were completing their mud nests under the eaves of a thatched barn.

I showed them my Itchen Water film last night. It made me sad, mainly because I felt how much I might have given in that place. It would mean much the same if I said how much I might have made of being there.

Jude has promised to send me several articles on local history, on William Rufus & on Sway Tower. I find the factual nature of his own writing—in *Comyn's New Forest*, for example—far more poetic than any evocation of atmosphere or mood. If I'd become a historian, as I wanted to in my last years at school and first year at university—it was Chris Shore who gave me the nickname "Historian" at St Peter's, largely because of my history essays—I wouldn't have been able to be the kind of historian Jude is. Yet our feeling for place is much the same, and is as passionate in his minute attention to fact as in my poems.

§

Endless progress, an endless process, means the triumph of death. Only the resurrection of everything which has lived can give meaning to the world's historic process, a meaning commensurate with the fate of personality.

Man is an historic being; he comes to self-realization in history; he can neither cast aside the burden of history, nor free himself from responsibility for it. And man cannot abdicate his God-like worth and dignity, cannot consent to being turned into a means for the merciless and inhuman process of history.
Nicolas Berdyaev

18 May
Cycled with Joe to Zuidlarenmeer. Through falling blossom and in a warm breeze, catching the sun. Red campion, stitchwort, milk maids, cow parsley just beginning to flower; every roadside and waste place a constellation of golden yellow dandelion suns. The sky over marshy fields near the lake was huge: a blue sky with a solution of white cloud. Lapwings tumbled away from us, snipe flew off, curlews stayed, probably on nests close by in the grass. The drainage ditches and weedy ponds were heaving with frogs, which made a loud chorus: *brekek koax brekek koax*—just like that! Almost drowning the cries of birds. Got back stiff and saddle sore after five hours and several detours—one a "short cut" which ended in a grassy field surrounded on three sides by water, Martinitoren appearing temptingly in a straight line at a distance.

28 May
Chernobyl and the American madness in the air. Also newness light and shining in growing things. Elm seeds blown from trees in the park, snowing on cars and cyclists at the traffic lights. A small garden is enough to show the fullness: one small sycamore, leaves turning from red to green, one small rhododendron in flower, clematis—white with a faint shade of purple—delicately binding up the rusted iron bracket and broken light outside the front door, an abundance of green hiding soil that was bare only weeks ago.

I have finished the book of essays and sent it off yesterday. A lot of effort, but worthwhile. No poems for a long time, though; no time, when I *could* have written. The unpublished collection already belongs to the past in my mind. I know that I have to pick myself up from the broken pieces of the Mosaic, and try for a stronger, more continuous rhythm.

Anger and pride have made me calmer, colder, at the prospect of leaving Carcanet—before they leave me! It's a worry, mainly because I want the book of poems out, in order to go beyond it. There's a rhythm about these things: if the book is genuine, if it carries me forward, then it should appear in due course, and if it doesn't, I dwell on it too much, my feelings about it become confused, I'm not free to go on.

I hope there's no self-justification in the conclusion to the book of essays; there was quite a lot in what I eventually left out.

I feared again recently that this whole journal might be a devious form of self-justification, or at least that that is one of its motives. I fear, too, that I may have succumbed to the temptation Glyn Jones warned me against: of mixing the poetic and critical impulses in an impure form. At least, the danger is present in 'Barbarous Reflections' and in the journal generally.

There's only one way of being clear. Not by care alone, though I need to be especially careful, now that my sense of intellectual community is more tenuous than it's ever been. Once I've freed myself for poetry, the way is to put all my passion and interest and effort as a writer into it. I've given *far* more to criticism since I gave up my job, and in consequence I'm now far more confident in my critical prose than I am as a poet: not vainly confident, but freer, more flexible, daring to say more. And for me this is the easier way, because I can communicate more easily—I have a sense of the people I'm talking to.

For poetry I need more faith; I'm more in the dark, in several senses.

First, the act of concentration, the will and persistence for that. Then faith comes with the live rhythm; once working with the current I don't want to turn back. Or faith is that it will come: that there's more than my isolated mind, working fruitlessly, as it often seems to, and therefore painfully aware of its limits.

7 June

Schiermonnikoog—grey monk isle. Here I heard the cuckoo for the first time this year, as I cycled with Joe and Alisdair MacKinnon between hedges of flowering may, hazel and alder, through pine copses and out onto the open dunes. After several wet and cold days, sun gleamed on water and the cloud cover broke as we landed. It rained again in the afternoon, but was warmer than on the mainland.

Heart's-ease on grassy slopes of the grey sand hills, around the concrete bunkers. Shellduck, oystercatchers, a peewit chick in its nest, with the eggshell beside it. Many rabbits in the cultivated areas, then marsh & cotton grass, pinewoods, We lost Joe when we turned off the track to look at a bunker. I was anxious, but we found him back at the village, grinning, when we returned there.

Looking for him, I went to the highest point, where the Germans had built a lookout tower. The whole island can be seen from there, and it is easy to see how it absorbs people, as Alisdair says it does—an irregular dune country, hiding its paths in hollows, vast beaches of grey sand.

After lunch we went over the beach in a tractor-drawn coach to the Balg, the eastern point which is otherwise inaccessible, except perhaps by foot. A desert of sand and sea, seabirds and, visible through binoculars, a family of seals; razor shells & jelly fish underfoot.

15 June
Sunday morning. At Woltersum with M., walking on the north side of the Eems canal, which stretches broad and brown for a long way in both directions, between rows of poplars. Sun and wind; the sky blue, ashen grey at the horizon, as it is on hot days; eyes of light blinking sharply among wind-currents on the water. The may is over now, the elder flowers just coming to a head. Spiderwork of tiny black caterpillars cocooned in silk on hawthorns. A cuckoo called from a wild area behind the poplars on the other side of the canal.

16 June
For me, my essay on Edward Thomas' prose, just completed, is one of the most important I've ever written. It crystallises ideas & changes of attitude which have been forming for several years, and has both negative and positive effects.

I have never seen the "dream" so clearly before: the private ideal inner world, the childhood country or landscape, never outgrown, but retarding growth. Suddenly, this seems to be *the* English story, certainly the story of many writers in imperial Britain, and later. It is my story, too, with a difference. That is why I need very much to understand what I have seen, instead of indulging in shock at other people's "emotional retardation".

The whole subject is horribly difficult, not least because a certain childlikeness, and a refusal to bury the child in false adulthood, is among the most necessary and desirable human qualities. But false "innocence"—that above all has to be seen for what it is.

Of course Edward Thomas was sick, desperately sick: that is why he matters as a poet, because he suffered a common ill, and became at last partially whole. That is much for anyone to achieve. But his biographers don't see it; most of his critics and readers don't see it. I haven't seen it clearly until now, but have idealized and sentimentalised him.

Thomas himself knew far better; he was quite unlike the image that has been set up and worshipped.

There is a problem with "natural" speech and vision: briefly, that a man is not a bird! Yet, positively, Thomas has much to teach me. Above all, in his idea of style as the whole man's speech. It was, perhaps, his idea of "purity" that was wrong: as if anyone could write as a blackbird sings! But he was right about the whole *man*, whom he knew to be social, but at a deep level. The poetry of "the larger man", in himself as well as in Jefferies, eventually released emotional and unconscious powers that the mere "writer" has no access to. These are personal, but not exclusively subjective. We are human at a deep level; on the surface we are either mere "animals"—in fact, disintegrated appetites such as no animal knows— or mere social beings. Each in his depths is different, uniquely personal, but that is where we are one substance, too, and draw on the same powers. This is what I sense, or see darkly. And it makes me irritated with the conventional treatment of Edward Thomas, as if he were mysteriously different, not really "one of us". I don't know whether he ever formulated it, but I think Edward Thomas knew at last that the great poet is *most* "one of us". I mean *at our deepest*.

It is perhaps only in certain things in this journal that I've come close to expressing myself fully. Not "self-expression", as David Jones spoke of it; but expression of the deeper self. I might almost say the "common" self, except that our common depths are where we are each most single.

Later. Common self/deeper self. I think the crucial distinction is this: human beings communicate, relate to each other, share; they do not merge, they are not one, except at the cost of their humanity, to which personal being is essential. In order to love we have each, first and always, to be different. Human beings are the same in their depths only in so far as each is different.

Evening. On the roof garden. "The heron flew east, the heron flew west"—and swifts, swimming in the sky over the city, tiny, black, sharp-winged, in the vast volume of blue air, under a half moon. Yellow stonecrop matted among stones on flat roofs of neighbouring houses. Distant clockfaces gleaming dull gold on church spires in the sultry atmosphere.

22 June
I have begged the question again: the question which I'm always being forced back to, but can't even formulate precisely.

The question is: what is a rooted man? Natural man is a construct of sophisticated romantics. Social man is a construct of soulless materialism. Civilized man, on the other hand, is rooted in the Christian and classical inheritance of Europe. What else can I mean when I talk about the deep self? For however unique a creation there is no self existing outside a world, or not mediated by shared things.

What I know best is confusion, and the feeling that something is missing from my deep attachments. It is there in love of England, in my Englishness— something narrow, choking, blocked off. Recently I thought: suppose it is my "fate" as a poet to see the inadequacy of the very things I write from, and the very idea & sense of the "poetic". Would that mean, in effect, being unable to write, or being able to write only as a critic? A critic who sees through "structures" and how they work…

But this is the "fate" of all serious modern poetry: it is what makes it self-critical, and drives it to break through narrow ideas of poetic feeling, subject, and form. My problem in this respect is rather an over-tenacious fidelity to original impulses & influences. And now, having seen *my* danger in Thomas' prose, I should be freer.

I must know the chaos of "Englishness" now, instead of hiding from it in a dream order. I must understand what civilization means.

And at once I come to the edge of detachment—as if by mere curious enquiry one could become a rooted man!

§

For those who have the habit of prayer, thought is too often a mere alibi, a sly way of deciding to do what one wants to do. Reason will always obscure what we wish to keep in the shadows.

How little we know what a human life really is—even our own.

I know quite well that lots of people die before they manage to find out anything.
 Because they were not really looking. They were dreaming.... The people you mean go round in circles. When you go straight ahead, the world is small.
 Georges Bernanos, *The Diary of a Country Priest*

What a man Bernanos was! A man who loved life, but measured all against the reality of God. A Frenchman who loved his country passionately, but judged it without mercy against an ideal of the past. A man rooted in a faith and a nation, who moved restlessly from place to place, and spent many years living abroad.

In Robert Speaight's biography there's much that I find foreign, alien, even repellent. This is due partly to the old mutual incomprehension of the English and the French, partly to my limited knowledge of French politics, and partly to his anti-Semitism & contempt for democracy. Not, however, to his conservatism or idea of military tradition.

The latter are closely bound up with his sense of *honour*.

This is, specially, a French concept and value. For Bernanos and Simone Weil, for example, national defeat, and humiliation and corruption made it shine brighter, with a sharper edge. In America, George Oppen renewed the concept—as personal integrity, but also in opposition to his country's dishonourable social ethic and war in Vietnam.

In England "honour", outside its limited meaning for a small class (who are nevertheless prepared to die for it), has been a dead word since the First World War. Ivor Gurney was an exception; and to his tormented mind it was at once personal and national. But perhaps Gurney's extreme "case" represents a more widespread hunger, which is very difficult to express and therefore largely inarticulate. In so far as Geoffrey Hill's theme is honour and love of country, I feel that the extreme difficulty of exploring it in the context of England now had some influence on his choice of Péguy as a subject.

A patriotism without honour is mere chauvinism or jingoism—the kind of thing the English gutter press stirs up over a Falklands war or a game of football. A narrow concept of honour, identified solely with a corps or caste or nation or race, can be a deadly servant of evil or injustice. No doubt there were Nazis, some of them highly "cultured", who ordered or executed the most inhuman acts for the "honour" of Führer and Fatherland. Perhaps Bernanos, in his days of supporting *Action Française*, was narrow in his concept of honour, but not, I think, fundamentally. If not, that was because his thinking and feeling about it (as about everything else) was rooted in his faith. This in turn freed him to be a passionate critic of Church, nation and state.

But if honour is a spiritual absolute it is also embodied in particular peoples, so that its exemplars, and the national spirit they create, are inextricably bound up with a man's love of his country. These are clumsy words—quite inadequate to express what a man like Bernanos sees and feels when he looks at his native land. There is the priest's feeling for his village through the centuries, and his perception of the continuity that will swallow him up with all the rest. Life in the depth of time: yet perhaps we don't love this simply because it is or was, enduring and reproducing itself, like the beasts of the field, but because honour shines in it— honour often darkened, often betrayed, but always alive too, in the lives & work of the humblest & the most conspicuously great, in all who live in the world by the light from another world, and would die sooner than lose it. And if, in a people, the very concept dies?

Whether right or wrong in particular judgements, Bernanos was a man. In his anger and tenderness and courage. His spiritual courage was the measure of his great fear. He too knew the loneliness which his Cure de Torcy speaks of: the loneliness which the Church hasn't "torn from the very heart of Adam", by making him know that he is the son of God. It would be impossible to be more a man with all his spiritual resources gathered together in face of death than he was, or to be more serious about what is at stake in every living moment.

I know: thinking for oneself, even, perhaps, imagining that it is possible, can be a terrible, futile vanity. If Jefferies on his deathbed really did repent of intellectual vanity, it wasn't without reason. Yet he was a poet, who did not live in an age of faith. There have to be men like that, even if what they believe original in their thought is in fact a restatement of *part* of a philosophy or religion that is thousands of years old. If only they make the part *live*, in a time when for many the whole original truth is moribund. What else did the great mind of Heidegger achieve? For me, the difficulty is language, the dead words: "honour", "glory", even "God". I know that I'm not wiser than the great Christian philosophers & theologians, let alone St Paul! I may be deceiving myself, but I feel that I have no choice. My work is to think as a poet, and I cannot think except by finding or renewing living words, or believe except in speaking them.

28 June
In a flat country climbing onto a dyke is like looking over the rim of the earth.

"Noordster" (North Star), a labourer's cottage more than 100 years old, stands alone in a big landscape, at the foot of a dyke, between fields of sugar beet and peas. I lay on the dyke, smelling the warm grass: below me, a wide landscape with a few horses and cattle grazing on clay fields, then mud-flats, and the blue-grey sea—tide out—a narrow rim of water ending in the faint outline of an island, Schiermonnikoog. Behind me, sun beating down on the small house in a wide landscape, with two or three church spires visible at long intervals along the horizon, and a long straight track parting the fields. Sun in a cloudless, blue sky: a breeze ruffling water & crops. A cuckoo calling almost continually from a clump of trees hiding the only other house nearby: an inland voice among piping and crying seabirds. Old red brick, white painted brickwork; a heavy sea turned to stone in the pantiles and a wagtail with a beakful of grubs on the roof ridge.

At Niekerk: bright blue flowers & creamy elder blossom mirrored in water green as thick paint, sun winking on brilliant black pantiles. On such days in this country even the light is material, and it seems certain that this is the only world. No wonder the old Dutch religious painters painted the substance of things redeemed, as good as God made them, instead of dissolving the world in light.

29 June
Summer nights, when boys and girls secretly leave the house to meet each other. As Elin did last night; as I did years ago to meet Janet, creeping downstairs in quiet, rubber shoes, climbing out of the dining room window and walking to the Common. Once we missed each other in the darkness; we must have passed on either side of a gorse bush. I glimpsed a shadowy form, and inexplicably thought it was someone else. And once I passed someone of Janet's height in Ramley Road, and stared hard until a man's voice roughly asked: "What are you staring at, mate?" Soft, warm nights with glowworms shining in the grass. What we talked about, I don't know. It was innocent enough, and perhaps there was only one occasion when we actually met, and one when we missed each other in the dark.

It is the conviction of Jack Clemo's militant Calvinist faith that "the poet is by nature a pervert, and most of the world's religious and mystical poetry is theologically heretical", and "Art finds its most satisfying level when it is content to be a footnote to spiritual renaissance". He is an apostate to the modern religion of poetry and worship of the poet as seeker: "A man is spiritually unfit to write books as long as he is a baffled seeker. The sick soul needs health before it needs self-expression" (*The Invading Gospel*). He throws down a challenge, which can't be dismissed by appeal to the "spirituality" of art. There is, however, a disparity between the wit and eloquence of his argument, which reveals a large knowledge of modern "heretical" ideas and writings, and expresses an intellect tempered by his own struggles as a seeker, and his outbreaks of aggressive Philistinism.

I like Clemo's sharp knocks at our modern self-conceit. I like his sheer bloody-minded passionate contrariness towards nature & poetry & individualist thought. But do I really side with bullying evangelism against those it sees as wanderers in the wilderness, such as D. H. Lawrence and T. F. Powys. No! And there's something in Clemo that I find repugnant. Yet he's a man with something to say that we need to hear.

What a world this would be without individual vision, and therefore without any form of modern art—neither Rouault nor Picasso, neither Lawrence nor David Jones. And would it be a world of brotherhood and sisterhood, because a world with one Father? Or would the human race, having arrived all together at the truth, turn savage with boredom and rend each other, or perish in mass suicide?

Truth also is the pursuit of it. I want to be in spirit with those who die honourably in the pursuit, not with bullies who have arrived, and berate the rest of us from their eminence for our blindness. Even with Jack Clemo, it is the fierce independent man on his clay verge whom I find intellectually companionable, the man who is more like Ivor Gurney, or T. F. Powys, or Lawrence than he is like an evangelist.

6 July

On the train from Groningen, Joe dreamily plugged into his walkman. A close morning, misty and damp-webbed, darkening the already dark midsummer green. Pink spires of rosebay willowherb by he track.

Later. Crossed on the new *Koningin Beatrix*. Sea calm. In England: cut hayfields, foxgloves, convolvulus swarming over chainlink fences & embankments.

13 July

I came to Hayford on Wednesday and have been to London and again in Winchester since then, as well as cycling in the area.

Friday: read at the Tate with Kevin Crossley-Holland. Pat Adams organized the reading, which was held in the Constable room. After some talk with Pat, who was a kind and efficient host, and Kevin and others, I went with Lee & Kate for a meal at the unlikely hour of 4 p.m. We ate in an Italian restaurant within easy walking distance of the Houses of Parliament, and afterwards I walked back along Millbank under plane trees trailing their leaves in the Thames, over Lambeth bridge and along the Albert Embankment, Big Ben resonantly striking a quarter hour and a zeppelin advertising Fuji film indolently circling over the Houses of Parliament and the river.

Saturday: in Winchester, where Elizabeth put me up overnight. A damp morning, raindrops pittering on the ground from the lime trees beside Hyde Church Path. The new houses standing where the derelict Victorian schoolhouse used to be, like the estate on the site of the big house in Park Road, look absolutely settled: as if no other building had ever existed there.

I went first to the Domesday exhibition in the Great Hall. A series of tents, based on medieval models, had been erected inside the hall and all the young attendants & sales personnel were dressed in Norman costume. Bob Radford had spoken scornfully of the exhibition—"models of monks with tape recorders inside them". In fact, it was quite a spectacle, with fibreglass models of the king and his knights and officers enacting scenes associated with the survey, maps, explanatory material, copies of the book, a diorama and a model of East Meon (in polyurethane) in 1086, and so on. All this against a background of contemporary chanting and tapes of Domesday inventories played on concealed tape recorders, though I don't think they were inside the figures, as Bob assumed!

Here and there the past lived, mostly in its own words: William, "a burly warrior with a harsh guttural voice, great in stature but not ungainly". "You will send men all over England into each shire… Let this search be so thorough that not a single cow, nor ox, nor pig escape the net." The book itself was made of sheepskin, probably from flocks abounding on land around Winchester; the pens were made from primary feathers of birds' wings, the ink from oak galls and gum arabic combined with iron salts. What struck me most was that William & Matilda signed their names with a cross.

Then, on top of all the Saxon learning the castles went up, and churches and cathedrals of the military God, and the Saxon foundations disappeared as completely as the school at Hyde—or disappeared in fact, but were incorporated in spirit, as the Master of the Leaping Figures developed the hands of his Saxon predecessors.

Schools around the country had entered a competition on a Domesday theme, illustrating reports of their town or village now and then. 1st prize: a mobile film unit consisting of a 2-litre 15 seater Ford transit custom bus, with an ITT VMC 3865 video camera with built-in recorder and an ITT 200 projection television unit…

What ghosts do we capture? What *is* the history being coined?

Outside the last tent a huge statue of Queen Victoria was in its place in a corner of the hall, with the medieval round table on the wall just above it. Sir Alfred Gilbert's Victoria, a figure wrapped in voluminous drapes and seated regally on a dais, all in black-painted bronze. Commissioned for the Golden Jubilee (1887) by the Whitaker of Pylewell Park, who was then High Sheriff, it was a good deal more forbidding than fibreglass Norman knights on horseback, and in a way stranger, from a world that is harder to imagine, because closer to us, but irrevocably gone.

Sunday afternoon. To Highcliffe Castle with Jim. A first impression of "bare ruined choirs". The idea of a ruined abbey is fortified by the amount of medieval stonework that the 19th century neo-gothic building contains—the magnificent King's Oriel in yellow Caen limestone, for example, and other pieces of the same stone, originally from Jumiages Abbey or the Manor of Grand Andelys. After its use as a religious house in recent years, there's a rumour that it was used for black magic rites. Its appearance makes this plausible, not least the heraldic stag high on the arch of the portico, which seems to have had its head twisted backwards on its neck, and with hoof hanging down looks more like a satanic goat.

We sat on the grass and Jim showed me the two porcelain rosaries he has made—a rosary of the Sorrowful Mysteries and a rosary of the Joyful Mysteries—and explained the symbolism of the various curved and painted beads. Behind us the King's Oriel hung intact in the gaping ruin, beside the quotation from Lucretius built into the parapet and looking out over the Mediterranean setting of ilex trees to the sea and the Island:

SUAVE, MARI MAGNO, TURBANTIBUS AEQUORA VANTIS
E TERRE MAGNUM ALTERIUS SPECTARE LABOREM

The oddest thing about this odd place is the mentality that made this part of it, and it is hard not to see a sinister unconscious symbolism in the elevated wealthy and renowned visitors, including Edward VII, Kaiser Wilhelm II & many other members of European royalty, and their parties and the land and sea below, under their feet. We read in the guide that the Kaiser was very popular locally as a result of his manners and the party which he threw for local school children during his stay in 1907, and Jim remarked that he was soon killing them.

Here an angle of the cliffs recalled Swinburne, there a sail appearing or disappearing over the rim of the horizon near the Island brought Tennyson to mind. But as I sat on the grass fingering the beads and listening to Jim quote a psalm or the *Book of Jonah*, with the ruin behind us and other visitors including small children and a party of youngsters playing a transistor spread out around us, I felt at once a strong natural sense of reality and as if I was participating in a drama too strange to be believed in.

14 July
It has been a long day, starting when I drove my parents to a guesthouse in Budleigh Salterton. We called in at Sidford to see my aunt and uncle, Winifrid and Roland, who are both unwell, and move about with difficulty. Roland with his bull's head, the strong man in his weakness, the old policeman who will be beaten but won't give in. Voices of my childhood—the same voices but the bodies faded that had such authority and dignity and seemed invulnerable. No books, nothing that an intellectual would call an idea, a contempt of anything "arty". Thomas Alfred's obdurate sinew and intolerant mind. And for a while Roland & Dad were boys again, together on the playground, against the rest and men with nothing and

everything in common. The same generosity too; not emotional in Roland's case, yet perhaps with something of the same understanding though it doesn't speak… I can't say what I saw.

Later I walked on the beach at Budleigh, shadowless on a hot, muggy afternoon. I came here first as a boy on holiday with my parents, and loved the smooth pink and dove-coloured pebbles. Today I called on Peter Dent and had tea with him. We talked poetry and publishing and were generally in sympathy with each other. He said that all the poets he knows feel isolated. He spoke too about feeling the extraordinary magical power of individual words.

Driving from Budleigh this evening—via Beaminster, where I couldn't find accommodation—I had the odd feeling that there are places in Dorset more beautiful than any place has a right to be: some sweep of downland or hollow or wooded coombe. The feeling doesn't make sense, but there it is.

15 July

After breakfast I drove to Cerne and went to look at the Giant from the viewpoint near the old workhouse. His outline was discernible through mist—but what *is* the Giant except an outline? He is like Dorset: the depth is barely perceptible on the surface, but may be sensed.

From Plush to Mappowder the road is a track cut into the earth. Hedges full of wild roses, elder, honeysuckle, cow parsley, meadowsweet, nettles, grasses, which almost touch across it; a road plastered with mud & dung, in places passing through a dark tunnel of overarching trees.

Gerard took me first to see Lucy, who talked about Emily & Joe, about Romsey and Horsebridge Mill, and about her father knowing William Barnes and sometimes helping him to take services. Later Gerard and I went for lunch to The Green Man at King's Stag. He told me about Mary's spiritual struggle with Platonism and Christianity. Later, he showed me a typescript of her novel about Plotinus, which is soon to be published. He told me that Jack Clemo, now living at Weymouth, who visits them from time to time, gained his wife by *The Invading Gospel*. She read the book, and was overwhelmed by the feeling that she must contact him, and devote her life to looking after him—as she has since his mother died. He is completely deaf and blind and she does everything for him.

In the afternoon I walked to the church, with Theodore and Violet's stone "book" in the graveyard, in which smoke from a garden fire was drifting, and then down the road in the direction of Plush. It was hot, sultry, with cloud-anvils moving slowly round the horizon. The smells—always the smells—are indescribable, not quite sweet, not quite bitter, merging together—warm hedgeside smells that are the smell of life, today and time past, my time and the time of hedges and fields. On the shelf behind Lucy were photographs of Mary & of her mother, looking with their Powys look even more alike than either looks like Lucy, though all are alike, and a line from Mary was half in my mind as I sat looking at them: "when I am nothing of my own".

Later we all sat out in the garden and had tea. When I think how hidden even for Dorset these places are, it seems extraordinary to me that their great influences on my life should be unrelated; that I should have met Sue just down the road in Plush and this part of Dorset should have meant so much to us before I met Gerard or had any interest in any Powys. And years before, when Hardy was still alive, Dad travelled here, and knowing almost nothing of Hardy, bought Mother a copy of Herman Lea's *Hardy's Wessex*.

Sometimes I think superstitiously that the Giant has exercised a kind of magnetism... And only this morning I wondered what the old people must have felt, the paupers, looking up from the workhouse at the figure of fertility—themselves barren of all earthly resources—or at the wintry bleak destroyer.

Later. His isolation makes Gerard talk when in the company of friends who share his interest, and after supper I had one of his "sermons"—not directed at me. It is evident that, close as he has been to several of the Powyses, he has also kept his distance in spiritual & intellectual matters. On this occasion he spoke of the intensity that all had, which could be painful for others, and the detachment in face of death—of those dear to them as well as their own. He obviously finds this detachment towards the death of the beloved—for example, Willy (like Theodore) speaking of death as "obliteration" when his wife died—troubling, impossible to understand, and even repugnant. For Gerard, love that does not will the eternal life of the beloved in God is not love.

16 July
I took my leave of Lucy in the morning—such intense life in a face that is the image of death—and set out for Winchester. Some way beyond Shaftesbury I turned off the main Salisbury road and drove along narrow lanes through small villages and chalk hills to Bishopstone, where Lottie Elkins, Mother's mother was born. Here and in Dorset there are places which, even now, bring to mind Cobbett's meeting with the woman who had lived all her life without moving more than a mile or so from the one place.

17 July
Crossed to the Island with Jim on the Lymington—Yarmouth ferry in the afternoon. It was during the summer of the year that I started at Aberystwyth, when I already had the job, that I last worked on the ferries. From Yarmouth we took the path through meadows, woods and barley fields to Freshwater, where we visited the church alongside the river Yar. A persistent lady helper followed us about the interior pointing out things of special interest, such as the faces of Ellen Terry and Lady Emily Tennyson in the window reproducing a G. F. Watts painting, and I sidled away leaving Jim to be civil—not for the first time, he remarked later.

From there we walked to Freshwater Bay for a swim, the water very cold. Climbed the downs to the Tennyson Memorial, the hill ridges and chalk cliffs behind us rearing up like the back of a great dragon. Thyme, mullein at the edge where the cliffs break off into air, the first harebell. A cool breeze blowing in a vast blue and white sky. The Channel and the Solent expanded below us on either side—Fawley, Calshot Chimney, matchstick masts in the Lymington River, Hurst Castle, Sway Tower, the northern Forest edge fading into mist. The Angelus rang from St Saviours at Totland, and as we came in sight of Purbeck and water surrounded us on three sides, West Wight was set in a silver sea!

19 July
From the Brockenhurst to Lymington train, Sway Tower moves behind the ridge of Latchmoor, like a giant stepping down into deep water.

To the Island again, for a reading at Calvert's Hotel, Newport. David & Judy Gascoyne were there, Judy with her photograph album, proudly showing photos of her & David in Cyprus, Iceland and other places where his celebrity has recently taken them, and one of her with President Mitterand. She is so warm, innocent of guile and eager to share her pleasure that it would be hard to take exception to the simple-hearted vanity. Both she and David were very friendly. In the discussion after my reading he talked about fragmentation—in response to my Mosaic—and also recalled, in a different key, singing as a boy in the choir at Winchester Cathedral.

With Brian Hinton and others, I felt myself to be among friends, in the first place in the south to give me real encouragement.

As we were talking in Brian's flat in the afternoon, an old soldier who is founder of the IOW Tennyson Society called in. Apparently there has been a recent sighting of Tennyson's ghost, in black hat & cape, disappearing into the mist! I am beginning to realize how much his presence is part of West Wight, of the downs, cliff-scapes and sea vistas: an effect of the presence of the place in his poetry, but greatly enhanced by the Victorian past surviving in the place. There's also the great emotional vulnerability, the suffering of heart & mind, the discontent: feelings which reach out, and are palpable in the very air and landscape. In contrast with this sense of the unfinished, a feeling of completeness, or at least of closure, of sealing the life in and the temporal afterlife out, pervades Hardy's Dorset.

21 July
Tea with Peggy & Jude at Hordle. Older red-brick houses, dark green oaks on either side of Silver Street, like the trees overarching Yaldhurst Lane: will it be possible for people after my generation to have a sense of belonging—a powerful, binding emotion, however tenuous in fact—to an old deep historical England? It is rooted in me, not all my criticism of nostalgia or knowledge of myths of "Old England" can root it out. There are times when I feel very far from the rational intellectual critics of such "conservative" emotions, and close to JCP in his rage to escape the mechanical world and protect nature's sensitive tissue from it. Yet as I feel this, and go back on what I've said about not wanting to retreat into a

retrospective life in a quiet rural corner, I know that I had to go away, would not have seen and felt this if I hadn't.

22 July
Moor Farm. Walked with Lee up the track by barley fields, between banks of midsummer flowers, and round the garden, the neo-Gothic front of Booton church across the fields, and several of his sculptures standing up in clearings in the wild meadow alive with butterflies & moths. He showed me his latest work and work-in-progress in the barn-studio, which has had some improvements. Two of his pieces in public places have been vandalised this year—one he no longer much cared about, and was glad of the insurance money, the other he has here and is replacing the broken head, knocked off with a sledgehammer. In recent works, especially in a dancer, the sinuous, dynamic movements are even more marked, and in some there's a tension, or balance, between the gravity of mass and the leap or flight of movement. A major current preoccupation is the imagery of angels (in part, a development from his bird imagery), and the model of the Islington Angel, presently being cast, suggests how fine the finished work will be. Before a late supper, we played a long game of cricket with Guy & Louis between the apple trees on the lawn.

23 July
Rain after drought; a surprisingly cold day, like autumn. In dry intervals I weeded a border beside the house and Lee worked outside the studio, on *Sundance*. Grey sky, darker grey jets flying low overhead, splitting the silence.

To Heydon with Lee for a drink in the evening. We discussed the idea of collaborating on a work.

24 July
Outside Salle church, on either side of the door: two angels censing, bodies and upper parts of the wings scaly—representing armour, perhaps, but making them look like mermaids—wings ending in points, like fern. A woodhouse with club held across his chest over the north porch, which contained, under a roof boss of the Last Judgement, a dead Christmas tree on a bed of fox-red needles.

Inside: an immediate sense of light and space, lifting up the spirit with the pointed arches, windows, and high roof. Simultaneously, a familiar musty smell keeping the spirit earthbound. Silence, except for the clock ticking in the tower: heavy monotonous footsteps at my back. The fury of the iconoclasts was soon apparent: empty niches, broken statues, disfigured carvings round the font, fragments of paintwork, missing brasses leaving the outlines of medieval figures set in the floor, colourless window glass. In this vast, almost bare shell, perhaps only the wooden angels under the roof remember a lost meaning.

The high, pinnacled, slender tower on its low hill commands a wide country of cornland and beet fields. Fine, stylised angels stand on parapets on either side of the roof. Today it was like an island in a sea of cloud, with gulfs of blue sky and great crumbling tidal waves of cumulus. Wind streamed through grass growing over graves. Inside, tall pew ends catching the edge of my sight were momentarily like the large congregation that once filled it. But it was quite empty, all the power raised on the backs of great flocks of sheep gone into the ground.

From Salle I cycled to the Victorian church at Booton and found it locked, a black-painted St Michael standing guard over a doorway into which dead leaves had drifted. Wilderness topping the heads of stones and crosses filled the graveyard and grew almost to the church walls: grass, hogweed, nettles, elder, and the silent blare of bindweed's white trumpets everywhere, a tigerish dragonfly zooming over rank vegetation, sparrows chirping on the neo-Gothic tower, and larks singing high over cornland falling smoothly away to Cawston church tower. A fairly new gravestone at the edge of the vegetation, close to the church wall, commemorated "our little farmer Robje van Moorsel", who was born on 22 May 1977 in Eindhoven and died at the age of 6 months in Brandiston. On the other "sheet" of the stone book his father and mother, sisters and brother expressed their gratitude to God "for his resting place next to the church of St Michael and All Angels".

As I cycled back, seeing again the physical unity of the area, I thought of the things I had seen, and especially of the angels which are still alive on the roof of Salle church, and of the relation between these and Lee at work on *his* angels, struggling both for true meaning and for recognition in a world that cares little for such things or for the individual effort in their making. And I thought about how we might work together—exactly how, not whether it would be possible, since we have a fundamental imaginative sympathy.

Later
Lee talking in the studio—a swallow flying to its nest in the roof, nestlings squeaking, over the black-painted bow-and-arrow swift sculpture picked out by light falling from a high window; smell of wood shavings, and wood chips to finger as he talks:

Earth and sky: moments of feeling part of the whole, being nature, being one instead of separate. The relief called *Within*, a humanistic version of Christ in Glory.

Duality: how make one material speak about two different things? The same material, but different forms, different feelings. New feelings—ancient language.

Our world is a dangerous place because the root is lost. We have wealth and technology, but are spiritually poverty stricken. The human root: being part of things instead of fighting against them.

25 July
On the train from Norwich on a damp, grey morning. When I got up early there were five or more rabbits on the lawn, hump-backed with ears flat against their heads, nibbling the grass. A moorhen with growing chicks feeds with chicken at the back door.

Afternoon. By tube to Swiss Cottage and a walk to Belsize Park to visit Anne Stevenson. Either her door bell wasn't working or she didn't hear it, because I had to walk another half mile and call her from a public phone box before I could let her know I was there.

We had a pleasant lunch together and with Peter Lucas, who arrived home a little later. But her response to my collection of poems is disappointing. She likes 'Itchen Water' best, finding them "watercolours" (like Cotman), and "charming". She can make little or nothing of 'The Headland', and thinks it, like the Mosaic, not realized. She thinks the Mosaic doesn't transcend the personal and the local either, and finds no "plot" or development in the collection overall. Evidently she doesn't "hear" the poems, praises their visual qualities but finds them lacking in resonance.

It is clear from this, and other signs, that my chances of finding an English publisher for the poems aren't good. As Anne readily acknowledges, they have nothing sensational to offer in the prevailing English fashion, but have affinities with an American style which is not understood—not *heard*, I would say—in England.

I don't want to think too much about this. Neither to dwell overmuch on past work nor to dull my own sense of its inadequacy by brooding on other people's insensibility to its strengths. What matters is to go on. Lee quickens in me our common creative ground, and seeing him work I know what I must do, and, at the same time, the weakening effect of my bookish academicism. He, more than any one, knows the poet in me—that that is my very being—and by his perception and faith, as well as by his example, helps to stimulate and strengthen my creative will.

Anne is writing, with painful difficulty, a book on Sylvia Plath. She reminds her of her own earlier struggles, of what she says, humorously but melodramatically, it took her four husbands and alcohol to survive. She's also much distressed at present by fragmentation (which affected her response to my Mosaic) and feels that, without a sense of the whole, she won't be able to write poetry again.

26 July

At Hayford. David has just been in with a cup of tea, before leaving for Brighton. He has been listening to a tape of me reading my poems, and has evidently appreciated it though he says there's much he doesn't understand. What I've failed to remember is that our specialisms, our "languages", are completely different, and that I know even less of his than he knows of mine. He listened to the tape with our parents. No family could have been more encouraging and supportive than mine.

29 July

To Holland with Emily. A blowy day, clear, pale blue sky, misty horizons. Women leaning back or lying on the deck with eyes shut in an attitude of complete passive abandonment, offering themselves up to the sun. Black-headed gulls gliding, swerving, hanging, cutting the air over a black and white sea, which is beaten silver where the sun falls upon it.

It is the northern worm that soils sensuality, leaving its slimy tracks on the lover's mind, or cankering the heart of the rose. Suddenly I know that I can't believe in the sunny sinless lover, in a Goldmund or a Llewelyn Powys. For always there's someone left to suffer as he passes on his way, free of conscience or commitment.

But worse is the "soulful" sensualist, whose intimacy and show of understanding have only one end in view, which he can compass in no other way.

On deck we tower over a white crested, black sea; only when a ship of similar size passes at a distance, looking like a toy, do we know how tiny we are.

A brief, faint rainbow, barely perceptible, in spray.

3 August
Spent part of the day with Rudy van den Hoofdakker ("Rutger Kopland"), one of the leading Dutch poets. Rudy, in his early fifties, is a professor of psychiatry at Groningen, and lives at Glimmen, off a quiet, sandy lane near Appelbergen. We sat in his garden on a hot day, in a brick-paved suntrap under a vine at the back of the house, the long narrow wooded garden stretching above us to the main railway line, where a train passing occasionally drowned our conversation. After some preliminary remarks we talked quite freely about poetry, marking out differences and similarities, and understanding each other well. He said there is no direct relationship between his work as a psychiatrist and his poetry, and he certainly doesn't write about his patients; but his sense of words has been greatly heightened by listening to the different ways in which people use them, and observing their habits of concealment, and all the indirect or non-verbal means of communication (or its avoidance) that accompany words. He sets a high value by precision and clarity in his writing; and although he is sometimes frustrated by having, due to his profession, little or no time to write, he wants to say only what he has to say, and finds much contemporary native writing trivial and meaningless. But Rudy has a high regard for modern Dutch poetry too, and we discussed the reasons for its neglect in England. He has no time for vagueness or confusion, and believes that although there are mysteries, all is ultimately knowable. Thus a good poem makes more of the unknown known. He is a confident man, with no false modesty about the worth of his poetry or its recognition in Holland. He is also direct, and sought my future help in publishing his work in Britain.

After a light lunch he drove me, with his wife Ineke & an aged aunt (all of them, together with the two elder daughters, heavy smokers, the old, withered aunt rolling cigarettes in brown fingers) to the river Drentse A. This place on the Hondsrug near Zeegse is obviously a favourite of theirs, and Rudy has written several poems about the river. Here we met a group of people, including his translator & her husband, Ria & Jim Leigh, and we sat at a table outside a caravan (Ria's workroom) and near the river, now low, and quick flowing, and drank wine or beer and talked.

M. and Emily picked me up after we had returned to Glimmen, and we went to the sandy beach at Meerwijk, where Emily & I swam in Zuidlaarder Meer.

12 August
One of the delights of this holiday has been the companionship of Elin & Emily, who are like older and younger sisters. Now and then I've had time to work at the proofs of the book of essays. This morning my break with Carcanet was finalized, and I wrote to Stephen Stuart-Smith, who is taking over Enitharmon, and has shown a warm interest in my Winchester poems, after hearing me read from them on the Island.

14 August
To Schiermonikoog with Joe & Emily. We had to queue for tickets and the two ferries were both crowded, with people & bikes. The day began mistily but later became hot, as we cycled about the island. No shelter on the vast sandy beaches, but we found a shaded pool beside pinewoods and swam in it. Time now of yellow hawkweed and purple thistles, and willowherb bearded with seeds. Oystercatchers & plovers picking between rows of cut grass. The heat increased throughout the day, and when we returned in late afternoon the atmosphere was close. Air and sea curdling, water oily and marbled, with a thick, supple skin, and coppery gleams of sunlight on lips of waves.

15 August
Back to England with Emily. The sea, in contrast to yesterday, alive, ridged and white-crested under a strong wind in a blue sky, rainbows in spray accompanying the boat.

On Waterloo Station a thin woman with straggly hair weaved from group to group of men cadging money or cigarettes—she touched my arm in passing but didn't approach me, perhaps because I was loaded down with bags—her filthy trousers clinging to her thin buttocks stained with shit. A man standing alone shook her off as though she were a loathsome insect: "Get away from me, get away".

16 August
By train from Winchester on the line parallel to the Itchen, on just such a day as when I walked with Robert Wells by the river. Ragwort meadows; ponies and black and white heifers drinking at the water's edge. Butterflies & seeds on the air. A hot sun occasionally darkened by small, white clouds; light aircraft over Southampton airport. On a smoke-blackened railway bridge: GET MILITANT TORIES OUT. Purple buddleia by the bridge, and a glimpse of St Mary's church, close to where I used to live, in the area in which archaeologists are now uncovering Hamwic, and changing our picture of the urban & commercial power of "Dark Age" Anglo-Saxon Britain.

17 August
Sunday morning. Pennington Marshes: tide in, at first under heavy-ribbed cloud, a broken, blue and white sun washing back and forth among brown bladder-wrack by the seawall. From the path at Oxey the area at once comes into view, between white masts—a forest of dead trees—at Lymington and Hurst and the Island. A first impression of silence and stillness—as though peace were an actual place, which opened, and I walked into it—yachts and the IOW ferry moving slowly on the Solent, and a feeling that this place is *ancient*, despite the relative newness of converted salterns and seawalls. Then a sound of distant voices, bird cries, rumble of a high jet, and the silver-grey water moves with innumerable ripples and creases, and grasses wave slowly on the banks.

Walking or standing still I see only a fraction: oakapples and spiderwebs on low oaks growing on the seawall, brambles, dead thrift, long, white-headed grasses and glaucous or red-leaved, fleshy salt-loving plants, sorrel like bits of fretted, rusted iron. Water sucks audibly at an old fishing boat and its ropes hung with weed slowly rise and fall. As the cloud thins and breaks open the sun is scattered white across the water; my eyes narrow between the sun above and its reflections blinking and glaring up. In stiller water, against the wall, the sun has an oily halo. Shingle, dusty paths, bumble bees on thistles—at every instant there is some thing or some change to note, and still I see only a fraction, yet feel the place as a whole, in and beyond my sense of any part of it.

What if I could come here every day, recording, making different pictures, slowly building up an image of this particular world with its many forms of life? The emotional pull is strong, but despite the deep pleasure of a visit, I know the danger too. For this morning, and for sometime past, I was also thinking about failure.

Not only thinking about it either, but fighting off the old destructive attraction *down*, which I succumbed to at the end of the last visit here, after seeing Anne in London and in spite of the time with Lee, and the time with Jim and Gerard. I know it: it gets into my voice, as M. said, and is a corrosive self-pitying complaint, which feeds on failure, and is actually greedy to amass and consume it. It isn't *this* alone, or even mainly, that I touch at the Marshes; this isn't the secret of the place. Only, there, I'm aware of the passivity in me, of that giving in and resting on a kind of vegetative inertia that is part of the drag downwards, and is a potentiality within my love of the place—as if I could settle like mud or weed in a dark underworld, with no further need to struggle or act or make anything. But this isn't all. For the world of salt water and seawalls seems all that the deceits and miscreations of consciousness are not. And in this place they carry the past, my past, but as if it were an essence, free of my mind's distortions, and part of this world like stone and light and air.

Where does it come from, this will or even desire to fail? There's something similar in my father, and it's related to pride as well as self-pity—a complicated pride of *not competing*. But while this would be a strength, if the work were one with full power, in fact it infects the springs of creative energy, it limits effort and vision. And in that respect it is symbolized by the vegetative watery underworld as *an end in itself*, a place that excludes all personal conflict, and is outside history, society and person, all struggling significant life.

Late August
At Tanner's Lane, walking on the foreshore with Mother, picking over flints and talking about old times. We arrived to see, unexpectedly, the QE11 sailing slowly and majestically through the Solent, outward bound. She looked larger than Hurst Castle, towered over the Needles, and made the ferry look like a water-spider beside a swan. Ponies on the narrow shingle shore, between mudflats and stunted oaks, above the solitary redbrick house which Sue once wanted us to buy. Island hills dark-blue, sea in changing light, under dark clouds and sunbursts, cleansed and still lively after the tail of the hurricane from America, which brought heavy rain & storm—November in August—to the country in recent days.

We talked about Dad & about their moving from Hayford. He has declined markedly in recent weeks, feeling wretched with bronchitis, but accelerating a process that has been going on for some time, as his sight has got worse and he has begun to dwell repetitively on the past, and, now, his will seems to have weakened and he has given in to his dependence. He has at last accepted the need to move into a smaller house with a small garden, in walking distance of the shops.

As the sea colours darkened and brightened, spray from waves of the incoming tide leaping at mudbanks, a gull with an injured wing made hopeless efforts to fly up out of the water. Here & there in the windrow wings of dead gulls, still attached to perishing skeletons. Sails cutting the air in the wake of the liner, now small beyond the Needles.

§

The bitter juice of the acid, unripe fruit is poison to the eater, until these same juices have been tempered and mellowed by the rays of the summer sun. The wholesome essences of every life are poisonous if wrongfully laid bare.
　　　　　Stephen Hobhouse, interpreting Boehme

29-31 August
At the new university of Bath, a concrete & glass labyrinth, with security guards menacingly uniformed and a generally authoritarian & impersonal atmosphere—only lifted at morning by views from the high-rise buildings of balloons floating gracefully and peacefully over surrounding hills and catching sunlight with bright colours.

Lectured on JCP & Thomas Hardy at the Powys Conference. I went, and came away, feeling strained, but enjoyed meeting and talking with a number of old friends, including Glen, Kenneth Hopkins, Belinda Humfrey, Marius Buning, Timothy Hyman, and Charles Lock. Charles' lecture was brilliant, with quotations from Bakhtin which I found very sympathetic. By one of the contrasts that make the Society a pleasure to belong to, there was a moving account of Phyllis and John Cowper in their later years by Frederick Davies, who knew them well and loved them. I met the poet Francis Berry, who now lives in Winchester and knows the Dean, Michael Stancliffe, who befriended me. Francis told me Michael is fatally ill.

Iris Murdoch and John Bayley provided us with a dialogue, followed by open discussion, on the Saturday evening. It's hard for me to be fair to Bayley, who is at once large-minded in his treatment of European literature & English poetry of the past, and small-minded in his evaluation of contemporary English verse, and, indeed, he said little of interest. Iris Murdoch was altogether more serious and more interesting, especially in the questions she asked about religion and morality in JCP. But the evening was, in the main, disappointing.

Drove back after Sunday lunch by the way I had come, on smaller roads: Bradford on Avon, Trowbridge, through some of the finest chalk country in the south of England, with a distant view of the Westbury white horse, and down the Wylye valley. But too tense to see much.

§

Language, for the individual consciousness, lies on the borderline between oneself and the other. The word in language is half someone else's.
M. M. Bakhtin

1 September
No one works harder or to more purpose than a great sculptor. In my experience, I have never known anyone who works like Lee. Now, in the strain of this time and the difficulty of the time to come, I am more grateful than ever to these great workmen, for their work and lives and for what they show me. I know what is "dark" in me—the poisoned spring—that makes me brittle & tense. I both know it and will not simplify. It is an attachment from which I also draw strength—the strength of awe & piety—and whose very weakness of nervous debility may also be, at times, a strength of sensibility. But it is necessary not to live in the parental shadow, to love without unreasoning grief, to be a father in one's own world. There is a shadow anyone may live in; no individual human life is inherently simple, and anyone may fail to find or create a balance between love and creative freedom, fidelity to origins and a direction outward and away from them. But the son has to become, in turn, the father, literally & metaphorically, as maker of a home and creator of an imaginative world. And for this a kind of violence is necessary, which is not an enemy of love, but breaks ties only to extend them and order them anew, creating the centre which each person must be, without denying the centres of others, but relating to them, remaking the connections.

By M. I know this and by reflecting on experience. And I know too that whatever the future holds I have to make my life by work.

§

I call that man awake who, with conscious knowledge and understanding, can perceive the deep, unreasoning powers in his soul, his whole innermost strength, desire, and weakness, and knows how to reckon with himself.

Yet all men of good will have this in common—that our works in the end put us to shame; that always we must begin them afresh, and our sacrifice be eternally renewed.

Narziss, in *Narziss and Goldmund*

7 September
Sunday. Sailing with Hans on Leekstermeer in his small fibreglass yacht. The water was quite rough, the crosscurrents of wind were unpredictable, so that as we cut up & down or round & about the lake—and I sprawled clumsily under the mast in the wet bottom of the boat as we went about—we would sail suddenly into a windless space or the wind would hit us abruptly. Then, suddenly, we were over— as we went over I hung on desperately to the rope instead of letting it go—and down, under the water, which I swallowed and came up coughing and gasping, and under the boat and the sails. It was the very image of my fear, and as I went over and down, swallowing water, I felt complete helplessness, something fearful happening to me, beyond my control. Then I struggled out from under the sails and the boat and got my fingers on its side. And after a while found that I could just touch the mud bottom of the lake with my bare feet, but still felt precarious, as well as being soaked to the skin and cold! Then, with a huge effort, Hans and I turned the boat back over the right way, and with another great effort, scrambled in. Wind on the water was making a small storm as we limped back to the jetty, got the sails down and the boat back on land with some difficulty, and dripped our way back to the car.

7-12 September
That evening, when I was still drowning again in my mind, Adam Hopkins arrived to stay with us for a few days. Adam is writing a book on the Netherlands and, at present, seeing as much of the country as he can, forming impressions and taking in information.

We made several expeditions together, the weather on the first two days being warm, sun shining and wind-sculpted white clouds towering and disintegrating in the sky, light and shadow drawing things in the vast land-and sky-scape sharp and clear:

To Drente on the Hondsrug on the track of *hunnebedden*. Megaliths mounded, humped up. One still grassed over, a green mound with a square, open chamber at the top. Harebells in the grass, acorns full-grown in cups on low oaks, with silk strands & spiderwebs shining between the leaves, and a sweet smell of decaying vegetation meeting us as we walked on the slopes.

It seemed to me at that moment, as I thought of man's religion early and late, megaliths and churches—and David Jones too was in my mind—all one work.

Glaciers & men: the stone-shifters.

Big iceberg clouds on the route of the glaciers, where the boulders of pink and grey Baltic granite were scattered.

Groningen to Friesland: Appingedam—Eemshaven—Noordpolderzijl—Lauwersoog—Dokkum—Franeker—Harlingen.

From the dyke: tide out, blue-grey mud under blue sky and clouds; inland, standing alone in a vast landscape, a windmill called Goliath with a ditch leading to and beyond it—a ditch not quite straight, in a country where irregularities stand out more than in England, where they are the rule. Here one may appreciate what hills and mountains are even more than when among the Alps.

At Noordpolderzijl men were rebuilding the inland face of the dyke in patterns of different coloured stones. Otherwise we were alone, sitting outside at a café table, when a large party of middle-aged & old people arrived on bicycles, from a village which is 15 kilometres away, and surrounded us talking and laughing, full of good spirits and the health of the ride.

At Westernieland, a small medieval church with a redbrick tower and walls plastered a pale yellow, standing in a small graveyard. A number of gravestones set flat in the ground were evidently by the same mason or from the same workshop, or perhaps they are to a pattern which commemorates a particular sect. All are dated from the mid to late 19th century and are carved with a Tree of Life & butterflies—symbolizing the soul set free of life's brevity? Later I learnt that the graveyard has some very old stones commemorating seal hunters, but I didn't see them.

On the edge of the Waddenzee, small villages set in a broad, open landscape of sand & clay, always with the pressure of the sea behind the dyke. Old dykes lie farther back inland, and in places there are flames from a natural gas field flaring against the sky, and a distant spire under cloud which the wind is turning and moulding like a great spiral shell.

In Friesland we visited the water-towns: Dokkum on its terp, Franeker, Harlingen. Neat, elegant, even rather ornate architecture of a bourgeois civilisation, but resting on a hard working base, practical and daring, open to the sea. In Harlingen, a church beside the docks, coasters being repaired just a road's width from its doors; dredgers with rusty buckets and walls of old tyres in a canal.

The older churches, as at Appingedam, often have fine green glass in the windows, and are filled with a pure, green-tinted underwater light.

To Ezinge (*het Troje van het noorden*) on a grey afternoon. Black sheep grazing in the churchyard, a five pointed star in red and grey brick set into the pavement just inside the gate. Cattle in the fields around, feathery rushes in ditches, a feel of sea-soaked earth from which the terp rises, a man-made island thousands of years old.

On Thursday, in Drachten, M. opened an exhibition of paintings by Nelleke Vogels, an autistic woman who has never communicated in any way unless with these images, which she paints quickly and takes no further interest in. They are beautiful and expressive—they are "art"—showing a strong sense of colour, texture, relations of shapes, form. They lay structures bare—bodies inside clothes, a kite like a skeleton, a mouth of teeth—and are disturbing when the subject is human, because everything is seen a-humanely. Except that Nelleke Vogels' condition is a human possibility, but frightening, a dreadful mystery. There is, then, an aesthetic *instinct*, an instinct to make beautiful things? And *flight* is somehow part of it—her birds, her kites, her serpent-headed phallic lighthouses—dynamic forms, forms that move and rise, forms with the rhythm of life. They are exuberant, and they convey, with colour, movement and shape, a sense of happiness.

Yet the painter wouldn't understand this or any other concept, wouldn't know why the paintings were hung up and why a crowd of people was looking at them. But she shares her images with us—kite, crow, and lighthouse belong to our common world. Or she shares their colours, shapes and structures, but not their meanings. I can't grasp this either, when she can paint the kiteness of a kite.

After the opening Adam and I drove to Leeuwarden, where we saw a fine piece of metalwork by M's grandfather: the railings encircling a tree outside the Stadhuis. Geert Kroes was Mieke's maternal grandfather, a Friesian (though there's good reason for thinking he was of Polish descent, from the Poles who came to Franeker University in the 17th century). A professional metalworker, he made small artistic objects in silver, as well as small and larger works in metal. His work was exhibited at the World Exposition in New York in 1904. His photograph stands in the living room: a black-haired young man with rather drawn cheeks but a sensuous mouth under his moustache, and intense, piercing eyes burning in the hollows of his face. He died at the age of 37.

Adam left for the south of the country this morning. Everywhere we went we talked, shared our impressions and ideas, tried to get below the surface. And we talked about our work & our lives. He is disillusioned with his poetry (but perhaps because of several rejections by publishers) and feels it may be *only* personal. On the other hand he is working flat out as a full-time writer and is obsessed by the need to make a living, to the extent of measuring the time and income of each project very carefully. He does good work under that pressure, even if it isn't always the work he would like to do, and he made me realise the requirements of that kind of independence. It was a great pleasure to have such a lively, intelligent, good humoured and considerate companion.

24 September
With M. on a morning of warm sunlight, blue sky and daylight moon, over sandy heath to river Drentse A near Schipborg.

Red leaf, yellow leaf, wild cherry by oak & sycamore. Now the few leaves falling, spinning down leisurely, look as if they have chosen to fall. Funguses, a sweet smell from the woods.

Drentse A like a river in an English landscape, opaque, greeny water carrying grasses & leaves, slow-flowing and serpentine through meadows.

Walking back, we talked about the present concern of intellectuals to demythologise every "reality" and expose it as a social *construction*. In *Wales: The Imagined Nation*, for example—the general trend, following historians' exposure of the exclusion from nationhood, and virtually from history, of the larger part of the population by myths of romantic nationalism, and, in particular, the message of Gwyn A. Williams and Tony Bianchi writing on R. S. Thomas: that truth to the feeling of a class may sanction and reinforce a social lie.

Is the exposure, in effect, destructive of all poetry, or does it make possible a new *poetic* vision, and a new way of *reading*—without diminishing—poetry embedded in what it sees as a structure of myth? Is there an absolute opposition between poetry and religion on one side, and historical materialism and the sociological mind on the other? When all structures have been laid bare, or as bare as possible, the ultimate ground of reality—socio-historical or religious—is a matter of faith. But I don't accept that, as ways of seeing, they are incompatible—in fact, not mutually enlightening—except to fundamentalists at either extreme.

But for a poet with instincts embedded in *the poetry of earth*... Yet what may that mean! It isn't "*never dead*" because rooted in a set of attitudes constructed by one narrow social order. It can never die, as long as man and Earth last, because the vital relationship between them always exists to be felt and interpreted anew. And what comes from the past—a power that may rule the heart and overthrow the mind—has to be welcomed with the eye of critical understanding.

25 September
Afternoon. Cycled into the country, sweating out the poison of inactivity. By a canal, in hot sun, yellow leaves falling occasionally from poplars at my back, then a gust of wind and a sudden shower of leaves, falling on grass, road, and water. To Woltersum, on the canal bank opposite the village, windmill & house roofs appearing over the far bank. *Waddenzee*, an old tug, engines thumping, making the water churn and heave, pushing waves slantwise against the banks in advance, and drawing them behind, waves with a crest of spray speeding along the banks, cutting through reeds—a heron flying away at the vibration of the approaching boat. Harvest of grass & reeds on the roadside. Mud black as tar from newly cleaned ditches. Sometimes, looking far across flat fields, I still expect to see hills, and momentarily, in cloud or faint blue mist, dream that I do.

§

> But the man who tries to express his age, instead of expressing himself, is doomed to destruction.
>
> Ezra Pound, *Gaudier-Brzeska*

> I could not agree more enthusiastically with "If you feel enough others will"... But the "enough" has to be so "enough" as to make the form dead right—utterly convincing.
>
> David Jones, *Inner Necessities*

28 September

Day of warm, faintly misted sunlight. Cycled through Glimmen to the Hoge Hereweg, the Neolithic track following the crest of the Hondsrug, at Appelbergen, where it is a narrow, sandy way between tall thin oaks with an understorey of rowan & hazel, & elder with slender branches bowing under clusters of black fruit. I sat in the wood by a path to eat my sandwiches—branches & leaves trembling in a refreshing breeze—and a dog came up and barked at me. The family it belonged to soon followed, and the father, a pleasant young man, explained to me—he spoke English—that the dog was barking because of my beard! A brief, inconsequential exchange of words between strangers, but I went on my way feeling the better for it.

Sunday: a day of cyclists taking their pleasure in the country: couples of all ages, families, mothers or fathers with little children held in front of them, sometimes an infant, face looking through a plastic windshield; a young man leaning his elbows on upright handlebars, pedalling vigorously, but nonchalantly, devil-may-care—a recurring gesture that seems typically Dutch. A bright yellow & blue train passed just as I was close to the track, which ran beside water—train above, its bright image fleeting across the water below.

Onnen to Noordlaren, a village with a fine old church with beautifully sculpted red brick buttresses. White sails visible on the meer at some distance across the fields, and an arm of water, boats moored on it, reaching almost to the churchyard. The conjunction of church & water reminded me of Freshwater, though the place was otherwise quite different. Back via the station for tea & cake, acorns on the *fietspad* popping under my tyres, and from the fresh smells of the country—muck-spread fields, an orchard, gardens—to the sour smell of the sugar factory.

4-5 October

Weekend at Tilburg in Brabant with M's friends Hetty & Tom. Two beautiful days, sky becoming cloudless as we drove south. American oaks turning rust-red in woodland from end to end of the Netherlands, flocks of peewits in fields, gliders spiralling over the Hoge Veluwe near Arnhem.

Saturday afternoon: Tom took me sailing in his yacht—a half-ton sloop from Poole—on the lower Maas at Drimellen. On one side of the waterway the smoking cooling tower of a power station, on the other the *Biesbos*, a large area of swamp and reclaimed land, some of the polders on the site of settlements drowned under water & mud in former times; polders with sinister names: *Angst, Moordenaar, Verdronken Land*. A quiet afternoon on the water, with a few yachts and an occasional barge, cormorants and other water-birds, boys fishing, an otter among the reeds. Yet as we sailed back with the wind, after a leisurely sail down channel, I was afraid. Tom, a big, black-haired, generous man, is an expert sailor. On this occasion, my fear invented the story of him falling overboard—perhaps tripping as he raised or lowered the sail—and leaving me helpless on board.

From pub to pub in Tilburg at night, under a sky of bright stars.

Sunday morning

Tom drove us all over the border into Belgium, to the abbey at Postel. Organ music from the surviving Romanesque church—limestone beside the brick of later additions—which M. and I entered. Half-light, a faint smell of incense, music filling the church from the organ above a Christ hanging in greater darkness under the dome, against a background of stained-glass windows: an immediate, dominating focus, lifting the eye from the few people, some of them lighting candles, in the shadowy interior, and to me at once the conviction: they really mean something here!

Driving back we visited 's-Hertogenbosch (The Duke's Wood) which, seen from a distance, had intrigued us: several tall modern buildings above old roofs & a dome & spires on the far shore of a large lake—a view which was even more like a dream in the autumn light. Town of the great Hieronymous—his house was almost the first we saw after getting out of the car and walking towards the cathedral.

Sint Jan Kathedraal: an immediate impression of size and power—like Winchester, but much more ornate. Then a sense of the fantastic in its combination of basilica and Western Gothic features. Inside, the feeling of strangeness increased, especially with the eye of the Trinity looking down from high in the cupola. Many visitors and a christening in progress in a side chapel, the candidate bawling. But from deep within a great cathedral the noise of people moving about and talking is like the sighing and rustling and murmur of the sea lapping and gently breaking on the shore. Floor paved with worn, slippery black marble gravestones, the smoothed symbols & Brabant coats of arms like hieroglyphs. Altar of the Passion, 15th century gilt woodwork and painted panels from Antwerp. Christ riding on a donkey into Jerusalem, Christ in the Garden, gripped by a man who has locked an arm round him and has seized his long hair, after Peter has sliced off the servant's ear. The face of this Christ is a deep thinking, inward, but also *simple* face—the face, perhaps, of a spiritual & intellectual peasant—and has a close family likeness to the face of Bosch's Christ in *Heaven*. But other figures on the panels, the servant in particular, and the vigorous dramatic action, reminded me of Brueghel.

The cathedral was full of visitors, but in the Chapel of the Virgin most people were praying, with an intent stillness that took me aback and made me feel like a voyeur. Rows of red candles with yellow flames stood in front of the statue, and people were continually adding a fresh flame.

Now, in retrospect, it is this that is set apart as something entirely different from the interior as spectacle: a stillness in the bustle, a concentrated seriousness of deepest need, in place of all the rapid glancing, or, in my case, the raid on a few images.

Granted that the place as a whole is very different from how it was in Hieronymous Bosch's time, the town and especially the cathedral brought more of his mystery home to me. But I brought to it, as well as a romantic dream, a sense of ancient dread from the waterlogged land vulnerable to flood, and painful embarrassed knowledge of my own neurotic fears. It isn't that I want to translate his vision into modern psychological terms, which seems to me patronising—as if some affinity with our (Freudian) way of seeing things is what makes him important. In the horror and cruelty I recognise an essential—and terrible—part of common human experience. Certainly of northern experience; but it isn't only in the north that people have tortured and destroyed each other and themselves, or so misused the mind that it blinds them or makes them weak with fear.

Bosch's vision is "medieval" in the sense that it couldn't have come into being at any other time, without the Christian Hell (and Heaven) working on an individual mind during a period of transition, when what many had long felt could at last be *seen* and externalised, (as Freud could give a form to what many people had long felt). But it is one of *our* great stories: not literally true, but true in the sense that we recognise something of the worst of ourselves in it.

Then to turn from that to the Mother & Child, and to the goodness & truth of the peasant-Christ, and only then to know that we do not *have* to think, or to act, the horror and cruelty. It was not this Christ who brought evil into the world. He is not the torturer of Inquisition or the devil of flagellant or puritan castaway. We turn or fall away from the goodness and truth, but I don't think we invented them. Though their images rose and developed under the artists' hands, it was something beyond all the images that came into the world, something men & women would not have been able to think for themselves. It is hard for anyone to think the *fact* of it—but easy to recognise its manifestations. Of course I don't understand this; what I'm reaching for is beyond me. I only know that if the fact hadn't been given I could never have thought it, and believe that no human being could. The mystery is that something beyond our grasp, but speaking to our deepest need, came into the world.

Man is very strange; in Bosch and in Sint Jan something of that strangeness can be seen. But I think it is, in part, a strangeness arising from the attempt to give form to the truth which man did not invent, but was given. Truth that is a person, that is God—man turns himself inside out and ransacks the world of images trying to give God a form. And in doing so he gives shapes to his dreams & nightmares—and catches now and then some glimmer of the original uncreated light?

But I mustn't forget the element of play and the delight in shape and design in Bosch, a man who may sometimes have been frightened and chilled by what he imagined but who, as a painter, evidently took pleasure in his exuberant inventiveness. Certainly, the insect-devils or insect-men, the beast-men or fish-men, all the bird-headed men and strange composite creatures, are figures of nightmare, of the mind sick with the torments of Hell and Sin; and there is cruelty, born also of an age of physical torture, in what Bosch does to the bodies of the damned. Yet he delights, too, in the way one thing or shape suggests another—e.g. earthenware jar and pig, or roots and antennae, or egg shell and hollowed tree trunk. It is a delight in visual suggestion or metaphor, but it is also a vision of metamorphosis and of correspondences, in which man's roots are entangled in nature, and his spiritual condition can be best shown by the way in which he wallows in the natural matrix, acting like the lower forms of life.

A swamp breeding horrors, a fecund world both terrifying and fascinating, and with a touch of humour that is inseparable from delight. In this world there's nothing whole about the natural man—that idea would come to Europe later—but except for the divine or blessed, all human beings are hideous with vice. It is immeasurably more sophisticated and more psychological, but this world is still connected with the world that conceived Grendel in the meer and the monsters and freaks of northern folktale & myth. And in a curious way it looks forward to Darwin even more than to Freud. The darkness of forest and morass and the bright, bewitching, dangerous colours of Creation—swamp colours, colours of creatures and of vegetation—come together in the mind of Hieronymous Bosch. And the world of breeding nature with her weird forms becomes the world of Apocalypse and Judgement. But if Hell and Sin tormented Bosch's mind, and the mind of his age, what would his vision have been without images of the blessed & the divine, without Saint or Virgin or God?

9 October

Windy. Ghost sun in sky the colour of smoked glass, brighter on the water of Paterswoldemeer when wind thinned the cloud—burnished sheen on pewter.

Poetry of windmills: De Helper, De Vier Winden, Goliath, De Jonge Hendrik, Aeolus, De Meeuw, Stormvogel, Windlust.

Passion & courage of thought: Richard Jefferies in his last notebooks. Not, what consoles, but, what is true? Acute pain, but he attempts to see beyond its distortions. A man broken in body, but mind at its noblest: observing, speculating, thinking at the extreme edge of knowledge, on the brink of death.

His isolation is terrible. And it is the *logical* conclusion of his thought, together with something deep in his personality. It finally cuts him off from everyone & everything—people, nature, the universe—as completely as anyone can be cut off while still conscious.

I can't speak of the *direction* of his thought without criticising it, but I can only honour and admire the man. What I understand about him least, where I can't feel with him, is his total friendlessness. That perhaps was his misfortune, which I could understand. But it suggests rather that something in him chose it. He *never* speaks in his most intimate writings, the notebooks, of communicating with others, with his wife or anyone else, and at last books and nature too are "nothing", and there is only the "Beyond". He was self-willed, but he was also representative of tendencies in his world, less isolated from social & intellectual influences than he thought, but not less alone. The notebooks are terrible, but fascinating; there are few writings in which one comes as close to the person—and is that terrible or consoling, that Jefferies in his extremity should be in reach of fellow feeling that he never knew?

Even in his last months Jefferies was still obsessed by flight. Not a mechanical interest alone, surely, for one equally obsessed by the soul, and dying. What is the significance of this, together with the fact that Goethe's *Faust* was one of his favourite books, in relation to Oswald Spengler's idea of the Faustian?

> To fly, to free one's self from earth, to lose one's self in the expanse of the universe—is not this ambition Faustian in the highest degree? Is it not in fact the fulfilment of our dreams? Has it never been observed how the Christian legend became in Western painting a glorious transfiguration of this motive? All the pictured ascents into heaven and falls into hell, the divine figures floating above the clouds, the blissful detachment of angels and saints, the insistent emphasis upon freedom from earth's heaviness, are emblems of soul-flight…
> *The Decline of the West*

In fact, the connection is in part a shared romanticism (Spengler, as Huizinga rightly says, was a German romantic), and in that respect a secularisation of religious impulse. I think that in Jefferies it is also an expression of the imperial spirit or will, the desire to *penetrate* and *conquer* space, and to go beyond both the whole material universe and all previous thought. In that Jefferies was a man of his time. But what is *his* time? Our time, too, or a time past for some of us: time of Baconian science, time of Faustian, Romantic will, time of Christianity in dissolution, forming other compounds in artistic & intellectual minds, which some of them wrongly think a new thing. Yes, Jefferies was a "Victorian"; but if we really understood what our time is, we'd feel brotherhood with him, and with many others across the centuries.

§

> A flat country with few tall trees, without the many great ruins so typical of Southern countries, offered the eye the peace of simple lines, of hazy distances and gradual changes. Sky and cloud, then and now, helped to calm the troubled spirit. The modest towns with their moss-covered

walls were surrounded by greenery or water—the oldest element in all creation, upon whose face the Spirit of God had moved in the very beginning, and the simplest as well. No wonder, therefore, that even the people were simple—in all they thought and did....

...Our people have always loved simple things—it is part of our religious outlook to prize them as God's gifts, to enjoy their beauty as such, and hence to care for them as best we can. In this we are greatly helped by the ample presence of water, and by the fact that a moist atmosphere and frequent sea breezes generally keep our air free of dust.

It may have been a homely virtue, our cleanliness, but it was anything but crude materialism. For cleanliness went hand in hand with a strong feeling for reality, in as much as, philosophically or otherwise, objects were deemed to exist in their own right and valued as such.

J. H. Huizinga, *Dutch Civilisation in the 17th Century*

16 October
Wolddijk—Winsum—Garnwerd—Ezinge: with Joe, to take photographs.

Cycling into wind, under a lowlands' sky-sea, blue and vast, with small, pale purple-grey cloud islands far to the north. Windmill across fields, something Odyssean about the motionless sails shining, perhaps because they look like crossed oars!

Dandelion flowers & clocks. Fallen leaves lying on duckweed in ditches, like green tracks. Occasionally a train, very small in the distance, cutting across the landscape.

Three boys fishing in a small watercourse—reeds shaking and hissing in the wind, yellow-gold when the sun caught their autumn tints—the water pointing across meadows to spires, water-tower and smoking factory chimney of Groningen at the horizon. Vapour track high up—fading print of dinosaur vertebrae.

At Garnwerd, looking up the church tower from close to its base, at once high, apparently moving fast, and bringing back an early memory, from Warsash: the big girls (whose names I've long since forgotten) telling me that, as red-tiled roofs of houses across the lane seemed to fly through space, what we could see was the earth moving.

Beside a branch of the Reitdiep to Ezinge, boats to the edge of the village and ploughland to the water's edge, only the narrowest margin of reeds where otherwise the tractors would have gone over.

On the way back, a large old boat drawn up out of the water, a rusty hulk lying in a field, with a cow rubbing its chin against the boat's side.

§

And was there not plenty of larch timber lying about, that had been thrown and not sold, that would make a very good spar-gate... Why couldn't old Hooker, the hedge-carpenter, knock it up cheap?

Richard Jefferies, *Hodge and his Masters*

24 October
On the Sunday after our ride to Ezinge the succession of beautiful weeks was broken. Continents of cloud massed overhead, grey but radiant at the edges where the hidden sun glanced off them, and between the continents a deep abyss of icy blue. A storm followed at night, and has returned with rain & hailstones several times since.

27 October
A beautiful day for our wedding: blue sky and a wash of white cloud. To calm myself I walked round Bernoulleplein in the morning. About twenty gulls were picking over the grass, most apart but some shrilling and squabbling, and long shadows of Lombardy poplars were laid out, leaf shadows shimmering darkly. Sun shone on windows of parked cars, on damp leaves lying on the grass, and made a ladder of light inside our window blinds.

In the afternoon, with Hans & Agnes as our witnesses, and in the company of family & friends, M. and I were married at the Stadhuis. A lady registrar officiated, with touching enthusiasm. She spoke partly in Dutch and partly in English, and to such effect that Karel, who was taking the photographs, had to hide behind her and behind his camera. In fact everyone was amused, but her effort, earnest sentimentality, and quaint English had a charm that added to the warmth of the occasion. Afterwards we returned to the Korreweg, where we had a lively party in the evening, the house filled with guests.

28 October
From fair to foul weather, driving in dirty, misty light and then in clearer darkness to the Hoek. Rough crossing, but the sea near England was calm towards dawn.

29 October
Another beautiful day. From Harwich to the South Orbital, from which we turned off and drove through Sussex—rust red and burnt gold woodlands, here and there a communal bonfire ready for Guy Fawkes night—Horsham, Billingshurst (with a glimpse of the church where I was married before, on a cold February day), Midhurst, and so to Petersfield for lunch, and Winchester.

After tea with Elizabeth we took Emily to Hayford and celebrated again with my parents.

30 October
With M. in Lymington, after putting Emily on the train at Brockenhurst. A dull, damp day. At once I was ill-tempered, finding fault with the people & the place, seeing everything with sour, ambiguous, *class* feelings—which is always my initial response on going "home" now, since I ceased to be at home.

31 October
My parents in the drive at Hayford, Dad with his arm round Mother—always lovers, and with a way of holding on my father's part that I've recently learnt to recognise in old and new photographs of myself.

To the station at Oxford with M., who then went on to Cambridge for the weekend. I met Elizabeth on the platform and travelled with her to Worcester. From the train: ploughland, cabbage fields, orchards, a green mist of winter crops close to the ground. Constant variation of hills & hillocks with the rhythms of English country. Sombre and vivid colours side by side, but as Elizabeth said, there are no aesthetic clashes in nature. Looking out of the window at Moreton—in—Marsh I was startled to see the name of a building firm: Spook Erections Ltd! Later, in Worcester, Bladder & Son. And in the Netherlands my surname always raises a smile!

31 October—2 November
At The Loch Ryan hotel, Worcester (in a room looking out on Fort Royal, site of the Battle of Worcester) tutoring a creative writing weekend, with Gillian. Two reminders of Southampton: Bernadette, a doctor practising at Bitterne, told me that the Itchen Bridge is now the favourite place for suicides; Bill, a man in his fifties, reminisced about his time at Calshot with the Air Sea Rescue service, and we remembered the Sunderlands & the Queens.

3 November
In Worcester with M., who joined me at the end of the course on Sunday. First we went into a shoe shop, where pop music was playing so loudly in the overheated interior that the assistant could hardly hear what M. wanted. Then back into the street, where pop music was blaring from Woolworth's into the shopping precinct and intruding everywhere in the public space. It was quiet by the river, Severn broad and brown and leafy. Alders growing from the embankment of mossed sandstone blocks, their trunks looking hard and cold as stone, a pair of grey wagtails flitting delicately from tree to tree, swans swimming against the current and a branch floating downstream. Another world here, between the cathedral rising above and the river, a world of water and massive, worked stone, undercrofts above flood levels marked on a wall, bell chime and a noise of distant traffic over a bridge. In the cathedral there was a chinking of hammers as workmen were erecting scaffolding.

Not a May morning, but up into the clouded Malverns—Tortelier playing Elgar's cello concerto on the car cassette recorder. Then a climb on foot above bracken and tree line, following the earth walls of the fort, hills above us climbing ridge over ridge. Any field below might have been the field full of folk: irregular fields separated by hedges, arable and grassland, a tractor ploughing, the Severn Plain stretching into England and into Wales, into mist and cloud. A jay circled the hill and the fort's bare, carved sides lifted above us like a maze. Wet mist came down while we had lunch at a pub, but Langland's joyful May morning prelude was still ringing in my head as we descended to Little Malvern Priory at the foot of the hills.

Later, in Tewkesbury Abbey, I felt sour again. Outside the warm, yellow stone was welcoming, but inside the space between the great pillars was like an empty barn, with crusader chantries like stalls against the walls. Immediately inside the door a crucifix on a pillar over a sign to the abbey shop seemed to point the way— and the shop was the worst of its kind for knick-knacks I've ever seen. Of course they have to make money, but somehow the well-lit room full of trinkets in the otherwise empty interior seemed to be the real heart of the place.

We arrived at Swindon early in the evening, and walked about the concrete and glass labyrinth of the shopping area, beside carparks & the bus station crowded with people who work in the centreless interior, on their way home to outlying villages & towns. Once Jefferies' town, where now, in a shabby studio of the Wyvern Theatre, I gave the Birthday Lecture—one hundred years after Jefferies was celebrating his last birthday.

Kim was at the lecture, and afterwards we drove back with her to Tackley.

4 November
We woke to ploughland strewn with straw stretching in a wide expanse outside our window, and frosty dew on the grass covering the site of the lost village.

Later, in Oxford on a bright morning, we called on Oli in his room at Magdalen and he took us round Addison's Walk.

Chestnut, beech, maple—each day the leaf colours seem more vivid, as if undergoing a final, impossible alchemy—autumn smells from undergrowth & ditches, mistletoe on trees in the deer park in which the animals were grazing, and a view across the park of Magdalen tower—pristine in scoured stone, clean now of industrial dirt whose acid has eaten into it. Oli took us to the Holywell ford and the studio-cum-boathouse where, he told us, Dylan Thomas had had his affair with A. J. P. Taylor's wife. A piece of information which for me, now I record it, is curiously uninteresting!

After lunch at The Turf M & I drove to Church Hanborough. Midge dance and shining threads of cobweb between yews beside the church path. Starlings clustering on the weathercock at the apex of the tall, slender spire. A primitive power in the Norman tympanum over the north door: St Peter between a lion and a lamb, with a cock at his feet.

Wastie graves in the graveyard: "In Lasting Memory of our much loved Father and Mother James and Emily Wastie who died January 1 1921 and January 17 1932. *In Jesus Keeping*". To Walter Wastie 1904 and Eliza Wastie 1908. Inside, Alfred Wastie was among the names of the local men killed in the First World War. From the interior I could hear, faintly, the noise of rooks from high above the church. Light through clerestory windows fell in patches on whitewashed walls, in the clean space of a working church.

It was "a love match" between his father and mother, Tom Hooker and Annie Wastie, my father said: "*Make no mistake about that*". I thought of young Tom working in the Orchid House at Blenheim, and of Annie, "in service", from Woodstock. I thought too of the old man my father knew: James Wastie scratching the back of his beloved pig, all the vigorous life gone years since into the ground. And of my father after his mother's death, walking in tears through *her* places, from Freeland to Church Hanborough.

Suddenly, talking with Kim & M. some things came clear. It isn't only the "corruption of the language" that has made me so rigorously selective and indirect in my poetry, but, more, my dislike & distrust of the dominant type of English *man* who reads and writes poetry. There's writing whose aim is the *thrust* of meaning (often, now, a verse of smart punch lines), and there's writing that weaves a web (Gwyn Williams on the *Celtic* forms of David Jones), which is tentative, exploratory, and made for the love of the thing. In the latter the meaning may be in the making (as I love noting what I see), rather than an end product, as it is in the former case.

6 November

In London, on another bright day, I walked with Lee to Parson's Green. Down a turning off the New King's Road, in a yard, the workshop of Mr Fiorini, bronze caster. Five or six men & women at work, dust & fragments of plaster everywhere, casts, sculptures including a Henry Moore (Mr Fiorini was his caster), and a figure representing a naked Winston Churchill, with a penis befitting a bulldog—apparently the work of an elderly sculptor disgruntled at not winning a commission for a Churchill statue.

Mr Fiorini, who has recently cast Lee's *Islington Angel*, showed us around. A good-humoured, thoughtful man of about sixty, a workman in overalls, he said that he could have made more money at another occupation, retired years ago, but the work "gets hold of you", drives you on always with the desire to do better, to achieve a more perfect colour.

7 November

From Harwich on a grey morning, blowing a little. On the Essex coast across the estuary, a medieval church tower rising above trees—as we have seen them all over England.

Sea dark, greeny grey, great black-backed gulls flying close to the water, and a pair of starlings crossing with us, now flying alongside, now landing on deck or lifeboat.

I stood on deck for a long time staring into the misty dusk, ships lit up like Halloween turnip skulls passing on the darkening sea. At last pinpricks of light appeared on the horizon behind a lighthouse beam, which had been flashing for some time, it was brighter now, and visibly turning.

From the Hoek we drove in less than three hours to Groningen.

8 November
Mother told me on the phone that they have sold Hayford and will be moving to New Milton, probably before Christmas. She also told me that she had read in the paper that Lucy Penny had died at Mappowder during the week. Lucy signed the card which Gerard sent on 25 October for our wedding.

13 November
Instead of starting work this week I've been laid up with a nasty cold, reading Jonathan Raban's two most recent books, *Coasting* and *Foreign Land*. I bought the former out of vanity as well as curiosity, wondering if I might appear in it in some form. I don't; which is probably just as well. But irrespective of that I've found reading *Coasting* in particular fascinating and disturbing.

I admire parts of Jonathan's books and have reservations about others. If I feel any envy it's of his ability to release and develop his talent, not of his work itself, which was always going to be quite different from mine. And if I envy his *success* it takes the form of wondering, sourly, and with increasing worry, whether anything I could write could possibly *sell*.

To my mind, the finest parts of *Coasting* are the accounts of the actual sailing, based on experience which it must have taken him real courage to gain, and the descriptions of the north of England and of London. It's when he writes of the south coast, though, that he invokes for me a flood of memories, and makes his account of a time and a place we shared seem frail and superficial. I've only in imagination to set my foot on the pavement by St Mark's or on the Common to know a world of experience that Jonathan's writing doesn't touch, and that overwhelms and silences me with its vast strange actuality.

18 November
To Den Haag with M. by train. *Moord Schokt Parijs* headline of the morning papers: the President of Renault gunned down by terrorists. Sun in my face, low, bright white sun in a sky cleared by strong wind; water ruffled, trees almost bare, the sun's image racing on parallel watercourses. Cloud and rain farther south, a wet, colder day in Den Haag.

We went to the Mauritshuis, and found it closed for repairs. From there to the building housing the Willem V collection of paintings. Up dingy, red-carpeted stairs, smelling of stale cigar smoke, into a long, high room in which paintings were hung close above and beside each other. An overwhelming impression of old, brown varnish which resolved, incompletely, into portraits, still-lives, landscapes, with a few notable works—e.g. a Rubens portrait of a young woman, a small Rembrandt, a small Jan Steen—and many mediocre and some bad ones, most memorably a large monstrosity depicting bears being attacked by dogs and a man with a sword on horseback, the dogs with bloody muzzles leaping on the bloodstained bears, a dead dog with mouth open like a man-trap, lying on its back, and the unscathed man coming in for the kill. An ugly thing that somehow stripped decorum from the 18th century collection and revealed a clumsy naked barbarousness. We then walked to Johan de Witt Huis, an annex to the Mauritshuis, and found it occupied by artists "striking" against government cuts in bursaries. Afterwards—the purpose of the visit—to the Palais van Justitie, a new, big, labyrinthine building, where M. had to see a judge about a juvenile client, and I waited on the eighth floor looking out over streets of terraces, tower blocks and trams at the wooded city edge disappearing into mist. Below, rain blowing across almost empty courtyards & squares and falling on heroic, green-bronzed statues.

30 November
"A blanket of fog is covering much of England." On a bright day here I cycled to the station for an English Sunday paper, but none had arrived, probably because the fog hadn't lifted. A short walk in the Sterrebos, behind the clenched and upreaching, tortured hands commemorating the Jews. Sycamores & hazels with abundant green leaves, alongside leafless oaks & oaks with scraps of rust-coloured, dead leaves clinging to them. I walked round a lake of black water, under the high windows of the fortified prison, and behind the sculpture, which stands beside the road and at the wood-edge close to the prison walls, the hands reaching up with the trees. Back in town: *Parcival*, an old barge, now a houseboat, flying the Dutch flag astern & the Friesian flag amidships, moored at the side of a haven and connected to the shore by planks & a wooden bridge with a bike leaning against a hand-rail.

§

The North: a world of inner distances.

H. R. Ellis Davidson, in *Gods and Myths of Northern Europe*, describes the "picture of a long and perilous journey from one world to another over mountains and desolate wastes of cold and darkness, or of a tedious and fearsome road down to the abode of the dead'". She comments: "long before astronomy revealed to men the terrifying extent of the great starry spaces, the idea of vastness and of distances to tantalize the mind was already present in heathen thought".

Robert Rosenblum begins his book *Modern Painting and the Northern Romantic Tradition* with Caspar David Friedrich's *Monk by the Sea* and ends it with the Rothko Chapel, Houston, in which "it is as if the entire content of Western religious art were finally devoid of its narrative complexities and corporeal imagery, leaving us with these dark, compelling presences that pose an ultimate choice between everything and nothing". According to Rosenblum:

> The sense of divinity in boundless voids, where figures, objects, and finally matter itself are excluded, belongs to a Romantic tradition primarily sustained by non-Catholic artists—Protestants, Jews, or by members of such modern Spiritualist sects as Theosophy—for the iconoclastic attitudes of these religions were conducive to the presentation of

transcendental experience through immaterial images, whether the impalpable infinities of horizon, sea, or sky or their abstract equivalents in the immeasurable voids of Mondrian or Newman.

Spengler, a Romantic on Romanticism, writes of "our first-person idiom", and claims: "This first person towers up in the Gothic architecture; the spire is an 'I', the flying buttress is an 'I'". Shakespeare's drama appears to Spengler as a single monologue, revealing even in group-scenes "the immense inner distance between persons'. To Spengler, all Western lyric verse is monologue, unlike Classical lyric verse, which is "a singing before witnesses". What, then, is his "soul-flight" but the self's fall into the void of inner distance?

At the end of Rosenblum's book, despite the great beauty of many of his illustrations, or perhaps because of their kind of beauty, I felt a curious sense of emptiness. It was as though meaning had been bled from the world with its substance, by rendering it objectless and immaterial. And how escape the conclusion of the stress upon iconoclasm: that the "new" modern vision is *dissolution* of the old, and therefore dependant upon its destruction or transformation for its force?

Sparrow's flight through the king's hall on a winter afternoon, from dark to dark. From palpable immense distances of forest & sea men might infer the geography of an underworld, or visualize Hell. The soul's flight in that otherworld is terrifying or ecstatic, but still remains within "space" with a common meaning. But when the immense *inner* distance is the space *between* people, when no metaphor of cosmic "depth" or "height" will serve, that is the nothing and nowhere, opening at any instant in the self, that sickens with fear. It is late in the process dividing us, and setting one human competitor against another, that "gifted" individuals think about founding a "new" religion; as if, even in their terms, with God or all the gods dead, it weren't staggeringly arrogant stupidity that makes an individual think he can, purely with his will or imagination, both bind himself to other people and give them what they need... But no true artist thinks that; but, as his time and talent allow, renders the bird's flight between darknesses, which he did not make.

15 December
Frost white on the grass in the morning, jackdaws & gulls picking round the edge, among frozen leaves. Ice on puddles on the pavement, trapped air bubbles changing shape, like amoeba when I cracked it. At dusk and after dark, snow. Snow swirling and falling aslant in the light of street lamps and around an illuminated, black tree, with naked branches hanging down. My parents left Hayford today.

§

Here in England, we have a fair house full of many good things, but cumbered also by pestilential rubbish. What duty can be more pressing than to carry out the rubbish piecemeal and burn it outside, lest some

day there be no way of getting rid of it but by burning it all up inside with the goods and house and all?
  William Morris, 'Art, Wealth and Riches' (1883)

England—I am sick of the sound of the word.
  Charles Sorley (August 1914)

Stated briefly, what's happening now, in books like *Englishness* & *On Living in an Old Country* & most of the increasingly numerous analyses of English "patriotism", "tradition", "national identity" or "heritage", is a kind of iconoclasm. The icons were made mainly in the years leading up to the Great War, developed in the interwar period and renewed during the Second World War. They were newly embellished after 1945 by events such as the Festival of Britain and the Coronation, but continuing economic decline and social conflict have, by the mid-eighties, worn them thin.

 The icons are still serviceable for Conservative political ends, as in the Falklands War, but for many intellectuals they are myths or mystifications to be deconstructed into their formative historical and political power relations. This particular iconoclasm is part of a wider intellectual movement in the West, which is replacing concepts of people or society or nation as "organic"—in fact all "naturalising" ideology—with historicist thinking about processes, constructions, formations. In England the most potent icons are pictures of an idealized countryside, where the past (in this view, a petrified hierarchical social order) "lives" as ground of national identity: Kipling's Sussex or Baldwin's Worcestershire, (or Hardy's Wessex and Jefferies' Wiltshire, remade in the minds of sentimental readers).

 I agree with much of the critical reading of "Englishness". As in William Morris' metaphor, England is a house full of cloying and suffocating junk, and the fire blazing at present may have a cleansing effect. Whether the house itself will be burnt down remains to be seen.

 Charles Sorley spoke from love, disgusted by the parody and perversion of his country by propagandists, and the rhetoric of sacrifice, induced by war hysteria. The England currently being deconstructed doesn't leave much standing on the national ground to inspire love. But the increasingly orthodox intellectual movement doesn't leave any one to love, since its aim is to demolish all concepts of integral identity including that of personal being. In place of a complex mysterious poet called Edward Thomas, for instance, we have the thought patterns or "structure of feeling" of a rural populist.

 Looking down on formative relations from a theoretical overview it's the history *lived* that I miss: not only that being alive of others that we can only approach through fellow feeling & imaginative sympathy, but the actual complications of a society, felt blindly or partly seen, in an individual mind.

 I have seen the decay of a "green language" (Raymond Williams), a language of nature separated from social context, and internalised, drawing the poet down into nostalgia, or projected as violent myth. I have made an attempt to "place" myself, and I haven't abandoned the idea of the "centre", or the idea of a poetry of place. But both ideas are changing, in ways that I can't see clearly yet. I have to ask myself whether returning is only a dream, a mirage of belonging. If the iconoclasts are to be believed there's *nothing* there, or an "emptiness" to fill with compensating images. Could I realize my idea of the poet as citizen—a cold word in English, suggesting bureaucratic officiousness rather than familiar, shared streets—of writing from inside the life of place, instead of from a separated ego, making a career in the literary market? Does going back mean only lapsing back into the past, into some "green" England of the mind—as Lawrence was tempted by Garsington, before his soul rebelled? And if I write from *here*, from the truth of my situation, must that mean only either being an observer or exploring my isolation?

We have walked along the Korreweg through snow, on a bright afternoon, and bought a Christmas tree from a man selling trees outside Aldi, the supermarket across the street. A big man with a face like a retired boxer's—I immediately thought he had been a lumberjack when he told us he had lived in Canada, but he is a chef—who was delighted to speak English. Later, when we came back down the street, he got quite sentimental about his liking for the English, the mutual liking of English and Dutch, and the war. Meanwhile, waiting for M. while she was seeing the doctor, an old man spoke to me in Dutch, and went on even after I'd told him that I couldn't understand, and I hid my face in my newspaper, embarrassed and ashamed. Here, as in Wales, I'm trapped in my language, or by my ignorance of the language spoken outside the house, and while no one here resents that, because the Dutch language isn't threatened and there's no long history of antagonism between the two nations, I'm driven in on myself, and made more dependent on M. In this narrow, self-made space I've turned back on myself, and must now turn outward.

Christmas Day
In the morning I walked alone in falling snow to the park. Walking through snow there's a sense of the upper world breaking apart in soft white fragments, but the world below has a new unity and coherence, and differences and dividing lines are smoothed over. Then it is also a pied world, more black & white, but narrower, more womblike, a world half seen through snow blowing into the eyes.

Children were sliding on sledges down the man-made hill, some deliberately falling off and rolling over & over, others being cautiously propelled by parents. Suddenly, into an otherwise deserted space, with snow silently falling between trees with white, sculpted branches & trunks, a black dog bounded, wild with delight. Black birds huddled on the bare branch of a tree in a garden, gulls & ducks stood frozen in attitudes of miserable bewilderment on slushy ice—some of them no doubt birds hatched this year, but others surviving from last winter; but would they remember? Frozen twigs stuck up through snow like a buried forest, and I walked back over outgoing tracks that were almost covered.

4 January 1987

New Year with Emily & Jim, who returned together to England early this morning.

One afternoon M. drove us to Eemshaven, where we merely poked our heads over a snowy dyke and wind off the rough, grey North Sea cut into us. There were curlews picking about in one field where grass blades spiked the snow, and in another a covey of six partridges huddled together. One cold night of keen starlight, with Mars burning iron-red in the west, I ran with Joe & Emily on a sledge down grassy slopes on the other side of the street. On New Year's Eve, fireworks, sudden explosions of noise and colour all over the city, with red lights drifting slowly over rooftops. Once, as we were walking back along the Korreweg, Jim remembered that, years ago, Groningen was a kind of joke name for him and Snug: a place they couldn't imagine ever visiting or having any contact with. And there we were, as we have been many times in other years in England or Wales, when the future here was completely blank to us.

Mid-afternoon of a long, slow day, snow falling, bringing down early dark; my daughter & my friend sailing back to England. There's a very strong sense of the presence of a person in the hours after their departure.

They're sailing back to England, which I can never turn away from; but it's from here now that I need to go out—out of my shelter, and into an old, changing world that's new to me. I need again to renew my faith in poetry—in my ability to write poetry that is worth having faith in.

11 January

Bright, clear days of bitter cold, subzero temperatures here and throughout Europe from Spain to Siberia, where it is—60; blizzards cutting off communities in Sweden; a lorry carrying nuclear warheads crashed into a field after an accident on an icy road near Salisbury in Wiltshire, and was closely guarded overnight by military & police until it could be removed.

I went out for short cycle rides yesterday and today, and riding into the north-east wind my beard & eye lashes quickly froze and the cold bit into my forehead. Blue sky, a three-quarters, skull moon. White sun reflected on the ice on a pond, like a long, pointed candleflame. A light-brown wisp of rush, from rushes frozen into the ice, was blown sliding and skipping over the surface. Bird tracks printed in slush and frozen over. Shouts, thwacks and knocks from boys skating and playing ice hockey.

Later, a smell of wood smoke in the front room, sun an orange-red dome behind a fine, black tracery of branches at the top of the Korreweg.

20 January

§

> I'd not urge anyone back. Back is no value as better. That sentimentality/
> has no place… //Back is only for those who do not move…
> >   Charles Olson

But he does urge us back, back to an understanding of "man as only force in a field of force containing multiple other expressions". Back, in some sense, is where almost all the Anglo-American modernists direct us. In American poetry, in particular, the way back is the way to order:

> Order that rules music, the same/controls the spacing of the stars and/
> the feathers in a bird's wing
> >   Louis Zukofsky

> We are "hemmed in by mysteries/all moving in order"
> >   Gary Snyder

> The plan is in nature rooted
> >   Ezra Pound

Wendell Berry links Snyder to the old poets, to Pope and his predecessors, and finds the idea of the Chain of Being lying under English poetry like a root, (but denigrates the Romantics, whom he sees cutting themselves off, by interposing their selves between poetry and the order of the world). Snyder delights me more than any other living poet does. He is evidently exceptionally intelligent as well as wise and generous. But I read him with an edge, even a wide margin, of reservation— partly because I see him from here, in Europe, and from a particular concern with English conditions, and partly because I'm not sure that he doesn't simply sidestep difficulties that poets who are most alive to the present, like Oppen, face. The contrary view (which I also hold) is that he's rubbed the dirt off the mirror of mind. And he is an actual spring of hope: it is not only his poems that delight me, but thinking of him now, living and working, looking back thousands of years with his new, "larger humanism", and looking forward thousands of years to the continuing life of his tribe in their place, my heart opens, I know that *this* is a spirit of truth, even if we bring destruction on the planet tomorrow. I can laugh with Snyder; it is laughter of hope, a sense at once of close fellow feeling and of being surrounded by a great space, in which we belong. But I think too of what has to be done here, where history crowds us in, and the shadows of Russia & America lie heavily on what is still the ruined groundwork of the West; and here things are very different.

Wendell Berry leaves me colder than Snyder does. The main problem is that in writing about place Berry seems to have little sense of history as displacement, of the forces actually unsettling people (or offering them a better life elsewhere). After all, it is special circumstances, as well as particular gifts, that enable a poet to *choose* to farm in Kentucky (or the Sierra Nevada). Place as I understand it includes experience of displacement—all that binds or looses, and binds to enslave as well as to belong, and looses to free as well as to disconnect and destroy. Berry may be aware of the history, but it isn't ingrained in him, he doesn't write from it, and therefore his sense of place has a kind of "innocence" that I can't identify with.

According to John Elder, Snyder, with his anthropological and ecological awareness, pursues what Gilbert White called "the idea of parochial history"—the fullness of nature that only close observation of a district during many years can bring to light. But to be centred as White was, scientist and man of God: the Creation understood in *that* way is hardly what any poet could come back to now. If Selborne is still much the same *natural* world as it was in Gilbert White's time, the lines that cross there now, and in the mind of an observer standing where White stood, make it a very different place. All the same, there's a quality of care that's essential to all seeing. It's in Ruskin's looking with love; it's what makes sense of Kenneth Rexroth calling William Carlos Williams "the first great Franciscan poet since the Middle Ages", and it justifies seeing a link between Snyder and White.

"Let's sing the walk up to Darwin." Snyder, in *Good Wild Sacred*, writes of the Pintubi people of central Australia singing "a cycle of journey songs, walking through a space of desert in imagination and song".

Wordsworth walked to think and feel and meet fellow solitaries. John Clare beat the bounds of his place, going over and over the ground his identity was founded on. Hardy's love was more measured; he accepted loss, he based himself on a philosophy which saw loss as inevitable and necessary. Now the received wisdom is that the conditions of these poets' feelings are over, as much a fact of the past as any prehistoric singing the walk to Avebury. The task of academic criticism is to dismantle the feelings into their social constituents. What we can't do is love simply. Or is it received wisdom that love is a bourgeois category?

I have an idea forming of poetry as an inner map of sacred ground; of place as an imaginative field, but known with the bodily knowledge of growth, work, sensual experience, love, and through family and communal experience, and in the light of all relevant scientific and historical facts. Imagination maps the relations among these forms of knowledge, the data & images, and locates the poet in place, not place in the poet. Not "the mind is its own place", but the place its own mind. By contrast, the picturesque distorts and fragments place by confining it to a narrow kind of visual experience: not the mind that sees "things in motion, motion in things" (Fenollosa), and maps the ground, but the consuming eye of the self apart, and hungry for certain conventional properties; the eye that sees others too as consumers or competitors, and now fills the world with images of what we are to desire, and with stereotypes of us & our places, so that we're blinded to reality.

I am closeted here with ideas; outside the polar wind has dropped, the air is moist, and trees beside the street are white with rime. I have been in the house day after day this winter, reading & rereading, seeing the web of thought grow and become more intricate, in places more dense and tangled, connecting things I thought separate, renewing or making other connections between points I first saw years ago. And what haunts me at times is the fear that I may *think* anything, and it means nothing, not because untrue, but because the truth doesn't connect with other people in a common daily life. On the bus on the way back from the centre of town on Saturday I saw the way the young driver looked at a girl on a bike beside the bus, waiting at traffic lights, and the way she looked at him, with friendly interest. Of course they may have known each other, but what I felt I saw was a look of mutual understanding between strangers, which contained sexual liking but was more an instinctive recognition of common humanity. Now I elaborate, trying to find words for what was more a glance than a look, and which I just caught, knowing the world between people to be more real than anyone could ever say, and real as thought that dismantles the world, or keeps the world too much in the head, is not.

23 January
Is it due only to what's lost in translation that when Rilke, in *The Rodin-Book*, writes about *things* I don't believe him? It's a matter of trust, which is of fundamental importance in poetry. For example, when David Jones is difficult, he can always be trusted to have a meaning, while I suspect Dylan Thomas at his most obscure of writing to make an impression, and perhaps impressing himself first, by what only sounds profound. Quite apart from the problem of translation, I couldn't say exactly the same of Rilke. But I find him teasing, and having followed what he says about things expecting him to reveal a profound perception, both evoking the *presence* of things and drawing his ideas home to a central truth, feel cheated by a vapid religiosity.

Perhaps the problem is caused by the extreme contradictions, which *The Rodin-Book* amply expresses but seems unaware of: between the artist as infinitely patient, humble and receptive in learning from nature and from practising his art, and the artist as the master, capturing and subduing things, and like Rodin's *Balzac*, "a creator in his arrogance, erect in the midst of his own motion as in a vortex which catches the whole world up into this seething head". The sexual violence is unmistakeable ("Rodin was a lover whom nothing could withstand"). This is not the humble pride of the artist serving truth, like Michaelangelo, or absorbed into the world he pictures, like Vermeer. It is a romantic, egotistic expression of the same urge to *master* nature that may eventually destroy us.

The figure of Rilke's Rodin gazes into the future like a prophet; it also "loses itself in a certain mediaeval anonymity, it has that humility of greatness which recalls the builders of the great cathedrals". But it wasn't the cathedral builders who were prophets; they made representations of prophets who saw and proclaimed the truth that was their pattern.

I sympathise completely with Rilke's sense of himself as a perpetual beginner. But even when he quotes Constable—"The world is wide, no two days are alike, not even two hours; since the creation of the world there have been no two leaves of a tree identical"—and says, "A man who has arrived at this knowledge begins a new life"—even then I don't trust him. For Constable was rooted in a faith that he knew to be far greater than his art; that which he saw as ever new was, so to speak, a *given* creation—he didn't invent it or compete with it or try to master it or even become it. Rilke too recognises nature and things as absolutely other—with part of himself, but his exploratory approach isn't only the medium of this humble recognition, it also serves the arrogance of the creator, catching the world up into his head.

I was out before dawn this morning, walking—some nervous trouble, the world too much in *my* head. Light drizzle, mist, pavements & cobbles damp, raindrops on branches shining in the light of street lamps, lights orange and white on the canal, on ice at the edges and water alive with rain farther out; houses with a few lights in the windows across the canal, and behind them lights in the cliff-face of the hospital, rising high into mist. A church bell rang repeatedly from the far side of the park as I returned, and the grey morning was homely with cyclists, alone or in pairs, talking together, on their way to school or work.

Later in the morning I finished reading Svetlana Alpers' *The Art of Describing*, which is for me, intellectually, one of the most exciting books I've ever read. I would never claim that there's no new truth, totally different from all one has ever thought, which comes as a revelation, and a judgement. But in recent years, and increasingly in recent months, I've experienced things coming together, connections being made, all within a field that I call *the art of seeing*.

I don't claim that this includes everything, only that it seems to gather in all the ideas and perceptions and questions of which I'm capable, or see and feel really matter. It's a large field with many intricate, complex interconnections, with (I think) an overall order, and subordinate orders, which I can't see as a whole. For the sake of convenience, I have to mark off areas within it: for example, the art of seeing of different writers, art as different kinds of visual experience, natural observation and its limits, image-making and image-breaking as religious apprehension, seeing things and seeing with things, the history of perception and the perception of history, seeing as detachment and seeing *from*, poetry as a "mapping" of place, seeing as vision and seeing as structured by society or myth, moral imagination, the eye that consumes... What excites me then is anything—experience, perception, or book—that deepens or extends connections in this field.

Svetlana Alpers' fine book is necessarily a product of our time, with the available means of vision. Also, as a great work of scholarship, it *describes* its subject—draws a line round it, and concentrates the focus of attention within the circle. Not surprisingly, perhaps, she makes little or nothing of what might be called the Dutch artists' *mysticism of the particular*, a sense of which strengthens the continuity of northern painting that Alpers is at pains to show—strengthens and extends it: not only to (among others) Van Eyck, Van der Goes, Geertgen tot Sint Jans, Brueghel, Saenredam, Vermeer, Van Gogh, Mondrian, but also to the Limburg brothers, and back behind them, to the great illuminated sacred books of the north, like the Winchester Bible. In discussing the status of the word in Dutch paintings Alpers doesn't relate it to these books. It would have complicated her argument had she done so (but would it have confused it?).

The illuminators too had a microscopic eye. For a time at least, the new world discovered through lenses didn't contradict the world between heaven and earth pictured by the masters of illuminated manuscripts. But perhaps it is with Vermeer that *this* world becomes *the* mystery: a world whose meanings from near and far in space and time cluster round the presence of a woman in a room, and can be seen and felt but not touched or understood. Or perhaps Vermeer, like Donne, held the tension between human and divine love. Later, when the order mapped in the Christian universe had broken—when, for many, the image no longer held—Dutch painters, and painters in the north generally, found terror and ecstasy in the forces loosed into the world of things.

In the evening we went to Rudi's party to celebrate the publication by Gallimard of a book of French translations of his poetry. I promised to lend Rudi the Alpers book. He is trying to write poems about water, which fascinates him by being at once fundamentally life-giving and completely indifferent to us, absolutely *other*. He is stuck with the idea, and said that the book about Dutch art sounds like what he needs. Rudi's poems are lyrical, melancholy, tender; their surprising imaginative logic is quite different from the dated, mechanical surrealism and self-fascination that I find in rather a lot of modern Dutch poetry (in English translation). His poems draw me back with their distinctive voice and movements, and with his sense of the world.

1 February
Sunday afternoon: a walk with M. through the park and round the town.

Snow on the ground, blue in shadow. Bright white sun, sky almost cloudless.

The park was full of skaters of all ages, from old people to small children, on the ponds. An old man stood leaning on his wife's shoulder as he took off his old-fashioned, wooden skates. They were talking to a young couple, possibly their grandchildren, who then moved together a short distance away, so that the young man could take a photograph of the old man and woman, each couple standing side by side.

All the waterbirds had crowded into two places where the ice had been broken for them, and people still came to feed them, though lots of uneaten bread was floating on the water.

Shimmer of reflected sunlight on the canal's brick walls, the mirrored image seeming at a glance to be a continuation of the walls underwater. But the water is opaque, dark brown, almost black, when it can be seen out of the sun.

6-10 February

Friday: before dawn start from Groningen. Greyness of station platforms, white-faced clocks.

The surprise of stopping alongside another train, glancing across at other people in lighted compartments, as if looking into living rooms.

I watched dawn's dark blue lighten—once it begins the light spreads rapidly—and standing pools of glassy water in fields reflect misty blue.

Flame over a gasfield.

Trees emerging are sacred beings—here only a very few remain, descendants of Europe's great forests, but at once, appearing in the light, they are sacred. Here, too, at this hour, are remnants of an older, darker countryside, ages of candlelight under long, humped farm & barn roofs, standing wide apart.

Then we pass cyclists & traffic waiting at a level crossing, and the present system is visible—we are parts of a smooth-functioning machine.

Later, aboard the *Beatrix*, sitting at an aluminium table in a bar decorated with aubergine—with purple synthetic materials, hearing the film entertainment on board announced: violent "hit films", including Stallone's latest..

At Liverpool Street station, after a tiring, delayed journey from Harwich, we hurried through a door to find a taxi just drawing up. As I handed M. in, I felt a sharp jab in the back and turned to face an angry, red-faced man holding a stick, who at once started shouting at me. He was in the "queue" (which I hadn't seen—there were taxis arriving all the time) and in our haste we had stepped in front of him. Feeling the sharp thrust in my back and being shouted at, I shouted back—we hadn't seen the queue. "Because you're bloody ignorant," he shouted, and walked off full of violent hatred to another taxi.

And afterwards Waterloo, the filth of litter, the carelessness and signs of human dereliction and self-neglect, which still comes as a shocking contrast to the Netherlands, after a few months away.

Saturday

Spring in Winchester. Purple crocuses out over night, thrushes & hedge-sparrows in Elizabeth's garden. Blue sky, clear air, fast-flowing water.

Late afternoon: by train to my parents at Caslake Close, New Milton. A small, comfortable house with a small garden, in a new development just off the main road—right for them now, much better than Hayford.

Mother, who was thin before, has lost a stone in weight over the period of the removal. But she is, if anything, more full of energy, and enjoying the new place; and of course with phenomenal strength of will.

Sunday

To Barton with Mother in the morning. Sea grey in sea-mist, the hotel on the cliff top looming, as if about to slide down. All colour burning in the bright-orange gravel over sand of the cliff face.

Out with M. in the afternoon, first to the shingle-bank leading to Hurst, at Saltgrass Lane, the sea breaking white and grey in mist.

From there to Wilverley Plain, where we walked to the Naked Man. The sky had lifted at the horizons, over Fawley and Southampton Water, over the dark-blue, pine-jagged distances of the north-western Forest.

Space. Stillness. Ponies at the wood edge standing utterly still, as they often do, but as if listening to the stillness in the air.

Shortly after we had reached the old dead tree and while we were looking at it, a loud man (by his own admission "pissed") came up with two friends, a man & a woman. "I'd like to cut it down," he said. "Here, where's my penknife." (He was full of a sense of his own wit and humour.) "The old thing's a product of the bourgeoisie." "They say they used to hang people here; I'd like to hang Margaret Thatcher on it." After they'd gone, I wished I'd been friendly, but at the time the assumption that we wanted to be entertained—that we'd come there for the benefit of such a performance—made me clam up, and hardly acknowledge his friend's apologetic caution that we might be friends of Mrs Thatcher!

From Wilverley to Bolderwood, open heath with Scots pines to ancient beechwoods, with a few oaks & an understorey of holly & dead bracken. A soft floor of bright green moss & brown leaves over black leafmould. Black damp stains on trees. At a little distance, in half-light, a stag! In fact, a fallen beech, its upended roots forked and twisted. Everywhere, to the anthropomorphic eye, tree gargoyles—ape or devil, an elephant trunk—but the real mystery is that trees are completely other.

Grey stillness of beechwoods, like the ponies' stillness, as if listening, or communing silently in a mode unknown to us—or at a level any living thing can reach by listening to its nature?

Monday, 9 February

Our parents' Diamond Wedding Anniversary.

The day began badly with Dave being rude on the phone because I found his plans for being met vague and confusing. Then he & Margaret were late but arrived at the Redhouse, Barton, in time for the delayed meal.

Christ! What a day, what a family! Male egos born and borne up by the strength of a woman, mine in these circumstances taking the form partly of strained mediation, partly of escape within. But in the event, after an inauspicious beginning, the celebration went well.

Tuesday

Birds singing before dawn. Venus bright over roofs in a clear sky.

New Milton station just the same as it was more than thirty years ago, with the same ramshackle appearance and unpainted, rusty iron footbridge

Brockenhurst: trees emerging fine and black against dawn-blue sky.

Morning star over the Test estuary; clusters of lights like stars on the cranes.

Basingstoke, rim of the sun rising from downland hills.

In London, an AIDS warning poster addressed to us whether "straight or gay".

Harwich: wind blowing off the land, driving small white clouds—later a thickening cloud-stream—towards the continent, speeding cloud shadows over the brown estuary and over the ploughed fields & meadows of the Essex coast.

At lunch on board over a bottle of wine I let my violent feelings boil up. The words "gay or straight" started it—the fragments we are, not human beings but identified by "sexual preference", bits & pieces destroying ourselves and each other. Man, a violent, cruel, self-destructive animal. But the real causes were the family ego clashes, the miserably depressing state of things in England, my personal difficulties there and my fears for the future.

How make violent or painful feelings creative instead of self-destructive?

I remembered my last thought of the previous night: male egos born and borne up by a woman.

No one has better cause than I to believe in the strength of women.

On deck later: moon a few days from full brightening ahead, sun astern slanting a bright silver track. We had outrun the cloud, with just a few wisps (sheep's wool on barbed wire) in the blue sky. Sea a dark, glassy blue-green, a wide sea, with white wave caps and one other white ship, small on the horizon to the north-east.

20 February

From the car as we pull up at traffic lights, glimpse of a hand waving from an upstairs window, hand of an elderly woman, with a ring embedded in the flesh, waving to two girls who look back as they walk away along the pavement, and this breaks through the crass factual statement in my mind, and at once a sense of the immeasurable depth of human meaning, always everywhere, replaces it—"Now that our planet is known to be attached to a fairly insignificant star in a fairly insignificant position towards one edge of one galaxy out of millions of galaxies, our feeling of self-importance ought to have been pulverized." (Anthony Smith, *The Seasons*)

A bare fact (but how slanted and weighted) and then the brutal word, "pulverized"—these caught in my mind, and were literally waved away.

21 February

Blackbird singing in lightly falling snow.

22 February

A drifting dance of seagulls in irregular circling patterns, rising high over Meerwijk. Ice on the lake still, silver-blue, pitted and cracked: a curved moonface. Catkins, alder, pussy willow buds. The cloud-cover broke as we walked by the lake, the gulls rose higher on a thermal, the sun gleamed, replacing its small, clouded image on the ice.

Winter here in the north seems almost over now.

In Jerusalem, the trial of the man accused of murdering nearly 900,000 Jews at Treblinka: reminders for a new generation. We have to know what our kind is capable of. If we don't know, we don't know anything.

When my life began, when I was surrounded by love & kindness and a grazed knee was a major event, children were being sent to their deaths with their parents by our neighbours and relatives in Europe—who cared as much for their own children.

No words can understand this "madness", which is common among human beings in certain circumstances, with our genius unique among creatures for inflicting death and pain.

I delight to see and hear the blackbird singing in the snow and silky buds breaking by the ice-covered lake, and at the same time feel that I've hardly begun to see the *danger* of being human; not only the horror, which our Western literature is expert at invoking, but the danger that I might do such things/that such things might be done to us.

25 February

In Amsterdam Marius Buning met us at the station and drove us to the Vrije Universiteit, where I gave a lecture and a reading. Afterwards went for a meal at an Italian restaurant. Marius' colleague, Jacques Alblass, came with us. Alblass, his family name, comes from an old polder near Rotterdam. His family background, working class and Calvinist, has influenced his interest in writers, like Heaney and Hardy, who both have a strong sense of "roots" and need distance from them. This made him responsive to what I had to say. (He was already familiar with some of my poetry, and proposes to translate 'Shepherd' into Dutch.)

26 February

In Haarlem with Johan, we visited the Frans Hals Museum.

Here, I noticed the complete absence of Romantic distance in the paintings—the solitary's view beyond the world seen as a human encampment. At the same time, I felt some dislike for the frequent moralizing, which seems to be the obverse of the Dutch social sense, and relates to the perception of *this* world in all its material and fleshly particularity. In a Molenaer, for example, peasants near a tavern guzzling and drinking, pissing and shitting, and all the ways of "dung and death"—Eliot, by contrast, positively idealized his rustic forebears at East Coker!

With Hals, but generally, a gallery of faces. In Hals, the character—mean, vain, officious, humorous, drunken, conceited, complacent, and so on—and all together organising and administering a society, making a world in their own image, with no need or capacity to imagine any other. These people will always belong to their Haarlem.

In one room, Hal's faces look out of blackness—men & women, poorhouse guardians, at either end of a room, but mostly his groups stand as though on a stage representing their self-esteem.

After visiting the museum we had a light meal in a café close to the walls of St Bavo's—gilded bells, pinnacles & weathercock on the steeple shining high above in the sun—with a tape of Billie Holiday playing in the background, but filling the atmosphere—

God bless the child...
Ain't nobody's business if I do...
Good morning, heartache...

Then we went into the cathedral. Long aisles, tall white walls, high wooden roof, a ceiling with a delicate flowery design and a clockface looking down, large baroque organ, which made me think of a fairground, even though Mozart had played it. The interior felt like a place for a cold wind of thought to blow through.

Our feet tapped on the uneven paved floor, over the numbered slabs; we looked at model galleons suspended from the ceiling, at brass "spider" candelabra, at wooden dogs guarding the railed off area surrounding the altar table, and at Frans Hals' grave, with an old-fashioned lantern with candles standing on top. Some stained glass shone brighter against the cold, white and grey space. It was a place in which to walk or stand like tiny figures in Saenredam (he too is buried there), wondering, and feeling lost. It felt to me utterly godless, and I couldn't fill it with any of the faces we had seen in Hals' paintings, though they must once have gone there regularly and greeted each other from their seats.

2 March
Everything was turned to glass overnight by freezing rain. In the morning, icicles hung down wherever we looked outdoors—windowsills, eaves, cars, road signs—like nails, fangs, daggers, teeth, and trees and posts were smoothly coated with ice, thicker than bottle glass. The hedges were like vitrified glaucous polyps. Soon, branches started to break off under the weight of ice, and trees and small shrubs bent to touch the pavement. Adam Hopkins arrived with a photographer, Tim, in the morning, and Joe went out with them to take pictures for Adam's book, driving in conditions that soon worsened, becoming at times a white out, to Ezinge and the coast. It snowed here too during the day, and by nightfall the scene outside was wintry. Joe came back with the men highly elated after dark, when the trees under street lamps shone like chandeliers.

3 March
Sun bright on a frozen world. Ice started to fall dangerously from roofs. I walked out with M., tentatively, seeing branches that had been torn off littering the ground, trees wounded and painful to look at, as if they felt the pain, and buds encased in ice, like foetuses frozen in. It was beautiful, a day of shining crystal, silver, prismatic—I've never seen anything like it—yet there was something sinister and even horrible about it, a sterile beauty, entombing, and killing. The blackbird that was so slender the other day, when I saw it singing in light snow, but in what

felt like early spring, came to the front garden all puffed up, almost round. The sun shone all day, ice fell, but still the ice was in possession. I saw for the first time what the ancient Welsh poet meant when he said that a man could almost stand on a blade of grass—though in fact the frozen grass was too slippery to stand on.

7 March
Many people drowned when the cross-channel ferry, *The Herald of Free Enterprise*, capsized in calm weather just outside Zeebrugge harbour. A priest on the radio quoted 'The Wreck of the Deutschland' but it seemed a far cry from the tragic accident. Mrs Thatcher spoke with genuine feeling, shocked and compassionate, thinking of the children wandering about the boat, separated from their parents—which is indeed one of the first things one thinks about.

8 March
Broke the car out of its coat of ice and drove into the country. At Schipborg, the Drente A meandering through bright icefields, diamonds and stars sparkling from trees. Ice like brambles with cold, sharp thorns covering slender budding branches. Slow thaw, tinkle of ice falling on ice through trees and on the ground. An ice mobile hanging on horsehair on a barbed wire fence. Birches bent into hoops or broken off at the trunk. A cold east wind, but warm out of it; lichen on oaks free of ice, a warm green.

21 March
More snow following the thaw yesterday, but this morning, on the shed roof, a blackbird with straws in its beak.
    Started work on the Gezer poem.

23 March
Phonecalls from Tony in the morning and from Emily and my parents in the evening. Worked all day at 'Tel Gezer', and in the evening friends came in and we had a party. A week ago I felt that I'd overwhelmed myself with reviews to write, but in that time I've completed two review-essays and written a draft of a longish poem, so that at present I no longer feel buried under unproductive work. Elizabeth Waltheer mentioned the strong possibility that I will be asked to work part-time in the university next academic year.

27 March
Posted a copy of 'Tel Gezer' to Ned at *Planet*. In the evening, Joe asked me to read the poem to him, and I went through it, answering his questions.

29 March
Sunday. A drive into the country and to the sea with M., the broad, flat northern landscape with small, brick villages & farmhouses set far apart even quieter than usual, but with many birds, including curlews & lapwings, in the fields or on

the water, (and a magpie at a nest in a treetop beside a farm), and early spring flowers—snowdrops, crocuses, aconites—out in gardens.

High, pale blue sky with a little white cloud. Warm and bright in the sun (one upright blade of a windmill's sails shining), but a cold, strong wind blowing off the sea. Four scarecrows in one field, their coats flapping.

Flood time at Noordpolderzijl. Fields of Brent geese, with gulls & oystercatchers among them, on islands of marsh grass between the sea and high water against the dyke.

1 April
Finished 'Walking to Capernaum'. From the start, the title was an integral part of the poem, but it had a teasing, and quite unintentional echo, which I finally realized was of 'Sailing to Byzantium'!

Out for a cycle ride on a warm, sunny day with a light breeze. Fresh, green leaves among faded grass under the hedgerows, and life pricking on buds of sycamore and beech, in spite of all the branches torn off and lying under them.

12 April
Lee, Kate & the boys arrived for a holiday with us last Tuesday and went back on the night boat yesterday. We all had a really good time together, talking, drinking, going out on expeditions.

Wednesday
To Noordpolderzijl (where I saw the first swallow skimming the mud) and along narrow roads near the dyke to Lauwersoog. A day of April showery cloud cover—grey, but also white, silver, violet, dark blue, and continually changing darker or lighter masses and shapes.

How to describe the colours of things without merely abstracting their surface appearances? By Lauwersmeer & Waddenzee, in particular, a great space full of different movements—or space that is always in motion, that space which is vaster in this small country than in any other I've been in.

Earth, water, sky.

Tall golden feathery reeds; many seabirds—ducks, geese, gulls, curlews, oystercatchers, plovers, shelduck in a field. Church spires in mist at long intervals on the horizon far inland both emphasise the space and give it a human dimension. Yet here, too, each small island of church & village has the look of a relic. But what do I know of their life? The way of seeing that I bring with me both looks for depth in place and sees it against the hurtling, shrunken headline "world".

Lambs skipping in the fields. Several windmills working, including *De Vier Winden*, by which we stopped and heard it rumbling as the green-painted sails went round.

On the way to Westernieland, deep in the country, a heronry of about fifteen nests in trees beside an isolated farm, birds at the nests or, grey birds in grey sky, slowly, gravely, flying to or from them.

Thursday
To Bourtange ("Hobbitville"), where swans were making a nest from reeds at the side of the black water in the moat.

Then over the border into Germany. Haren: a small, new town which was almost completely asleep at lunch time, when we walked round in the rain. Oddly placeless and dispiriting, but a joke for us at the lifelessness—as if everything had been shut against our coming—and at our damp fruitless wandering. Meppen was awake and more interesting, but there's an odd feeling about Eemsland generally, which may have something to do with the new building since the war, and with a certain centrelessness, as if the heart really has gone out of it. But I don't know it, and in any case I was put into a fury at the rude way in which an old, respectable-looking woman stared at M, as if her vitality & difference were an affront.

Back over the border, we visited the monastery at Ter Apel, a medieval, brick building in woodland. It is a museum now, but was formerly "Domus Novae Lucis" (House of the New Light), situated on a sandtongue surrounded by wild peat-moors.

Friday
To Anloo in Drenthe, on the hondsrug, on a day of fresh breeze and heaped, white cloud. Dark brown peaty rolling ploughland, and a walk through woods of birch, beech & oak to a hunebed. Coming out of the woods, the church at Anloo was visible across the fields—brick tower with stepped gables.

Stopping by the church afterwards, cloud was coming up behind and could be seen through the windows, which included that beautiful, green-tinted, puritan light. Only suppose that *there never was any other light*, never any light but that of the sun, and of the human mind, self-illuminated, with never a gleam of supernatural light.

Lee was more confident, in a quiet, relaxed way, than I have seen him before. He no longer thinks of a sudden "success", but of making a body of work, which may be recognised when he is much older. This, in fact, is what he is doing. It is clear to me, though, that fame could strike him at any moment. Indeed, I think it more likely than not—his work is *obviously* so good—it only needs one well-known collector or influential critic to *see* it. His greatest fear is that he should die without fully expressing the artistic truth that he has it in him to express. I understand the fear, but he has the gift and the energy and the will to succeed. He talked about the completeness of Gaudier's work; his is not complete; he still has much to clarify and achieve.

We talked about our work together too. I understand better what he has in mind now, though at present I have a better idea of what he might do with my images than of what I might do with his response to them. Still, I think the collaboration has considerable possibilities for both of us. Certainly, his works make me want to write.

Of all the people I know, Lee has at once the greatest sense of present artistic need and the greatest sense of tradition. He told me about a History of Art that he has long liked to read. On the front inside cover it has a chart of sculpture in the ancient world, long lines representing the thousands of years of Egyptian sculpture, etc; on the back inside cover the chart representing modern movements has many short, broken lines—Impressionism, Expressionism, Cubism, etc. He simply doesn't believe in the latter; to him, the tradition is continuous, with Cubism and modern Primitivism, for example, continuing the lines represented at the front of the book. He is a workman, a sculptor, in that tradition.

I would like one day to write a book about Lee's work and ideas. In the meantime, though, he gives me the greatest possible encouragement to do my own work, and we have work to do together.

Good Friday
At the flower market in town with M. & Elin & Emily, the two girls walking hand in hand. Flower stalls on either side of the road and the road crowded with people so that we could only move along very slowly. People with armfuls of flowers, here & there a person apparently with a green leafy shrub or small tree growing out of their head. A lovely fresh spring day.

26 April
From Tuesday to Friday I was at La Sainte Union College in Southampton for the annual N.A.T.E. Conference, at which I conducted a series of workshops on "poetry of place" and gave a reading. On the first evening of several lovely days, after dinner, I walked down the Avenue to Watts Park and back by the memorial to the Titanic's Engineer Officers and heard the Civic Centre clock chiming "Our God, our help". But most of the time I was too busy meeting people, working and generally participating in the conference to leave the College during the day. Like the weather, the seminars got better as they proceeded and we became easier with each other, and I think everyone benefited, both those knowledgeable about the poems, like Tony Charles & Terry Gifford, and those who came with little knowledge, including the teacher from Devon, who arrived exhausted after months of sleepless nights with a first child. I enjoyed the company enormously and spent a lot of time talking in the gardens or in the bar, as well as at meals & in the seminars.

Everywhere in Southampton change and decay, or, rather, renovation. A marina, restaurants, small businesses and up-market shops where the docks used to be, in what was formerly the Chapel area, looking over the Itchen to Woolston. Just upriver the work goes on, with fires and mounds of bricks on wasteground, and, temporarily cleared, a fine view of the new bridge gracefully curving high over the river (the old floating-bridge, latterly a disco, was burnt out recently). At the new Ocean City along Canute Road the water, weedy ropes hanging in it from jetties and small hands of bladder-wrack floating past, really was bottle-green. At La Sainte Union I had been moved by an exhibition of poems about Southampton

Water by pupils at Hamble, and to see the same things in them that I saw as a boy, and later, and wrote about: from small green crabs to Fawley Oil Refinery. So Southampton enters another cycle: the great liners have gone, the docks are dead, but a new phase of the leisure industry begins, as it did in the city's days as a spa, in the 18th century.

Near the sea and in the country the south is very beautiful at this time of year, with magical qualities, in a breeze off the sea blowing over shingle, or in the depth of birdsong among leafy trees, or in the grass' colours, vibrant with life. It is beautiful, and I am happy to be here, although I know that I can't afford to live here, and although I see the exclusive signs (not just those that exclude me, of course). It's important that Emily is happy in Winchester; that's her place. And I am freer than ever, in a way. I can give myself elsewhere, to other people and other places, without ever losing the original love that connects me to the south.

Later. A drive with Jim to Queen's Bower and a walk under a cloudless sky by the heath and by the river—gold, or cloudy greeny gold with blue-framed shadows—and under the trees.

Driving back from Brockenhurst, I felt as if, in a sense, I'd never been away. Nothing is strange to me in this area: the social life doesn't surprise me, and I don't feel estranged from the places. Again, I felt completely at home.

But of course, it is the few people I have long-known who give me a reason for being here, and without them, and without any function, I would only dwell on the past, while it is also the work I have done in the last week, and the work I have to do here, that helps to make me feel at home.

27 April
Winchester. Early evening. North transept of the cathedral scaffolded for repairs to leaking gutters & damage by death watch beetle, the great stone mass appearing leaf-light among new leaves on the limes, blackbirds singing, yellow sunlight. I met Stephen Stuart-Smith in The Eclipse and talked with him about the forthcoming book. He is a sensitive, attentive man, who is genuinely concerned to promote poetry which would otherwise not get a hearing because outside current fashions; in fact, a worthy successor to Alan Clodd.

28 April
A late start for Waterloo after a pantomime involving a train which failed completely alongside the station and had to be shunted into a siding. The commuters seemed fairly relaxed and amused, as I wouldn't be if I had to sit knee to knee with others or stand in a draughty rattling corridor every morning.

To the Hayward where, with Jonathan Barker in the morning, I helped Michael Harrison choose paintings for the *Experience of Landscape* exhibition, for which I am to write an Introduction.

29 April
At the Poetry Society library with Jonathan Barker, selecting "landscape" poems to include in the exhibition catalogue: Jones, Bunting, MacDiarmid, Sisson, Hughes, Bellerby, W. S. Graham, and others. Afterwards, very hungry, I went round the corner into Shepherd Market and had a late lunch of bacon, egg & chips. Later, nodding off in the train, back to Winchester and a glimpse of Emily playing in the road.

1 May
Early afternoon: a short walk with Kim Taplin at Yew Tree Bottom. I went hoping to hear the cuckoo, and we did—at the very moment that I saw a green woodpecker flying away over the gorse, a cuckoo began to call from among trees in the valley of the Avon Water stretching into the distance below us, with Sway Tower standing out toward the sea but under grey cloud that hid the Island. We walked across the heath, along the abandoned railway track and among the trees, and a pair of green woodpeckers appeared from time to time in the open, with that abrupt looping flight low over bushes that looks as if it may end by the bird falling heavily out of the air.

A day of good talk, with Kim, with Séan & Joanne Street in Bournemouth in the evening. Mother said Dad half-woke up crying recently, because he had no one to talk with about painting. Yesterday he sat holding his watercolour of Ibsley Bridge to the light from the window, peering at it closely and admiring it. Thanks to him, paintings have always been as natural to me as nature itself, and I learnt from Mother to feel the same about poetry: these things, like lively talk in the house, were simply part of daily life.

Dad, on the field at Fairacre (now known as Hooker's Field), "as full of couch grass as hell is of devils".

2 May
Drove to Mappowder to visit Gerard, who is now in his seventieth year, but still strong. We went to The Green Man for lunch, and afterwards he rested and I walked to the church and along the road toward Plush. The strong wind became stronger as the day went on, and blasted violently against the windows at evening, but the interior of the church was very still, with trees shaking beyond the glass. I looked again at the figurine of a crusader in a niche in the wall, but suddenly it was the mere historical curiosity that seemed strange, especially in this place where so much that affects and questions me is in the earth and in the air.

I walked between deepening hedge-banks, among stitchwort, pink campion, herb Robert, past a meadow full of dandelions, and a meadow in which black & white heifers, with yellow tags in their ears, followed me and stared at me over a gate, between hills rising at some distance, with blackthorn like a chalk-white scar on a slope, and thought about my first meeting with Sue and all that happened afterwards, and about Theodore and John Cowper, and Mary and Lucy and Gerard. I walked in and out of shadow and warmth, under cloud masses being driven over and broken by the wind, by windblown oaks against blue sky, in rapidly changing patterns of light & dark that made everything in the landscape sharper and more distinct, and with shining wind-currents flowing in waves through long grass. Looking over a gate, thinking of the light of the sun and the light of the mind, it seemed that what I had to do was accept gratefully. It seemed that this is all that can be done, for nothing can be called back, and the essential life in others and in things, which is so real at such times, can't be grasped. I thought too of the mess I have made, and that I live to write, ironically making "order". How is it possible to keep body and soul together?

After tea with Gerard & Pamela Murray, who has made an illuminated copy of 'Master of the Leaping Figures', which she gave me, Gerard took me on a "mystery" tour. We drove toward Plush and I parked the car by the roadside at Rockpit Farm. We then walked back a short distance in the direction of Mappowder, stepped over a fence and climbed an overgrown track onto a spur from Ball Hill. This led to an area of nettles with the tanks of an abandoned reservoir among them, surrounded by beech trees. There was a rookery in the trees, and rooks cawed in their nests and swirled in large numbers against the windy blue and broken cloud, and the nettles were speckled white with their dung. There were also a few ramsons among the nettles, a few elders, a fallen beech tree, and the stump of an ancient oak.

As we stood looking in to the open enclosure, or down to the cypress tree and church tower at the top of the rise above "Four Corners", or at the hills on either side, Gerard told me what he knew about the history of the place.

It had been the site of a chapel of ease, which had stood for 800 years until demolished in 1847, when the stones had been used to build the church at Plush. The chapel had served the local community, but belonged to the parish of Buckland Newton, to which, after a night in the chapel, the dead had been transported by ox-cart for burial, three miles over the hills. In the time of Elizabeth the chapel had gained a certain notoriety, since it contained an image of the Virgin Mary which had become a cult object, especially among elderly spinsters, who had themselves carried up to the chapel when they were dying in order to spend their last night there. Elizabeth 1 directed a commission to investigate; which it did, calling witnesses. It is assumed that the image was removed and the practice of the old women was banned. The chapel continued to be used for monthly communion until 1847. Gerard also told me that this whole area had been very badly affected by the Black Death, which is thought to have entered England at Weymouth, in a ship from Spain.

Gerard visits the place regularly, and sits with his back against the largest, oldest beech, a tree between 200 and 300 years old, by which we stood as he told me the history. From here he often sees deer, and now, as we set out to walk from the site of the chapel by a field of young corn to another area of beeches on the hillside just above Folly, we saw a deer below us, in the shadow of trees at a field edge under the smooth fluted curved side of Ball Hill. Gerard said this was a Dorset deer, which he described as the oldest breed in these islands, living here since before the Roman occupation.

From the next double row of beeches, between Ball Hill and Nettlecombe Tout, above the valley between Mappowder and Plush, a distant view opened out, in which the hill on which Shaftesbury stands and Hambledon were small whaleback islands standing out in a wide inland sea. On the hillside opposite us, above Folly, a long mound revealed the site of an ancient settlement. Wind in the beeches, a sea-noise, wind-currents racing downhill in the grass, wind moulding great white cloud towers over distant Hambledon, intermittent harsh calls of cock pheasants from undergrowth, and beech shadows long across fields in evening light, under downs that are predominantly barebacked, with a few trees. As we walked back toward the car, blown sunlight filled the valley.

On the way back to Mappowder, Gerard pointed out the field gate which had been the favourite object of Theodore's walks in old age. Theodore called it Heaven's Gate. We returned past the churchyard in which Lucy is now buried beside Theodore and Violet.

3 May
Before leaving Mappowder after breakfast, I read a passage in Meister Eckhart marked by Theodore, in the copy of the book which he and Mary had both read and marked. The words seem apt to what I was haunted by—an absence, but an absence denoting what is most present to the person—as I walked alone on the road to Plush.

> "And the life was the light of men." Meaning that the soul has a spark in her which has been in God eternally: life and light.... "The darkness comprehended it not," which means that neither in time nor place shall this spark ever be comprehended. No doctor could ever give it or call it by its proper name.

Back, then, winding in and out of margins of Dorset, Wiltshire and Hampshire, from deep in Dorset: Mappowder, Shaftesbury, Sixpenny Handley, Cranborne Chase, Ringwood, Avon Valley, with Christchurch Priory downriver.

After Sunday lunch I took Mother to Taddiford Gap. Sea in stormlight: grey inshore, with a wind off the land driving gustily across it, incising the backs of incoming waves with rapid, vanishing curves and arrow showers. A margin of glacial blue by the Island, and one bright blade of light in the grey sea between Barton and the dark mound of Hengistbury Head, then the whole sea became a glittering surface, and then went dark again, blue-green, sea-green, as cloud and veils of rain swept over. Dark blue cloud massed on the Island, and was broken, suddenly, by a jagged stroke of lightning. From day to day, minute by minute, Island and sea are constantly changing.

Dad once won second prize at Ilkley Music Festival by singing 'Sombre Woods' ("Ye glades dark and lonely/Where midnight gloom enters only/O hide my slighted love/In your unbounded night./If now these eyes never more may behold thee/Then ever more I hate the light.") I felt a sharp pang when Mother unexpectedly recalled David, as a child, calling out "Dada" when Dad once got up onto a stage to sing in a hall Below Bar. Dad seemed to brush the memory aside, but it has gone on echoing in my mind more than any other reminiscence.

Of his father he said: "He wasn't a man forgotten by his friends and those he worked with". Thomas Alfred was brought up by his uncle, Mr Humby, who was estate bailiff at Warsash House. He was very fond of his uncle and the first thing he did when he returned south was to visit his grave. It was at Kent Lodge, Uxbridge, where he had his first head job, that Tom Hooker developed a specialism in orchids. While working at Blenheim, he was married at Church Hanborough. Orchid growing was a great interest of moneyed estate owners in the 19th century and well into the period of the First World War, and orchids were zealously sought in different parts of the world and hybrids were bred. His last words to my father were, "I loved orchids". Dad says it was the only time he heard him use the word love.

5 May
At Stoke Park Junior School, Eastleigh, where I was warmly welcomed by the teachers. I spent the first hour reading and talking about some of my poems set in the area to a large class of boys and girls from 9 to 11 years old and the second hour encouraging them with their poems. I was rather anxious when I went, because I'd never taught a class of children as young as this. But they were marvellous, following me wonderingly, agog, with friendly, open faces, asking questions and then writing with real interest. After I'd read my poem about Weston Shore, one boy was delighted to tell me that he went fishing there. At the end the children brought any pieces of paper they could lay hold of and asked me for my autograph. I felt like a star footballer after a match, but more privileged, as this doesn't happen to me every week. The afternoon was a very special, moving experience for me.

Evening Elizabeth introduced me, and I read at St Lawrence's church, Winchester, standing at a lectern at the head of the aisle, on some rather slippery, black gravestones, which reminded me of a dancing floor. The reading was well attended, and a number of friends were there.

After the reading, and after some beers and a large brandy at the Wykeham Arms, tired at the day's end, I suddenly turned a sour, bitter edge in talking with Elizabeth, at the influential people who were *not* at my reading, but no doubt would be at Wendy Cope's, whose book is in all the local bookshops while one shop alone had two copies of my "Winchester" book, *Master of the Leaping Figures*. It was the old thing, too, of having a gift that brings me no nearer being able to live in the south. But this was a momentary, fatigued reaction, too glancing to spoil a marvellous day.

10 May
Late Sunday morning, a walk with M. just outside Groningen, in the Eelde-Paterswolde area, in old, beautiful woodland, with public paths, which probably once belonged to the estate of a great house. Rooks were clamouring in a rookery just inside the woods, in the tops of tall beeches & oaks swaying in a strong wind, leafy tree crowns echoing the rounded, bright-edged masses of cloud. Farther in, at the top of a small beech, I saw what I thought was a stork sitting at its nest, looking down with a yellow eye, and as we watched it other nests, which we also thought were storks', were revealed by loud clacking of bills, like sticks or bones being knocked together, and an occasional noise like a curious retching bark, from treetops. As we walked deeper into the woods, by dark, still water channels between shallow ponds, in which copper beeches made cloudy, dark red reflections on dead leaves covering the bottom, and ducks splashed among fallen branches, the wood seemed full of storks. Then I got a clearer view of one, in an untidy raft of twigs & branches at the top of a pine, and saw long black hairs, like antennae, growing on the head and the hunched, grey back, that looked as if covered in a cloak. And of course, it was a heron. After the first partial sighting, we had seen what we wanted to see—all the "storks" were in fact herons.

20 May
Finally got my introduction to *The Experience of Landscape* into the post on Monday.
    M. is naturally tired after a long winter of hard work. I have been restless, discontented after the time in England, frustrated at the narrow life I have outside the home here, and generally in an anxious, dismal, negative state of mind. I saw the ingratitude and folly of this earlier, but last night brought it home to me, with, I hope, a change for the better.
    We had supper with Nan & Jan Snijders & two other mutual friends at the Snijders' home at Haren. For once, it was a beautiful evening, and at first we sat outside. Jan showed me their large garden, with the bed of blue flowers and the bed of white flowers which he has planted in corners. He is 77, a slight, frail-looking man, but full of life and energy. Nan is a little younger, also quite small, but active, and they are both considerate, kind and understanding. Jan was formerly Rector of the university, and, before that, Professor of Psychology, and Nan also was a professional psychologist. It was their love for each other and for their children & grandchildren, their humour and lack of pretension and, generally, their warmth and truly civilized behaviour that made me realize how ill and how stupidly I have behaved recently. But in any case, I was looking at M. across the table, knowing how little she asks of me and how much she gives; seeing her, knowing how fortunate I am.
    I can't conceal from myself, either, that it is their position in the world—their former work, their achievements, the recognition and the standard of living they have earned, all that they are part of—that shows in what the Snijders are. Not, of course, that one can't *love*, or be civilized, without that. But it is difficult

to live well without it, and I am more *worldless* here than I have ever been, and contemplate a future when I shall have to earn, for all of us, the living and the home that M. is currently providing.

Late May—Early June
Last weekend we walked with Elin & Joe by the sea near Eemshaven. Strong wind off the land, a break, a blue cave-mouth, in tumultuous cloud. An old mountain smell of sheep & warm grass on the dyke, then the smell of the sea. White caps on grey water, a yacht, slender curve and sharp angles, courting danger far from shore, and a freighter like a ghost on the blue-black line of the horizon, between the German islands. We walked to the end of a long breakwater, a sweep of stone into the sea, and could hardly stand in the wind.

But mostly I've stayed in, reading, writing or preparing to write reviews, and the early summer outside has been cloudy and wet and sometimes stormy.

In Lyons the trial of Klaus Barbie. "If we wish to save the world it can only be by opening this secret and painful door to our common memory." (Elie Wiesel)

In England the election campaign. Emphasis on the leaders' personalities, on carefully packaged presentation, on polls. Sometimes it seems to me that democracy in Britain has been *reduced* to the vote, with politicians bidding for it with promises. Passive democracy's a contradiction in terms, at the mercy of newspapers, image-makers, opinion based on ignorance & prejudice and manipulated by a few people serving hidden economic powers. What I see's a shopfront of glass-eyed Thatcherism, and behind it the divide widening between rich and poor, employed and unemployed, north and south. Above all the dereliction of working-class communities especially in Wales and the north, and the hopelessness of people without work. The greatest evil of my time and place is that people are made to feel useless.

Last night, a man from the City spoke on TV of industries made "fitter, slimmer, with less fat" under the Thatcher government. He was an educated man using words to exclude their human meaning. This is a language widely spoken in my country, especially in the south.

And here I am, without even a vote, talking to myself. There have been times in recent weeks when I've felt that the life I've made for myself, isolated here, and still hoping to live and work again in the south of England, is utterly mad.

And still I want to go back—to live in the present, where I feel at home; to have a function and to make a living.

Wynn Thomas, in his fine book on Walt Whitman, writes from an historicist point of view, and what he says of 19th century America is true of the West now, at a later stage of the process:

> Social powerlessness produced, in those worst affected, intimations of their cosmic insignificance, including a fatalism which was itself a thoroughly characteristic symptom of that state of mental disorder which the changing society promoted.

Wynn is a subtle historicist, whose understanding is born of "the humility of doubt". He is also a fine *reader* of poetry. But what I find most moving about his historicism is that it is also a sense of solidarity: of the poet living with others, sharing in and being shaped by a society and a history, reacting passionately with partial understanding to the corporate experience, struggling to keep faith with a common ideal even at the expense of deceiving himself about the unfaithfulness of his society. And Whitman emerges as a more moving and human figure from the actual conflicts of his time and place, though Wynn knows what he cannot know about him or anyone else, what he has to let *be*. Whitman in Wynn's book is more human than a "timeless" Whitman, where "timeless" means abstracted from time.

This is not a deconstruction of personality into the forces allegedly constructing it. This is an understanding of the great poet of democracy, who practised his belief in the equality of all souls, and indeed of all that exists, by a Welshman, who also knows solidarity among the living, and between the living and the dead, in his own culture—as an ideal (Waldo Williams' brotherhood) but also as the practice of several kinds of Welsh community, urban and rural, religious and secular.

11–12 June
Stayed up most of the night watching the election results on TV. A sorry spectacle. Most significant the reaction of world money markets, their alarm at the prospect of Labour success and excited relief at the Tory win. Experts widely acknowledge that their motives are greed and fear, but few question *why* the rest of us should have to suffer their freedom to pursue those motives. What do they care how things look in desolate pit villages this morning, or to teachers in the classroom, or parents worrying what there'll be for their children to do when they leave school? Just so long as industries become still "fitter, slimmer" and the profits roll in.

Jim rang from a phone box in Lymington in the middle of the night. He said he wanted to tell me about the election, but was more concerned that he hadn't offered me tea & cake when I was with him in his home. I hope he got safely back to bed.

§

Ah, the dead to me mar not—they fit well in Nature;
They fit very well in the landscape, under the trees and grass,
And along the edge of the sky, in the horizon's far margin.
                Walt Whitman

The world hates death. But love does not hate death. Love has something of death in it. Love and death together are stronger than all the meanness and silliness of the world.
                John Cowper Powys, 'Walt Whitman',
                The Pleasures of Literature

13 June

Annual trip to Schiermonikoog with Joe & Alisdair & the Foreign Guest Club. Cloud thinner over the island than over the mainland, and a warm day, with sun glare, but thunder around in the afternoon, and rain. We cycled again on sandy tracks, between cow parsley and hawthorn and strong-smelling elder. Off a muddy track through woodland, at a short distance from the bunker which commands a view of the whole island, we discovered the Vredenhof, with Commonwealth war graves.

Cemetery in a sheltered hollow among dunes, with Scots pines on either side. Well-tended, with roses not yet out, dead daffodils, bluebells & buttercups among low-growing cypresses, and a scattering of hawthorns & birches. A compact, oblong cemetery, with a stone cross at either end, and between one hundred and two hundred graves arranged in rows, each plot filled with blue and white cockleshells. At first it was very quiet as we looked at the small headstones in that sheltered place, only a faint bee hum in the stillness, but as we walked about reading the stones we heard seabirds crying, piping and shrilling, shelducks flew over, and a large harrier scoured marsh beyond the dunes.

Graves of the dead in both world wars and of several nations, ally and enemy, known and unknown, lay side by side. All were bare, with the same beautiful covering of shells, except one, a German soldier's, which had a wreath of lichen & fir cones lying under the headstone.

Returning with Joe after lunch, down a green track yards from the war cemetery, we came on another burial ground. Here were white, steel crosses, askew, among the lowest branches of a large birch tree, which must have been a sprig, or perhaps not even a seed, when they were first put there. A plaque on a large wooden cross informed us that, according to old inhabitants, these were the graves of the crew of a Swedish sailing ship, wrecked in a storm.

The bodies of those killed in the Great War buried in the cemetery must also have come from the sea, washed up on the sands, as also must a number of those— seamen and airmen—killed in the Second World War. The soldiers of the Great War must have been drowned when troopships went down, and so came ashore in neutral Holland.

This is a place to haunt the mind, with "complete absence of rhetoric", as Alisdair said. But even while it moved me, I was suspicious of my feeling for a peace too easily won. It is too easy to love that beautiful simplicity, and thereby simplify the lives of those whose remains lie there, and the history, as if absorbed and somehow cleansed in the soil of Europe—a continuing history, setting nation against nation, and now threatening to destroy the world. Yet the place represents a noble act of commemoration, a necessary ritual effectively and movingly carried out. Even as we came out of the cemetery, other members of the Guest Club— American, Dutch, African—joined us and the conversation turned to our lack of rituals to help us honour and mourn the dead.

When we came back to the mainland the tide was far out, and had left sculpted mudbanks on either side of the channel. Mud of the Waddenzee—mud fields, a planetary mudscape, like a huge relief map, with miniature canyons and river valleys and mountains, with flocks of geese, dark against silvery blue or grey. Twice the crowded boat juddered almost to a stop as it hit mud underwater and just carried over it.

14 June
To the heron wood (the place is called De Braak) with M. Sorrel reddening the meadows. A leafy muddy fungoid smell under the trees. Among the throaty retching noises and bill-clacking from the nests were noises which sounded, at a distance, like pigs squealing as they're driven to slaughter. Again, round yellow eye—seeing me? Seeing what?—an utterly nonhuman eye, grey hunched back & long spear of a beak over the side of a nest.

28 June
Lucy's last message to her friends, the lesson read at her funeral, was the parable of the mustard seed. The Revd. Gordon Wynne, whom I last knew as a clever, studious boy at Rope Hill thirty-five years ago, spoke in his address of the depth of true simplicity. "The simplicity of Mark and of Jesus leads us to eternal life in God the father, and God is absolutely simple." He also said that, "Lucy and her family have always stood for God's kingdom and its eternal values." I think that is true, at the same time as I think of the complexities of John Cowper's and Theodore's writings, and feel the knots in my mind loosen at Mark's words—at the words, together with a sense of sharing them with Lucy and Gerard and Mary.

In Czesław Miłosz's *The Land of Ulro*, among often intellectually demanding discussions of Blake and Dostoevsky and Swedenborg, there is this: "For surely the ideal to which I have always aspired… is membership in a human community, of the sort where communion with others comes of a shared set of values and an emotional closeness". He says the source of his poetry is his Catholic childhood in Lithuania.

For Miłosz, as for Blake, science, Baconian and Newtonian science, has imprisoned our minds and spirits in the world of matter. At times, again like Blake, he seems almost to identify science as the cause of the Fall, rather than its misuse as a consequence of the Fall. Through all I can't help thinking of the reverent, exploratory attention to nature's minute particulars, which is mixed in with Baconian imperialism over nature, but also shines with a different light, illuminating the world given to the senses on whose dignity Milosz says Christianity depends.

I sense in Milosz, with his belief in the Imagination abiding in truth, which "acknowledges God as energy and love", an absolutism that dismisses almost all modern art for its puerile barbarism. Isolating the few great figures whom he regards as having seen the roots of our crisis, he seems to have little fraternal sense of the many fellow strugglers who in their art have found broken reflections of the truth, or who have helped us to know our sickness by their affliction.

When I read condemnations of mere "creativity" I see, not artists possessed by demonic egos, but the faces of the children at the school at Eastleigh. When I think of young minds opening, learning the delight of imagination, even a simple perception of the world around them, I come closest to believing in original innocence.

1 July
After days of humid, oppressive weather the sun was shining in our wake as I came out on the deck of the night-boat this morning, close to the English coast.

On the *Benjamin Britten* to Liverpool Street. First June roses by the railway line out of Harwich. Bramble flowers, elder, foxgloves. Poppies on banks & in young corn. Convolvulus in flower on chainlink fences.

In Winchester with Emily, fishing with jam jars in the bourne, by the bridge in Nuns Road and upstream towards Abbots Barton, catching bullheads and a small crayfish.

2 July
On the train out of Brockenhurst, crossing the heath at Latchmoor, with a brief view of the Island's blue downs and the top of Sway Tower—*why* do I love the place so much? I thought again of that intense, but innocent, romantic egotism which J. C. Powys ascribed to his father, who had a passion for the places closely associated with his life. A passing thought, as the train dipped below embankments shutting out the view.

At Barton with Mother in late afternoon. Sea between Purbeck and Wight a large, blue millpond, Needles and chalk cliffs dazzling white. Masses of lupins, yellow and white and mauve, from fallen gardens, have seeded in sand and clay fallen from the cliffs. Greenfinch greeny gold on a gorse bush. A martin disappearing in a sand hole in the cliff face. An occasional swallow or tern over the almost motionless surface of the sea.

3–5 July
From Lymington to Yarmouth, where Brian Hinton met me. In the evening I read with Séan Street and Paul Hyland at the Apollo Theatre, Newport, as part of the Isle of Wight Festival

I stayed that night with Jim & Séan at Brian's flat at Chine Cliff, Totland, and the next morning we walked on the beach. Another hot day: blue sky, blue sea, with patches and shoals of kelp, like purple shadows. Hurst Castle across the water: the outer rim of an indented granite wheel. Marestails, teasels, cuckoo pint, deadly nightshade, and hart's tongue fern growing on chalky clay and under trees in the falling cliff—an almost tropical profusion of vegetation opening on the Mediterranean blue of sea and sky, but all native, part of the special, indescribable aura of West Wight.

Later, Brian led us on foot up a sunken lane to Freshwater church, where we saw the graves of Emily Tennyson and her family (but not the poet's, of course), close to the wall above the Yar estuary.

At an exhibition of sculpture in a church at Ventnor the most unforgettable image was fortuitous. A young robin had flown in, and now flew round looking for a way out, perching on pew ends and window sills and, for several seconds, on the top of a tall altar candle.

Brian took me for my first visit to Farringford House in the morning, and we had a drink on the terrace under the great cedar tree, looking out across the lawn and valley, at the path snaking up over Afton Down, with barrows on the summit, and at a corner of Freshwater Bay. This was the view Emily Tennyson said she must have when she first saw it.

A quick visit to the poet's study, a heavily carpeted, stuffy room in the heat, where he wrote some of the *Idylls*, and 'Crossing the Bar'.

Easy to imagine Tennyson feeling at home in that place, which, with the surrounding country, must have seemed to him, and others, like his kingdom. What's hard to imagine is the nation cherishing a poet as he was cherished. That whole Victorian world, which one can at times still think oneself in, physically, in West Wight, is more foreign now than the world of the lonely Anglo-Saxon celebrating the sea-farer, or even singing royal deeds in his lord's hall.

After a drink we went to a party at Jill Rook's beautiful house near Alum Bay, just below the dragon's back of West Wight, with one stack of the Needles visible below. David Gascoyne was there, looking pale and ill and withdrawn (he had been working on his new *Collected Poems*). I talked to him a little but found his manner off-putting.

9 July

New Milton—Waterloo—Liverpool Street—Cambridge. Lunch with John Matthias & Rona, a graduate of Notre Dame, at Clare Hall. Among many other things, we talked about the possibility of me teaching in America next year. John is confident that there will be no difficulty. Later he & I had supper with Ulla & Göran Printz-Påhlsson in their home overflowing with books and periodicals in Norfolk Street, where I stayed up all night talking with M. when we first met. Göran is depressed after a long, unsuccessful struggle to retain Scandinavian Studies at Cambridge.

10 July

Cambridge to Ely. Corn, baled hay and wartime pillboxes in flat fields. Ely to Norwich. Wide flat spaces, black earth, fields of potatoes, onions, corn, reed-edged waterways. Shippea Hill, a tiny station in the middle of a great space. A momentary twinge of panic at the sense of exposure on a toy train on a raised line with no shelter for miles on either side. Lakenheath: a church spire rising from trees across the fields, no sign of the nuclear base from the line.

Lee met me at Norwich station and we drove back to Moor Farm. Heavy grey cloud, midsummer smells & dusty roadsides. Green barley round the house and garden. I was too tired on arrival to take in much of what Lee told me about his work on our project. He had just taken delivery of a load of very heavy African wood (*iroko*) for his Peterborough sculpture, and the long blocks, together with a big elm torso (perhaps for 'Naked Man'), filled the barn-studio. Tired, I walked up the track to where the three church towers can be seen. As always a sense of loss, more that, perhaps, than a sense of exclusion. I want to avoid mere nostalgia for an idea of the past, of a mythical Middle Ages or Age of Faith, as I want also to avoid mere churchyness, that mainly aesthetic feeling for old religious buildings which is a substitute for thinking about religious questions—a kind of picturesque sentiment which stops thought, and seems to blunt any sense that the questions are addressed to *us*.

11 July
Morning: walking alone into the barn, in shadow with oval spots of light on floor and timbers from shafts between loose tiles in the high roof, where, with flashes of white and whirring wings, a swallow flew back and forth looking for a way out. Looking in half-light over the baulks of timber to the far wall opposite the windows, I was startled to see three wooden uprights (for *Parable* I learnt later) leaning against the wall, and had for a moment a strong sense of having stepped into the workshop of a maker of crosses.

Later, walking with Lee in the field wild with long grass, nettles, purple vetch, where his *Angel* (small head bowed, long, curved, graceful arms upreaching) stands echoing the vertical lines of Booton's twin towers across the valley, he talked to me about what the cross means to him. He is not a Christian, but for him the cross is an axis, a juncture of powerful relationships (e.g. between man and tree, or sky and earth). He asks, "What is whole?" and seeks "to recover nature in us". In his Peterborough arch, the entrance or opening and the thing that opens are one. We talked about awe, and how in England one has to struggle with guilt and embarrassment at being serious about such things.

He showed me the first shapes of sculptures (*Deepening half-light, listening & Bolder Fountain*) belonging to our project. As we stood in the yard looking at them, a white dove fluttered down and clung to my notebook, and we later rescued a half-naked, fleshy baby dove, which had fallen from the dovecot, from Malevich, the white cat. When I looked through Lee's notes on 'Their Silence a Language', copying out what I felt I might use, I kept reading "half-light" as "half-flight".

Later in the morning we drove to North Walsham, where Lee returned some lifting equipment he had hired to the workshop. On the way back we stopped in Aylsham, and picked strawberries at Salle Moor Farm, a little way past the high-pinnacled church tower.

Evening: jazz in Reepham Square, a Norwich youth orchestra, dressed in purple and black, playing to raise money for a local leisure centre. We joined the crowd and stood around listening and drinking beer.

12 July
A day of cricket, picnicking, lazing in the garden. Underlying these days, often surfacing, I think anxiously of Joe and Emily.

After dark Lee and I walked on the track through the fields to the Cawston-Reepham road, and the white cat followed us all the way. Cloud hid all but a glimmer of the cap of the full moon, in a sky faintly lit with neon towards Norwich. I asked Lee about his beginnings as a sculptor, and he told me that, as a boy, he always had a stone in his pocket and would endlessly pick at and clean it. Like most boys (e.g. me), he would usually kick a stone when out walking, but more obsessively than most, trying not to lose it. As a boy in Bucharest he was left to roam the city with street boys, in no danger despite attempts to bugger him in cellars, and his parents were always busy with Communist Party work, and seem to have had little time to care for him. He was always alone (inwardly, if not in fact), and when he came to England he felt foreign, like his name, as if he didn't belong anywhere. I think he has that sense still, in spite of Moor Farm, and of London.

Mother had talked of aloneness as we sat on Portland stone breakwaters at Barton—of being alone in the family as a girl, but also of that inner core of aloneness that each person has. Lee's *loneliness* as an artist is different; he is driven in his work in a way that I can understand, but which has, sometimes, an edge of desperation ("I can't work, I *must* work") which I feel less often and less acutely. But I can live for long periods among books, with other people's words, whereas his work demands constant physical urgency and effort, which is inseparable from the exploratory shaping of images and the creation of a developing body of work.

Now, walking on the stony path in the dark, and smelling strong midsummer night scents of grass & corn, elder & fields of beans, he talked about the difficulty of work (he has a phenomenal amount to do on public sculptures, as well as work, including ours, which excites him) and the tension between what art demands and the call on his unselfishness as a family man. We talked about the fullness of life, and the joy & privilege of working.

13 July
Morning: cycled alone back along the path we walked last night—to Cawston church (St Agnes). Looking up at an angel poised like a diver at the end of a beam of the wooden roof I distinctly had the illusion, in the flicker of an eyelid, that its outstretched wing feathers moved! And was that a Sheela na Gig holding her vagina open which I saw suspended from the central beam? The guidebook records a Green Man among the "old gods" carved among their conquerors on the roof. I did see the fine Woodwouse brandishing a club against a dragon carved in stone on either side of the west door. Inside today a feeling of emptiness in the cavernous space, with damp spots scattered on memorial slabs and stone floor.

Afternoon: helped Lee and the driver unload more offcuts of *iroko* wood from the lorry. He has enough for a gallery of reliefs. Later he drove me into Norwich, where we had a drink at a pub by the river before I caught the train.

Night, after the sun had gone down red: sat in the bar on the ferry watching the orange lights of the English coast get very small, then crawl away into the dark.

14 July
Early morning on the nord west express travelling through Rotterdam and into the country. Sun, a faint mist in the distance, full summer. Cows in meadows and round the steel feet of pylons. Herons standing stick-still by watercourses. Lilies in yellow flower on still ponds. The sun's reflection an almost blinding white eye racing on water in a channel beside the line, and broken and dulled where weed covered the surface.

I read further in David McLellen's *Karl Marx: His Life and Thought*, which so far I've found, on the whole, unsympathetic and in places boring, with its account of infighting and backbiting among revolutionaries and portrait of a dogmatic, self-righteous man—another great mind with a system that extends thought in one direction, and stops it in another.

"*The tradition of all the dead generations weighs like a nightmare on the minds of the living.*" Why this extreme violence against the dead on Marx's part? The desire for "something that has never yet existed" corresponds to it: a completely new day with not a breath from "the spirit of the past" to contaminate it. Marx may have hated injustice and oppression, but what I feel he hated more was the past, perhaps because it was not *his* day, or because he could not control it with his thought as, by prophecy and polemic, he could predict and also help to shape the future. The dead were all that was immune to the power of his words. By his hatred of the past he denied human brotherhood, as, correlatively, he defined man not as a fellow creature but as one with an imperial claim upon nature. All that intellectual certainty of Marx & the young Hegelians should seem as dated as a stovepipe hat now; but in fact the confidence of academic system-makers is stronger than ever, and farther from historical experience.

15 July
Back, I am here, with M. & Elin, in the house on the corner of Bali Straat and the Korreweg, seeing sunlight on the brick wall across the yard as I come into the kitchen in the morning, but also I am vividly elsewhere in my mind: with my parents, or walking across the grass under the oak tree (planted to commemorate the Coronation of King George V & Queen Mary) beside the road at Old Milton, or peering into the water spotting fish for Emily as she stooped with jam jars into the stream by the bridge in Nuns Road, or at Moor Farm…

I can believe in memory so powerful that its possessor can actually *touch* something in another place, and perhaps even project himself there in spirit, as JCP is said to have done. What I feel is that the purpose of life isn't (only) something ahead of us, a direction into the future, or a process of making, but what fulfils itself, through the gift of love, many times in a lifetime, and often in shared experience, or when, alone, we live in relation to what is around us.

Late July
It has been a stormy July, and the unsettled weather continues. Clouds piled on clouds, white as sunlit pure snow, grey, dark blue, black, swirl round and round, and lightning flickers, and thunder crashes. But afterwards the air never really clears, and hours later, or the next day, the storm circles closer again. On Sunday M. & I set out to walk at Zeegse. The wind was strong among the clouds, and blew refreshingly below. We walked a short way on the sandy heath, bright just now with delicate, red-stemmed quaking grasses, and reached the pond of black water. As we stood there under the trees, watching swallows skimming the surface, the sky suddenly darkened and it started to rain. As we hastened back to the car the rain fell violently, in rods, and we were soaked.

While working on my 'Writers in a Landscape' book, I'll continue to prepare the journal for publication—a task which causes me strong feelings of pain and regret and self-doubt, as well as the suspect, exquisite pleasures and pangs of memory. I've understood for some time that much in the journal complements my earlier poetry, in the sense that it contains what I could not say, or expresses part of what I could not express. There's much in the journal that *belongs with* the poetry, rather than being private matters that I should properly keep hidden. I envisage not a confession, but rather a "place": a world for other minds to enter, which is mine but also more than mine.

I'm acutely aware of the capacity of poetry to be both symptom and cause of ego-sickness. It's in our *unbinding* from one another, or, to speak in another image, our lack of a common ground, that I see the main cause of a poetry which seeks not relationship, but to distort or deny reality and aggrandize the self.

5 August
M & I left Groningen at 2 p.m. on the first stage of our drive to Spain.

6 August
As we drove through a broad, rolling country of cornfields & copses, with poppies & blue cranesbill by the dusty roadside, and under broken white cloud stacks, it must have been the name in my mind that made me see death hanging over the ridge we were approaching. But the name scarcely prepared me for what we found on the wooded hills above Verdun.

First we came to an iron machine gun post on a bluff, the thing with two eyeholes like a hideous mask, a monstrous extension of the human face. I crouched down and looked inside—the rusted and twisted remains of a gun hung in the empty cavernous space, which was claustrophobic, with a smell of fear. Young pines and birches and a few harebells grew on the slopes it looked down on, which would have been ripped to pieces when it was occupied. Coming to the Memorial, which somewhat resembles a temple and houses a museum of the battles, with guns and shells as good as new outside, we didn't go beyond the entrance hall. M. hadn't much wanted to make the visit and I was guiltily conscious of "tourists to the devastated areas".

From the Memorial we drove to the Necropolis, a strange, haunting building against cloud and sky: somewhere that is really the end of the world. It seems part cathedral, and part castle, a granite fortification with bunkers. The phallic tower standing up in the middle doesn't seem to reach up—the whole thing standing in a high place seems *enclosed*, battened down, and in spite of the Christian symbolism it seems barbaric, Sphinx-like—as if waiting for another holocaust, or beyond waiting.

Inside, in the orange light, I was more chilled than moved. To M. it was full of grief, the grief of the living whose dead were buried there, an endless, unfathomable grief. When she told me her reaction afterwards I felt ashamed; but it wasn't grief I felt, more an intense *curiosity*. It was the building, what it represented, what it was and what it was saying, that I couldn't understand. In one sense, what it was saying—with PAX over the door, and all the words about *sacrifice* and *martyrs*—was clear enough. But a tower that is like a shell? And it was the fact of the whole bloody mess in that place, the gouged earth, the terror and loss of one man multiplied over and over again, as the military and state machine drove them in to kill and die, and then the *order* of the monument and its surroundings, the elaborate reconstruction of the place: by and for the bereaved, but also by the very state machine that caused the slaughter in the first place, and now talks of meaning in sacrifice. But for the French it was a defensive action—only that's too simple in the whole European history enacted there.

Below the building I walked in the immaculate cemetery, each white cross with a red rose bush, and the whole smelling sweetly. Below again, the dark, dense back of wooded ridges, with openings on the distances of Lorraine.

On the way out we visited the small chapel on the site of one of the destroyed villages: Our Lady of Europe. It stands on rubble under pines, where the ground has been blasted, heaved up, cratered. There it was dark and still, but the chapel was in a glade full of sunlight, and a white butterfly was fluttering round flowers growing outside the porch. Round the wrought-iron door: EN MEMOIRE DE FLEURY DEVANT DOUAUMONT.

From Verdun we drove along "La Voie Sacrée"; combines harvesting in clouds of dust and chaff in the country of the Marne.

7 August
Burgundy: vineyards on warm-coloured, reddish-brown soil; chateaux; villages and walls in limestone. We followed a country road to Cluny, an occasional field of sunflowers among meadows and fields of maize, vineyards on hillsides. In Cluny we found the abbey could only be visited by means of a guided tour, the next one being some hours later. No doubt the motives are good (to protect the abbey), and the prohibition may be necessary. But it made me angry all the same, and I walked round the small town rather sourly.

8 August
At Mende in the Central Massif, under pinewoods & rocky precipices. A fine morning start from a real French hotel, unpretentious and untouristic. Over the mountains, and into Languedoc. At first a country of scattered rock outcrops, like natural castles. Fields of grey rock softening into cultivated fields, then a massive gorge, through which we came down to small terraced vineyards, bleat of goats. Crosses on high rock outcrops: the whole rocky country under the cross. Larger vineyards on dark red soil, the heat increasing—a Mediterranean warmth—and cicadas singing in a country of olives, cypresses and figs. Late in the afternoon we drove down the coast road, exposed in the heat, and over the Pyrenees into Spain. To Begur, and a terraced apartment among pines on a steep hillside: quiet and secluded though only a short distance from the coast.

Mid-August
At Begur.
    One drop of resin on a flaky pine tree—a brilliant spot, green, blue, gold, as I vary the angle from which I look at it.
    Cicadas scratching, one note repeated at changing tempos, like a stuck Morse code key. One very loud, the other quieter, perhaps in the same tree. So far I've been unable to locate them; the sounds seem to come definitely from one place—a particular branch—but when I look and listen hard it seems to be coming from elsewhere, even another tree.
    From the apartment we look out through and over pine trees growing on hills to the mountain formation at Torroella de Montgri—a large mass of grey rock cleft into three, the dome-shaped central part crowned with a castle—and from here the alluvial plain between us and Torroella is hidden by the hills.

Empuries lies on the far side of Torroella, on slopes rising gently from the Gulf of Roses. On a hot day we walked among the ruins: nearest the sea, a Christian necropolis—empty, stone-boat coffins—above it ruins of the Greek settlement first founded from Massalia c.600 B.C., with a model of a large statue of Asklepios, and above that ruins of the Roman port, where mosaic floors with geometrical designs among pillars and remains of the forum give evidence of fine living. Motionless, dark, perpetual flames of cypresses between stone walls and dusty paths and holes in the ground, all hot in the sun. What lives, for me, is the head of Aphrodite (a model) in the museum on the site—a timeworn head whose beauty is still palpable, still desirable, so that desire echoes desire across thousands of years. And the vases & pots (whether primitive or refined, and painted, their shapes and textures always evoke the touch and moulding of hands) and the life twitching sensitively in a rabbit's ears, or embodied in pigs and birds and fishes, in mosaics or ceramic figures.

I think all real poetry incorporates a feeling for native land. In Antonio Machado, for instance, though Charles Tomlinson's translations afford recognisable pleasures of *his* poetry, and of Anglo-American modernism, a feeling for Castile—the land and the people in relation to the land—informs the verse. The land is a presence in the poetry, as it is also a source of the poet's imagination, feeding his senses, enriching him with historical and personal associations, giving a body to his apprehension of life. The land puts him in touch with ancient continuities of feeling, and intimates or establishes a primeval sense of identity, at the same time as it relates him to people *now*, and facilitates his expression of a modern sensibility.

The relationship between poet and land is especially complicated in modern times; but it is still strong in poets as various as Machado, Bobrowski, Montale, Seferis, and most of the great Russian poets. For there to be a relationship between poet and land which energises the poet, I think there has also to be a relationship between land and people: not one that is only historical, but that can be apprehended now. Therein lies the difficulty for an English poet: not just the separation between poet and land caused by urban experience, but the difficult feelings engendered by an apparently empty countryside—the landscape of agribusiness—and by the complex history of exploitation, in which, for example, pastoral ideals have either ignored the people working the land, or been enjoyed at their expense. Nevertheless, without a strong source of feeling *under his feet*, a source which is in some sense the land itself, the poet is impoverished.

Vincent Sherry's book on Geoffrey Hill has contributed to these reflections. Hill is among the most gifted English-language poets of the century, with an astonishing *mastery* of words and forms. He has strong feeling for the land of England; but that feeling, perhaps because of difficulties which are *our* public difficulties, never *comes through*, as it does in Machado or Montale, but always turns back, ending in complex irony. It may be that Hill's importance as a poet lies partly in his confrontation and exposure of the difficulties of being an English poet now. What I cannot accept, though, is that there can be a great art that is closed, without roots in land and people, and from which we may not draw generously, as from David Jones or J. C. Powys. But if the difficulties are such as to sever the roots... *Are* the roots in England, everywhere in England, severed? Or is the idea of severance an ideological construct?

Here, villages or small towns arise, often heavily fortified, like islands out of the alluvial plain. Pals, for example, with huge walls of stone, or Peratallada with its medieval castle. At Ullastret the Iberian settlement *was*, virtually, an island, the hill on which it stood descending to a large lake, which extended into lagoons and marshes connecting the settlement with the coast and with Empuries. Now there are stubble fields and strips of green all lying very flat at the base of the steep hill, where the water once was. The ruins of Cyclopean walls occupy a beautiful site of pines, cypresses and olives, with figs, peaches, almonds and flowering shrubs, so that it is cool and fragrant, in spite of the cactus and the sun. There, in the museum, among shapely pots, we saw coins (including drachmas, and coins from New Carthage inscribed with horses which looked to me like Pegasus), and a statuette of the god Bes, brought to Catalonia by the Phoenicians: a gross, flabby figure (somewhat between a wrestler and a dissolute Buddha) with a worn, distorted face, like an actor's comic mask. Also, evidence of a skull-cult: skulls with iron spikes driven into them.

Crowded beaches of the Costa Brava, but early in the morning they are almost deserted. At Fornelli, for example, there was just one yacht anchored in the bay as M. and I climbed down the steps in the cliff, and a little later two old men gathering up litter. Water a little chilly before the sun has had time to warm it, but refreshing, in a suntrack lying from sea to shore.

At night, after an evening when the sun had gone down white in a close sky full of dust, the heat almost unbearable, motionless naked bodies bathed in sweat. Then, at 4 a.m., suddenly, the wind rises brushing the pines. We lay out on the terrace, under a bright half-moon, pine needles falling on us, the wind deliciously cool. I've rarely been as grateful for anything as I was for that wind. If only the mind could be kept in that state, knowing what it is to be alive.

The Salvador Dalí Museum in Figueras, an amusing, entertaining place, deliberately theatrical, with clever optical jokes, and also a trivial use of great art of other times, not the illuminating transformations of creative pastiche or parody. True, Dali does have *something* of the fantastic and even grotesque visual imagination which seems to characterise great Spanish art, but his jokes and display of personality are the ruin of a talent—or the only forms that restless talent could consistently employ? At any rate, the museum is an amiable place, but certainly not, as it claims to be, "the spiritual centre of Europe".

From Figueras over the mountains to Cadaqués, which was
>   too white
>   too blue
>   too picturesque

But I suppose a hot tripper in a bit of an ill temper might say something similar about Lymington.

All thoughts about bad or indifferent art were put into perspective in Barcelona.

On the Ramblas, moving leisurely among crowds of strollers, by pet stalls, flower stalls, cafes, newspaper stands, knickknack sellers, pavement artists, fortune tellers with Tarot cards, men shining shoes. Sunlight through plane trees on either side, a few leaves falling, houses with iron balconies rising storey on storey. A relatively quiet part of a dynamic, vibrant city, that is a wonderful combination of the old and the new, and where the sheer variety and mixture of human life can be felt: squalor and beggary, wealth and vice (young male and female prostitutes openly soliciting), simple goodness and communal warmth, imbecility and sophistication…

By the Columbus monument and the lions (in this eclectic city which incorporates ideas from London and Paris and other world cities, but is completely itself), a smell of fish and the salt sea.

In the Museu' d'Art de Catalunya, among the Romanesque and Gothic works (art, but more than art), which is certainly one of the spiritual centres of Europe. For us, passing through too quickly before the building shut, a few fragments:

> Among the many wooden Christs, one in a brightly painted, patterned robe with a profoundly sorrowful face.
> Some mere fragments without arms, and some peppered with wormholes, but you always *know* who it is!
> Angels with dynamic wings, like whirling swords.
> *All* the faces on murals or altars or whatever surfaces are faces of figures in a sacred drama, human like us, but as our faces might be only if transfigured.
> Faces of ox and ass at the nativity, faces that amuse and evoke tender feelings, and express an utterly adoring simplicity.
> Joseph with his hand lifted to his cheek, looking on at mother and child as if wondering what it is all about.
> In every fragment, the drama, the intensity, of that story.
> John the Baptist with a shock of brown hair and a jagged brown beard, wide-eyed, against a background of cacti, which might also be green flames.
> The Christ child held in a sheet between two archangels, as if they are about to toss him up and down.

Later we visited Antoni Gaudí's Sagrada Familia. First impression of the Nativity facade: a magnificent hand-moulded castle of mud or sand. The organic forms seem to melt and run and drip, like ice or water. And the thought came to me, wondering, intrigued, a little sceptical (there are a few features that recall Disney): so this is what can happen if you let little boys play with sand! And what I was responding to was the play and wonder and boldness of the child's imagination which Gaudi in his maturity had retained.

But the space within isn't sacred yet. People sit there chatting and smoking, children jump on the heaps of materials. A sound of workmen hammering from outside. Spiderwork wire netting and scaffolding over the unfinished parts of the façade.

A building that is at once fluid and monumental, with the rhythms as well as the giant forms of nature; and an act of personal imagination, so that I found myself addressing questions to the architect in my mind.

There's a laughter of delight that's close to tears.

Late August
Just before and after Emily's arrival, on the 21st, the first signs of autumn: a pair of hedgehogs in the garden at night; sea-mist when we went to swim in the morning; a large flock of redwings playing on air currents and uttering short warbling notes.

The Uncommon Tongue is a brilliant critical work. What troubles me about it is the idea of poetic "mastery", and "redemption", and "transcendence", as a *rival* to religion. Despite passages in which he claims otherwise, Sherry's Hill is a veritable Lucifer of conceit and pride and cunning. What the figure lacks is the profound humility which is a feature of the Powysian magus (I have simultaneously been reading, with some delight, and some impatience and irritation, *The Complex Vision*. The influence of Powys on Hill is, I think, significant, though virtually unacknowledged, and hard to specify). That humility is an openness—for example, whatever one may think of its ascription of personality to *every* being and thing, whether animate or inanimate, material or immaterial, the belief renders an equality of unfathomable depth to all throughout the multiverse. But there's inevitably something closed about a poet isolated in a position of superiority by his mastery of language; it is also at once a peculiarly male and a congenitally academic position. After visiting Verdun, and after seeing the devotional handiwork of the Catalan masters, I'm even less able than usual to think of poetry either seriously rivalling religion or transcending history. The power of redemption, as religion understands it, is not an individual mind's; and the poet remains subject to history, an historical being, immersed in the destructive element, however much his control of language may seem to set him above it.

Storm. Morning when the Pyrenees stood out in clear outline behind the rock outcrops at Torroella, but were obscured later by dark blue stormcloud as thunder came growling along the coast. Then the storm closed over us, lightning flashing in misty dark and torrential rain, which came through the roof like water running out of a bucket with holes in it.

Light clear and washed the morning after the storm. Snow visible on the summits of the Pyrenees.

A slow journey with M. on the stopping train from Girona to Barcelona. Endless sandy beaches crowded with sun-worshippers, beach cafes, the sea with a line dividing it into two vivid colours: green-blue and purple-blue.

Short boat trip from Tamariu to Calella, close to rock cliffs with pines growing on them more than halfway down to the water. On the way back the boat, especially when turning, tossed on a swell. I was afraid, and have imagined things to fear almost continually in recent weeks.

In Girona after taking Emily to the airport and leaving her with a stewardess, and after we had wound through the labyrinthine streets and climbed the long stone stairway to the cathedral, as I rested my hand on a stone wall at the top, the jet taking her back to England turned over the city and climbed over the mountains, disappearing with a noise of retreating thunder into the hot blue sky.

Is there any cathedral with a finer, more imposing situation than this? Its great walls are like a castle's and it towers over the city, looking out far over the mountains. At a visit, it seemed to me an even more powerful stronghold of the military god than Winchester, and I took the giant statues of St Peter and St Paul on the façade for a Jupiter and a Mars.

There we saw the Tapestry of Creation: an otherworldly model for early maps of this world. But it *is* a map of this world, a divine map. Christ Pantocrator at the centre, the sea and its strange beasts below him, issuing continually from the creative act, which is an act of blessing, Adam naming the creatures (including a unicorn and other legendary beasts) on one hand, Eve emerging from Adam's side on the other, then the four winds, angels riding on wineskins, and in boxes along the margins, the months and the seasons. It is all one incredible imaginative act: the world as God creates it, the ordinarily fantastic earth, to which everything imagined by man the creature of this order belongs.

Here also we saw a slender Christ in Majesty, dressed in a blue robe and with a serene face. Nailed to the cross, he stands with a gentle, peculiarly inward look, his arms stretched out in an embrace or a gesture of universal blessing, rather than forced into position. There's nothing of the preacher about him; his whole attitude is that of one who offers but does not compel. There's even a graceful simplicity about this Majesty, and a certain self-effacingness that corresponds with it.

29 August

Today we left Begur and started the drive back. Glimpses of names and landscapes: the Camargue, Languedoc, Provence, Arles, sun hot on vineyards & harvest fields & fields of dead sunflowers.

30 August

Lyon, Saône, Jura, Le Doubs, Les Vosges, Alsace. Into and out of Germany beyond Mulhouse, then beside the Rhone to Strasbourg, where we stopped for the night in the old city near the statue of Gutenberg and the pink and ruddy sandstone cathedral, which glowed darker red as the sun went down. Evening walk by the river, against the sun and the sun on the water, by walls and bridges of Vosges sandstone into Petite France. Here, one of the best preserved of all medieval cities, but quite different from Girona, where one can also imagine oneself in the Middle Ages. Strasbourg is more austere, more masculine, M. says, less enclosing; also, I would think, with less poverty, and much more mercantile wealth when the old city was built—the big houses standing by the river bespeak considerable wealth and civil and political power. Now, as we returned from our walk, the narrow streets were thronged with people coming and going, especially in the approach to the cathedral doors crowded with carved figures, with a kind of stilled hurtling motion, stopped in flight.

31 August

Strasbourg—Saarbrücken—Trier. In the north, as I first really noticed in Germany, red berries on rowans, conkers & rust-gold leaves on horse-chestnuts. Moselle: cloudy green vineyards covering broad steep hillsides crowned with pine forest, neat, white-painted, slate-roofed villages and small towns. Glorious cornland at or just before harvest time over broad rolling hills towards Koblenz.

In Cologne, the cathedral's formidable blackened stone spires by the Rhine. Its size and blackness frightened M. when she was taken there as a little girl. Now too we found it rather frightening, inspiring in the great height of the roof held up on tall slender pillars inside, so that the mind daunted by the exterior is suddenly released on an upsurge of power with grace and lightness and delicacy, but with more of that sinister atmosphere which some cathedrals have, with the sheer spectacle of worldly might together with the deadness of receding belief—as if only a candleflame and someone praying in a side chapel represented the still-living part, like a green branch on the trunk of a huge dead tree.

And in Cologne the image of rubble from bomb damage haunts the cathedral, as the city is ghosted by its former devastation. No, it isn't only that, which is fairly common among European cities; it's also the sense that all this, all that this building stands for, didn't stop what happened in Hitler's Germany. This great hulk didn't make an iota of difference—it wasn't *this* that inspired and sustained the great courage of Bonhoeffer and those like him. Then there's also the more troubling suspicion: of the elements in Christianity itself which have stimulated cruelty, intolerance, and hatred, and, in Auden's words, "driven a culture mad". At another level, there's my sightseer's uneasiness: this making a bee-line for cathedrals or other places of "historical interest". It's rare enough in these fascinating old buildings that I realize, as I do before a Catalan crucifix or Mother and Child, that the challenge of Christianity is to literal truth. Not, with a familiar modern psychological religiosity, how wonderful is the mind of man, which has created from itself all these fearful, beautiful and magical symbols of his condition, but: *This man is God.*

Outside the cathedral a Peruvian group (possibly the same one we heard in Ghent two years ago) was playing melancholy-joyful music, a sound that was alive as nothing we had seen inside was, and the broad surrounding area was crowded with people. Stopping to listen to the group I found myself standing by an inscription cut into the paving stones: THIS COULD BE A PLACE OF HISTORICAL IMPORTANCE. I don't know whether it was meant as a joke, or whether it was a pompous statement of the obvious, meant to raise consciousness and deter people from larking about, but it made me laugh at myself for my avid garnering of historical and religious sensations. On further reflection, I suppose it could have a wiser meaning: This *could* be a place of historical importance, *if* we recognise what has happened here and what it means. But at any rate, it did me a good turn.

From Cologne we drove on the busy autobahn through the Ruhr and were at Arnhem towards sunset. Back to Groningen under a misty yellow half-moon.

3 September
Dad's youngest brother, my uncle Leslie, died in August. He was the only one of the family to stay in the north, but in Blackpool, where he had a garage, not Yorkshire. (Dennis had a modest smallholding at Lock's Heath—and made a great deal of money when he sold the land a few years ago. Roland was a senior policeman in Oxford. Dad came south when he was a young man.) Leslie was the most intellectual of the brothers, and a kind, understanding, witty man. He had the accent and dramatic ability to do excellent Stanley Holloway monologues, such as 'Albert and the Lion', and I can remember, as a boy, being spellbound and shaking with laughter on the few occasions when he did them with us. In more recent years, I seldom saw him, and it is much longer ago, perhaps more than twenty-five years, that I last saw his children, my cousins Kenneth and Greta. Yet they were friends, too, when I was a boy.

When very young, up to the time when we left Warsash, I grew up with Janet and Christine, Dennis and Marjorie's children. I even have a vague memory of being pushed in a pram with Janet, along the road from Lock's Heath to Sarisbury Green, and at that time, when Granny Hooker was still alive and for a short time after her death, we were all virtually one family. What I find sad is not that time passes—there's nothing we can do about that; without it there'd be no life—but loss of contact between relatives, and this thinning out of family, by which a continuing shared life with its store of memories becomes less substantial, and may at last cease to exist.

5 September
I wasted a whole day yesterday reading *A Paradise Lost*, Dr David Mellor's text to the book accompanying the exhibition, *The Neo-Romantic Imagination in Britain 1935-55*.

For a paradise lost read an opportunity missed. And what an opportunity: to look closely at works by Henry Moore, Paul Nash, David Jones, Graham Sutherland, and others, and also to understand what shaped their vision and what obstructed it, and how it relates to what we see, what we desire, and what frustrates our desire.

This is a period in academic criticism of the dominance of the totalitarian mind. Order is a general need of the mind, but the systems that, in single dogma or in combination, commonly supply it now are the monolithic psychological or Marxist abstractions of modern thought, or the more complex and subtle ideologies based on them. In the confusions of the time, all seems frighteningly clear to some thinkers—"products" of ideas which flatter the mind's weakness for mastery over its subject.

14 September
Ned Thomas stayed with us this weekend, at the conclusion of his EEC sponsored tour to meet representatives of several minority cultures, including the Friesians. He is a delightful person, invariably good-humoured, humane, with a wide and

deep-reaching intelligence; a friend and former colleague who, more than anyone, made me feel the worth of working in a Welsh university, and whose tireless conscientious work for the causes he believes in is exemplary. We had a convivial time, and talked with all the old freedom about a number of things. I almost wrote the "old" things, but they are the same yet not the same, as the political situation affecting peoples throughout the world changes, and the pressures we're subject to, our thinking, and our grounds for hope or fear also change.

At a personal level, I touched once or twice on my baselessness; but carefully, more out of respect for the tragedy Ned and his fellow Welsh nationalists fear for their nation (Wales being sucked away from under their feet, as J. R. Jones wrote) than because I've overcome self-pity. Again and again, I need recalling to the connection between personal distress and the sense of loss or rejection that people are being made to feel. Still, at the personal level, it's salutary for me to talk to Ned because he both believes strongly that I did the right thing for myself as a poet in leaving Aberystwyth, and takes a very sceptical view of the kind of academic or literary "success" that periodically tempts me.

I thought with affection of members of the department as Ned gave me news of them, and remembered functions of my working life that I sometimes miss. But I could honestly say that I don't regret my decision to leave.

As we talked about Wales and our many mutual friends & acquaintances, I remembered what it's like to feel part of something, for even though my sense of belonging was partial and complex (and included a feeling of *dis*placement in relation to an idea of home in England) Wales did give me shared ground to stand on, and strongly affected my sense of purpose. But I could still say that I *had* to leave. Even though I wasn't able to settle, as intended, in the south of England, and even if the logic of my situation subsequently makes me more of a wanderer, I couldn't make the choice that Peter Lord or Raymond Garlick made. I don't say that others without Welsh connections can't *become* Welsh by commitment and adoption, but I know that I couldn't. Say I lacked the gift; it doesn't matter much what I say—the only true relationship I could have with Wales was based on *difference*; that was determined, for good or ill, by what I am.

If Wales can't be the focus of my concern, to the degree that it is for Ned, it's nevertheless part of what I see feelingly; and the fact that I see it with some insight, and see the related plight of other peoples, owes much to him and to other Welsh writers in both languages.

15 September
The day before yesterday a man was shot dead only yards from here, round the corner in Padangstraat. He was involved in the *drugswereld* as a *kleine drugsdealer*. At a certain distance from the horror there's something indescribably pathetic about the sight (in a photograph) of a pair of legs sticking out from under a blanket, the trousers still creased, the shoes laced—as he dressed himself in the morning.

I know the spot where he fell, shot by unknown assailants, outside a youth centre and across a border of low rose bushes, beside the brick-paved street.

Last week—resisting a neurotic pattern—I started going for a walk each morning. The walk I like best is to the end of the canal (*Oosterhamrikkanaal*), where it is stopped against a brick wall. Rubbish has been dumped there—a sofa, a supermarket trolley, bits of rope, a Christmas tree, all slimy & tacky, with marsh gas bubbles rising in greeny brown water—but Michaelmas daisies grow in crevices between bricks in the wall, and canal water even lends a kind of desolate beauty to the things thrown in to it. And each morning, according to the weather, the water is different, whether sunless or with a surface of blinding, sparkling light.

I walk beside the canal to *Kapteynbrug*, where a black-painted barge is moored. One morning I saw a hand appear (the rest of the body hidden from me) in a cage which projected from the barge's superstructure and move back and forth with a brush so that droppings and white feathers fell like a miniature snowstorm on the water and the feathers slowly floated away. Then I noticed the flock of pigeons perched on the wheelhouse. Next morning I saw the elderly man who lives on the barge, as he gingerly worked his way round the side to unhook some kind of bundled-up net. I know nothing about him but see him now with sympathetic interest. The bridge is directly in line with the sober, elegant *nieuwe kerk* with its blue clockface with white hands, at one side of which stands the tall brick chimney in the area called *Jodencamp* (a former Jewish area), and on the other Martinikerk. Now, when a flock of pigeons wheels overhead, I wonder automatically if they have come from the barge.

Early in the month a young woman committed suicide by jumping off the Martini tower; she was the second person this year to do so. The shooting was also the second this year in the immediate locality: earlier a young man caught in an act of burglary pulled a gun on a policeman, who shot him dead. As in other cities there are frequent acts of violence or despair. Before going on holiday we were burgled, not with great loss (some cheques which could be stopped, a hired video recorder) but Elin & M. in particular felt more vulnerable & afraid as a result; also, it seems certain that the culprit was a friend of Elin's, a girl with a drug problem.

M. says that every thinking, sensitive person sometimes agonizes over whether they have *ever* really got outside the circle of the self and known another person. I'm not alone in that, either. The world has never been so full of words, sometimes the air seems black and heavy with them; it has never been so full of images of violent or sentimental or meaningless human contact (or collision); and people generally have never been so cut off from one another or found it so difficult to communicate from deep inside, or with their depths. I don't think I exaggerate; even poetry, at once the most careful use of words and a passionate ordering of language, rarely communicates at that level. In consequence it is impossible for us to address *our* problems (which are at once social and personal) except in the case of two (or more) people who love each other—in which event they may feel themselves to be an island in dangerous seas.

22 September
Check with a doctor in the morning before starting evening classes for *Stichting Noordelijke Leergangen*. Overweight: I didn't need to be told that, or rather I did, in order to do something about it. Also, blood pressure a little high. Mortality my companion.

Evening: first class, with first year students (most of them teachers), on essay writing on literary subjects, and some modern English and American novels. In the Ubbo Emmius building, which is a pleasant cycle ride from here, to the north west, where the city ends and fields begin beyond the building. I talked to them about poetry and then we discussed two "war" poems by Hardy and Owen. It was good to be teaching again.

§

"No, it is impossible to convey the life-sensation of any given epoch of one's existence,—that which makes its truth, its meaning—its subtle and penetrating essence. It is impossible. We live, as we dream—alone."
Marlow, in *Heart of Darkness*

Conrad's idea of the artist emphasises his loneliness: he "descends within himself, and in that lonely region of stress and strife, if he be deserving and fortunate, he finds the terms of his appeal" (Preface to *The Nigger of the Narcissus*). Biographical reasons for this readily suggest themselves: the sailor alone with the sea, or the captain separated from the crew by his responsibility for them; the exile; the writer isolated in his study. The same reasons may be invoked to account for the emphasis he places on solidarity, and the link, at first sight paradoxical, between loneliness and solidarity. Fear of psychological breakdown *and* of breakdown of social order is very strong in Conrad, and loneliness in his stories leads, again and again, not to solidarity but to its breach, by some form of egotistical behaviour or illusion. "The latent feeling of fellowship with all creation" can't be relied on, indeed, it can't be trusted not to lead to destruction, as Kurtz succumbs to the rhythms of the "savage" dance. Order, then, is very precarious; it may even be seen as a social construct, which protects people both from the jungle without and the "darkness" within.

Descent into the self leads to nightmares, not to "solidarity". In Conrad, at the end of the nineteenth century, we are a long way from Wordsworth and Rousseau, and from the belief that introspection opens on the depths of human commonality. And of course Conrad is quite aware of the distance, since he is self-consciously anti-Romantic—(and a great writer partly for the reason that he opposes, with his fidelity to solidarity, his own strongly romantic impulses, which both arise from and exacerbate his loneliness).

2 October
Colder now, but a bright sunny start to my visit to England. Dew on grass, water shining, a mist of light. A pastoral of cows in meadows, fields of maize, allotments with bean stick tepees. Tense at first, I looked out of the train window and noted what I saw.

Schiphol to Heathrow: clear blue sky over the North Sea. After a long wait at Heathrow the coach to Woking was crowded and I huddled into a seat with my bags on top of me. Train to New Milton, where it was raining when I arrived late in the afternoon.

3 October
On Barton cliffs with Mother in a lovely soft warm southerly breeze. Island barely visible in luminous mist, white sun over the sea. Martins skimming the cliff tops, a few hawkbit, yarrow, and wild barley, with small, brown fungi in windswept grass.

Afternoon: a course with Jude on "poetry of place" for the WEA at the Memorial Hall, Whitefield Road. Jude talked about the history of the region and showed slides of its different landscapes, and I talked about poems by Hardy & Edward Thomas and later read from my *Master of the Leaping Figures*. In Whitefield Road I could see myself as a boy sitting upstairs on the bus between school and home, and as a young man in the coffee bar that used to be on the corner, looking covetously at the girls.

Later, watching the local news on TV with my parents, Mother pointed out a row of trees at Botley which Pop had seen planted, and Dad remembered playing cricket there. In their reminiscences, in my wanderings about the area, this kind of thing happens all the time; as if memory were in the very air, in the colours & textures of pavements, houses, trees, fields—memory on memory, mine, theirs, other people's, fetched out of time-sequence, rising up at present thoughts, sensations, conversations, but without breaking the one strong invisible tissue. It isn't that we are inside one another's minds, or that individual experience is any less incommunicable in its uniqueness, but the lives lived are somehow together in the places, creating a medium which is as palpable as it is elusive, with an existence which mere dead bricks—places without associations—don't have.

4 October
Sunday morning. Dad talked to me about painting. He said he was about forty when he had a revelation of *seeing*, of colour above all, and of mass, the light in the dark, after looking closely at Constable and the Impressionists, especially Monet. He spoke about colours—the names that have been magical to me since childhood—and his use of them, emphasising those he found most important.

"A touch of yellow ochre in sky blue." Yellows and blues make greens. A touch (he says "titch") of Prussian blue, a bit of flake white, a touch of lemon yellow, a bit of yellow ochre, a touch of red. "You see some dandelions. You want to paint them. What colour? The only way is to take the brush or palette knife with almost pure chrome yellow."

"There's no such thing as a white colour in nature."

"The fewer colours, the better."

"How commence a painting? By seeing my subject thoroughly, seeing its possibilities in paint. The artist walking about in nature—all of a sudden he sees a composition, in colour, a possibility of design, and he's happy, he puts his easel up and commences by drafting the composition, and then painting into it. And all the time feeling the beauty."

"The total impossibility of capturing nature. You have to go for what you see, the relationships in harmony. You have to have an understanding of light, God Almighty's light. It doesn't come easily, only by experience, and understanding of what it does."

He takes Constable's view of Turner, that he saw what was beautiful in his mind (i.e. was too subjective).

Constable painted "faithful to what he was looking at".

Dad had "a God-gift of seeing" from very early. Sitting in class in school, he looked at a still-life of a bowl of fruit, seeing it in complete harmony of shape. He was the only one in the class who could see it rightly. "Didn't realize it myself. Could see when others were wrong."

"I haven't done with my art life what I might have done, what I should have done. That's my fault." The main reason was his need to make a living. And he has destroyed many of his canvases, and in some cases regrets having done so. Even paintings which he knew to be good, if he had painted them with the aid of a photograph instead of directly, in nature, he destroyed.

Afternoon. A walk with Jim on the disused railway track near Cater's Cottage, Hinchelslea and Long Slade Bottom to Wilverley and near Yewtree Bottom. At first a black, muddy track churned up by horses' hoofs through thick undergrowth, with smells of mud, fungi, wet vegetation, and masses of acorns on the oaks. Inevitable green woodpecker flying away from us. A robin singing on top of a gorse bush. A solitary pink dog rose on a bush covered with hips. We walked across the open heath on a mild, quiet autumnal afternoon, and again under trees (the chestnuts of Wilverley) and out into the open above the Avon Water valley. In one place beside the track we found a solitary apple tree loaded with green fruit, which was sour to taste. Jim fantasised that he might have thrown the apple core from which the tree had grown out of the train window; or perhaps it was the one act that in God's eyes redeemed a wicked man's life…

5 October
My first of a series of school visits to read and hold workshops in the morning: at Canford School, which I've often passed. A sumptuous place by the Stour, a piece of old upper-class England, with an ancient church in the grounds, new and old buildings (the earliest are Norman), extensive landscaped grounds with lawns,

urns & statues, and cedars, plane trees, chestnuts (but no one had picked up the shining conkers lying on the grass. Why?) I began by reading to an older group and answering their questions. Afterwards, having given perhaps too much, a dismal feeling of fatigue & disappointment when not one of the well-to-do pupils bought a copy of the book. Next a workshop with 13-year-olds, polite, confident boys who had been writing a "Venutian" exercise. All the schoolrooms had been named after places in Hardy's novels, Casterbridge, Kingsbere, and so on. Sally Winter from radio 2CR sat in on the workshop, and after lunch I drove after her to Bournemouth, where she recorded an interview in the studio.

6 October

To Cams Hill Comprehensive School in Fareham, with a view across the playing fields of Portsmouth waterfront and tower blocks. I arrived lunchless having set out early but got lost around Fareham, on roads that have changed a lot since I was a child, though I wouldn't have remembered much about them in any case.

Pop's father, Charlie Mould, rented a farm near the brickfields in Fareham. He was an immensely strong man. When he died, in 1916, he was taken on a farm cart to the local cemetery. His wife, Thirza, died in 1918. Pop may have rented the farm for them—he kept his horses on it.

7 October

To Alton Convent in the afternoon, through pouring rain and strong winds. Here, as in all the schools, the teachers were exceptionally friendly and welcoming and the children listened closely and asked a lot of questions. I don't know what Mrs Thatcher means when she talks about the new confidence in Britain—or rather I know that she's talking about a kind of competitive-cum-patriotic spirit that's anti-communal in effect and excludes a large part of the population—but I invariably find among teachers and children a great reservoir of goodwill. They're simply people I'm happy to be with, and I'm proud that as visitor and poet I can give them something that interests them.

From Alton Convent I followed a teacher to Lord Wandsworth's College. It was well that I did, since the rain was now even heavier, and the narrow twisting roads were more like rivers of brown water. Tea with Stephen Stuart-Smith in his rooms—a boy brought us a dish with a mountain of cucumber sandwiches on it and a plate of cakes—which reminded me of a don's room in Oxford or Cambridge. Later I read to two groups—the young men seemed less formal than the pupils at Canford, and almost all of them bought books!

8 October

To St Nicholas' Girls School, Fleet, in the morning. A day of high wind, but clear and dry, so that I could see more of the country, a beautiful part of Hampshire I hardly know, which seems farther from Basingstoke and the motorway than it really is, and feels, even now, more like Gilbert White country than the south of commuter villages and large estates.

Back to Winchester at lunch time, where I met Séan Street in a pub. He took some photographs later and we went over to Elizabeth's to record an interview.

Elizabeth had organized a workshop at The King Alfred for me to meet old friends and celebrate the publication of the book in the evening, but, for one reason or another, none of them except Elizabeth herself were able to be there.

9 October

A free day in Winchester walking about in heavy rain, talking to Elizabeth, resting. I met Bill Crozier outside Harrington's and he went in with me and bought a copy of the book, which I signed for him and Katherine. He has retired from the School of Art and seems well pleased not to be concerned with it any longer. We talked a little about *Spycatcher*, which he is reading.

10 October

At Harrington's bookshop again in the morning, where Elizabeth had arranged for me to sign copies of the book. More rain, but even if the sun had been shining I doubt whether many more than two people (one of them Paul Williams, my former student) would have turned up to see me. It was embarrassing, but Elizabeth was more upset so I kept my feelings from her.

Then all was made good after lunch when we drove out to Tichborne church, and I gave a reading. The audience wasn't large, but that made no difference in the compact, intimate interior, with the people in Tudor box pews below me, as I stood in the pulpit, feeling quite at home, as I never thought I would, and not at all like an impostor. To my right the Tichborne memorials, and I ended by quoting Chidiock Tichborne's poem, which Robert Wells introduced me to when we visited the church during our walk by the Itchen. It was obvious afterwards that everyone had enjoyed the reading, and for many, who had either been born in or near Tichborne or had lived there for many years, it was moving to hear poems about their places. And moving for me to receive their gratitude, as it had been to read to them.

How a world of coldness can vanish at a gesture—as when a big man who looked like a farmer asked me to sign a book for his wife, who is seriously ill. It isn't only that the coldness, which seems like something done to oneself, vanishes, but that, at least for a time, one realizes something of the human truth that puts such feelings of embarrassment or humiliation in their place, and is reminded of what poetry, as opposed to a poet's vulnerable ego, is all about. I was also very pleased to meet again a young man and a young woman who work for the oral history unit in Southampton and who had come to hear me at New Milton the previous Saturday. He, Carl Major, is interested in George Oppen and the Objectivists, and Carl and Christine brought me tapes of recordings made about working and growing up in the Northam and Chapel areas of Southampton.

The Irish vicar, Ernest Simms, who at Stephen's suggestion had invited me to read in his church, was a delightful man. He told us with gentle humour a good Tichborne story. He had had the delicate task (his words) of asking the surviving members of the old family—three women—where they would like to be buried, since the family vault is full. The last Tichborne to be buried there was a man six foot six tall, and when, after great difficulty, they had got his coffin down into the vault, it was found that a churchwarden, a little man, had got in front of the coffin and couldn't get out. So the coffin had to be taken out and the whole process gone through again. Now the churchwarden always looks at the entrance to the vault when he comes into the church and gives a bewildered shake of his head.

12 October
Late afternoon, alone on the beach at Barton. Despite what I'd learnt at Tichborne, a letting go of my bitter disappointment at the bookshop and at what I've rarely been able to admit to myself about Winchester.

Why do I refuse to *see* what the situation there is, and widely in the south of England? That the dominant values are money-values, and that only a few people care for the things I care for. Of course my motives were never "pure". It's always been that early sense of belonging, however ambiguous, that I've sought to regain, develop and carry through. I *know* how "success" works. Why then do I go on expecting it will be different in my case? If I were a celebrated poet returning in old age, or if I were a poet with a "name" in London, my books would sell and might be widely read. What's hopeless is this wanting to live a life in the place, on the terms I've chosen or could accept.

I thought too of a poem by David Orme, whom I'd met at Elizabeth's. He'd spoken generously of his friends and gave us poems modestly, even shyly, becoming more outspoken with a few drinks and as we all talked. His poem was set at Hill Head: he had come up against the filth and evidence of waste on the beach as if it were a wall which shut meaning out. He was pressing for a way through, and had come to a stop in the poem, still pressing. I felt he had come up against the wall that confronts us all, if we look for something more than money-values or conventional literary success ("framing bits of experience for sale as commodities," as Tony Conran puts it), if we look for anything with community in it, which we can give our lives to. I have to work knowing that others too are scrabbling at that wall.

With this new book, and going on beyond it, I can come of age.

13 October
To Cheltenham for a reading with Deirdre Shanahan as part of the Literature Festival. Descending Coopers Hill, with the view of Gloucester below, brought Ivor Gurney to mind. There are those whose love of the world is so great (Gurney, Jefferies, and Llewelyn Powys) it seems incredible that they should die. My parents had talked about dying, saying that only those who really know us—our friends, our relatives, perhaps—will remember, that we as we are are soon forgotten. Pop had refused to put up a stone to his wife Lottie (it was like the end of the world when she died, Mother said), and refused to have a stone put up for himself, saying that people should remember without that, or else forget.

14 October
New Milton—Woking—Heathrow—Schiphol. On the station platform at Schipol there was a mysterious pool of blood and bloody footsteps leading away from it. It was interesting to see how everyone stared at it curiously, and smiled.

From Amersfoort I travelled to Groningen with a young man from the city, who had been south for a job interview. He was tall and thin with dark hair and a sallow complexion, full lips and a moustache. He told me that he was a Catholic and belonged to the Legion of Mary. He had intended to train for the priesthood, but had met an Irish girl with a young daughter and was going to marry her. He was an archivist and found the work interesting, though he complained of the dirt he got on his hands from handling dusty records, but he would just as soon take over the village shop of his mother-in-law-to-be, which was in a fairly remote part of rural Ulster. He was frank in describing his courtship with his Irish fiancée (as soon as he'd mentioned her he'd produced a photograph of her and her daughter), and his life, as a friendless Catholic boy growing up with a beleaguered feeling—like the Jews, and from his appearance he may also have been a Jew—in the Protestant north, and as a member of the Legion of Mary working for some months at menial tasks in Birmingham and other parts of England. I was both touched and a little embarrassed by his disclosures and his way of describing his relationship—proud, almost boastful, with an innocent but slightly furtive enthusiasm, which I've noticed before in a certain kind of religious person talking about a sexual relationship. He was interested in me, but needed mainly to talk about himself: he said he wasn't liked in the department where he works temporarily, and he seems to have no friends here. I didn't want to read between his words but couldn't help sensing precariousness in his relationship. Finally he asked me, on the basis of my experience, which I'd outlined for him, whether it was desirable for a relationship to continue for long at a distance. He was full of a sense of the difficulty of what he was doing and proposing to do, and thought that being a priest would have been easier, but agreed that we can't live in any way without meeting difficulty.

17 October
Supper with Rudy & Ineke at Glimmen. Rudy came in a little after we got there, bringing a bag of assorted edible fungi from the woods, which we ate later. Somehow his knowledge of these things reminded me of Tony Conran's expert knowledge of ferns—in both cases adjuncts of poetic care. The old house at Glimmen has a wonderful lived-in quality, with old wooden furniture & books, a warm disorderly order of things belonging to Rudy and Ineke and their daughters, and with a Boxer dog and old cats (one of them on the table after supper licking a plate) and alcoves with books on a desk & natural history charts (notably one of owls) on the walls. Outside a starry night sky with Venus very bright, trains occasionally passing closeby and the woods and fields and sandy tracks.

I took him a copy of my review of *The Prospect and the River,* which speaks to me of living in the Netherlands—specifically in Drenthe and the northern inland and coastal area—like nothing else I've read. I knew he was a good poet before reading it (alongside the original Dutch poems) but not how good. Last night he was very tired—his work as an academic and a psychiatrist must be very wearing. But he & Ineke have a way of accepting things—tiredness, people, cats on tables—that's part of their relaxing hospitality.

18 October
Sunday morning. Cloudless blue, sky swept clean by recent strong winds—the hurricane from the Bay of Biscay that brought death and chaos to southern England and also, to a lesser extent, to northern France and the southern Netherlands, but was much weaker here, bringing down branches and causing a dyke alert.

With M. in the country outside Groningen, beyond the heron wood. A country of smaller farms & smaller meadows, divided by oaks & birches, with alders growing by ditches and beeches on either side of brick roads. Here we walked along a sandy track between trees, picking and eating blackberries, and a solitary brown horse came to the edge of his meadow to look at us.

A light that stills the mind and lets it see, when everything stands out to be looked at, and is at once distinct, a part of nature with multiple connections, and perceivable only as a fragment of its reality.

Leaves dying, curling, ragged, decay burning brown holes in oak leaves and burning birch leaves yellow. A little bedraggled feathery seed clinging to willow herb by the shadow-dappled track. Sunlight on leaves, beads of dew, snippets of web, and the sun through tree tops broken into fine rays. Insects suddenly struck by light, momentarily visible. Spiderlines streaming in the breeze, or drifting across the track, here and there a tiny plump spider, black as an elderberry, floating with its silky line. *Chink* (bluetits from tree to tree), *twitter, caw, kronk* (a pair of ravens), ringing of distant church bells, and the faint warm sweet smell of decay, then strong with the suddenness of an assailant breaking from undergrowth. A few pink campion. A falling brown leaf which suddenly opens wings and is a butterfly flying out into a meadow. In the middle of the track, a slender broken branch, bright green side uppermost—lichen cracked and bubbled like old pigment on a canvas—fallen at a random angle, yet seeming to my mind to hold a greater secret than any mythological golden bough.

20 October
Day of smoky cloud & mist with a round, blood-orange sun rising as we set out, with Joost and Anita, to drive to Amsterdam. There were large flocks of grey geese by the Friesian lakes, lapwings in the fields, solitary herons almost everywhere. Flevoland: a flat new world of sandy soils, a wide-open strangely vacant landscape, with here and there a raw, concrete town like a vision of the future.

On our way to a film festival, *Festikon*, where Joost & M's film on autism was being shown, we passed through the industrial outskirts of Amsterdam: not the old city of canals, bridges, art galleries & high gabled buildings, but the heart of capitalist enterprise, new blocks of concrete and black or blue-tinted glass, including a new bank—the strongest in the world—colonising waste ground which still extended round or between them, with a hawk hovering, a heron fishing in tacky water.

Two of the three films on autism we saw were well worth seeing: M. & Joost's, and an American film of a young man. It was noticeable in this that the professor of psychiatry, when asked to define autism, repeatedly used metaphors drawn from modern scientific means of communication, likening brain disorder to faults in radio, tape recorder, computer. This makes good sense as far as work on the structure and chemistry of the brain, which may reveal the cause of the disorder is concerned. But there's something in the care of others for the autistic—admittedly often members of their families, especially their mothers—and in the haunting absence in the face of an autistic person, which, together, strangely and movingly, tells us something essential about the human being, which metaphors drawn from machinery can't describe.

It would be monstrous to describe the autistic as less than human—who would have the right? What I can say as an amateur observer is that autism seems to focus, hauntingly and perplexingly, the question of the relation between our humanity and our capacity for communication with one another. There could hardly be anything more poignant than the contrast between a parent's love given constantly to an autistic child, and the child's lack of response; though of course there are degrees of responsiveness among the autistic. But think, then, of a Nelleke Vogels, who apparently doesn't communicate at all with anyone, yet creates images which do communicate, and seem to be an essentially human response to the world.

24-25 October

I've often wondered what to make, practically, in terms of actual examples, of T. S. Eliot's argument that the present alters the past, in the sense that the new work of art modifies the order which the existing works of art form. But perhaps it's his idea of completeness that makes his argument at this point difficult to grasp, for he insists that "the existing order is complete before the new work arrives". Surely, this idea both ascribes to human vision a wholeness which it never has, and denies the possibility that new works may correct and enlarge it.

I've wondered about this again recently after reading A.S. Byatt's review of Toni Morrison's *Beloved*, in which she claims that the novel "in a curious way reassesses all the major novels of the time in which it is set. Melville, Hawthorne, Poe, wrote riddling allegories about the nature of evil, the haunting of unappeased spirits, the inverted opposition of blackness and whiteness. Toni Morrison has… solved the riddle, and showed us the world which haunted theirs." This is itself a peculiarly haunting suggestion. Not only can one person see what another can't, whether from repressive fear or limitations of sympathy or understanding, but each historical period is blind in different directions. The blindness is general but variable, and always has partial exceptions.

There is progress; the great work of art is always progressive in the sense that it expands vision and extends our sympathies. At the same time, we may be sure that there are large tracts of our world to which we remain blind—and as we see evil in one guise so, in ourselves and in our society, we probably won't see it in its present, subtle and insidious forms.

§

As Jesus asked in Gethsemane, "Could ye not watch with me one hour?" That is the exact opposite of what the religious man expects from God. Man is challenged to participate in the sufferings of God at the hands of a godless world.

Surely there has never been a generation in the course of human history with so little ground under its feet as our own.

The ultimate question the man of responsibility asks is not, How can I extricate myself heroically from the affair? But, How is the coming generation to live?

What do we really believe? I mean, believe in such a way as to stake our whole lives upon it?
   Dietrich Bonhoeffer, *Letters and Papers from Prison*

I find it hard to believe that I really did read this book once before. But it is necessary to reread Bonhoeffer periodically, because although much that he says is of the first importance, *he* is what matters most: not the words alone, or the man apart from the words, but the words spoken by the man, who stands by them.

 His witness against evil is brought powerfully home when, caught up in what he is saying, and momentarily forgetful of the man himself, one looks up, and remembers—imprisoned in Buchenwald, hanged at Flossenburg.

 What particularly moves me now is his concern for the coming generation. Reading his 'Thoughts on the Baptism of D.W.R.', I suddenly realized: he's talking to me too, because he's concerned here specifically with my generation. And I was moved, grateful, and the words were suddenly even more distinct. And of course it isn't only the personal application that moves me, but the knowledge that he's right—that I in turn ask about the coming generation, and wonder, in confusion, what I have to give.

 In one respect I find Bonhoeffer's "God without religion" less than convincing. Though I trust his prophetic insight when he talks about our groundlessness, he himself is evidently always a firmly grounded man—in belief, but also in his family, in a world of values at once civilized and profoundly religious. He could say: "To be deeply rooted in the soil of the past makes life harder, but it also enriches it and gives it vigour. There are certain fundamental truths about human life to which men will always return sooner or later. So there is no need to hurry: we must be able to wait: "God seeketh again that which is passed away" (Ecclesiastes 3. 15)". But these aren't the words of a man with "little ground" under his feet. It is clear that for him religion—and religion as inextricably part of an old-established cultural tradition—was very much alive.

It was to my generation—to me—that he said, "you are learning from childhood that the world is controlled by forces against which reason is powerless". No doubt some born during the war did learn that lesson. But for myself, always well-protected and later shielded by illusions, I'm conscious of still learning it. I think many of us in the West have grown up taking for granted "the importance of reason and justice in the historical process". Almost every day now brings some further proof that the world is not only not responsive to the idealistic desires of any individual but is out of the control of governments. There's a mad rage for its own interests in power high and low, in individuals, markets, states, and against it stand Bonhoeffer and those like him, free from self in their concern for others, and present in their unique being as only those who transcend self are.

2 November
To Enschede with M. to read and talk about my poems to the England—Netherlands Society. When first invited, by phone, the organizer had assumed that I offered talks on the New Forest and was audibly nonplussed when I told her I was a poet. Still, the invitation was repeated. We stayed with Hans' parents, who were very kind and welcoming. Hans' father, a retired accountant, warned me, with touching well-meant tactlessness, that most of the members wouldn't have any interest in poetry and I should be as simple and down-to-earth as possible. In the event I had a warm welcome and was listened to closely, with evident enjoyment. Afterwards a number of people came up to talk about their experience of places in the poems—sailing on the Solent, visiting the New Forest or the Isle of Wight, attending a service in Winchester Cathedral. A retired oil-man had worked for several years at Fawley: he was a keen fisherman and had fished at Brockenhurst. For him and for the others the places had come alive again in their minds. For me, too, it was a strange and moving experience—to come across the country of peat and sand, near the German border, to a place that couldn't be more Dutch, and share impressions of another country which were unexpectedly vivid there.

7 November
A day's fishing at Zoutkamp with Jan & his family. Across the canal, a church spire showed like the top of a grey sail over the dyke. Grey day, with a cold wind blowing near the sea; home in the warm, I could still feel the cold in my bones. I still get spellbound staring for hours at a float and feel some of the old excited anticipation. But I have to admit that, now, I don't have an easy conscience catching fish, and, despite the anticipation, am quite happy not to catch any!

§

The highest knowledge of truth is beyond the reach of an isolated mind; it is open only to a society of minds bound together by love. Truth looks as though it were the achievement of the few, but in reality it is the creation and possession of all.

The loneliness of a man is the cause of his impotence; whosoever separates himself from people causes a desert around him.
Alexei Khomyakov

The deadly influence of egoism is connected not with a tendency to ascribe to oneself some importance, or even with making oneself a centre of life—for each individual is in some way a vital focus of the life-process—but in separating oneself from all others.
Vladimir Solovyov

Why is the thought of the great Russians, with the exception of Dostoevsky and Tolstoy, so little known in the West? The modern thinkers we know best were all in some way broken minds: whether both the geniuses and victims of their terrible singularity, like Kierkegaard and Nietzsche, or making a false system out of the parts of truth they seized on, like Marx and Freud. The Russians alone retained the complete human image—man in relation to God as at once a unique person and a part of the Creation. It is surely their concept of man as a corporate being—of brotherhood among all people, living and dead, and of fellowship with creatures, plants, the whole material cosmos—whose truth we bear witness to by our violation of it, so that the suffering we bring upon ourselves and inflict on Nature proves in our minds and flesh the truth we deny.

I've been reading Brodsky's essays at the same time as Zernov's *Three Russian Prophets*. There's no need for Brodsky to refuse irony at the expense of the Soviet regime. And he doesn't. Nor does he refuse the prophetic stance in his condemnations. The results, in his portraits of St Petersburg/Leningrad, for example, or his celebration of the great modern Russian poets who were victims of tyranny, are brilliant, and moving. Yet for some reason I find Brodsky a weaker, more ambiguous moral force than Nadezhda Mandelstam, or Anna Akhmatova. The reason may be that I am aware, behind them, of *Sobornost*, of that order which, for the great Russian thinkers of the 19th century was identified with Orthodoxy, and of which godless Communism is a hideous parody. Akhmatova's being with her people, the profound humanity with which she suffered in fellowship, was also, surely, an example of what she shared with Khomyakov and Solovyov. Brodsky's main object of worship, on the other hand, seems to be poets and poetry, and for him the autonomy of the individual, which stands for all that Communism attempts to annihilate, is identified with poets. He has a corresponding disdain of the mass, and when he criticises "vulgarity" in the Soviet Union he even sounds, with extraordinary incongruity, like one of E. M. Forster's Herritons!

It may be that Auden is so important for Brodsky partly because the later Auden takes a stand on principles that may be identified with Western civilization. Other poets, however, maintain a kind of dissidence within the West, for which they may suffer indifference. While there's no comparison between their "punishment" and Brodsky's (labour camp, enforced mental treatment), a poet like George Oppen may suffer a great deal for finding the ethic of his society vicious. The main point, however, is that the knowledge Oppen suffers is knowledge of separation, of the breakdown of community in all spheres and at all levels, while Brodsky values the autonomous individual above all. John Riley, with his conversion to Orthodoxy, is another poet who comes to mind in this connection—and Riley's spiritual intensity, his vision of restored union, which is utterly in opposition both to his society and to the dominant ideology of English poetry in his time. Then consider Riley's obscurity, his *hiddenness*, and the prophetic elevation of Brodsky or Miłosz in America. Of course that elevation is due partly to the use made of their work by Cold War ideologues, which isn't the poets' fault. But it's the enforced obscurity of an Oppen or a Riley that I can't altogether get out of my mind when thinking of the fame of dissidents formerly from the Communist bloc who take their stand on Western civilization. It isn't that the English or American poet is persecuted; their revelations of our fundamental evil, and their moral witness simply aren't seen.

15 November
Sunday. Cycled round Paterswoldemeer. A mild day with blue sky showing through a film of grey cloud, but the wind felt colder as I sat by the lake to eat my lunch. Coots were riding waves facing into the wind and the sun; I thought them asleep or simply enjoying the movement until, watching, I saw one and then another dive. Two men on ladders were repairing a sail of the windmill, De Helper, and the lake surface was shining behind them.

16 November
A reading at the university on an evening of pouring rain. *Master of the Leaping Figures* is being taught on the first year course, and I aimed my comments to be as informative and useful as possible, without overstepping the line between commentary and criticism. I feel quite easy about this: the teacher in me enjoys it, and I don't fear that openness either releases creative pressure or betrays what I've written. Rather, it's part of the sharing that, for me, poetry is. That depends, though, on the poems being granted their integrity: I try never to tell people what to think. I've learnt not to talk as I did years ago, with a vibrancy and an emphasis betraying the fact that I was really talking about myself, for which Glyn Jones rightly rebuked me.

Czesław Miłosz speaks in his *Nobel Lecture* of the "double vision" of a hero in one of the books of his childhood. "He is the one who flies above the earth and looks at it *from above* but at the same time sees it in every detail." This, Miłosz says, "may be a metaphor of the poet's vocation". So it may be: certainly, the prophetic vision of the poet looking at the world from above San Francisco Bay is full of details of childhood, of war, of the things of civilization. For me the view from on high has been, rather, a temptation: a form of superior distancing, like Alun Lewis on Aberdare Mountain, or like Auden's airman. My desire has been—and is—to see from the ground, to be with people. But I have found, like George Oppen, that seeing is a function of distance, and increases distance. That, though, isn't the end of the case, leaving only one more step—onto the mountain or the skyscraper, or up among the clouds or the stars. For seeing that comes with distance also reveals our likenesses, our common needs, our blindness.

20 November
My father's 86th birthday. He sounded very happy when I spoke to him on the phone in the evening: they had had drinks with a few friends and he had told them the story of his and Mother's early years together and sung some of the old songs. Old age still sometimes surprises him, I think—as it must, for the boy & the young man & the man in his maturity are all still within—and weariness sometimes sounds in his voice. But now it was only happiness, that great capacity for happiness which I feel we all in the family have, but which is least inhibited in him.

For me now, at the same time as I prepare for more teaching in the university, the struggle is to write, and I am again an absolute beginner. In discussing my poems I may talk about my belief in verbal care, subtle rhythms, implicit meaning, an exploratory method, but at the time of writing I know little, and am either tense and restless, or relax into another, more concentrated level. I can't will the quickening, informing principle, which, when it enters the words, or when it is released among the words, will reveal something more, and possibly something quite different, from what I had in mind. Then the poem will see more than I see, and know more than I know, and I will learn from it—but not how to write.

22 November
M. drove us to Den Haag and back. Fewer leaves on the trees, with sober colours—dark red, brown, ochre—creating an effect of windows opening in the park, in copses and hedgerows. A watery, pearly light in the north, at first with cloud at the horizon—far off under a roof of cloud—like a downland ridge and fragments of ruined castle, lit with strokes of light. It changed as we drove towards it, becoming a distant mountain range. Then the light became mistier, with continuous cloud, and rain fogged the motorway as we drove south.

In the Mauritshuis:
Vermeer, *View of Delft*. Here the small figures conversing on the bank of the canal are at home. Light and dark, substance and shadow: no place more substantial, the shadows of clouds and buildings are part of it. Light and dark give depth, and the seen depth is also the unseen, lived-in depth. The colours of sacred painting are revealed in the world, which is seen with love.

Vermeer's *Girl with Pearl Earring* is one of the most delightful portraits in the world. The girl's soul is in her face and the light of her eyes (Vermeer & Rembrandt paint the soul). Her look is the least coquettish, the most open, innocent, and vulnerable. I could understand someone falling in love with the person in the painting.

Paulus Potter's *Bull* may also be a study of vanity—the young smiling bull with his pretty face & handsome balls, the smiling farmer (who may soon lead him to market or the slaughterhouse). Or perhaps it is simply a study of good nature.

Hendrick Avercamp, *Skaters*. Again the foreground figure—the dandy—on the ice is a figure of vanity. I find it peculiarly poignant to learn that Avercamp was a deaf mute ("the dumb painter of Kampen"). It may be being wise after the event but there's something about these crowded *silent* ice-scenes that suggests a deaf, isolated observer. But in any case the physical representations of noise in paintings—festive crowd scenes, open mouths, etc.—increase the silence with which paintings speak.

Rembrandt's *David and Saul*. Saul's half-concealed face is eaten away with suffering, with grief & remorse; it is a mad, murderous face, but *stricken*—stricken with *listening* as also with guilt and depression; soul-sick. He is listening with ardent desire to what he can never have or be, and to a harmony which is everything that he is not. His is an utter exclusion, a hopeless wanting, the most tormenting loneliness. And the darkness and size of the curtains emphasise his distance from David, the beautiful young Jew, who is equally intent, but intent with hands and soul on his music. Both figures are profoundly moved by the same thing, but it is utterly different for each. Saul's haunted, haggard face is terrible in what it sees; David's face shows his complete absorption in the harmony he is making. The murderer is a figure of great pathos—still murderous, but suffering, and knowing his condemnation.

In the faces of the surgeons bending over the dead man (an executed criminal) in Rembrandt's *The Anatomical Lesson of Dr Nicholas Tulp* their life shines in the dark of their eyes—one life, but unique in each—and the dead man's eyes are closed, his mouth slightly open: the mystery has left this dead flesh. But mystery shows in the eyes of the living—of the man who looks at us with puzzled eyes, whose look says that he is wondering about himself, what he is, and of those who look at the exposed tendons in the dissected arm, or look thoughtfully aside. They are a mystery, and they are mystified. "What a piece of work is man?" Yes, but "What *is* man?" "What am I, whose body is wonderfully and fearfully made, like this dead thing?" This is a critical moment: the answer to the question in a purely scientific sense, as if there were no other, is already pressing to be given, but for these men, who feel the first nagging pressure, it is still fundamentally a question about their meaning in relation to God.

Rogier van der Weyden, *The Lamentation of Christ*. Christ naked among the clothed, his essential, wounded flesh, which suffered so that these might be whole. But it isn't only the painting in which it occurs that this figure haunts, but the whole edifice of Christian art—as the angel with nails haunts Winchester Cathedral.

According to Eric Heller in *The Disinherited Mind*, in art "reality" which has lost its sacramental framework "dissolves into incoherence, ready to attach itself to any fragment of experience, invading it with irresistible power, so that a pair of boots, or a chair in the painter's attic, or a single tree on a slope which the poet passes, or an obscure inscription in a Venetian church, may suddenly become the precariously unstable centre of an otherwise unfocused universe". Later in the book he says that Van Gogh "painted the tree of Rilke's elegy, the sunflower, the chair and the boots that are the chance receptacles of all that homeless energy of the spirit which had once its lawful house with Giotto's angels and madonnas—once a king of kingdoms, now a squatter in boots".

But if it is true that Van Gogh perceives a pair of boots as "the precariously unstable centre of an otherwise unfocused universe", the presence of the sacred in the humble workaday object is also a fundamental Christian perception, which an art concerned with divine kingship and angelic hierarchies obscures. There's more continuity of spirit between a Rembrandt Adoration of the Shepherds and a Van Gogh painting of boots than Heller's description of the breakdown of "the sacramental model of reality" might lead one to suppose. Not that Van Gogh did not suffer the terrors of a homeless energy, but at any time Christ has been found among the homeless, himself a squatter in boots, rather than in the likeness of a medieval king. Van Gogh gave back the very vibrancy and colour that disincarnate religion had exorcized, and gave it back to the humble people and workaday or natural things that Christ valued, as no Caesar or Pharaoh ever has.

5 December

On the train from Groningen. Mineral before-dawn-dark street light shine on roads & rails. Window mirrors: the mirrored compartment (curly haired girl with sensual mouth & long legs talking with her companion) travels alongside the train—a fragile baseless image suspended over rails and penetrated by lights in the dark outside. An image that becomes more substantial against the dawn. Frost-salted fields & roofs. Ice on long narrow strips of water between furrows. Bare trees, deepening smoke-blue distance.

Later: on the boat. Grey cloud cover, a swell, subtle grey water colours—blue-grey, grey-green—an occasional black-backed gull or pair of them. After dark, the lit deck with people in easy chairs mirrored alongside the boat, with lights on other boats or on the Essex coast shining through.

From Harwich I went on a local train to Manningtree, and from there by train to Colchester, where I stayed the night at Herbie's in Roman Road.

6 December
A Sunday morning walk with Herbie & his old dog Wally beside the Colne. A large holm oak lay uprooted in the Quaker burial ground, and willows by the river—mud-grey at low tide—had also been blown over by the hurricane. Later, over breakfast, Herbie and I continued our talk of the previous evening, mostly about poetry. We talked about the quality of tenderness which we find in William Carlos Williams but precious few other modern English and American poets, with exceptions such as Reznikoff, Oppen and David Jones, though I contend that it's an important element in the English poetic tradition. Lyric poetry is inevitably a self-drama, but tenderness requires recognition of the other—person, creature, thing, any aspect of the world—as other, and delights in and loves it for its uniqueness.

Later. At New Milton
Dad said of his father: "he wasn't *nothing*, he wasn't *nothing*". He called him "orchid grower to the Duke of Marlborough". I think he rather suspects—not without reason—that I like to emphasise "humble" family origins. But then my father has always needed to feel somebody, while my pride takes a different form. He talked this morning about going to bed with a candle in the country, hearing foxes barking, and the cockerel and birds at dawn. It seemed permanent, but wasn't, of course. Mother remembered waking to the sounds of the cart-horses stamping and shaking their heads and then being curry-combed. My first memory of sound is of the AA gun in the field beside Fairacre. They tell me one of the gunners was a Welshman with a fine voice who could be heard singing opera by the guns at night.

Walking from New Milton station with my bags the other evening, along Whitefield Road, beside the Recreation Ground, seeing grass and especially the dead, white grass stalks and stalks of cow parsley, how my heart went out to them. How describe a love of such things, in which the past wells up, but it is because they are there, because one has always loved them. But if I could not show or at least imply this, if I could not admit it as fundamental, all my ideas and writings would be false, I wouldn't know myself and whatever others saw or heard, it would not be me.

10 December
Another bright frosty morning with the old moon in blue sky. To the Thursday communion service at Old Milton church with my parents, Dad walking painfully slowly and having to rest from time to time. The church (opposite Edgar's Dairy where I worked one summer while still at school) has a spacious, pleasantly simple interior, and windows mostly of clear glass which let in plenty of light. The vicar held the service at a side altar, slender gilded crucifix & two slender candles casting their shadows on the wall. Six old people kneeling at the altar-rails—a humble, humbling sight. The old lady sitting next to us made the responses with distinct emphasis, and would have done the same, no doubt, if she had been the sole person apart from the vicar there. That quality of being given—as long as I notice

it in others I don't have it. Part of me is moved by the service, stilled and awed, part looks on at a strange ceremony, with some words whose meaning I can hardly understand.

§

 As for us:
We must uncenter our minds from ourselves;
We must unhumanize our views a little, and become confident
As the rock and ocean that we were made from.
     Robinson Jeffers

Evening with Séan and Joanne. Since his father's death in October, four days after he spoke to me of him in Winchester, Séan has worked with tremendous energy. Coincidentally, at the same time as I've been struggling with a poem about Bethlehem, he has written the libretto, including a number of carols, for a choral work on the Nativity. Last night he told me about his father's experience with the navy in China, on the Yangtze: how the people would throw their old and infirm or their malformed children into the river to drown, and the sailors could not rescue them—if they did, they would be totally responsible for them for life—but saved some by guiding them to land with long sticks.

 It is incredible: the shapes our humanity can take. It certainly gives pause to any thoughts about a *common* humanity, or dogma of what we are capable of, ordinarily, under different cultural and social conditions, or, simply, what *in*humanity is. At the same time, it underlines the need to fight for the *ideal* of humanity—a compassionate concern for all by all—developed in our culture, which the philosophy of competitive individualism within a free play of market forces has done much to weaken, so that the quality of social life in England now is palpably poorer than it was only a few years ago, and the fang of the human wolf gleams in the comfortable south.

11 December
Another hard frost overnight. Pennington Common was white when I drove past.
 To Oxey with Jim, where we walked on the seawall. Perfectly still at first, the reflected sun electric on the water, Island hidden in mist, the ferry slipping silently out beyond the further wall. Patterned ice, like stacks of splinters, in salt water inlets. Tiny piping waders, a solitary swan majestic on the open water, and a flock of Brent geese, newly arrived from Siberia, picking at mud-flats and making querulous grumbling noises when we appeared. A noise of ships' engines from the mist, an image of the old half-moon in a brimming saltern—and for a time we vainly searched the sky for the original—and a sudden smell of salt where seaweed had been washed up in heaps against the wall. Tiny figures at a distance—fishermen on the seawall. Then there was a sonic boom—probably Concorde. Hips growing alongside the inlet had been pecked out leaving a mishmash of red

husks. Ivy was still in flower beside the sheltered path, with small branchy oaks in the hedges, by which we walked back as the wind was rising, rippling the water in the salterns.

Jim understood what I meant when I said that this is a place where I often feel at the brink of revelation, but remarked that it's better not to expect too much of places, since such knowledge comes unexpectedly.

I suppose what was given was gratitude—for these occasions among other things—which rises from greater depths—a deeper belonging—than bitterness at not being able to live my life here. That, perhaps, is the greatest revelation we can hope for: to see by the light of a grateful love.

A glimpse of Hayford (now called "Apple Tree Cottage") as I drove back. Some of the great firs in the garden of Ramley House had been blown down, smashing gaps in the brick wall.

15 December

After an early lunch on Friday I drove through the Forest and over Salisbury Plain and through the Cotswolds (where frost still gripped the meadows, though it had melted from Pennington Common even in the short time that I was at Oxey with Jim) and eventually, after dark, via the motorway and Tewkesbury to Worcester. There, at the Loch Ryan Hotel, I tutored a weekend poetry course with Paul Hyland. Intensive, as usual; and rewarding, with a group that was generally harmonious, good-humoured, and dedicated.

Paul and I got out for a short time after lunch on Saturday, and walked in damp cold beside the Severn (purple fruit on alders) and through the cathedral, which we'd hoped to look at but a W. I. choir was about to perform. The next day, which was fine, we had another breath of air, with Gwyneth, who took us beside the canal and back in a circle over high ground, from which we could see the cathedral's dark red pinnacled tower and the misty shape of the Malverns in pale yellow sunlight. On the other side a large gasometer, allotments immediately below us and an arrangement of box-like cabins where down-and-outs live; also Lee and Perins sauce factory with its sharp smell. This had once been the Italian quarter and is now inhabited mainly by Pakistanis. I know little of Worcester, but there's clearly more to it than Elgar's music & views of a haunted, literary landscape. What sticks in my mind as much as the cathedral's crumbly sandstone walls or the river is the hate in the voice of a derelict man who muttered at us as Paul and I walked past him. What did he see? Two well-fed arty-looking men in comfortable overcoats?

A clammy misty start, walking in drizzle to the station. Dusk already at 3. From the train: dark, bedraggled gorse bushes, dripping birches on the heath. Shockheaded oaks in Brockenhurst Park. Trees drawing dark down, gathering it. Light in pools of water.

I have no sense of a subjective haze in looking out on the Forest. Nothing could be more distinct than the quality of dark or light, or the wet bushes & trees, yet I see them both with lifelong knowledge, and especially from the child's touch, and in the emotion that comes from not being able to stay, but passing through.

Southampton: lights in tall office blocks, which appear transparent. I find them harder to feel with, although that is where words are used. And now it comes to me that man is a love animal—he creates with the non-human world relationships that can exist only in his own heart and mind. On a larger scale, including all that he knows and extending to all that he can lovingly imagine, he is an artist who—in Stanley Spencer's words—desires to gather all in.

Winchester: in the cutting below the flats, under the bridge where Joe, new to these things from the depths of rural Wales, sat on the parapet watching trains. Sue has sold the book on Dorset with the poem inside it that I wrote for her at the beginning of our relationship: she didn't intend to, but had forgotten about it. In a way, I admire her ability to live in the present. To her, the cathedral which haunted me was no more than a heap of old stones. I don't regret the past, except for actions with which I have harmed others. The desire to gather all in may be confused with a refusal to let go, or it may be contaminated with it, but they are not essentially the same.

18 December
To Zwolle, feeling uncomfortable with tiredness and the beginning of a cold, to give a talk on teaching poetry at an NSL colleague's retirement party. I began with some of the poems written by the children at Eastleigh, which made me realize the obvious: that children have an essentially poetic apprehension of the world, and that what the great poets draw on and develop is present at source in children's poems. For example, a sense of the active universe, and actual or metaphorical relationships between things and processes, and bodily knowledge. Also sympathetic imaginative projections or identifications. There's a sense in which a child already has what (some) poets aspire to: a participant's oneness with the world. In thinking about the separated self or the alienation or marginalisation of modern poets, I don't think I've ever really seen this before. Yet it helps to explain the particular magic of my time with the children at Eastleigh—not just that I was that thing of wonder, their first poet, but that we understood the same language.

Conversely, after my talk at Zwolle, several Dutch teachers told me that their difficulty in teaching poetry (both reading and writing) to adult students arose from the students' contempt for anything physical as "vulgar" and their fear of emotion. This surprised me, for I think of Dutch people as being less inhibited and more down-to-earth than the English. Yet this may be partly a stereotype, while I'm becoming increasingly aware of the emphasis of the Dutch educational system on developing the *critical* mind—the very system that makes it hard for a student or academic here to express enthusiasm by saying more than that they "quite" like something, but makes them more eloquent at finding fault.

Of course I don't say that the aim of poetry is to *return* to the child's world, or to seek an unselfconscious at-oneness, but, rather, that it is to draw on our common source while exploring the utmost reaches of its capability. That is to say, it is the complete human image with which poetry is concerned.

I remember little of my grandmother—no more than an impression of kindness. I do remember feeling special because she had died, and telling another little boy, as we sat together on the grass beside Greenaway Lane, and him asking me who had killed her. I had learnt from her death that one didn't have to be killed in order to die.

Nancy Wastie was one of a family of eleven children. Her mother was Irish, an O'Brien, who lived to the age of 93. Nancy's mother had married James Wastie, and they lived at Rose Cottage in Church Hanborough. James Wastie was a labourer on the Eynsham estate (he also had an allotment) and earned—according to Dad—"16, at most 18, bob a week". He kept pigs—"all the Wastie family kept pigs". I remember we did, at Warsash, after the war. I even had a pig of my own—Dolly—which was very small, but grew big enough to be taken one day, with much squealing, to the slaughterhouse.

My grandmother died on Christmas Eve, 1947. She had insisted that all should go on as usual, for the children, and her presents for us (Christine, Janet and me) were by the tree. She died at home, at Camiola, where we spent Christmas, and her body (Mother tells me) lay in the other room; but I remember nothing of how we kept that Christmas. What I can still see from that period—apart from the boys talking by the roadside, which must have been some months later—is Dad sitting in a chair at Fairacre and suddenly starting to cry, and David saying "Don't cry, Dad" and comforting him. Nancy Hooker is said to have had a beautiful singing voice. Dad says she was a deeply religious woman, of simple faith. When I think of her I remember an encompassing warmth, a kindness, but no particular incident or word. I think she must have been a woman of great inner strength, as all the women of the Wastie family are said to have been.

When I wrote that my father has always needed to feel somebody, I didn't mean that he is vain. He is a naturally gifted man who would be distinguished in any company. I was referring, rather, to a certain social insecurity, which he may have had in part from *his* father, with Victorian values derived from working for landed aristocrats. Thus my father, contrary to his professed socialism, has always had a high regard for figures in authority, including the retired Commodores and Captains and Brigadiers and so on whom he advised when they set up nurseries or smallholdings in the New Forest after the war. Indeed, some of these men were his friends. All I mean to say is that I'm aware of a quality of social deference in him, and a corresponding pride at being able, with his personal and artistic gifts as well as in his role as an adviser, to relate to such people. All this is quite understandable: not only because of his early struggles, and his extreme lack of confidence before he married, but because the people to whom he deferred were men of genuine distinction.

But I don't think I could ever write of my parents without grossly simplifying. What I've set down here is one small truth about my father; but whenever I verge on a biographer's language I feel how laughably far it is from the man.

Christmas Day
To the sea at Eemshaven with M. on a damp misty day, humped shapes of farmhouses mysteriously veiled in the countryside and phantom gulls haunting the water. The only colour (apart from many shades of grey) was the mussel shells, which lay in heaps in the angle between dyke and breakwater. These shone dark blue as a night sky on the outside, but were iridescent within. Bits of naked wood in the water slopped against the dyke. Black birds—large ducks or geese—bobbed up and down out at sea. As we walked back the breakwater under our feet, a portion curving into the mist, suddenly appeared like the back of a sea monster.

We spent the day quietly, alone, with phone-calls from Tony in Berlin & Joe in England, and to my parents.

27 December
This morning, as I opened the living room blinds, the first things I saw were gulls wheeling and diving over the grass of Bernoulleplein. And instantaneously they brought my mind to the sea, and instead of city houses I saw the grey sea opening beyond the dyke. I saw the Waddenzee, and the North Sea, but also the gulls of my childhood—the ubiquitous black-headed gulls at Warsash—and the gulls that haunt inland places, and always carry the mind seaward, breaking the enclosing mental images of walls or thoughts entrapped in the self, opening on an expanse that may refresh or desolate, but that I've always found cleansing and renewing.

§

> The universe is full of violent activity: the explosion of stars, huge eruptions of energy from disturbed galaxies and quasars, horrendous collisions between monstrous objects, bodies torn apart by gravity, matter crushed to oblivion in black holes.... Amid the turmoil of unleashed energy, nature may sow the seeds of future tranquillity. The heavy elements that make up our equable planet were created in the fire and explosion of supernovae long ago. The entire universe was born in an outburst of incomparable, unlimited violence.
> Paul Davies, *God and the New Physics*

In the night of *Brahman*, Nature is inert, and cannot dance till Shiva wills it: He rises from His rapture, and dancing sends through inert matter pulsing waves of awakening sound, and lo! matter also dances, appearing as a glory round about Him. Dancing, He sustains its manifold phenomena. In the fullness of time, still dancing, He destroys all forms and names by fire and gives new rest. This is poetry, but none the less science.

> Ananda Coomaraswamy

What happens to identity in the new physics, which appears to be non-reductive, (as interpreted by practitioners & theorists such as Fritjov Capra in *The Tao of Physics* anyway), seeing the universe as "a dynamic web of interrelated events"? In this web, no property of any part is fundamental; "all follow from the properties of the other parts, and the overall consistency of the mutual interrelations determines the structure of the entire web". Instead of Newton's idea of God's formation of matter "in solid, massy, hard, impenetrable, movable particles... even so very hard, as never to wear or break in pieces; no ordinary power being able to divide what God himself made one in the first creation", we have subatomic particles which are "dynamic patterns which do not exist as isolated entities, but as integral parts of an inseparable network of interactions".

The emphasis, then, is on relations rather than things, and on the whole determining the behaviour of the parts. For Capra, the parallel is both clear and welcome between this view and Nagarjuna's "Things derive their being and nature by mutual dependence and are nothing in themselves".

From an artist's point of view the problem of the new physics is that it concerns events beyond images and beyond language. In theory one may be able to agree with Capra that "the bubble-chamber photographs of interacting particles... are visual images of the dance of Shiva equalling those of the Indian artists in beauty and profound significance", but in fact, without his understanding of what the photographs show, it is hard to appreciate the beauty. Some artists (especially visual artists) have found beauty in the new physics. What they see may however owe more to the revelations of the microscope than to what is in the mathematical formulae.

But if I'm somewhat sceptical, it's not about the exciting imaginative potential of the new physics. This may yet stimulate poets to better effect than Newtonian physics ever did, and perhaps encourage in them a sense of the wholeness and interconnectedness of the universe such as we have not had since the lifetime of the idea of the great Chain of Being. My scepticism arises from what is laughably called the "zone of middle dimensions", or the realm of our daily experience: our actual position as sensory beings in the world. It's back to identity, to what we can actually hear, see, feel, to the love between people, and of people for a God who is a person. I can't share enthusiasm for the idea that things are nothing in themselves, or for the Buddhist idea that the self is illusory. The idea that excites me is that of a web of unique identities, in which all are interdependent yet irreplaceable living souls.

But a poet has reason to be grateful to the new physics—for fearful awe, for knowledge that quickens rather than kills wonder. Although the subatomic world is beyond images, the idea of it should strengthen awareness of the rhythms and connections we can apprehend, which a child in particular may *see*—dynamic web, matter as fire or stream—and which is developed in the vision of a Heraclitus or a Van Gogh. This knowledge of field, of space-time, of matter that is bound energy, of a universe that is not an observer's but a participant's, is capable of reanimating the world deadened by a different idea of science. Poets may yet fulfil Wordsworth's ideal and "follow the steps of the Man of Science", perhaps by somehow carrying the ideas into the midst of sensation, as a new understanding of the world enters our way of seeing and feeling in the "zone of middle dimensions". Thus things may reveal their interdependence without becoming nothing, and people shed false selves in order to regain their souls.

§

In the heaven of Indra, there is said to be a network of pearls, so arranged that if you look at one you see all the others reflected in it. In the same way each object in the world is not merely itself but involves every other object and in fact *is* everything else. "In every particle of dust, there are present Buddhas without number".
Sir Charles Eliot, quoted in *The Tao of Physics*

28 December
After dreaming of meeting my old teacher, who showed me a book containing names of all the boys I once knew, and details of successful careers, I lay awake thinking miserably about having no part on my home ground, with even less prospect now of finding work there. Yet this is the recurrent thinking that prevents me from using what I have, and by use extending it, moving on and moving deeper, although I know how much I owe to estrangement. But without believing in and desiring to be all of a piece—living, writing, teaching in my own place—I could do nothing that's real.

This is my life, and I have to use it. My story matters as much as anyone's. What shames me is courage and restraint with regard to personal feeling, in face of the enormity of experience. I realise now that Brodsky's thinking can only be understood as the result of a struggle against evil, and that in response to a system and an ideology that kill souls he should value the autonomy of the individual existence above all.

The more I see into Brodsky's mind the farther it seems from the mental world I actually know with its hesitations over judgement, anxiety to understand others and readiness to make allowances for them, care for particulars and fear of absolutes, and concern for what is common. It is when he writes about Auden with openhearted gratitude and unqualified admiration that I *like* him best. But the issue is essentially a conviction of truth, and the distance between needing to belong to a community and needing to affirm an extreme individualism. What I look for in the society that Brodsky calls "free" is quite different from what he, in exile from a tyranny, most values.

2 January 1988
Joe returned to the Netherlands with Emily and her friend Nicola the day after Boxing Day and the following night Jim arrived to see in the New Year with us. Today we went with M. and the girls to Lauwersoog and walked a short way on the dyke in a gale, blinded with splinters of rain and, where wind blasted by the sluice with nothing to impede it, almost blown into the sea. A scarecrow dressed in a dark suit with loose trousers & sleeves was running frantically on the spot in a large, open field.

3 January
An early start for England with Jim and the girls. Strong wind and black cloud at dawn. A heavy sea, but quieter towards sunset as we neared the English coast. On deck with Jim: wind whistling in the ship's tackle and a full moon in a sky swept clean. Small vapour trails, at first black like charcoal streaks, were gradually drawn out in long, thin streamers. The moon grew brighter, moonlight sharper on the water as we watched, and daylight flared up in orange flame over the approaching coast as the sun went down behind the island. Venus, Jupiter and the moon described the great curve of the ecliptic in the sky.

6-7 January
When Dad came down from the north of England and met Mother, before Christmas 1925, it was a "green winter" in the south. He remembers an earlier winter when he was based at Ilkley, crossing the frozen Wharfe and walking through snow to work at laying out an estate near Grassington, when he was employed by Backhouses of York. In those days he lodged with "old Porson", a former shepherd, who was a mean old man, estranged from his two daughters who lived next door. They didn't even pick him up when he fell down in the street. Old Porson told Dad the story of his housekeeper—a pleasant Yorkshire woman, Dad says—who, having been put upon for years, eventually left him, with a bag full of his belongings. Uncharacteristically, Porson had helped her downstairs with the bag.

Now, too, it is a green winter. At New Milton station, only a month since I was last here: still light at 5, and very mild, soft, almost like early spring (April is often colder), with a few birds singing now and then. Eggshell blue evening sky, luminous from the hidden sun, with dark-figured clouds in relief.

    Leaving Elizabeth's house before dawn. Bright moon in starry sky. Birds waking in St Bartholomew's churchyard, thrushes & blackbirds singing near the station.

    From the train near Harwich, on banks beside the track and near the water, I saw primroses in flower. On the train I read Joseph Brodsky's 'The Condition We Call Exile' (*NYRB*), and was puzzled and disappointed, especially by the tone, after a sympathetic beginning, in which he sets the writer's "exile" in the perspective of the plight of Turkish *Gastarbeiter* in West Germany, Vietnamese boat people, and others. The metaphor of the writer gravitating outward from earth in the space capsule of his language is about as far as could be from anything I desire or believe in.

27 January
I heard on the news this morning that Raymond Williams has died. I became more critical of him as a theorist latterly, but for my generation he was one of the thinkers and writers who mattered most. He helped to recover a tradition we could believe in, a great English tradition of radical humanism, and part of him belonged with Crabbe and Cobbett and Jefferies and Hardy, with writers who were flesh & blood of their subject, and part had to engage systematically with theory, in response to the needs of his subject—of that continuity of values which *applies* them to the present struggle for a better society. I say *English* tradition, because they were, in the main, English writers and thinkers that he brought back to us. But of course it was his knowledge in himself of the border between Wales and England that both gave depth to his sense of history "from below" and provided him with a rare, wider perspective on Britain.

It is hard to realize the death of a person who was so alive to the present, of the total withdrawal—I can think of no better word—of a mind in which our conflicting social reality existed more fully than in most minds, and which was strenuously engaged with the reality. There are people we need to think for us, even if we don't agree with all they think—but disagreement is also part of the thinking *with* them that sustains the democratic mind. At the same time I feel, like a chasm, the distance between Raymond Williams' understanding of our social reality and the way in which it is being forced and manipulated by the presiding Thatcherite political powers.

Now I remember my second and last meeting with Raymond Williams. I had come late from a seminar to meet him & Robin & Ned for lunch in a pub. As we greeted each other, he asked me, with a smile "teaching?" His look and his way of saying the word quite naturally took for granted that teaching was *work*. He would have spoken in the same tone to a shepherd or a factory worker, not implying that all work is the same, but that all work requires proper effort and has proper worth.

It is only a few days from the beginning of term—or as they call it here, in American fashion, semester—when I shall again be, for the time being, an academic. I'd rather call myself a teacher—if I've learnt one thing in the past two years it's that I need to teach, and enjoy teaching, part of the time. But I use the word academic because the situation here is, in the worst sense, academic: mentally constricted, and further constricted and confused by political and economic factors that contradict any ideal of a university. Still, there are students to talk with and literature to talk about. To be able to read Shakespeare day after day, as I have in recent weeks, and to be paid for it, isn't something to complain about.

8 February
The rain turned briefly to snow while the morning was still just dark, as I walked with Joe to the bus stop as I do every school morning now. Raindrops shone dully on the bare, black trees, cyclists passed us on the cycle path, cars with their headlights on on the road, and the big articulated lorry backing into Aldi supermarket to deliver goods, stopped the traffic as usual. As we joke or talk, even when I have to chivvy him (as I usually do) and even when I get impatient, these shared times mean a lot to me, not, I think, because I know they are coming to an end, though his return to England is much on my mind. Afterwards I got down to work, and wrote what I hope is the first poem of my collaboration with Lee.

I am working much harder now, with three full days (and sometimes more) of teaching and preparation, and the other days to write (when I can). No time, then, to keep up the journal. And that, for several reasons, is probably just as well. For one, my recent application for a post at Portsmouth Polytechnic didn't even lead to my references being taken up, which meant that I have now finally applied without success to *every* HE institution in the south of England! A sorry tale which, given time, I might have elaborated on, to relieve the feeling of humiliation. But, working, I realize that I've cared far too much about rejection—a care that is my folly, and when working I simply don't have time for it. For another, I see that I haven't always used the journal to think, or to make useful notes, but have turned to it overmuch when "humiliated", instead of working. There's a kind of thinking that's action—that moves on—and a thinking that turns back on the self. I want the active thought—in the poem.

§

To begin again—it is what writing teaches me—with these words on every page, on every day, engrained on my mind:

> "There is special providence in the fall of a sparrow. If it be now, 'tis not to come; if it be not to come, it will be now; if it be not now, yet it will come. The readiness is all."

25 February
Emily's thirteenth birthday. Yesterday morning a light dry snow was falling—I could see it through the window as I was teaching—and the secretaries in the department office had some beautiful yellow catkins in a vase. There was more snow overnight, and this morning it lay in white lumps on the privet hedge in front of the house, painted sharp outlines of the twisting witch hazel, and obscured road signs. Snowdrops and aconites have been out for a while, and forsythia in gardens along the street looks about to flower, but now the weather is appreciably colder.

Saunders Lewis speaks of Tillyard's description of the *Chain of Being* as "the best available English introduction to the matter of the great classical poetry of medieval Wales". Thus, for Lewis, it was virtually synonymous with the *reality* which he struggled to recover, in a renewal of the Welsh national community. For Lewis and for David Jones, order was not separable from community, or community from order. So it is with Shakespeare too: universal order and his national community are closely connected. In Wales, therefore, an Englishman may find a still-living sense of the nation that seems to correspond to an ancestral need, which the present state of his country denies; he may find it mainly in rural Welsh communities, and in their importance for a powerful, eloquent current of living thought. For such an Englishman—the case is partly mine of course—the ironies are obvious.

For me, it wasn't only a matter of ideas, literary or otherwise; it was also a matter of restoring connections, with my ancestry and with an earlier sense of belonging. It was an emotional need, which I checked against awareness of the ironies, and against other loyalties, other knowledge—of the history of industrial democracy and its present crisis. It isn't for me now to tell the whole personal history, which I am still living, but to try to gain more clarity about certain things. Thus I'm aware of a connection between my interest in David Jones and in Saunders Lewis, in their ideas of community, locality and universal order, and in the appeal for me of the Russian Orthodox thinkers. And aware that what I have to hold onto, as a light to shine on the darker appeal of *any* ideas, are the absolute equality of souls, and the centrality of the ordinary. I want no idea of order that obscures these truths, or that forms an ideal in my mind which affords a superior position from which to *over*look the particular, or contrives a supposed personal resolution of common problems, that cannot be resolved by anyone alone. I suppose that is why, for me, truth cannot be a system, and why I am drawn to Christianity, to truth that is a person, and to an image of our human community in which we are at once personally unique and one flesh.

1 March
Snow in the morning and a heavy downy fall in the afternoon. It was still snowing quite hard when Joe & I walked into town in the evening. We had a meal at the Pakistani restaurant which is owned by the father of one of his school friends, and then went on to the Oosterpoort where we saw a LAMDA production of *A Midsummer Night's Dream*. A good meal, a good walk there & back, a bad production, but all thoroughly enjoyable for both of us, and I enjoyed his enjoyment of the play, while feeling angry, partly for his sake, that it wasn't better.

First we had a quick look at an exhibition of news photographs covering the past thirty years or so, which was being shown in the gallery above the theatre. I hadn't known it was on, and didn't realize what it was until we actually began looking, and the effect was immediately shocking—horror after horror starkly portrayed, or, rather, captured with the artistry of the news photographer, who finds an angle on the horrific subject that burns it into the mind: starving children with huge heads and matchstick limbs, a Buddhist monk who has set himself on fire, a woman jumping to her death from a blazing building, hostages about to be killed by their terrorist captors, a politician being assassinated, the open eyes of a dead child as earth is thrown on the body, the Vietnamese holding a pistol to the head of the Vietcong officer, summarily executing him, an early AIDS victim in America, his bare upper body blotched with sores, and then a humorous shot, e.g. a streaker being led off a football pitch by a policeman who is holding his helmet over the man's private parts… Biafra, Vietnam, Belfast, Cyprus, the Berlin Wall, Shatilla, Chile, the assassination of President Kennedy, of Robert Kennedy, of Lee Harvey Oswald, of President Sadat, of…

It was a shocking exhibition, but it was also like turning the pages again, burying image under image, pictures on the newspaper pages you have turned, and, mostly, seen with a passing horror or impotent anger, and buried under immediate concerns—a good meal, a job application, a walk in the country. And I can't say that it haunted me then, as we went into the theatre and the play began.

The actors came out and tumbled and wrestled and ran and jumped around, inventing action and horseplay where the play didn't provide it and emphasising every scene that did: which produced funny moments and was generally quite entertaining, except that *all* the poetry was either left out or turned into prose, and the play was emptied of most of its meaning. No wood magic or realistic country life, no "quaint mazes on the wanton green", no "minds transfigured so together", nothing "strange and admirable", no Dream… But for us, the truth of the evening wasn't the incongruity of the different elements, or the shortcomings of the production, but the relaxed enjoyable time we had together.

3 March
There was one moment when I was looking at the press photographs when the question suddenly flashed into my mind, "what world have you been living in?" Afterwards, as I was trying to describe the evening, I realized that such a question, together with the attempt to make *some* sense of the incongruous elements, was grossly self-regarding, for the sense could only be in *my* mind, and could in no way be an "order" affecting the people who suffered or the violence and cruelty and fanaticism in the world. I don't mean one shouldn't care or, when necessary, take sides; I'm referring to what the mind can actually take in, the mind which is not a god to allot every event its "place".

19 March
M. is away this weekend, with Elin & Ellie & her daughter, in the Sauerland. She is already much better after suffering slight concussion from an accident in the car; but in fact she was very tired, after 'flu, and worrying a lot, especially about our uncertain future, or she wouldn't have had the accident in the first place. Together, we can face the prospect, and I'm not unhopeful, but there isn't any concrete hope I can offer at present.

I've now finished typing out the "Welsh" journal as far as the end of the years at Brynbeidog and have already started making a selection for publication. My feelings when typing it out were often extreme: shame, regret, irritation, embarrassment, pleasure, but also, at times, depression at sheer bad writing, and at other times, surprise and interest at what is said, and confidence in the writing. Even now I'm not certain whether it's worth publishing.

What I have in mind isn't, primarily, confessional. It's that to some degree of course, for it's fundamentally *personal* writing, and enough material must be left in to show the negative side of that fact—the egocentricity, the depressions, the blindness. But what I want to make at this stage is *a book of openings*—of the heart and mind, of the senses. To this end, I'll be guided by what I find interesting and alive—from a single note or image or perception to a mini-essay or developed argument—and with an eye to the continuity of certain themes.

There is, I think, a crucial need for a certain kind of vulnerability: not confession which merely exhibits the ego—a spectacle, with the self on the stage and the reader as audience. Rather, an openness, a sharing of oneself, which speaks to others similarly afflicted—turned inwards, with frustrated positive social instincts—and sets ideas, the struggle to think through, in experience. It's the commonness of the struggle, experienced personally, that I want to publish, not a poet's journal focussed narrowly on the self & the work. Opening occurs, in Buber's terms, between people; it's something *in* each that's opened, but it needs what's between them, their humanity, to be able to open. Opening is *in* the person, *on* the person, but it's also *on* the world—at its simplest, in a sense impression that renews for us the physical universe. Thus I want my book to be full of "things" as well as ideas & feelings.

Richard Rhodes' *The Making of the Atom Bomb* is a fascinating story, which I *have* to understand. One interesting thing is how sympathetic most of the protagonists are—utterly dedicated men & women who, it seems, were compelled to do what they did, and who (some of them) only began to question the *end* fairly late in the day, when the intense specialisation which led to the splitting of the atom made possible the disintegration of everything. Like artists, they worked with their little bit of material, divorced, as an artist's work may be, from everything except the job of getting it right.

Copenhagen, Berlin, Manchester, Cambridge, Paris, Los Alamos—in the laboratories the controlled adventure, while with war and the rise of Nazism the world outside ran out of control. And if we look for perception of a larger order, outside the nucleus of the atom, or for thought that establishes meaningful relations and priorities, what did most contemporary thinkers have to say, artists to show?

We're not at the end of this yet and can't see what the work will produce as a whole.

I feel sympathy with these men & women, wonder at their scientific brilliance, understanding of their dedication and persistence, but also something more difficult to describe—a sense that they are *us*, but with a special gift, doing what had to be done, discovering what we had to discover. To condemn them for the military use of their discoveries is to treat them as scapegoats. Given the world they were born into, including the state of science, they had no more choice than an artist has—which ultimately is to develop his gift, or not. The holistic concepts available to scientists now relate, in a way that I don't wholly understand, to discoveries within the atom, so that the source of our potential destruction is also a source of hope.

> Thence up he flew, and on the Tree of Life,
> The middle tree and highest there that grew,
> Sat like a cormorant; yet not true life
> Thereby regained, but sat devising death
> *Paradise Lost*, Book IV, 194-197

"We did the devil's work."

Robert Oppenheimer is a fascinating man: reader of *The Waste Land* and lover of the desert, student of Dante and of the Hindu Scriptures; the super-intelligent, complex mind at odds with the body; the ambitious man, the man of keen conscience, who yet ultimately conformed to a powerful orthodoxy. At once attractive and untrustworthy, sympathetic and repellent, eloquent and vacuously wordy, even only on paper, at a distance in time.

This, though, isn't the point; for any "character" or historical figure can be fascinating, and "the father of the atomic bomb" is assured of a special measure of morbid fascination. With Oppenheimer the great interest is that he is "one of us", only, as it were, more so: more intelligent, more gifted, more modern, more a man of the waste land—neurasthenic, self-invented, aware of gaining, at best, "partial order in total chaos", more powerful. The temptation is to call him Faustian, and thus turn him into a spectacle, as if he were a character in a drama in which we don't have parts—but we do, that's why no one can afford the luxury of judgement. His is a story of our time, an historical story, a story of a man subject to great pressure (external *and* self-generated), and with a life to find by discovering and rooting himself in "reality".

All that—then the voices of the victims crawling out of the city that has in an instant ceased to exist. Brilliant theory, intricate calculations, all the effort of Enrico Fermi's "superb physics" and a sense of purpose found in making a weapon that you believe will end the war to end all wars—then "deadness, the absolute essence of death in the sense of finality without hope of resurrection" (a U. S. navy officer, on Nagasaki in mid-September 1945). What horror, what fear, is the father of the atomic bomb not the father of? But the metaphor is false. Oppenheimer played a special part in making the machine that had eventually to be made, because it could be made, because man must know, even though his knowing makes him part of a mechanism that manufactures death.

If it is true that we *must* know, then Oppenheimer is no more (and no less) guilty than anyone else. But this too begs a question, for it's not the scientist who determines the use of a weapon, but the government and the military command. The difference in Oppenheimer's case may be his intelligence and the use to which he put it—that we should expect him, not only not to be brutalized, but to have a special wisdom, which for one involved in the war may have been impossible, so that it's shocking, after the event, to see him conforming to, even supporting, the decision to drop the bomb, and with more than a hint that, though it is meant to end the war, it is also an experiment, ("the first target should if possible be one that has escaped earlier bombardments, so that the effect of a single atomic bomb can be ascertained", Report of the Manhattan Engineer District). Perhaps Neils Bohr and a few others had the wisdom. And perhaps Oppenheimer is so curiously moving, so disturbing, not only because of his later political persecution, but because he had the imagination to recognise devil's work in the making, but apparently did not. Certainly he wasn't whole, but a brilliant specialist, a fragmentary being. As we all are, whether gifted or not.

Los Alamos: Indian rock carvings and holy places, desert country that had been, also, the centre of the world, but where the sacred hoop had long been broken, and now other beings, men of another world, worked in laboratories, behind steel fences, to create a weapon that would ultimately threaten life on earth. Los Alamos, "at the edge of the world"—in fact at the centre of the new world, busy with the greatest scientific minds, deep in the country of our knowledge. And is that the same knowledge which occurs, crudely, in the mind of the President, Harry S. Truman, after visiting the ruins of Berlin, before the bombing of Hiroshima: "we are only termites on a planet and maybe when we bore too deeply into the planet there'll be a reckoning?" Is that what underlies all the eloquence of J. Robert Oppenheimer, and all the anguish, and the obscure sense of wrong that he seems almost always to have felt as part of himself?

23 March
At dusk and before dawn, a thrush singing. Lying in bed I heard it, today and for several days.

It is the most haunting, beautiful sound. Even in winter it calls up the depth of spring, the full foliage, the sap, the old stream that's always fresh and new.

1 April. Good Friday
On the train with M. & Joe. M, 8 or 9 years old, became depressed because she wanted to explore the world but found it had all been discovered. She felt there was no room for her: "the world became very small then". She found people were not as beautiful or powerful as she hoped they would be and lost faith in them. (She stopped going to church at that time.) "That's when I found out the meaning of the word nostalgia."

Joe: "There'll be lunar colonies just starting when I die".

Easter
At New Milton. Green under hedges—nettles, cow parsley—and celandines and daffodils, all fresh-smelling, fresh to the eye. The second thing we notice—the usual story—is the stupendous house prices. As I expected would happen, building has started in the gardens at Hayford and next door.

Mother, on the road to Barton, told us she doesn't expect to outlive Dad, and asked anxiously what on earth would happen to him in that event. M. said we will find a way. But how?

Next morning we walked alone down to the sea. Gulls on roofs, a smell of daffodils from gardens, then the smell of the sea. The main of light, glittering, Island downs barely visible in mist. Sea-smoothed Portland stone boulders with here & there a fossil scallop, standing against the gradual avalanche of blue slipper clay. A pair of wheatears—elegant birds—on a grassy slope. A warm, coconut-smell of gorse. Patches of ramsons & periwinkles among tree-lupins which are yet to flower, under holes in the cliff-face to which the martins will soon return.

As thought often comes to me, out walking or, as now, entering a room, words come into my mind to formulate an idea of recent weeks, which reading Shakespeare in particular has engendered. English is a language haunted by the ghosts of dead meanings. That is to say, for anyone sensitive to the literary heritage, there's a yawning emptiness under words of value—honour, say—or the natural-and-religious terms from which the order of the great age of English has long since died out. This isn't to say that that order was in practice what it stood for ideally, or didn't validate cruelties and oppressions, or that there's nothing better we can do with language than seek to embody the ghost of a vanished order. It's meant as a statement of fact: English, largely because of Shakespeare and the order he represented, is a haunted language. Using it sensitively, we have to be aware both of its emptiness and of the echoes that fill it, for we won't be able to make it speak our meaning—renew it for the meaning we can make good—if we do not.

I've felt for some time that few English poets are aware of the particular deadness of their language, and can therefore stimulate the capacity for renewal that every living language has. This, inevitably, is intimately connected to the nature of their world and its relations and values, and thus to knowing ourselves in the historical present.

On Monday afternoon Jude & Peggy took us into Dorset. At Winterborne Tomson we got out of the car to a dungy smell and to the cawing of rooks in a rookery in tall trees across the field beside the church. Across the road the pocked and pitted face of a sloping meadow showed where the medieval village had been. This was my first visit to the small Norman church restored by A. R. Powys (who is buried with his wife Faith in the one brick-walled tomb under an old slab in the small graveyard), with money from the sale of some Hardy manuscripts. "A piece of old England," as Peggy said: walls of flint and iron sandstone, Tudor windows, apse and wooden bell-cote, high sided pews of unpainted wood, roof bosses the same, a simple, whitewashed interior, and door studded with nails driven through the wood and roughly hammered flat. Just outside, over a lichened brick wall with dandelions growing in the cracks, a farmyard with cows in stalls. All in a haze of light, a breeze blowing the rooks' caws and a smell of cut grass. It was strongly borne in upon me that the God worshipped for centuries here was God of the fields.

From there we drove down the valley of the Winterbornes—the bourn no more than a ditch full of clear, quick-flowing water, where I glimpsed a water rat, nose against the current under flowering blackthorn—and stopped again at Clenston Manor Farm before driving on to Milton Abbas, where we had a cream tea, and to the abbey.

Jude told us about the history of the places we were passing through, pointing out patterns of settlement and many details, such as the addition to a war memorial of a plaque commemorating a local man killed in H.M.S. Sheffield in the Falklands war. He & Peggy also told us about the threat to his job, as the WEA Southern Region teeters on the brink of financial collapse. The government's sole criterion even for adult education seems to be economic success so that at a stroke Jude's local history classes (often of 30 or 40 people) in the Dorset villages could go, together with much similar provision. There's a new sourness in England, which accompanies the new money in the south (we were aware of it especially in Lymington), and in the unbelievable contrast between what a significant minority can afford and the social marginalisation of several million people. The taste of money is everywhere, in the haves who have more and the have-nots who have less. Apparently there's no end to the Thatcherite "revolution", and daily the memory of post-war social care recedes. It isn't hard to find words; what is hard is to express the feelings of anger & frustration at what is being done, in a country in which to *think* beyond the self is an eccentric, almost hopeless task.

Even as a youth, at 16, Dad had a sense at the back of his mind that he was going to have a lot to do with John Constable and with the New Forest. There were two books in the home, (one was Samuel Smiles' *Self-Help* which his father read), but one by a woman about the countryside included something about Constable, which he read. His father as a boy had known the New Forest well, (Bramble Hill Lodge and Apple Tree Court were two of the large houses where Tom Hooker had friends) and his talk about it had an influence on Dad, so that "something about it" was always in his subconscious. The only time Mother spoke crossly to her father-in-law was when he referred snobbishly to some grand dame as "a real Lady" and Mother said, "Nonsense, the real lady is in the kitchen" (his wife).

One morning, as he started to reminisce again, talking about himself, I worked myself up into a rage against Dad and let myself go to M. as we walked down to Barton and sat on sea-defences by the water. She told me at last that I have to see my parents as people, not only relating all they do and are to myself, and to let them die when the time comes. It's what I have said to myself, but hearing it from M. makes it more solid: as she, who is the most caring person I have ever known, allows people to be. It's the only way. She pointed to a post held up by wooden planks attached to other posts, but with the base, where it had been driven into the shingle & sand, worn away so that it was suspended over the water, and said that I was like that when I refused to take responsibility for my life and stand firm upon what I chose to do—in fact to shape myself rather than let myself be shaped. Then I remembered, as well as my favourite quotation from David Jones , William Law's "You are now your own carver, and must be that which you shall have made of yourself".

Another morning, walking to Great Ballard Lake (a small pond, cleared now and set in a public space, which was choked with weed and half hidden in undergrowth when I used to pass it years ago), I spoke to M. about still wanting, more than anything, a life as teacher & writer somewhere in the area: not to pursue an ambition for the usual kind of literary success, which sets individuals competing with each other, but to interpret and celebrate common ground. The very pavements make me inarticulate with feeling yet I know, even as I cite Whitman and Wordsworth, that I've no equivalent *idea* of people (the ideas which made their actual social experience into sources of imaginative power) and that for me, as I've often said before, the very absence of the idea, together with separation from people and place, makes me the poet I am. Yet, perversely or not, I ache to make my life in the south as much as ever.

At The Wheel with Séan, a big orange moon rising behind Turville's Nursery and over the field in which the flower show that Bert Morgan used to organise and Dad to judge was held. Ramley Road dark, familiar, strange.

At New Milton with Joe & Emily, Dad singing some of his old songs, the rest of us remembering bits of poems, over tea and cakes. At Sparsholt, looking with Emily & Joe at her pony, Tammy, the sun a bronze ball going down over the chalk hills.

At Wooton Bridge. Two deer feeding under conifers, looking up at the few ramblers watching them from the path. Hazels and hawthorns coming into leaf (elsewhere horse-chestnuts), trees lying where they'd fallen in the great gale, and a wind blowing sunlight about the woods. A large, brown anthill made of pine needles, heaving with ants, a number of them each carrying a pine needle, where someone has recently thrust a stick into the mound and stirred them up. A little wood sorrel—delicate white flowers, delicate green leaves—on the banks of Avon Water. A yaffle, unseen, laughing as it flies among the trees.

At Christchurch, daffodils among tombstones outside the Priory, which, idly, waiting for M, I went into, paid my contribution and walked round, with the familiar empty feeling, among other sightseers, (the tourist industry is booming in Christchurch). It didn't seem the same place when I saw it later, with Jim & M, misty with distance, across Christchurch Harbour, when it came alive for me again, with a mystery to which I'd been insensible. Then I thought again about the empty chantry of Margaret Pole, whose head was hacked from her shoulders— she refused to kneel for the execution ordered by Henry VIII—and whose body was laid in the plot reserved for traitors at the Tower. There's an extraordinary pathos about that capacious, finely carved chapel prepared for a guest it will never receive. But what I was really thinking about much of the time was the dearth of shaping ideas *now*, which makes things for which people once lived and died mere curiosities and allows talk about monetarist "philosophy", as if all that really matters is the behaviour of money.

7 April
From before dawn until midnight, returning by trains and boat to the Netherlands. In the dawn, birds singing all round New Milton station, I started to read George Fox's *Journal*, learning how he declared Truth in steeple-house and chapel, but whenever he could outside, from trees and on hillsides, in fields and market-squares, and was beaten with sticks and even Bibles, threatened with death, stoned, imprisoned, or received lovingly by tender people. His "openings" startled me: "openings concerning the things written in the Revelations"; "openings of that divine Word of wisdom and power"; "the word of wisdom that opens all things". To him, the church was a spiritual household, not "an old house made up of lime, stones, and wood".

It is impossible not to admire such a fearless man, or to wonder at his absolute conviction. The prophets of the Old Testament must have been like that. Yet there is, perhaps, a difference. I find myself reacting against his aggressive certitude, disliking the satisfaction he takes in "the vengeance of God" on his opponents, and questioning his theology of "purity". His *individual* certitude, as God-appointed truth-teller, scourge, and iconoclast, seems to me barbarous, contemptuous of everything in tradition that checks the ego with its suspect motivation. Yet perhaps true prophets are like that, immune to doubt of their prophetic gift, and determined to break down everything that limits or distorts original Truth. Hence channels of God's renewing power.

> And one morning, as I was sitting by the fire, a great cloud came over me, and a temptation beset me; but I sate still. And it was said, "All things come by nature"; and the elements and stars came over me, so that I was in a manner quite clouded with it. But inasmuch as I sate still and silent the people of the house perceived nothing. And as I sate still under it, and let it alone, a living hope arose in me, and a true voice, which said, "There is a living God who made all things". And immediately the cloud and temptation vanished away, and life rose over it all; my heart was glad, and I praised the living God.

9 April
Saturday morning in Groningen. Snow & hail, the brick streets slippery. As M & I sat in the West Indian restaurant drinking a rum cocktail snow was falling on the market in the square. Then blue sky appeared and in place of the covering snowcloud towering white cloud pillars, which fragmented and blew away in smaller and smaller pieces, leaving a spring sky and a fresh breeze blowing the flags on the top of the Amro bank on the other side of the square. Near the bank the great brick and stone stem of Martinikerk and the building which the SS used during the war and from which several partisans jumped to their deaths to avoid giving away information under torture. The streets were dry again by the time we walked back through the shopping crowd.

12 April
Kenneth Hopkins died on 1 April; he would have been just the man to write an epitaph for himself dying on April Fools Day, let alone an April Fools that was also Good Friday. He was, in many ways, the opposite of Gerard: I remember Kenneth's disgust at being subjected at a Powys conference to one of Gerard's slow-paced, prophetic reading-cum-sermons. Later I came to appreciate his wit and enjoy his kind of salt wisdom, which, like his epitaphs, was mischievous, unmalicious, and with the perception of human folly that must have owed something to his romanticism, which he never betrayed. He seemed to me a man wise in his folly, a hedonist after Llewelyn Powys, but with a less egotistic sense of his place in the scheme of things. In his dedication to writing a traditional poetry he gave a distinct flavour of personality to apparently timeless experience. I'd been curious about Kenneth since long before I met him, as the poet in *Advice to a Young Poet*, which F.T. Prince lent me. It was the first Powys book I read, long before I read any others.

23 April
I want to sketch an idea of loneliness, which occurred to me during recent reading.
    I suppose the feeling of loneliness is much the same for any one who experiences it at any time. But what is experienced surely differs widely between cultures and ages and above all according to the climate of belief. In *Hamlet*, for example, Shakespeare conveys a sense of a living soul, isolated (except for Horatio and he is off stage at crucial times) in the Danish court, and existing between the inexpressible height of heaven and depth of hell. "Nature" is at war in the Prince's mind, angel and beast struggle within him, and it is partly this struggle, together with the heights and depths on which it opens, that composes the heart of his mystery. To put it another way, Hamlet suffers the tensions within a deeply disturbed order, in which, in the final Act, the moral absolutes are restored.
    The treatment of language is implicated in the fundamental subject of order shaken and restored. Or the purging of the corrupt state. Thus different characters speak different kinds of the same language: Claudius the player king, the Player King himself, Polonius with his cynical worldly wisdom, Rosenzrantz &

Guildenstern the false friends, Osric, Horatio, etc. But Hamlet, an honest man living among liars, can't speak without guile. He, who does not know "seems", has to become a seemer, indeed a play actor (and producer), because it is the only way in a dishonest world for an honest man to find out (and in his "craft" of madness tell) the truth. He is isolated from others instead of connected with them by language. Yet what the messenger refers to—"Antiquity forgot, custom not known— /The ratifiers and props of every word"—is never completely destroyed, and is restored at the end of the play.

These ideas were moving vaguely in my mind when I came on a passage in *The Autobiography of Mark Rutherford* which made me think of loneliness in the nineteenth century—in Hardy's novels, in Jefferies, in Ruskin, in the desolation which, like a mental colour, surrounds most Victorian intellectuals. I'd also been reading *The Wild Duck*, which reinforced the impression. Rutherford, taking up a job as a schoolteacher in raw, soon-to-be-built-over country in sight of the lights of London, looks through the dark towards the illuminated city:

> I was overcome with the most dreadful sense of loneliness. I suppose it is the very essence of passion, using the word in its literal sense, that no account can be given of it by the reason.... I was beside myself with a kind of terror... It is possible for another person to understand... any emotion which has a distinct cause, but how shall he understand the worst of all calamities, the nameless dread, the efflux of all vitality, the ghostly haunting horror which is so nearly akin to madness?

Looking back after many years, he says "the yellow flare of the city is still in my eyes". He remembers thinking of "the happy homes which lay around me, in which dwelt men who had found a position, an occupation, and, above all things, affection". There are marked differences of situation and aspiration between them, but the image of the lonely man looking at the lights of the city has, as an image of loneliness, a close resemblance to Jude on the barn roof looking at the lights of Christminster.

Loneliness relates to what is felt to be absent and to the kind of space surrounding the self. Thus, for Hamlet, "space" is a space in which he is connected—disturbingly for him—to the whole of nature and to the supernatural. But mind in the nineteenth century was generally disconnected from everything—nature, God, society—or connected by laws—Evolution, Marxism—that destroyed ideas of harmony between self and world. Nevertheless it remained a haunted mind, while, to a large extent, mind in the twentieth century isn't, or isn't consciously. One can *feel* an absence in the nineteenth century writers, one can feel them feeling it, like a pressure on the brain, a *drained* emptiness, whereas most of us grow up in a different kind of mental space.

While there's much here that's hasty and not thought out, I'm more than ever certain that for us in the West, within the ruins of a civilization and forms of thought that were created by the interaction of Christianity and worldly power, the decay of Christianity is in almost everything we are and do and say.

24 April
By the Drentse A near Schipborg on the powdery sand of Drenthe.

Blue sky with a few small white clouds and a breeze brushing the river, its surface blue-brown, rippling, pulsing with life, flowing fast and dark through meadows.

Lapwings tumbling—*peewit peewit*—and a brownish grey wader with a long beak (a greenshank, I think) balancing on a fence post making anxious noises—*ewt ewt ewt*—as we approach on the opposite bank, then flying down to pick among the grass, revealing white undersides as it lifts its wings like an angel in landing.

By a wood of oak & birch, tree shadows branching and forking across the path. Through a passage between flowering blackthorn to a small pond—a pair of mallard flying off noisily when they hear us—sunlight gathering on masses of floating small-leaved water plants and spread in patches across the surface. Sun in water—where life began.

A smell of crushed vegetation, water, mud.

May Day
Near Oudemolen, by the Drentse A again, on a moist, cloudy morning, warm and still.

Approaching the river through an oak wood with a number of hollow or dead trees—*rat-tat-tat* of a woodpecker.

Then when I'm not thinking about it or expecting to hear it, from downriver, faintly, *cuckoo cuckoo*. And the distant call is repeated again and again.

On the way back we look at a meadow yellow with dandelions. "Like a gift," M. says; and it is, a meadow shaped like a crown, framed by woods, and divided by the path from a meadow that's all dark green grass except for a few dandelions trespassing near the edge.

13 May
Jeff Wainwright came over for a short tour of lectures and readings last Saturday and stayed with us until mid-week.

On Sunday, M's birthday, we took him in the morning to Noordpolderzijl, surely, as I like to think of it, one of the ends of Europe. From Warfum the long straight narrow road runs between drainage channels and meadows and large fields to the old dyke, a green embankment friendly with ancient use, where in an intimate corner by a small pond red and white cows and calves were grazing with sheep and lambs. Over the dyke the land is of course newer, and feels more exposed, with spaces that grow vaster as we approach the new dyke and look around and back. Yet there's intimacy here too, not only at the solitary café and the sluice, but along the channels alive with ducks and fishing herons and at the edges of the fields. Here, by a field of bright yellow charlock, we watched a marsh harrier, a large hawk with a yellow head, which showed some irritation when we came too close but otherwise ignored us, and hovered over the charlock or rested on the bank.

Over the new dyke the narrow channel where the fishing boats are moored is like a continuation of the long narrow road as, marked with tall feathery willow branches, it cuts through mud to the distant sea. The tide was out, the wind cold under a grey sky, and it was as if we could see the process of sea becoming land, with horses grazing on grass that ran into mudflats, oystercatchers in the grass or piping as they danced their mating dances in the sky, and slender avocets stepping elegantly in the water or on the smooth mud. Here we saw swallows, too, and heard, among the cries of water-birds, the sound of church bells from far over the dykes. Later, after passing ducks on the arable, three fine scarecrows in a newly seeded field, and watching a tractor ploughing long straight furrows, with gulls following it, we passed a farm called *Polderlust*, in which "lust", according to M, means much the same as in English, although a politer translation of the name might be "Joy in the Polder".

By a happy chance, as we stopped again to climb the dyke near Eemshaven, with *Goliath* behind us out in the wide space of fields, I remembered the marvellous image in *Twelfth Night*, referring to Willem Barentz's voyage to Nova Zembla in 1596-7, when Fabian tells Sir Andrew Aguecheek: "you are now sailed into the north of my lady's opinion, where you will hang like an icicle on a Dutchman's beard".

On Monday Jeff went to Utrecht and returned late, but we had more time to talk on Tuesday, when he lectured and gave a reading in the department. He had read—and indeed, written a thoughtful review of—*The Presence of the Past*, his lecture, 'Explaining History', was on Geoffrey Hill, Tony Harrison and Robert Pinsky, and some of our talk too was on poetry and history. I feel he has more confidence in himself as a poet now—whether he ever lacked inner confidence I don't know, but he evidently had to overcome embarrassment at being a poet, both because of the manifold abuses of "poet" and "poetry" in our culture, and because of the special difficulties which a poet with his loyalties has to face. I feel he has overcome this embarrassment. But perhaps we have both changed, and communicate more freely as a result. At any rate, we had a good time together and enjoyed real intellectual companionship.

On the day that Jeff left I had a phone-call from Bath College of Higher Education inviting me to a job interview next week. Momentarily I lost my confidence hearing the voice that asks what kind of a person gives up an academic career with its financial security and prospects of advancement in order to apply for a part-time job lower down the scale. Agitated, I asked Jeff, and he promptly replied: "a poet". Whether I succeed or not, it was the right answer.

Mid-May
In the park: lime leaves moist with life, and all round, so light yet forming a cool, shadowy walk by the water, "glad green leaves like wings".

Horse-chestnut candles.

Snowy hawthorn blossom, delicate as eyelashes.

A pair of terns, gliding, hovering, diving into the lake water, sea birds which always bring to my mind Hurst shingle-spit, but these were breaking a surface painted with bright reflections of copper beech by yellow maple.

What I think when I think of starting again is that I have to begin at the beginning, because I don't really know what anything is—skin, the bark of trees, tissue of petals: the basic materials of life, the relations. The mind living in a world of ideas (which few minds do, but living in a mental world turning on the self is far worse) may glide over everything, grasp nothing. I go wrong when I think too far from the touch of things, or when I get away from exploring causes.

Many years ago, when I was still at school, Timia Wilmer asked me if I thought myself an intellectual. I can't remember how I answered, but remember wondering what an intellectual was, and naturally wanting to claim for myself, especially in Timia's company, anything that was a form of mental distinction. The other evening, after writing about the Jacobean experience of corruption, and not for the first time in recent years, only with sudden, jolting fear, I asked myself—it was as if something in me asked—whether I'm not destroying myself as a poet with that kind of reflection. It's not that I want to go back and deny thought, it's more that I have to use time for poetry.

It's also a matter of voice, of communication, not only of thinking intellectually instead of poetically, or losing the touch of things. It's also a matter of that who-to-whom. I believe in poetry as, among other things, a necessary way of thinking. I don't believe thought will break the mould of a poet's mind, unless the mould is conventionally poetic, or intellect becomes abstractly theoretical. But there may come a time when necessary self-critical thinking takes over from poetic practice instead of being, as it must for a poet, part of it. I've now to see what I can *write*, not what I can merely think, for thinking may go on endlessly, out of touch with poetry's felt truth.

18 May
Train from Groningen to Schiphol. Spiky bright yellow broom by the track. Elderflowers, dandelion clocks, rough pastures rust-red with sorrel, and beyond them the broad flat meadows intersected by water channels with black & white cattle grazing. Poppies. A rabbit running away across a meadow as the train passes.

Flight to Gatwick. London. Paddington to Bath, on an evening train crowded with commuters going home to villages in Wiltshire or Avon. First impressions of Bath: kids on the pavement near the station, a black girl shouting filth copied from a movie. Big stone houses, thick well-worn stones underfoot and hilly vistas down a long street with houses & churches rising on bluffs; view over a parapet of a park, like a wide, green well: a stone city partly underground and partly in the sky. Tired, I walked around looking for a hotel, and chose one that turned out to be quite expensive and not very good.

19 May
Interview, with five other candidates, at Bath College of Higher Education, Newton Park. Informal discussions with staff members in the morning, formal interview by the board in the afternoon. I didn't have time to look round, though both the main building & the grounds are, at a glance, beautiful, but spent the day indoors talking or listening. The staff were friendly, easy with each other, and everything I saw and heard more than confirmed the impressions I'd received from the details of the post, which had strongly attracted me.

Early evening: two hours of suspense before I could ring Les Arnold, Head of English Studies, to learn the outcome. Walking round the city again, I found myself outside the Roman Baths & Museum and went in.

In spite of the suspense, and without dissolving it, I became absorbed and walked slowly through the underground corridors looking at things and making notes.

A memory of Akko, the city buried, filled in with rubble, excavated. But here the great stone structure had fallen into decay, and had been broken up, part carted away, part buried in black mud, built over.

> Splendid is this Masonry
> The Fates destroyed it
> The strong buildings crashed
> The work of Giants moulders away.
> *The Ruin*

A Victorian photograph of bowler-hatted gents, several wearing chains of office, and ladies standing round the then newly discovered Roman baths and mirrored in the water.

Aquae Sulis. Sulis Minerva:

> Over the Springs the divinity of Minerva
> Presides and in her temple the perpetual fires
> Never whiten into ash.
> (From the Latin of Julius Solinus, 3rd century A. D.)

A gilded head of Minerva, wrenched from the statue (presumably when the Temple was desecrated by Christians) and found in 1727 by workmen digging a sewer. Walking round to the back of the head, displayed in a glass case, I was startled to find it an empty hollow, more a mask than a head, with spiderlines drawn out along the edge.

A schist relief of three Celtic Mothers, like a small child's drawing of mother.

Suddenly, a smell of hot water.

Steam smoking from an overflow conduit, like a cave mouth opening on the fire at the centre of the earth.

Water gushing over orange stone.

Everything seems stiller because of it—tombstones, stone coffins, even the water of the baths, in the open, with a pair of mallard: scummy, milky green water, which reminded me of the Itchen seen from the old floating-bridge.

All so still against the hot water gushing out of the earth—and the great stone head, which is referred to as a Gorgon's or a Medusa's, but looks to me like a forefather of the Green Man, a flame-haired sun god presiding over the hot, restorative waters.

From six until seven I sat in a pub and had a couple of drinks and a sandwich. When I rang Les at 7 he told me that I had the job.

On the train from Bath, drinking in the deepening vegetation and flowering May, the Cotswold wooded steeps & sloping meadows, river and tithe barn, stone mills and farms. Bradford-on-Avon. Trowbridge, the train almost empty, running through quiet evening light. A man stands on the platform evidently not seeing what I see, and in my state of wonder and joy I'm amazed, it's incredible to me that anyone could live in this country and not be constantly alive to its beauty and depth. Yet at the same time I'm aware of the self-centredness of my thought, as if everyone weren't surrounded by his life, as if whatever concerned him somehow mattered less. I'm aware, too, that the view from the train window shows only a very little even of the life of the country it's passing through, or shows only parts and surfaces and signs.

Westbury: the White Horse on a distant hillside, beyond a tall smoking chimney. Chalkland. Rounded hillforts & clumps of trees. A hill shaped like an enormous barrow, with a barrow like a nipple at the summit.

Warminster. A blackbird in a field of new-mown grass. Cow parsley on both sides of a narrow farm track.

Scarps. Fluted valleys. Moulded hills, smoothed, rolling—but what are the words for Wiltshire, for the ancient, tended earth? A world of big farms, exclusive, privately owned, yet also a national symbol; land suggesting not, as thousands of years ago, the ground of a tribe, but the property of a class. Yet here I always feel in some sense Man.

Sun setting gold, a molten drop over chalk ridge, sky a clear pale blue.

Wilton: windows catching fire.

Salisbury: a cradle of scaffolding just below the apex of the spire.

To Romsey, with a new moon.

By the Test to the estuary & Southampton.

Through the New Forest in the dark.

www.ingramcontent.com/pod-product-compliance
Lightning Source LLC
Chambersburg PA
CBHW022003160426
43197CB00007B/242